Joseph Wallace

The history of Illinois and Louisiana under the French rule :
embracing a general view of the French dominion in North America
with some account of the English occupation of Illinois

Joseph Wallace

The history of Illinois and Louisiana under the French rule : embracing a general view of the French dominion in North America with some account of the English occupation of Illinois

ISBN/EAN: 9783337156855

Printed in Europe, USA, Canada, Australia, Japan

Cover: Foto ©ninafisch / pixelio.de

More available books at **www.hansebooks.com**

THE HISTORY

OF

ILLINOIS AND LOUISIANA

UNDER THE FRENCH RULE

EMBRACING A GENERAL VIEW OF

THE FRENCH DOMINION IN NORTH AMERICA

WITH SOME ACCOUNT OF THE

ENGLISH OCCUPATION OF ILLINOIS

BY

JOSEPH WALLACE

Counselor at Law
Author of "Life of Colonel Edward D. Baker," etc.

History recommends itself as the most profitable of studies.—T. CARLYLE

CINCINNATI
ROBERT CLARKE & CO
1893

PREFACE.

"No period in the history of one's own country," says an elegant historian,* "can be considered altogether uninteresting. Such transactions as tend to illustrate the progress of its constitution, laws or manners, merit the utmost attention. Even remote and minute events are objects of a curiosity, which, being natural to the human mind, the gratification of it is attended with pleasure."

With this conception of the interest and utility of his work, the author undertook to compose the following history. Much has been written and printed at different times (in State, county and general histories), respecting the French in Illinois and Louisiana, but it is mostly in an abridged or detached form, and one rarely finds any connected and consecutive view of the French domination, from its commencement to its close. Although the territory comprised within the limits of the present State of Illinois was ruled by France for ninety years, it was never as a separate colony or province, but always as a dependency of either Canada or Louisiana. Hence, no history of Illinois, during that early period, can be considered complete, which does not embrace that of the Province of Louisiana, of which it so long formed a part.

In the preparation of this volume the writer, without laying claim to what scholars call original research, has ex-

---

* Robertson.

amined every available source of information relating to his theme, so as to verify facts, reconcile or explain conflicting dates and accounts, and render it as accurate and trustworthy as possible. No parade need here be made of the various authorities consulted and freely used by him, since they will be disclosed in the progress of the narrative itself.

In writing Indian, French and Spanish proper names, the author has, as a rule, conformed to the received orthography, though it is not always easy to determine just what that is, since standard writers still differ considerably in this particular. Among the early annalists there was no recognized rule, nor could well have been any, in regard to nomenclature, and therefore each writer was a law unto himself. This, together with the different geographical locations often assigned by them to the same aboriginal tribes, gave rise to more or less contradiction in their narratives, which have been a source of perplexity to modern historiographers.

Although this work is primarily confined to the doings of the French in the Mississippi Valley, yet such a general view is taken of their transactions in other parts of the continent as to render it, in some measure, a compendious history of the French Dominion in North America. Without overlooking any important or familiar fact, the author has introduced much matter that will be new and curious to the general reader. In gleaning so wide a field, and in carrying the book through the press at a distance from his residence, he may have fallen into some errors and inaccuracies, but it is believed these will be found few in number and restricted to minor details.

It might be thought superfluous, at this time and place,

to descant upon the absorbing interest that must ever attach to that pristine period of American history of which we write, hackneyed as it is. But the new and strange experiences of the early explorers and colonizers of this continent can never be repeated, and the record they made will stand unchanged for all future time. The Indians, too, who then peopled the solitudes of our forests and prairies, have vanished never more to return, leaving behind them, as the only enduring vestiges of their presence, the names which they gave to the physical features of the country.

> "Their names remain, but they are fled,
> For ever numbered with the dead."

There are now no other new continents or large islands to be discovered; all the habitable globe has been overrun; and henceforth the business of civilized man upon it will be to possess, enjoy, cultivate and develop its marvelous resources.

To the descendants of the pioneer French colonists in North America, and particularly to those residing within the great Basin of the Mississippi, the theme of this general narrative must have a peculiar and perennial attraction. In the daring and memorable achievements of their heroic predecessors, they may not only cherish a just and laudable pride, but find solace and satisfaction for that inscrutable decree of fate, or Providence, whereby this vast, most fertile and favored region, was wrested from their grasp to ultimately become the geographical center of one of the mightiest, most enlightened and progressive empires on the face of the earth.

In concluding these prefatory observations, it remains for the writer to acknowledge his obligations, in the prosecution of his laborious researches, to the repeated kind offices of the intelligent and efficient librarian of the

Illinois (State) Historical Library, and also to the assistant librarian of the State Library.

The copious and comprehensive index at the close of the work will be found very convenient for reference, and not without occasional use in elucidating the text of the history.

SPRINGFIELD, ILLINOIS, *September*, 1893.

CONTENTS.

PAGE.
PREFACE...... iii

CHAPTER I.
1497–1690.
INTRODUCTORY NARRATIVE; OR, DISCOVERY AND SETTLEMENT OF CANADA...... 1

CHAPTER II.
1539–1671.
DISCOVERY OF THE MISSISSIPPI RIVER, AND OF THE NORTH-WEST.... 24

CHAPTER III.
1673–1675.
THE GREAT RIVER VOYAGE OF JOLIET AND MARQUETTE...... 45

CHAPTER IV.
1666–1680.
LA SALLE AND HIS EARLY EXPLORATIONS...... 71

CHAPTER V.
1675–1701.
FATHER LOUIS HENNEPIN...... 96

CHAPTER VI.
1680–1681.
LA SALLE AND TONTY...... 115

CHAPTER VII.
1681–1683.
LA SALLE'S EXPLOITS CONTINUED...... 130

CHAPTER VIII.
1684–1687.
LAST GREAT ENTERPRISE OF LA SALLE.......................... 153

CHAPTER IX.
1687–1689.
SURVIVORS OF LA SALLE'S TEXAN COLONY...................... 175

CHAPTER X.
1689–1712.
ILLINOIS AS A DEPENDENCY OF CANADA.......................... 194

CHAPTER XI.
1698–1711.
PERMANENT SETTLEMENT OF LOWER LOUISIANA.................... 212

CHAPTER XII.
1712–1717.
LOUISIANA UNDER M. CROZAT—DEMISE OF LOUIS XIV............. 233

CHAPTER XIII.
1717–1723.
FRENCH FINANCES, AND LAW'S MISSISSIPPI COMPANY 249

CHAPTER XIV.
1718–1732.
LIEUTENANT BOISBRIANT'S RULE IN THE ILLINOIS — THE NATCHEZ WAR... 270

CHAPTER XV.
1732–1752.
LOUISIANA UNDER THE DIRECT GOVERNMENT OF THE CROWN........ 288

CHAPTER XVI.
1742–1756.
PROGRESS OF EVENTS IN THE DEPENDENCY OF ILLINOIS............ 304

CHAPTER XVII.
1753–1760.
THE MEMORABLE SEVEN YEARS' WAR............................ 319

CHAPTER XVIII.
1760–1765.
INDIAN CONSPIRACY AND WAR OF PONTIAC 342

CHAPTER XIX.
1764–1769.
OCCURRENCES IN LOWER LOUISIANA............................... 363

CHAPTER XX.
1764–1778.
ILLINOIS UNDER THE BRITISH DOMINATION........................ 384

CHAPTER XXI.
GENERAL DESCRIPTION OF THE FRENCH COLONISTS................ 404

HISTORY

OF

ILLINOIS AND LOUISIANA UNDER THE FRENCH RULE.

CHAPTER I.

1497-1690.

INTRODUCTORY NARRATIVE; OR DISCOVERY AND SETTLEMENT OF CANADA.

THE first Europeans to reach the shores of America were the Northmen, or Scandinavians, who, during the early middle ages, formed settlements in Iceland and southern Greenland. Those hardy and daring sea-rovers gradually extended their voyages westward from Greenland to the coasts of Labrador and Newfoundland, and, by the beginning of the eleventh century, appear to have established themselves on the rocky shores of New England, about Massachusetts and Narraganset bays.

They named the new country Winland, or Vinland, from the profusion of wild grapes found growing in its virgin forests. But the Northmen effected no large or durable settlements upon this continent; and when their colony of Vinland was eventually abandoned, or exterminated by the natives, it was, doubtless, soon forgotten. The only remaining traces of their presence on the New England coast are two or three rude monuments,* and a few doubtful Runic inscriptions. The fact of their primal discovery of the continent, however, is attested by the Sagas, or ancient historical records of Iceland.

But the time was not then ripe for the opening of the

---

* Notably, the old stone tower at Newport, Rhode Island, which is believed to be a relic of the Northmen.

New World to European colonization and civilization; nor were the people of western Europe sufficiently advanced in wealth, intelligence and nautical science, to profit by so important a discovery.

To Cristoforo Colombo (Christopher Columbus), must ever be accorded the imperishable honor, *of having made known to* the nations of the Old World the pathway to the Western Hemisphere; yet it is by no means certain that he ever touched the continent of North America, and he died in ignorance of the extent and transcendent value of his achievement.

But the true and lasting discovery of Northern America was made by Giovanni Caboto (John Cabot), a Venetian navigator, who had become domiciled in the commercial city of Bristol, England, prior to the year 1493, and who afterward voyaged the North Atlantic under the patronage of King Henry VII. It is a singular fact, and worthy of remark here, that the maritime powers of Europe, with the exception, perhaps, of Portugal, should have owed their early possessions in America to the skill and daring of Italian navigators, although not a single American colony was ever established by the Italians themselves.

Within one or two years after the return of Columbus to Spain, from his first renowned voyage of discovery, the adventurous spirit of John Cabot induced him to propose to Henry VII., of England, to undertake a similar voyage, with the two-fold object of discovering new lands, and of finding a northwest passage to the Indias. The proposal of the Venetian was received with favor and encouragement by that cautious, yet sagacious monarch. And on the fifth of March, 1496, he issued a commission to Cabot and his three sons (Louis, Sebastian and Sanchez), authorizing them to " sail to all parts of the east, west, and north, to discover countries of the Heathen, unknown to Christians; to set up the king's ensigns there; to occupy and possess, as his subjects, such places as they could subdue, giving them the rule and jurisdiction—to be holden, on paying to the king. one-fifth part of their gains."

Under this broad commission three ships were at length equipped for the enterprise—partly at the expense of his majesty, and the remainder by private persons. With these vessels, manned by some three hundred seamen, the elder Cabot, and his son Sebastian, sailed from Bristol, in May, 1497. Taking a westerly course over the trackless ocean, the bold commander, on the 24th of June, sighted a shore which he named *Terra Primum Visa* (land first seen), and which is supposed to have been some part of Newfoundland. He thence steered northward, parallel with the coast of Labrador, as far as to the entrance of Hudson's strait, when he was obliged to turn back on account of the ice and the increasing discontent of his crew. After discovering many islands and coasting the mainland southward to the vicinity of Cape Hatteras, a mutiny is said to have broken out among his sailors, in consequence of which he returned to England. During the ensuing year (1498), Sebastian Cabot was sent out with two ships, on a second voyage of discovery. He again visited Newfoundland, and other points on the eastern coast of North America, but did not attempt any conquest or settlement of the country. No authentic journal of these two voyages was ever published, nor were they soon followed up by other like enterprises on the part of the English government or people. Yet, it was upon the discoveries of the Cabots, and the subsequent attempts at colonization under the auspices of Sir Walter Raleigh (1584–1587), that England based her title to the principal part of the immense territory which she afterward acquired in North America.

The Portuguese were the next to engage in this inviting maritime enterprise. In 1500, one Gaspar de Cortereal sailed from Lisbon with two well-manned caravels. He visited Labrador, ranged along its inhospitable coast for six hundred miles, and entered the Gulf of St. Lawrence. Returning the same year to Portugal, he set sail on a second voyage of discovery in May, 1501, but was never again heard of. His brother Michael sailed with two ships in search of him, but he also failed to return. It is conjectured that both they and their unfortunate crews fell victims to the savage vengeance of the natives of Labrador, some of whom had been seized and carried off as slaves by Gaspar de Cortereal, in his first voyage. Upon the strength of these northwestern voyages, however, the Portuguese set up a' claim to the discovery of the whole continent.

The business of oceanic discovery in this part of the New World, was afterward taken up by the French government. During the active reign of Francis I., an expedition was fitted out, the command of which was given to Juan Verrazano, or Verrazani, a Florentine navigator of great skill, who had signalized himself by his successful cruises against the Spaniards. He sailed from France in January, 1524, with four vessels, but three of them becoming disabled in a storm, he completed the voyage in a single ship. After touching at the Maderia Islands, he held a due westerly course, and encountered heavy seas, but at length sighted land on the 7th of March, in the latitude of North Carolina. Finding no secure harbor, he anchored in the open sea, and sent his boats ashore to open traffic with the natives. He next sailed southward some distance, and then turned his course to the north, exploring the eastern coast of the continent for six hundred leagues, and naming it New France, in compliment to his royal patron. When he reached the fog-laden banks of Newfoundland, his provisions began to fail, and he bore away for home, whither he arrived late in July, 1524. Of the subsequent career of Verrazano, but little is known.

It was not until the lapse of ten years that the French renewed these hazardous enterprises; when Jacques Cartier, or Quartier, a bold and experienced mariner of St. Malo, in Brittany, having proposed another expedition, was supplied by the vice-admiral of the king with two ships and one hundred and twenty seamen. Cartier put to sea from the port of St. Malo, on the 20th of April, 1534, and after four weeks of successful navigation reached the eastern shore of Newfoundland, which, though visited by fishermen, was still for the most part a *terra incognita*. He sailed nearly all round that great island, coasted the mainland for a long distance, discovered and named the *Golfe* de St. Lorent, or Gulf of St. Lawrence, and entered the Bay of Chaleurs. But by this time the season was well advanced, and our navigator returned with his ships to France, without having ascended the St. Lawrence River, or even knowing that it was a river. He opened trade relations with the natives of the country, and carried home with him two young Indians, who afterward served a useful purpose as interpreters.

The degree of success that attended this initial voyage encouraged the French monarch to further effort in the field of trans-Atlantic discovery. Three ships were now fitted out for a second expedition, which was joined by some of the young nobility, and Cartier was given the command thereof, with the designation of "captain and pilot to the king." On the 19th of May, 1535, after a solemn mass at the cathedral in St. Malo, the three vessels put to sea, but were soon separated by a tempest. After a boisterous and tedious passage they all arrived safely in the Strait of Belle Isle, to the north of Newfoundland, in the last week of July. From this point of rendezvous the captain took a southwesterly course, and, having navigated the channel between the south coast of Labrador and the large island of Anticosti, sailed slowly up that long and broad estuary, afterward named St. Lawrence. By the 1st of September he reached the mouth of the Chicoutimi, or Saguenay, coming in from the northwest; and on the 14th, after passing several low islands, including that of Orleans, dropped anchor near the entrance of a small river on his right, to which he gave the name of St. Croix, now St. Charles.

This was immediately below that bold and striking promontory which rises in the angle formed by the confluence of the two rivers, and which the natives of the country called Quelibec (Quebec), from the sudden contraction of the St. Lawrence at that point. While anchored in the river opposite the present village of Beauport, Cartier was visited on shipboard by one Donnacona, a neighboring Indian potentate, who resided at the village of Stadacona, on the peninsula of that name, and who came with a numerous retinue of his braves in *pirogues*.* The French captain received his copper-colored visitors with due formality, and held converse with them through the two interpreters from the coast of Gaspé, whom he had taken with him to France in his voyage of the year before.

Having moored his two larger vessels inside the mouth of the St. Croix, our brave and determined mariner, contrary to the entreaty of Donnacona not to go further, continued his voyage in the third vessel up the St. Lawrence. Arrived in that expansion of the river since known as Lake St. Peter, and finding the further advance of his ship impeded by obstructions in the channel, he quit it and proceeded in a boat, rowed by three of his men. On the 2d of October he reached the Indian village of Hochelaga,† situate on the island of that name, which he denominated Mont. Royal (Montreal), from the insulated mountain that rises from the plain two miles behind it. After spending a few days at Hochelaga, and opening an amicable intercourse with the inhabitants of the place, Cartier returned to his ship, and descending the river rejoined his other ships at the mouth of the St. Croix. Here, at the foot of the rugged promontory of Quebec, his sailors had already begun the erection of a temporary wooden structure, which was soon finished, and in which they passed the ensuing winter months, suffering greatly, not only from the rigor of the climate, but from the ravages of the scurvy. Twenty-five men died before the opening of spring, and out of one hundred and ten then remaining very few were free from that disease.‡

Before sailing on his return to France, Cartier, according to the custom of navigators in that age, took possession of the country of the St. Lawrence in the name of his sove-

---

* Pirogue (Sp. *Piragua*), originally an Indian word, signifying a dug-out canoe.

† This was also the original Indian name of the St. Lawrence, and the French sometimes spoke of it as the *Grand fleuve de Hochelaga*.

‡ Upon the site of the temporary structure occupied by Cartier and his men was long afterward built the church of *Notre Dame des Victoires*, which fronts the market place in the Lower Town of Quebec.

reign, by erecting a high wooden cross bearing the arms of France, with this Latin inscription, *Franciscus primus, Dei gratia Francorum rex, regna.* Leaving one of his ships that had been shattered by the ice in the little harbor of the St. Croix, he sailed for home with the other two on the 6th of May, 1536, and arrived at St. Malo on the 16th of July. During the preceding winter Cartier's friendship with Donnacona had become strained, and on his departure he took with him that chief and several of his braves, whose persons he had seized partly by force and partly by stratagem, and who subsequently died in captivity in France.

Some five years later, a scheme of regular colonization was devised by the French government, in which Cartier was associated with Jean Francois de la Roque, Sieur de Roberval, who had been commissioned by the crown lieutenant-general and viceroy of his American possessions. Accordingly, on May 1, 1541, Captain Cartier sailed with five ships on his third voyage to America, and arrived at his former winter quarters on the St. Lawrence early in August. Sending two of his ships home, he proceeded with the rest to search the neighboring shores for a better haven than that of the St. Croix, and found one to his liking nine miles above it, at the mouth of Cape Rouge River. Here he landed and built a fort which he named Charlesbourg Royal, and waited the coming of his coadjutor with colonists to begin a settlement. In the meantime he again ascended the St. Lawrence to Hochelaga, and examined the nature of the obstructions to navigation in the river above that place. Owing to the long delay in the arrival of Roberval, and to his impatience and jealousy of that officer, who outranked him, Cartier at length relinquished the attempt to make a settlement, and set sail on his return to France in May, 1542. Meeting with Roberval's ships at the harbor of Newfoundland, he avoided their commander and held on his homeward course. But, according to Lescarbot's history, he was sent back to Canada * in the autumn of that year, by King Henry II., to

---

* The name of Canada is believed to have been derived from the Huron word *Kan-na-ta*, meaning a collection of wigwams. According to Cartier, it is an Indian word, signifying town. For he wrote: "*Il's*

bring home Roberval and his colony. They appear to have wintered together on the banks of the St. Lawrence, and finally quitted it in June, 1543.

Captain Cartier's services as a navigator and discoverer were recompensed by a patent of nobility, and also by a seignorial mansion at the village of Limoilou, near St. Malo. The latter years of his stirring life were mostly passed at his seat of Limoilou, where he died childless about anno 1555, aged sixty. The printed journals of his American voyages are preserved by the Quebec Historical Society, but whether originally written by himself or not is undetermined. It is said that he advised the first French colonists in Canada to cultivate the good will of the natives by every means in their power, and even to form matrimonial alliances with them, in order to advance their material interests. It is evident that this last advice was subsequently adopted, though with ephemeral rather than permanent advantage.

The discoveries made by Cartier and his associate mariners turned the attention of France to the extensive Valley of the St. Lawrence and its capabilities, and established her claim to the country according to that peculiar international code by which the maritime powers of Europe were wont to apportion among themselves the territories of the Western World.

Although Canada exhibited scarcely any of that smiling and luxuriant aspect pertaining to the middle and southern sections of the continent, it opened into regions of indefinite extent, and the tracing of its vast chain of fresh-water seas to their distant fountains presented more than ordinary attractions to human curiosity and adventure. But for the next sixty years, owing to internal dissensions and factional and religious wars, French colonization in America was virtually abandoned.

It is true that in the years 1562 and 1564, Admiral Co-

---

appellant une ville Canada." Another early French authority makes the word mean *terre*, or land. The name seems to have been primarily applied only to the Valley of the St. Lawrence.

ligny undertook to plant some Huguenot colonies in East Florida; but the two expeditions sent thither under the separate leadership of Jean Ribaut and Réne Laudoniere ended in utter failure. After suffering deeply from shipwreck and sickness, their settlements at Port Royal and near the mouth of the St. John's River were attacked and destroyed by the Spaniards under the stern Don Pedro de Menendez.* Ribault and his followers were massacred, after a pledge of safety had been given them, and their bodies were treated with the most shocking indignities— "not," it was averred, "because they were Frenchmen, but because they were heretics and enemies of God." Two years later (1567), this barbarous massacre was fully avenged by a Huguenot soldier named Dominique de Gourgues, who sailed from Bordeaux with one hundred and fifty armed men for that purpose. Aided by some Florida Indians, he took and demolished the little Spanish forts on the river St. Johns, and hanged all of his prisoners, not because they were Spaniards, but that they were "traitors, robbers, and murderers." After accomplishing this deed of savage retaliation, De Gourgues made no effort to retain his conquest, or to revive the French colony, but having secured all that was of value at the forts, he re-embarked his troops and sailed back to France. If the efforts of the French Protestants to form settlements in East Florida had been countenanced and sustained by the crown, it is believed that France might have had a flourishing colony there long before England effected a single permanent settlement in America.

We come now to describe the first successful attempts of the French to form durable settlements in the cold and inclement districts of New France. The most conspicuous figure of his day in these arduous and uncertain enterprises was Samuel de Champlain. Born at Brouage, in the province of Saintonge, about the year 1567, he belonged to a noted family of mariners. His father was a sea captain, and he himself was early schooled in the art and practice of navigation. After spending several years in the military

---

* Who founded St. Augustine, Fla., in 1565.

service of his country, he went with an uncle, who held a high post in the Spanish navy, on a long voyage to Mexico. Returning to France in 1601, he was urged by De Chastes, Governor of Dieppe, to explore and prepare to found a colony in the French possessions of North America, the governor having received a concession from the king for that purpose. This was an undertaking well suited to the enterprising genius of Champlain, and he accordingly embarked at Honfleur on March 15, 1603, in a ship commanded by Captain Pontgravé, an experienced mariner of St. Malo.

On the 24th of May, after a rough and protracted passage, they dropped anchor at Tadousac, where the deep and dark waters of the Saguenay enter the estuary of the St. Lawrence. Leaving their large ship here, Pontgravé and Champlain, with five seamen, continued their voyage in a shallop up the St. Lawrence to the rapids, above Hochelaga. As they slowly retraced their course, Champlain examined and noted the rocky and wooded shores on both sides of the river down to Tadousac. He then drew up a map of the country, collected information about Acadia* (afterward called by the British Nova Scotia), and in the following autumn returned to France, where he immediately published a narrative of his voyage and observations, entitled *Des Sauvages*.

His patron, De Chastes, had meantime deceased, and the exclusive privileges that had been granted to him by Henry IV. were transferred to Pierre du Guast, Sieur de Monts, a gentleman of Saintonge, and an officer of the king's household. Letters-patent were issued to the latter in November, 1603, nominating him vice-admiral and lieutenant-general of his majesty in the country of *La Cadie* (Acadia), with full and exclusive power to trade in peltries, and to make war and peace with the natives, from the 40th to the 46th parallel of north latitude; also to make grants of land to French settlers. His patent embraced the whole

---

*This old poetic name, written Acadie in French, appears to be an abbreviation of the Indian name for one of the rivers of that country.

coast of New England, no part of which had as yet been occupied by the English. The Sieur de Monts was a Calvinist, and had stipulated for the free exercise of his own form of religion, but this was inconsistently enough coupled with an agreement that the Indians of the country should be instructed in the mysteries of pure Catholicism. Having resolved to plant an extensive colony in his new domain, De Monts now engaged the active assistance of Champlain in his enterprise. They at once proceeded to hire and equip a number of vessels, large and small, with which they set sail from Havre de Grace on the 7th of April, 1604, carrying numerous colonists, traders, and stores. The commander arrived with a part of his fleet off Sable Island in the first week of May, and thence stood along the south and western shores of Acadia for several weeks, being undecided where to make a permanent landing. At length, after exploring the Bay of Fundy, he determined to begin a settlement on the Island of Sainté Croix, in the estuary of that name, lying between the present Maine and New Brunswick. But this location proved unfavorable from the lack of building timber and fresh water, and during the next summer the colony was removed across the bay to a place called Port Royal, now Annapolis. When this transfer had been effected, De Monts found it necessary to return to France, leaving Pontgravé in charge of the new settlement. The cold, damp, and sterile peninsula of Acadia, or Nova Scotia, fulfilled none of those hopes of speedy wealth that had allured the French colonists hither. It yielded with difficulty the common necessaries of life, and the fur-trade was too limited to be profitable. Its mineral resources long remained unknown.

In the meantime Champlain diligently explored the rock-bound coast to the southward, as far as the sandy beach of Cape Cod, making surveys and charts of the same, and in 1607, re-embarked for France. His patron, De Monts, was accused of abusing his ample commission by capturing and confiscating all vessels that approached the American coast within the bounds of his territorial jurisdiction, and of interfering with the rights and endangering the safety of the cod fishermen on the shores of Newfoundland.* Nevertheless, he had sufficient influence at court to get his privileges renewed for a time, on condition that his company should form an establishment on the river St. Lawrence. As now reorganized, the company was composed principally of merchants, who had only the fur trade in view, and this led to a change in their plans and to the gradual abandonment of Acadia as the seat of their operations.

In pursuance of this change of policy, the company caused to be fitted out two ships at Honfleur, and confided them to the charge of Messieurs Champlain and Pontgravé, with instructions to proceed to the St. Lawrence, and there establish a trading post. They accordingly sailed in the spring of 1608, taking out with them a sufficient number of soldiers, traders and adventurers to form a settlement. Arriving in the Lower St. Lawrence, about the middle of June, they first touched at Tadousac, and thence continued their course up the river. Having fixed upon Quebec† as the most eligible site for the projected establishment, Champlain landed his company of adventurers there on July 3, 1608. This was one year after the settlement of Jamestown, Va., by the English, and twelve years before the landing of the Pilgrims on Plymouth Rock. The spot thus chosen was on the north side of the St. Lawrence River, just above its junction with the St. Charles, and about one hundred and twenty leagues from the sea. No sooner had the commander begun to clear the ground for a settlement here, than he discovered a plot among five of the men to take his life; but this was hap-

---

*As early as the year 1504, the fishermen of Brittany and Normandy began to ply their vocation on the banks of Newfoundland, and in 1517, upward of fifty vessels of different nations are said to have been employed in it.

†"The Indians of the country gave to this place the name of Quebio or Quelibec, which, in Algonquin and Abenaqui, means *narrowing*, because the river St. Lawrence here narrows till it is only a mile wide; whereas, just below the *Isle de Orléans*, it still maintains a breadth of four or five leagues."—Charlevoix' *Historie da la Nouvelle France*. English translation, edited by John Gilmary Shea (New York, 1866–1872), vol. 1., p. 50.

pily frustrated by his vigilance, and the conspirators were dealt with by martial law.

Mechanics and laborers were now put to work, and in the course of a few weeks a cluster of wooden buildings arose on the shelving bank of the river, under the shadow of that lofty precipice, since known as Cape Diamond, which towered above them. These rude edifices were surrounded by a stout palisade or wall, pierced by apertures for small cannon, and were thenceforth occupied as the headquarters of Champlain and his semi-military colony. Such was the inconsiderable beginning of the historical city and fortress of Quebec. Having thus provided a secure place for his men and munitions, the resolute leader pushed out into the circumjacent country, with a view to making it tributary to the French power. It was from about this time that Canada and Acadia began to be officially designated as *Nouvelle France*, though this ambitious appellation had been long before applied to the coast of the country by the navigator Verrazano.

In order to secure the friendship and support of the neighboring Montagnais and Algonquin Indians,* in furtherance of his designs of interior exploration and intercourse, Champlain now undertook, with dubious propriety, to aid them in their ceaseless warfare with the Iroquois, or Five Nations,† who inhabited the region lying mostly within the limits of the present State of New York. Victory, of course, attended his superior arms in the first encounters with them, but it intensified the hatred of those proud and fierce warriors for the Indian allies of Champlain; it led to an alliance of the Iroquois with the Dutch settlers, and afterward with the English, and long prevented the French from advancing southward into the beautiful and fertile Valley of the Ohio. On the other hand, it is doubtful if the

---

*The Algonquins, proper, dwelt on the Ottawa river, and hence were called Ottawas by the French; but they gave name to the entire family of kindred tribes (about thirty-eight in all), known as Algonquins.

† The use of the word *nation*, as applied to a single Indian tribe, though sanctioned by the usage of the best writers, is, nevertheless, a misnomer.

first French colonist could have maintained, for any considerable time, an attitude of strict neutrality between those ever-warring Indian nations; so that the policy they adopted may have been the only feasible one open to them.

In the early summer of 1609, Champlain, with a few armed men, joined a hunting and war party of their Montagnais allies on an excursion into the territory of the Iroquois. Ascending the broad St. Lawrence to the mouth of the Richelieu, or Sorel River, and pushing up the latter to its source, he discovered and partially explored that beautiful lake which still bears his name. On its sylvan shores he found game exceedingly abundant, and particularly the fur-bearing beaver. While exploring the south part of the lake, our French and Indian party fell in with a band of Mohawk warriors, when a sharp fight ensued, in which several of the latter were slain and others taken prisoners. Champlain had now to witness an exhibition of that protracted and cruel torture to which the savages often subjected their male captives, which filled him with such horror that he obtained permission of his allies to shoot the poor creature dead with his arquebuse, and thus ended his anguish.

Leaving Pierre Chauvin in command at Quebec, Champlain returned with Captain Pontgravé to France in September, 1609; but he came back the next spring, bringing fresh supplies, and a number of artisans for his embryo colony. In the autumn of this year (1610), the Montagnais again called on the French for military assistance against their enemies, which Champlain gave in order to secure the co-operation of the former in his own interior explorations. Moving with his Indian allies up the St. Lawrence and the river Sorel, he assaulted and captured a stronghold of the Iroquois, but received a severe wound in the action. If the French at this epoch could have forecast the future of their Canadian colony, they would no doubt have occupied the Iroquois country in force, and seized control of the Hudson River, so as to exclude the Dutch, and secure another and shorter outlet to the ocean. Such a course was recommended by M. Talon at a subsequent period, but it was then too late.

In August, 1611, Champlain again crossed the Atlantic to France, where he shortly married a girl named Hélene Boullé, who was only twelve years old, and who was called his "child wife." She had been reared a Protestant, but became a Catholic after her marriage. On the assassination of Henry IV., in 1610, De Monts lost his influence at court, and the merchants of his company having become tired of the continual expense of the Canadian colonization scheme, it was about to be abandoned. At this juncture, Champlain induced the Count de Soissons to take hold of the matter; and on the 8th of October, 1612, that nobleman was commissioned governor and lieutenant-general of New France. Champlain was now appointed lieutenant under him, and continued to act in this capacity until after the rights of De Soissons had been transferred to the Prince de Condé. Returning to Quebec in the spring of 1613, Champlain undertook to explore the Ottawa River, but did not proceed very far at this time. In the autumn of that year he sailed to Old France, and organized a trading company for Canada.

In 1615 he brought over four Recollects, or Recollets* (three priests and a lay brother), to attend to the spiritual needs of his colony. They embarked at Honfleur, and arrived in Quebec the 25th of May. The names of these first missionaries were, Fathers Denis Jamét, Jean d'Olbeau and Joseph le Caron, and Brother Pacificus de Plessis. It was with mingled curiosity and astonishment that the natives of the St. Lawrence Valley first beheld these gray friars, with their shaven crowns, sandaled feet, and long cassocks of coarse woolen cloth. Their first care, on arrival, was to select a site and begin the erection of a convent or religious house for their use. The paramount object of these monks was the conversion of the pagan Indians to Christianity; and, undismayed by the many

---

*The Recollects were a reformed branch of the old Franciscan order of friars.

obstacles and perils that confronted them, they met in council and assigned to each his province in the wide field of their proposed labors. By patient and persevering effort, they established missions at various points among the Montagnais and Hurons in Canada, but at length, finding the task too great for their limited numbers and resources, they applied to the Jesuits for assistance.

In 1616 Champlain accompanied his Indian allies in another expedition against the Iroquois, and afterward explored the river and valley of the Ottawa. Journeying thence westward, he appears to have discovered Lake Nipissing, and the Georgian Bay of Lake Huron, sleeping in their primeval solitudes, and engirt with dense forests of pine and cedar. By these different expeditions, our veteran explorer was enabled to form a more accurate idea of the geography of the Canadian country; inclosed by great lakes and rivers, and opening into vast interior regions, it seemed to him to afford unlimited scope for both commerce and settlement.

As early as 1611, the Jesuits, not without opposition and delay, had started a mission at Port Royal, in Acadia,* and when they received an invitation to enter Canada, they eagerly accepted it. But, owing to the prejudice existing against their order in the colony, it was not until 1625 that they gained a foothold on the banks of the St. Lawrence. During that year Fathers Charles Lalemant, Enemond, Masse, and Jean de Brébeuf, with two lay brothers, reached Quebec, where they were at first ill-received by the inhabitants, but were generously lodged in the house of the Recollets, on St. Charles River. In the following year (1626), three other Jesuits, to wit, Fathers Philibert, Noirot, and Ame de la Noue, with a lay brother, arrived at Quebec, and brought out with them several mechanics and laborers.†

---

* It was on the 22d of May, 1611, that Pierre Biard and Enemond Masse, two Jesuit priests, landed in Acadia. They had been ready to sail from France the year before, but were prevented from doing so by the directors of the colony. See Charlevoix' Hist. New France, vol. 1, p. 263, note.

† Charlevoix' Hist. New France, vol. 2, pp. 35, 37.

They were the first representatives in Canada of that celebrated religious society, which was destined to play so important a part in her ecclesiastical and civil affairs. The Jesuits had just fairly entered upon this chosen theater of labor, when they were interrupted and dispersed by the English invasion of the St. Lawrence Valley in 1629; but, four years later, they resumed their missionary work on a larger scale, and wrestled vigorously with heathenism in the northern wilderness. Cheerfully enduring every form of hardship, and confronting every extremity of personal danger, they penetrated the wildest recesses of the forest and lakes, and planted the cross, the symbol of their faith, among the most ignorant and savage tribes of the interior.

Quebec continued from the beginning to be the center of their operations, from whence missionary priests and teachers were dispatched far and wide.

During the year 1627 Cardinal Richelieu organized a company of one hundred associates, called *Le Compagnie d'Nouveau France*, upon whom was conferred the possession and government of Canada, with a monopoly of its trade and commerce, and freedom from taxation for fifteen years. Under the restrictive regulations of this company, the colonists were all required to be Frenchmen and Roman Catholics, a short-sighted policy, which hampered the growth and material prosperity of the colony. At this epoch the village of Quebec did not contain above one hundred regular inhabitants. It had in fact a fort, a church, a convent, and an hospital, before it contained a fixed population.

In July, 1629, after being blockaded for some time, Quebec was taken by an English squadron under the command of Sir David Kirk, a Huguenot refugee of Scotch parentage, who, with his two brothers, had been commissioned to ascend the St. Lawrence for that purpose. Champlain and his feeble garrison were now put on shipboard, and transported as prisoners of war to England. In passing down the river and out to sea, they barely escaped being recaptured by a French squadron under Emeric de Caen, who was coming to the relief of Quebec. The Jesuit missionaries on the St. Lawrence were also deported or driven away, and their missions broken up. But by the treaty of St. Germain en Laye, March 29, 1632, Canada was restored to its former proprietor, and Champlain was soon thereafter commissioned anew by Richelieu as director-general of the colony. At that time there was considerable discussion at the French court as to whether Canada were worth repossessing, so little was it valued.

On the 23d of May, 1633, the veteran Champlain, having sailed from Dieppe with three ships and two hundred new settlers, arrived once more at Quebec, and with him returned John de Brébeuf, the indefatigable Jesuit missionary. No sooner had Champlain resumed command in the colony, than he addressed himself to the task of restoring order, and of repairing the waste occasioned by the English occupation of the country. One of his first cares was to restore and strengthen the defenses of Quebec, which his quick military discernment and experience had taught him was the key to the St. Lawrence River and connecting lakes. During the next two years he also erected a fort on Richelieu Island, in Lake St. Peter of the St. Lawrence, and founded the post of *Trois Rivieres*, or Three Rivers, between Quebec and Montreal. But Champlain had now attained to the age of sixty-eight, and was worn out in the laborious service of his country. After an illness lasting two months, he expired at his quarters in Quebec on Christmas day, 1635, just one hundred years from the time of Cartier's first visit to the spot. He died without issue, and his young wife soon afterward entered an Ursuline convent, in which she passed the remainder of her days. Champlain appointed M. de Chateaufort to direct the affairs of the colony until the arrival of his successor, Charles Huault de Montmagny, a knight of Malta, who reached Canada in 1636, and remained eleven years.

We may not pause here to enlarge upon the personal and general character of Samuel de Champlain. He was a many sided man, and in his time played many parts. He "presented the rare intermixture of the heroic qualities of past times, with the zeal for science and the practical talents of modern ages." Apart from his high merits as a discoverer and scientific explorer, he was an intrepid negotiator with the aboriginal tribes, and possessed executive abilities of the first order. During a period of twenty-seven years (saving three years of enforced absence), he ably administered the affairs of the nascent colony, and devoted all his energies to the arduous duties of his position. Amid difficulties and discouragements that would have overwhelmed a less resolute and persevering man, he firmly fixed the authority of France upon the banks of the noble St. Lawrence, and thus achieved for himself a conspicuous and enduring place in the Gallic history of the country. Although traffic with the Indians was quite lucrative in his day, he does not appear to have personally engaged in it, for his thoughts were intent on higher things. As a military commandant he was just and firm, according to the maxims of his age, though his justice was ever tempered with clemency. A devout Catholic, he was zealous in promoting the religious welfare of the colonists, and in the effort to convert the aborigines to Christianity. In his writings he is charged with credulity for repeating the absurd stories told him by the Indians; but, though apparently fond of the marvelous, we are not to infer that he believed every thing he wrote, since much of it was related as hearsay. Charlevoix draws his character in flattering terms, and speaks of him as the "Father of New France."*

For twenty-eight years after Champlain's death, the management of public affairs in Canada was continued in the hands of the Hundred Associates, or partners, who ruled the colony arbitrarily in their own interests, and thereby restricted its normal growth and development. But in February, 1663, they voluntarily abandoned their charter to the king. In the following April, Louis XIV. issued an edict constituting a Sovereign Council, empowered to carry on the government of the province. New France thus became a royal province, with the laws and customs of the Parliament of Paris, and Quebec was con-

---

* Charlevoix' New France, vol. II, p. 89.

stituted a city. The white population of Canada then numbered but twenty-five hundred souls, of which eight hundred, including the garrison, were at Quebec.* At this transition period, Augustine de Saffray de Mésy was commissioned governor of the new province, and M. Talon intendant. De Mesy arrived at Quebec in September, 1663, and officiated until his death, which occurred May 5, 1665. He had been appointed on the recommendation of the Jesuits, but afterward disagreed with them, and his administration was infelicitous. At or before this time, however, the Marquis de Tracy was appointed viceroy, or lieutenant-general of New France, with Daniel de Rémi, Sieur de Courcelles, as governor, and Jean Baptiste Talon intendant. They arrived in the St. Lawrence during the summer of 1665, and entered upon the duties of their respective offices.

Under the new and more orderly system of government, the French-Canadians enjoyed domestic tranquillity and increased prosperity for a series of years. But this was interrupted toward the close of that century by border wars with the English settlers of New England and New York. In 1690, hostilities then existing between France and England, an army was raised in New York and Connecticut to march against Montreal, though it did not advance beyond Lake Champlain. This army of militia was intended to cooperate with an expedition by sea, under the command of Sir William Phipps, who sailed from Boston with a fleet of some thirty vessels. Entering the St. Lawrence in the month of October, and ascending it to Quebec, he landed a part of his troops, and laid siege to the city both by land and water; but he was repulsed and driven off by the French garrison under the veteran Count Frontenac. Subsequently, in the year 1711, the attempt against Quebec was renewed by Sir Hovenden Walker, with a fleet of thirty sail, and a large number of transports carrying troops, under one General Hill. But, after having lost ten of his transports by shipwreck at the mouth of the St. Lawrence, he

---

*Kingsford's Hist. of Canada, vol. I.

abandoned the expedition in disgust and returned to England.

By the treaty of Utrecht of April 11, 1713, Louis XIV. restored to England Hudson's Bay, ceded to her New Foundland and the larger part of Acadia, and renounced all claim to the Iroquois country, reserving to France the valleys of the St. Lawrence and Mississippi, and the region of the Upper Lakes. Prior to that time New France embraced not only the Canadas and all of Acadia, but parts of Northern New York and New England.

It was not until after the English attack by Phipps in 1690, that the French first attempted the construction of stone fortifications at Quebec, the town having been previously protected by palisades and earthworks. Thus was begun on a small scale that elaborate and unique system of fortification, now covering with its ravelins about forty acres, which crowns the summit of Cape Diamond at an elevation of three hundred and twelve feet above the level of the St. Lawrence, and which has been not inaptly termed the Gibraltar of America. Whoever has stood upon the parapetted and breezy heights of this renowned fortress could not have failed to be impressed with its exceeding military strength, or charmed with the magnificent and unrivaled view it commands of the surrounding rivers, valleys, villages, and distant mountains. The relative value and importance of the citadel as a place of defense, however, has been greatly diminished by the improved military science of the present age.*

Before closing this preliminary chapter, it is fitting that we should concisely yet distinctly trace the origin and primordial history of Montreal, the sister city of Quebec, and the great emporium of the Canadas. Montreal is situated on the southeastern side of the large, triangular island of the same name, at the head of ship navigation on the St. Lawrence River, and at the foot of that great chain of improved inland waters which stretch westward to the

---

* It was during a visit to this historic citadel that Daniel Webster caught the inspiration of one of his finest strains of eloquence.

extremity of Lake Superior. Within the extended limits of the present Canadian Dominion, no nobler site could well have been selected for a large commercial city. From this vantage point the majestic St. Lawrence, unbroken by any considerable rapids, flows on in one broad and deep channel for six hundred miles to the ocean, bearing upon its ample bosom the rich and varied products of an empire.

Montreal was founded in 1641-42, on the site of the ancient Indian village of Hochelaga. It was officially christened *Ville Marie*, or City of Mary, and for many years was known by that as well as its present name. As early as the year 1636, Jean Jacques Olier de Verneuil had formed an association in France, for the purpose of colonizing the island of Montreal. These associates purchased the Island of Jean de Lauson, August 7, 1640, and, in order to remove all doubts about the title, obtained a grant of it from the Company of New France, on the 17th of December, in that year. In the summer of 1641, they sent out the Sieur de Maisonneuve, a gentleman of Champagne, with a company of about forty colonists, including some ecclesiastics, to make a settlement. Maisonneuve arrived at Quebec on the 20th of August, and thence proceeded up the river to Montreal, where he was duly installed governor of the island. After wintering his colonists in Quebec and Sainté Foy, he returned to Montreal in the spring of 1642, and, on the 17th of May, having heard solemn mass, he began an intrenchment around his encampment. Subsequently, in 1656, the proprietorship of this company was transferred to the Society or Seminary of St. Sulpice, which had been founded by Father Olier, at Paris, in September, 1645, for the special training of candidates for the priesthood. The Sulpitians took possession of the island in 1657, and established there a seminary and missionary establishment, which has maintained its footing down to our time.*

Although of a distinctively religious origin, and never

---

* For a further account of the movement toward the first settlement of Montreal, see Charlevoix' Hist. New France, Vol. II, pp. 125 to 130, and accompanying notes.

the political capital of Canada, under the French *régime* (except for a short time after the fall of Quebec, in 1759), Montreal early became the commercial metropolis of the colony, the repository of its wealth, and the center of its increasing fur-trade. The town was not regarded by the colonial authorities as a place of special military consequence, nor was it ever regularly fortified until 1758, and then under the stress of war and expected English invasion. While its history is hardly so thrilling, or distinguished by so many vicissitudes, as that of Quebec, it is still replete with events of deep and abiding interest.

It was here, during the lengthened period of the Gallic rule, that most of those secular and missionary expeditions were finally equipped and sent out to the West, which first disclosed to European eyes the boundless extent and physical resources of the interior of North America. Here, from time to time, were wont to rendezvous and go forth to explore and subdue the savage wilderness, those little bands of Recollet friars and Jesuit priests, those high-bred and intrepid soldiers of fortune, those hardy adventurers, *voyageurs*, traders and trappers, whose deeds of daring and discovery, of courage and constancy, of penance and piety, of suffering and self-sacrifice, have been immortalized in prose and in verse.

CHAPTER II.

1539–1671.

DISCOVERY OF THE MISSISSIPPI RIVER AND OF THE NORTHWEST.

According to Spanish colonial chronicles, the Mississippi River was discovered by Hernando de Soto,* an ambitious soldier of fortune, who, after acquiring wealth and distinction under Pizarro in Peru, returned to Spain, and was commissioned by the emperor, Charles V., to be governor and captain-general for life of Cuba and Florida. Having obtained the imperial permission and authority to undertake, at his own expense, the exploration and conquest of Florida,† De Soto raised and equipped a force of six hundred picked men, Spaniards and Portuguese, besides twenty officers and twenty-four ecclesiastics. With these he put to sea from San Lucar, Spain, on April 6, 1538, and before the end of May arrived at the port of St. Jago de Cuba, then the seat of government, in the southeastern corner of the island. Here he tarried a few months to arrange his affairs of state, and then proceeded to Havana, where he was joined by his consort, Dóna Isabella, and all of his troops.

It was on the 18th of May, 1539, after fourteen months of busy preparation, that the captain-general and his splendid armament, with nodding plumes and waving banners, embarked for the shallow and treacherous coast of West Florida. Before setting sail, however, he appointed one of his trusted friends in Havana to act with his wife in the government of Cuba during his absence. His fleet consisted of five large ships, two caravels, and two brigantines,

---

* Variously written by different authors Ferdinand, Fernando, and Hernando de Soto.

† This large peninsula had been discovered and named by Ponce de Leon in 1512, but little was known of the interior of the country.

carrying six hundred and twenty soldiers, and two hundred and twenty-three horses.* They also carried a numerous retinue of priests, servitors, and camp-followers, and a large herd of swine. The horsemen were all furnished with shirts of mail, steel caps and greaves, after the military fashion of that age. The fleet quit the harbor of Havana with a favorable wind, but was becalmed on entering the Gulf of Mexico, and did not reach its destination until the 25th of May, when it came to anchor at the Bay of Espiritu Santo, now called Tampa Bay. On the 30th of that month De Soto debarked his troops, horses and baggage, and pitched his camp on the seashore. After some little skirmishing with hostile parties of the natives, in which several of his light-armed troops were wounded, he took possession of the deserted village of Ucita, situated about two leagues up the bay. This place he proceeded to fortify by throwing up intrenchments, etc., and made it his base of operations.

Learning from an Indian captive that a Spaniard was living not many leagues away, who had been a soldier in the unfortunate expedition of Pamphilio de Narvaez, in 1527 or '28, the governor sent an escort for him and had him brought to his headquarters. This Spaniard was a native of Seville, and his name was Juan Ortiz. He appeared at the Spanish camp with his face painted, and otherwise accoutered as a savage. On being interrogated he stated that he had lived among the Florida Indians eleven years, and knew their language very well, but could not tell much about the country, only that there was no gold in it. Taking him for a guide and interpreter, De Soto now set out to penetrate the interior with all his army, except sixty foot soldiers and twenty-six horsemen, who were left behind to guard the fort.†

After spending the remainder of that season in rambling through the tangled forests and everglades of the

---

*Narrative of Luis Hernandez de Biedma, or Biedura, factor of the expedition.
† Biedma's Narrative.

peninsula, he wintered in the territory of the Appalachians, near the northwestern coast, and during the next spring marched to the northeast, traversing what is now Georgia and a part of South Carolina. Arriving early in May on the banks of a wide river,* near a large village of the Cofitachiqui, the Indian queen of that nation sent her sister with a present of a necklace of beads to De Soto, and canoes with which to cross the river. When he reached the village, the queen gave him the use of one-half of it in which to lodge his men, and also sent him a present of many wild hens. Searching the graves of a dispeopled town in that vicinity for treasure, the Spaniards discovered a great store of pearls, which, however, had been injured by being buried in the ground. They also found two Spanish axes, and some beads resembling those brought from Spain for the purpose of trading with the Indians. It was conjectured that these last articles had been obtained in trade from the companions of Vasquez de Ayllon, who, sailing from Hispaniola, had landed at a port on the coast of Carolina in the year 1525.

Remaining at the village of the Indian princess several days, the Spanish governor next marched northwestward, crossing the southern spurs of the Blue Ridge Mountains, and thence bent his general course southward through the present State of Alabama, inquiring everywhere for the precious metals, often hearing of them, but finding little or none. The aborigines, living along this extended and tortuous route, were sometimes hostile, and at other times friendly, but nowhere offered any effectual resistance to the progress of the invaders. The privations and sufferings of the Spaniards were often severe, and their adventures bordered closely on the marvelous.†

About the middle of October, 1540, Soto and his army arrived at a large palisaded town called Mavila, or Mauvila (Mobile), which was situated on the Alabama

---

*Supposed to be the Savannah River, and probably in the Cherokee country.

† Thomas' History of the U. S.

River, a short distance above its confluence with the Tombigbee. The natives of that southern locality had conceived a strong aversion toward the Spaniards on account of their reputed inhumanity, and this was intensified by the arbitrary action of the latter in seizing and holding as prisoner, for a time, the Indian cacique, Tuscalosa, for suspected treachery. This bitter state of feeling soon burst out into a bloody conflict, which lasted several days, and during which the Indian town was fired and reduced to ashes, together with a great many of its inhabitants, and a part of the baggage of the Spaniards. According to some Spanish accounts, twenty-five hundred of the natives either died in battle, or were suffocated and burned to death, at Mavila.

Having now lost about one hundred of his men and forty-two horses, since landing in Florida, De Soto went into camp for a few weeks to rest his little army, and care for the wounded. Any one but this proud and headstrong captain would have here renounced his scheme of barren conquest and fruitless search for mineral wealth, and joined his brigantines which had arrived at the harbor of Ochuse,* only one hundred miles away. But still lured forward by the hope of finding some rich country, he broke up his camp and marched to the northwest. Fighting his way through the woods and across rivers into the heart of the Chickasaw country, he put his troops into winter quarters at the small village of Chicaca, on the upper waters (it is supposed) of the Yazoo River. Early in the following March, Soto, as had been his custom, made a requisition upon the principal cacique of the neighborhood for two hundred men to carry his baggage to the banks of the Mississippi. To this unexpected demand the wily sachem gave an evasive answer, and, instead of complying with it, secretly collected his warriors at night, and attacked and set fire to the village in which the Spaniards were lodged; thus causing the destruction of the clothing and stores of the latter, as well as the loss of fifty-seven of their horses

---

* Pensacola Bay, the Achusi of La Vega.

and fourteen men, who perished in the fight and flames.* This frightful disaster occasioned the Spaniards a month's delay, during which time forges were erected, swords retempered, ashen lances made, and every effort put forth to repair their irreparable losses.

At length, late in April, 1541, the indomitable commander again resumed his march, and, after struggling for a week or more through the intervening wilderness of forest and swamp, and meeting and overcoming stubborn opposition from the natives, he reached the long sought Mississippi†—the Rio Grande of De la Vega, and the Rio del Espiritu Santo of the Spaniards generally. The character of this mighty stream has not materially changed in the lapse of three and a half centuries. It was then described (at the place of crossing) as almost half a league wide, and flowing with a swift current in a deep channel. The river was always muddy, and trees and timber were continually floating down it. The Indian town where Soto first struck the main river, was called Quizquiz, or Chisca,‡ names now incapable of identification. The actual appearance of the Spanish captain, and of his tattered and battle-scarred followers, marshaled on the low banks of the Mississippi, was no doubt tame enough in contrast with the brilliantly pictured representation of the scene on canvas.

Here the resolute adventurers were detained nearly a month, constructing pirogues and barges to convey themselves, horses and baggage, over the river. They appear to have crossed to the western side at the foot of the lowest Chickasaw bluff, a short distance below the site of the present city of Memphis. Such, at all events, is the generally received opinion, though a few modern writers endeavor to

---

* See Biedma's Narrative.

† "There is probably no river that has had so many names as this great river. The name Mechisapa was afterward written Missisipi, and finally Mississippi. The Indians, according to their different localities and languages, had different names for it. Soto first knew it by the name of Chucagua. The French several times changed its name, calling it St. Louis, Colbert, etc."—Shipp's History DeSoto, p. 674.

‡ The latter is the name given by La Vega.

fix the place of their crossing below the junction of the Arkansas.*

After passing the Mississippi, Soto and his caravan moved in a northwesterly direction to the Indian village of Pacaha, situated not far to the west of the modern New Madrid, Missouri. Stopping there some twenty-seven days, he sent out small parties to explore the country, and afterward marched north and west to the highlands of White River, the northern limit of his expedition. Still seeking the rich realm described by De Vaca,† the Spanish captain now changed his course to the southeast, and came to a large town of the people called Quigata. This is supposed to have been on the river Arkansas, near Little Rock. But he was again tempted westward, up into the region of the Ozark mountains, and on his route may have passed by the Hot Springs, one of the fabled fountains of youth. He next wintered at the town of Vicanque, or Autiamque, which was probably on the Upper Arkansas, though some writers place it on the headwaters of the Washita. It was here that Juan Ortiz, the interpreter, died much regretted.

In March, 1542, De Soto left Vicanque and descended the Valley of the Arkansas, to get information in regard to the sea. Returning to the banks of the Mississippi, he fixed his fortified camp at a village called Guachoya, or Guachoyanque,‡ which was probably situated not far below the confluence of the Arkansas. The commander now found his health and strength declining under the fatigues and anxieties of his disappointing enterprise, and his lofty pride gave way to a settled melancholy. This was accompanied

---

* See the different opinions on this mooted question collected in a note to Bancroft's History of the U. S. (edition of 1875) vol I, p. 59. See also a lengthy note on the "Route of DeSoto," in the appendix to B. Shipp's History of Soto and Florida (Philadelphia, 1881), pp. 676–681.

† Cabeca de Vaca was second in command of the expedition of Narvaez in 1528, and it is asserted or conjectured that he discovered one of the mouths of the Mississippi.

‡ Some modern writers, including Bancroft, locate Guachoya near the mouth of Red River; but we prefer to follow Mr. McCullough, Mr. Shea, and others, who would confine De Soto's wanderings west of the Great River to the Valley of the Arkansas and its tributaries.

by a malignant and wasting fever, of which he died on the 5th of June, 1542, being aged about forty and six years. The knowledge of his death was kept a secret from the Indians of the locality, who yet surmised the fact, and his body, wrapped in a mantle, was buried within the camp or town. But to effectually guard the corpse against outrage by the superstitious savages, it was exhumed a few days after, and placed in the hollowed trunk of an oak, and then lowered at midnight into the deep bosom of the Father of Waters,* an appropriate resting-place for its daring discoverer. It is related that his sympathetic and devoted wife expired at Havana within three days after hearing the sad tidings of his end.

According to the more credible authorities, Hernando de Soto was born at Xeres de los Cabelleros, in the principality of Estramadura, Spain, about the year 1496. He was the scion of a noble yet impoverished family, and was indebted to one Pedrais d' Avila for the means of pursuing an university course. After this he went to the West Indies, and joined Pizarro's expedition to Peru. In his exploration and attempted conquest of Florida, he is said to have expended more than one hundred thousand ducats.

Garcilasso de la Vega, in his "History of the Conquest of Florida," gives us this concise yet flattering delineation of De Soto's person and character:

"He was a little above the medium height, had a cheerful countenance, though somewhat swarthy, and was an excellent horseman. Fortunate in his enterprises, if death had not interrupted his designs; vigilant, skillful, ambitious, patient under difficulties; severe to chastise offenses, but ready to pardon others; charitable and liberal toward the soldiers; brave and daring, as much so as any captain who

---

* The Knight of Elvas states, in his narrative, that Soto died on the 21st of May, 1542, and also gives a different account of his final burial from that currently accepted. He says: "Luys de Moscoso commanded him (Soto) to be taken up, and to cast a great deal of sand into the mantles in which he was wound, wherein he was carried in a canoe, and thrown into the river."

had entered the new world. So many rare qualities caused him to be regretted by all the troops."*

By his last will, De Soto appointed Luis de Muscoso d'Alvarado, his favorite lieutenant, to succeed him in command of the army, which had been reduced by disease and casualties to one-half its original number. The real purpose of the expedition was now abandoned, the only object of the survivors being to quit the country as best they might. Doubting his ability to lead the men back to Cuba by way of the Mississippi and the Gulf, the new commander set forth on a long and hazardous journey to the west and southwest in hopes of reaching the Spanish settlements in northern Mexico, as De Vaca claimed to have done after the failure of the expedition of Narvaez, to which allusion has been made. In the course of this arduous march, extending over seven hundred miles, Muscoso and his troop traversed a considerable part of the Valley of Red River, and passed by some tribes who were found still inhabiting that country when it was first explored by the French, nearly a century and a half later. The most westerly town reached by our band of adventurers was named Nacachoz, or Nazachoz, in western Texas. Here they saw pottery, turquoises, and cotton mantles from Mexico, and met with an Indian woman who had belonged to a Spanish expedition sent eastward from the Pacific coast a few years before. Continuing to advance ten days longer, they crossed a considerable river,‡ when they found themselves in a desert region peopled by roving and predatory tribes.

Disheartened at the cheerless prospect, and fearing treachery from their native guides, the Spaniards now faced about and retraced their weary course to the Mississippi. Arrived once more at Guachoya, where Soto had deceased, they determined to construct some vessels with which to descend to the sea and return to their own country. But not finding the requisite facilities for the work, they as-

---

* See Shipp's History of De Soto and Florida, p. 438.

† Supposed to have been the Pecos branch of the Rio Bravo del Norte.

cended the river to the village of Minoya,* where they went
into winter quarters and stayed six months. Here they set
up a forge, and worked all their iron and chains into nails
and spikes. They cut and dressed timbers, split boards,
laid keels, and thus built seven light brigantines, in which
they laid loose planks for decks, and afterward stretched
rawhides and mats to protect themselves from the Indian
arrows.

It was on the 2d of July, 1543, that the shattered
remnant of Soto's once proud array, now reckoned at only
three hundred and twenty-two men, embarked in their
slender brigantines, with a canoe attached to each, and
began to drift down the great river. During the voyage,
they suffered great annoyance and injury from the Indians
along the Lower Mississippi, who were exasperated at the
Spaniards on account of their cruelties, and who followed
them in canoes for many days, and harassed them with repeated attacks, both by land and water. In one of these
encounters with the savages, according to the Knight of
Elvas, the brave Juan de Guzman and ten soldiers were
slain or drowned in the river. Escaping at length from
their enemies, and having sailed as they computed two
hundred and fifty leagues, Muscoso and his followers
reached the Gulf of Mexico on the 18th of July. From
thence, instead of venturing to cross the open sea in their
weak craft, they coasted its low shores to the west and
south for fifty-two days, and, after undergoing incredible
hardships, finally arrived at the town of Panuco, in Mexico,
on the 10th of September. "The inhabitants of Panuco,"
says the old chronicler, Garcilasso de la Vega, "were all
touched with pity at beholding this forlorn remnant of the
gallant armament of the renowned Hernando de Soto.
They were blackened, haggard, shriveled up, and half-
naked, being clad only with the skins of deer, buffalo,

---

* Or Aminyo. The precise location of this village, where the brigantines were built, can not now be settled, its Spanish-Indian name
having left no trace, but it is supposed to have been on a small river
that put into the Mississippi a few miles above the mouth of the Arkansas.

bears and other animals, and looking more like wild beasts than human beings.*

This wonderful yet disastrous expedition, covering a period of over four years, was practically the beginning of the history of the United States of North America; for the migrations and wars of the savage tribes, who had hitherto occupied the whole country, are of hardly more historical value than the flights and skirmishes of so many hawks and crows. In this category we would not class the old Mound Builders, of whom and whose works so much has been learnedly written, while so little comparatively is really known. They, too, were probably Indians, though of a more intelligent and civilized type than those found here by the Europeans.

Subsequently, in the year 1557, owing to the implacable hostility of the natives, and to the loss of the crews of several Spanish ships that had been wrecked on the coasts of Florida, the King of Spain gave orders for the military reduction of that country. Accordingly, in 1559, an expedition of fifteen hundred men was equipped and sailed from Vera Cruz, Mexico, under the command of the veteran Don Tristan de Luna. He landed with his army at St. Mary's Bay, now Pensacola, and advanced northward into the interior, and thence westward to the Mississippi, in the country of the Natchez Indians. In the meantime dissensions and revolts arose among his troops, which impaired the success of the expedition, and necessitated a retrograde march to the coast, where vessels soon after arrived and carried the survivors back to Mexico.

Henceforth the Mississippi River appears to have been neglected and forgotten by the Spaniards, although they had explored it for nearly a thousand miles, and were acquainted with at least two of its principal western tributa-

---

* For full, if not always trustworthy accounts of De Soto's expedition, see the contemporary chronicles of Biedma or Biedura, of the Gentleman of Elvas, and of Garcilasso de la Vega, several English versions of which are in print. That of Biedma is the shortest, and perhaps the most authentic.

ries. It was afterward laid down on their maps of West Florida as a comparatively unimportant stream, and was not always distinguished by its original Spanish name; nor is it certain that any ship of that nation had ever entered and ascended the great river from the sea. Spain thus abandoned the Valley of the Mississippi to its primitive wildness and savagery, partly because of the great difficulty of penetrating the country, but chiefly for the reason that no El Dorado, no glittering gold, was found in all that semi-tropical region to attract and satisfy Spanish cupidity.

Nearly a hundred years had elapsed after Soto's primal discovery, when Jean Nicolet, an intrepid French *voyageur*, reached the vicinity of a northern affluent of the Mississippi. John Nicolet was a son of Thomas Nicolet, of Cherbourg, France. He came to Canada as a youth in 1618, and was shortly after sent by Champlain to reside with the barbarous Algonquins on the *Isle des Allumettes*, situated in the Ottawa River, above Chaudiere Falls. He stayed with them two years, following them in their periodical hunts, partaking of their fatigues and privations, and often suffering keenly from the pangs of hunger and the brutality of the savages. In the meantime, however, he acquired an intimate knowledge of the Algonquin language, then generally spoken on both the Ottawa River and the northern banks of the St. Lawrence. Nicolet afterward went to reside among the Nipissings, on the shores of the lake of that name, with whom he remained about nine years. Here he lived as an Indian, speaking their harsh tongue, having his own little cabin and establishment, and doing his own fishing and trading. But he still continued a Frenchman and a Catholic, and at length returned to the confines of civilization, because, as he said, " he could not live without the sacraments," which were denied him in the depths of the wilderness.

After the repossession of Canada by the French in July, 1632, the Sieur Nicolet was employed as a commissary and Indian interpreter for the company that governed the colony. In 1634, or thereabouts, he was sent as an agent or

Jean Nicolet. 35

embassador to the Winnebagoes, who dwelt near the head of Green Bay of Lake Michigan.* They had quarreled with the Nez Perces, or Beaver Indians, whose hunting-grounds lay to the north of Lake Huron, and who were friendly toward the French. Nicolet was charged, among other things, to negotiate a peace with those discordant tribes. But the main object of his expedition appears to have been to solve the problem of a western and more direct route to China, which country was supposed to be situated not far beyond the most westerly of the great lakes.

Agreeably to the best accredited account of his celebrated journey, Nicolet set out in a bark canoe, with seven Huron Indians for guides and huntsmen, and ascended the Ottawa River to a station above Allumette Island. Turning thence to the west, he traveled by way of Lake Nipissing to the Georgian Bay of Lake Huron, and followed its rugged and forbidding coast up to the Rapids of St. Mary, where he held interviews with the natives of those parts. Returning down the strait of that name, he next entered and passed through the Straits of Michilimackinac— about three leagues in length—emerging on the watery expanse of Lake Michigan, or Lake of Illinois, as it was first known by the French, of which he was entitled to the

---

* "In no record, contemporaneous or later," says Mr. Butterfield, "is the date of his journey thither given, except approximately. The fact of Nicolet having made the journey to the Winnebagoes is first noticed by (Father) Vimont, in the Relation of 1640, p. 35. He says: " *Le visite ray tout maintenant le coté du sud, ie diray ou passant, que le Sieur Nicolet, interpreter en langue Algonquine et Huronne pour Messieurs de la Nouvelle France, m' a donné les noms de ces nations qu'il a visitée luy mesme pour la plupart dans leur pays, tous ces peuples entendant L'Algonquine, excepté les Huronns, que ont rue langue á part comme aussi les Ouinipigou ou gens de mer.*' The year of Nicolet's visit, it will be noticed, is left undetermined. The extract only shows that it must have been made in or before 1639." Mr. Butterfield then goes on to show, pretty conclusively, that Nicolet made his voyage to the northwest in 1634, returning thence the following year. Mr. Parkman, however, fixes the time of the journey between 1635 and 1638, and Mr. Shea in 1639. To the last named scholar is ascribed the credit of having been the first to identify the "Ouinipigou, or Gens de Mer," of Father Vimont with the Winnebagoes. See "Nicolet's Discovery of the Northwest," by C. W. Butterfield (Cincinnati, 1881), pp. 42–45, and accompanying notes.

honor of discovery. After boldly threading his course around its wild, northern shores to the Bay of Noquet, an arm of Green Bay, he made his way over the latter to the mouth of a stream flowing in from the west, where he met a tribe of Indians called the Menominees. From thence he resumed his voyage up Green Bay toward the Winnebagoes, who, having received word of his coming, had sent a number of their young braves to meet him and escort him to their villages.

Nicolet found the Winnebagoes to be a numerous people, living in bark and skin covered lodges, and speaking a guttural language radically different from that of the Huron and Algonquin Indians. They belonged to the great family of the Sioux or Dakotas, and were the only branch of that stock who dwelt so far eastward of the Mississippi. Nicolet's arrival created a great sensation among the Winnebagoes, for he was the first white man to visit them, and four or five thousand of the tribe assembled to greet him. Each of the principal chiefs gave a feast in his honor, at one of which a hundred and twenty beavers are said to have been served. On taking leave of the Winnebagoes, he journeyed for six days up Fox River, and thence passed through Lake Winnebago to the homes of the Maskoutens, or Mascoutins, who afterward became banded with the Miamis. It seems that the Sauks and Foxes had not as yet migrated from the East to this section of the country. Hearing from the Mascoutins of a nation called the Illinois, we are told that he continued his progress southward and visited some of the villages of that people. While exploring the Fox River, he also heard of the Wisconsin; but as the account given by him of this tributary of the Mississippi is vague and confused, it is by no means certain that he either saw or navigated any part of it.

"It has been extensively published," says Mr. Butterfield, "that Nicolet did reach the Wisconsin, and float down its channel to within three days (sail) of the Mississippi. Now Nicolet, in speaking of a large river upon which he had sailed, evidently intended to convey the idea of its being connected with the lake, that is, with Green Bay. Hence he must have spoken of Fox River. But Vimont (Relation, 1640, page 36) understood him as saying that had he sailed three more days on a great river which flows from that lake, he would have found the sea," or "great water" of the Indians.

On his return trip, Nicolet stopped to form the acquaintance of the Poutouatamis (Pottawatomies), who occupied the islands in the mouth of Green Bay, and there met with a friendly reception. Shortly after arriving at Quebec from his tour to the far west, he was sent to the Three Rivers, where he resumed and continued his duties as commissary and Indian interpreter.

On the 22d of October, 1637, Jean Nicolet was married in Quebec to Marguerite Couillard, a god-child of Samuel de Champlain, and by this union became the father of one child, a daughter. Four years later (1641), he was associated with Father Paul Ragueneau in making a treaty with a large band of the Iroquois, who, having entered Canada, were threatening the post of Three Rivers.

"About the first of October, 1642, he was called down to Quebec to take the place of his brother-in-law, Olivier de Tardiff, who was general commissary of the Hundred Partners or Associates, and who sailed on the 7th of that month to Old France. The change was very agreeable to Nicolet, but he did not enjoy it long; for in less than a month after his arrival, in endeavoring to make a trip to his former place of residence, to release an Indian prisoner in possession of a band of Algonquins who were slowly torturing him, his zeal and humanity cost him his life. On the 27th of October, he embarked at Quebec, near 7 o'clock in the evening, in the launch of M. de Savigny, which was headed for Three Rivers. He had not yet reached Sillery (four miles above Quebec), when a northeast squall raised a terrible tempest on the St. Lawrence, and filled the boat. Those in it did not immediately drown. Nicolet had time to say to M. de Savigny, 'Save yourself, sir, you can swim; I can not. I am going to God; I recommend to you my wife and daughter.' The wild waves tore the men one after another from the boat, which had capsized and floated against a rock; and four of the number, including Nicolet, sank to rise no more." *

Thus was overwhelmed in the surging billows of the St. Lawrence, while on an errand of Christian charity, the Sieur Jean Nicolet, the first European, whose slender canoe cleaved the limpid waters of Lake Michigan, and the first who is known to have set foot in the level prairies of Southern Wisconsin. His untimely death was regretted in common by his countrymen and the red men. The story of his adventurous yet useful life has been worthily written, and his memory survives in the name of a county and town in Lower Canada.

It may seem strange that the Mississippi River, draining as it does the heart of the continent, should have remained so long unknown throughout its course to the English colonists on the Atlantic seaboard; but they evinced no early disposition to venture beyond the mountains that walled them in on the west. The vague story of an English voyage up the great river in 1648, has found some advocates, though it is quite improbable, considering the fact that the Gulf of Mexico was then a closed sea to all European vessels save the Spanish. In a book, descriptive of the Province of Carolina, published by Dr. Daniel Coxe, in London, in 1727, it is affirmed that a certain Colonel Wood, residing at the Falls of James River, Virginia, discovered different branches of the Ohio and Mississippi Rivers between the years 1654 and 1664. "It is possible, however (says Col. R. T. Durrett, in his elaborate historical address on the anniversary of Kentucky's Centennial of Statehood), that Dr. Coxe has credited Col. Wood with an exploration that was made by Captain Thomas Batts, at a little later date. In 1671, Gen. Abraham Wood, by the authority of Governor Berkeley, sent Captain Batts with a party of explorers to the west of the Appalachian Mountains, in search of a river that might lead across the continent to-

---

* "Discovery of the Northwest by Jean Nicolet; with a Sketch of his Life and Explorations." By C. W. Butterfield, pp. 82–84.

ward China. The journal of their route is rendered obscure by meager descriptions, and the change of names since it was written; but it is possible that they went to the Roanoke, and, ascending it to its headwaters, crossed over to the sources of the Kanawha, which they descended," probably to the Ohio. But it does not appear that either of those Virginia explorers ever penetrated beyond the region of the Upper Ohio.

In the meantime, however, the French Jesuits and fur-traders were pushing deeper and farther into the wilderness of the northern lakes. About the year 1634, three Jesuit priests, Brébeuf, Daniel and Lalemant, planted a mission among the Hurons on the shores of Lake Simcoe, and another on the southeastern border of Lake Huron. In 1641 the Fathers, Isaac Jogues and Charles Raymbault, embarked upon the Georgian Bay of Lake Huron, for the Sault de Ste Marie, where they arrived after a tedious canoe passage of seventeen days. They were met there by a concourse of some two thousand natives (probably Ojibwas), who had been apprised of their coming, and to whom they proclaimed the mysteries of the Romish faith. Father Raymbault died in the wilderness in 1642, while pursuing his missionary labors and discoveries. The same year, Jogues and Bressani were captured and tortured by the Indians. Then followed the havoc and destruction of an Iroquois war, by which the Jesuit missions were broken up, and many of their priests were either tortured or put to death. "Literally did those zealous missionaries 'take their lives in their hands,' and lay them a willing sacrifice on the altar of their faith."

For a number of years, therefore, all further French exploration was arrested. "At length, in 1658, two daring traders penetrated to Lake Superior, wintered there, and brought back tales of the ferocious Sioux, and of a great western river on which they dwelt. Two years later (1660), the aged Jesuit (Réne), Menard,* attempted to plant a mis-

---

* Recent publications," says the late John Gilmary Shea, " have placed a Jesuit mission on the lake (Superior), and even on the Mississippi, as early as 1653; but the Relations have not the slightest allusion

sion on the southern shore of that lake, but perished in the forest by famine or the tomahawk. Allouez succeeded him, explored a part of Lake Superior, and heard in his turn of the Sioux and their great river, the 'Mesissipi.' More and more the thoughts of the Jesuits, and not of the Jesuits alone, dwelt on this mysterious stream. Through what regions did it flow, and whither would it lead them—to the South Sea, or the Sea of Virginia; to Mexico, Japan, or China? The problem was soon to be solved, and the mystery revealed."*

The different enterprises of the Jesuits and fur-traders having made known the country of the northwest, the French-Canadian officials took steps to extend over it the jurisdiction and authority of the King of France. Pursuant to this end, on September 8, 1670, Jean Talon,† the active and able intendant of New France, selected and commissioned Simon Francois Daumont, Sieur de St. Lusson, as his deputy to go in search of copper mines, and to hold a general conference with the indigenous tribes about the outlet of Lake Superior. To avoid any pecuniary outlay on the part of the provincial government, the resources of which were rather limited, it was arranged that St. Lusson should remunerate himself for the expenses of his expedition by trading with the Indians. He set out from Quebec

---

to the fact, and speak of Menard as the first. The Jesuits named (Father Dugérre and others) as being concerned are not mentioned in the journal of the superior of the mission, nor in any printed Relation, nor in Ducreux, nor in Le Clercq. The fact of a mission at Tamaroa prior to Marquette's is perfectly incompatible with the Relations, and if established would destroy their authority."—Shea's History of the Discovery and Exploration of the Mississippi Valley (N. Y., 1853), p. 23, *note*.

* Parkman's Introduction to his "La Salle and the Great West."

† Jean Baptiste Talon was the second intendant of New France, and the first, we believe, under the royal government of the country, which prospered under his administration. He was intendant, or rather superintendent of justice, police, and finance—the position being next in rank and dignity to that of governor. He was first appointed to this office in 1663, and served till 1668, and again from 1670 to 1672, when he returned to Old France and accepted the position of principal secretary in the king's household. Talon was born in Picardy in 1625, and died at Versailles in 1691. His portrait in oil is preserved in the Hotel-Dieu of Quebec, and presents him as a handsome and courtly gentleman.

with a company of fifteen men, in several canoes, taking a full supply of goods and other needed articles, and was accompanied by Nicholas Perrot as Indian interpreter.

According to Parkman, few names are more conspicuous in the annals of the early Canadian *voyageurs* than that of Perrot; not because of the superiority of his achievements over those of many others, but for the reason that he could write, and left behind him a tolerable record of what he had seen and done. Like Nicolet, Perrot was a man of undoubted courage and address, and exhibited both of these qualities in his dealings with 'the various tribes of red men. He was now about twenty-six years of age, and had previously been in the employ of the Jesuits.

The Sieur de St. Lusson and party wintered on or near the Manatoulin Islands, in the northern part of Huron Lake, and occupied the time in hunting and bartering with the natives for their furs. Meanwhile Perrot, after first sending messages to the tribes of the north, inviting them to meet the deputy of the Canadian intendant at Sault de Ste Marie in the ensuing spring, continued his voyage westward to Green Bay, and pressed the same invitation on the Indian nations inhabiting that ulterior region. Flattered by his visit and personal attentions, they all promised to send deputations as requested. Accordingly, in the spring of 1671, the principal chiefs of the Pottawatomies (who also undertook to represent the Miamis in the absence of their own old chief), the Menominees, Winnebagoes and Sacs, set off in their light canoes, and paddled their way over the watery plains to the Sault, whither they arrived about the 5th of May. St. Lusson and his Frenchmen were there in advance to receive them. The Indians of the surrounding country now came flocking in from their hunting grounds, attracted in part by the fisheries at the rapids, and partly by the polite messages of Perrot. They comprised the Crees, Monsonies, Amikoues, Nipissings, and sundry other petty tribes, with names too barbarous to be written.

When the representatives of some fourteen tribes had arrived, and after the usual feasting and sleeps, St. Lusson prepared to execute the special commission with which he had been charged. Accordingly, on the 14th of June, in presence of the assembled Indians and Frenchmen, including four Jesuit priests* in the vestments of their office, he proceeded to take formal possession, in the king's name, of Sainté Marie du Sault, as also of Lakes Huron and Superior, the Manatoulin Islands, and all the countries, lakes, rivers and streams, contiguous or adjacent thereto. A tall wooden cross was now erected, for the adoration of the natives, and close by its side was planted a stout cedar post, to which was affixed a metal plate engraven with the royal arms of the Bourbons. A hymn was then sung, and one of the Jesuit priests offered up a prayer for the King of France; after which the Frenchmen discharged their muskets and cried *vive le roi*. When these formalities were ended, Father Alloucz addressed the Indians in a solemn harangue in their own language, to which they stolidly listened while smoking their stone pipes. Soon after the French party had left the place of assembly, some of those copper-hued sons of the forest removed the metallic plate from the post to which it had been nailed, and appropriated it to their own use. This was done, says Mr. Parkman, not so much from any knowledge of the true import of the plate, as from their superstitious fear of its influence as a charm. But the general effect of this notable convocation and conference with the indigenous tribes of the northwest was favorable to the French commercial and political interests, as well as to their designs for the future exploration of the great river and regions beyond. As a part of the history of this expedition, it is stated that the costly presents made by St. Lusson to the Indian chiefs, and other necessary expenses, were more than repaid by the gifts of valuable furs which he received from them in return.

---

*The names of these priests were, Claude Dablon, superior of the missions on the upper lakes; Gabriel Dreuilletes, Claude Allouez, and Louis André. Louis Joliet is mentioned as among the Frenchmen present on the occasion. Marquette was away at the Mission of St. Esprit, on Lake Superior, but was compelled to abandon it during that year.

Other French Enterprises. 43

It is deserving of mention here, that two years before this time, La Salle, then a young and little known man, had projected the discovery of the Mississippi. In July, 1669, he undertook, at his own expense, a journey to the southwest for that purpose. Proceeding with a company from Montreal up the St. Lawrence, and through Lake Ontario to Lake Erie, he thence rambled southward and discovered the Ohio River, which he followed down to the falls or rapids at what is now Louisville. A year or two after his return from this expedition, he is said to have ascended the great lakes, and, pushing on to and beyond the southern extremity of Lake Michigan, discovered the Illinois River, or one of its constituent branches. But of this, more hereafter.

Such, in general, was the progress of French exploration in the interior of this continent, and such was still the limited state of their geographical knowledge in regard to the Mississippi River and its tributaries, down to the time of Joliet's and Marquette's voyage of discovery in 1673; prior to which it is not known that any "pale face" had ever reached, or looked upon, the main trunk of that liquid highway, above the mouth of the Ohio.*

Father Claude Dablon, whose name finds repeated mention in these pages, merits something more than a passing notice. He came as a missionary to Canada in 1655, and was at once sent to Onondaga (New York), where he remained, with one short interval of absence, until the mission there was broken up in 1658. Three years later, he and Gabriel Dreuilletes attempted to reach Hudson's Bay, by the Saguenay River, but were stopped at the sources of the Nekouba by Iroquois war parties. In 1668, Dablon followed Father Marquette to the foot of Lake Superior, assisted in founding the mission of Sault de Ste. Marie, visited Green Bay, and, in company with Father Allouez, reached the sources of the Wisconsin. Returning thence to Quebec, he was made superior of all the Canadian missions, and held this office with intervals till

---

* It is claimed that one Pierre Esprit Radison, a noted *voyageur* and trader, reached the Upper Mississippi in 1658–59; but, if so, he never gave the world the benefit of his discovery. An account of his alleged explorations has been published somewhat recently.

about 1693. He was still alive in 1694, but the year of his death is unknown.

As the head of the Jesuit missions, Father Dablon contributed in no small degree to their extension, and, above all, to the exploration of the Mississippi by Marquette and Joliet. He published the Relations of 1670-'71, and '72, with their accompanying map of Lake Superior, and prepared for the press those of 1672-'73, and 1673-'79, which, together with his narratives of Marquette and Allouez, remained a long while in manuscript, for the reason that the publication of the Relations was interdicted in 1673. He was versed alike in the learning of the cloister and in the mysteries of the forest, and, according to Dr. Shea, his writings comprise the most valuable collection of topography of the northwest, which have come down to our day.

CHAPTER III.

1673–1675.

THE GREAT RIVER VOYAGE OF JOLIET AND MARQUETTE.

To Jean Talon, the able and enterprising intendant, already referred to, belongs the chief credit of having initiated the movement for the French discovery of the Mississippi. To effect this long desired object, he selected Louis Joliet, of Quebec, to conduct the expedition, with one of the Jesuit priests for his companion and assistant. But M. Talon did not remain in Canada long enough to witness the completion of the bold undertaking which he had projected, and which was prolific of such important and far-reaching results. Owing to repeated disagreements between himself and Governor Courcelles, in regard to the jurisdiction of their respective offices, both requested to be and were recalled. Failing health was also assigned as a reason for the governor's retirement. It is not improbable that the intendant, as the more brainy and energetic man of the two, had trenched upon the governor's authority.

Not long afterward, in the autumn of 1672, Louis de Buade, Comte de Palluau et Frontenac was sent out to Canada as the successor of Courcelles. Count Frontenac belonged to the high *noblesse* of France, and was the ninth governor of the colony after Champlain. He was now somewhat past middle life, and said to be broken in fortune; but he was a man of rare accomplishments, experienced in statecraft, and endowed with uncommon administrative ability. Although haughty and intolerant toward his enemies, he was ardently devoted to his friends; while his courtly manners and brilliant conversation made him a favorite and an ornament of the most cultivated circles. His powers, as chief executive, were derived directly from the crown, and were absolute within the sphere of his jurisdiction, though partly checked by those of the intendant. His government was aggressive and stormy, and was beset by strong opposition and enmity, which eventuated, after ten years, in his recall by the king. But when the colony had been brought to the verge of ruin under the weak administrations of LaBarre and DeNonville, Frontenac was reinstated in 1689, and the closing term of his official life was crowned with success, and with the plaudits of his countrymen, He died in Quebec in 1698, at an advanced age, and was interred in the Church of the Recollet Fathers, to whom he was warmly attached.

But to resume our principal theme. Upon the recommendation of Talon, before his final departure for France, Governor Frontenac charged Joliet with the conduct of the exploration of the Mississippi, "as being a man experienced in this kind of discovery, and who had been already very near that river." Apart from this official sanction of the enterprise, about all the aid afforded to Joliet by the provincial government, was one assistant and a bark canoe.

Of Louis Joliet* himself, some account must needs be given before starting him on his great exploration. The son of Jean Joliet, an humble mechanic, he was born in Quebec, September 21, 1645. When of proper age, he was put to school at the Jesuit Seminary in his native town. Here he made excellent progress in his studies, and evinced a special taste for hydrography. Completing his curriculum at the seminary in 1666, he took some minor orders in the church, but soon discovered that he had no call to the priesthood, and therefore exchanged the cassock for the trader's garb. In October, 1667, he appears to have sailed to France, and remained there until the next year. Entering upon his new career in the spring of 1669, he was sent by Intendant Talon, with a young companion, to look for copper mines in the wild, western region of Lake Superior, but returned without success from this mission. He

---

*This surname has several synonyms, as for example, Jollyet, Jolliet, and Joliette; but it is usually written Joliet.

Father Marquette. 47

further appears to have been present at the grand council held by St. Lusson with the Northwestern tribes, in the spring of 1671; but whether as a member of his party is undetermined.

The selection of Father Marquette, as the companion of Joliet in the proposed exploration of the Mississippi, seems to have been made informally on the recommendation of the superior general of the Jesuits at Quebec. He was doubtless chosen on account of his known zeal for the conversion of the western Indians, and his proficiency in the languages or dialects spoken by the different tribes. Jacques, or James Marquette came of a family distinguished in the walks of both civil and military life. He was cradled in the ancient town of Laon, in the department of Aisne, France, in the year 1637. From his pious mother (née Rose de la Salle), he imbibed an ardent and generous temperament, predisposed alike to piety and benevolence. In 1654, at the youthful age of seventeen, he voluntarily joined the Society of Jesus, of which he was to become so eminent a member. After two years of studious application, he was, in accordance with the custom of that society, employed a part of his time in teaching, and continued in the faithful performance of his unostentatious duties until 1666, when he was ordained to the Jesuit priesthood. No sooner had he been invested with this sacred character, than he showed an inclination to go upon a foreign mission; but the ecclesiastical Province of Champagne, in which he was enrolled, embraced no such mission. He was therefore transferred to the Province of France, and in the summer of that same year (1666) sailed to Canada, arriving at Quebec on the 20th of September.

Marquette was now twenty-nine years old, and buoyant with life, health and hope. At first he was destined by his superiors to the mission among the Montagnais Indians, in the Valley of the St. Lawrence; and on the 10th of October he started from Quebec for Three Rivers, to begin the study of that language under the instruction of Father Gabriel Dreuilletes. He remained there until April, 1668, when, his original destination having been changed, he was ordered to prepare for the Ottawa mission. In the meantime he had acquired a fair knowledge of the Algonquin tongue, and was thus qualified for entering his new field of labor. While waiting at Montreal for the departure of the Ottawa flotilla, he met a party of the Nez Perce or Beaver Indians, who were returning to their home in the northwest. Setting out with them, he journeyed up the river Ottawa, through Lake Nipissing and down French River to Lake Huron, and thence around its northern shore to the outlet of Lake Superior. Here, in company with Claude Dablon, a zealous and intrepid brother Jesuit, he 'founded the mission of St. Mary of the Falls, otherwise known as Sault de Ste Marie. After building a log house and chapel, and converting a number of the savages to an outward belief in Christianity, Marquette was directed to proceed to La Pointe St. Esprit, situated on the Bay of Chegoimegon, near the southwestern corner of Lake Superior, and arrived thither September 13, 1669. At this far westerly point, Father Claude Allouez had established a Jesuit mission among the Chippewas in 1665, and with it was opened the usual French trading post. It was from representatives of the different southwestern tribes, and particularly from the Illinois, who came hither to barter their furs and skins, that Father Marquette first learned of the grand river, of unknown length, which took its rise in several lakes in the country of the far north, and flowed southward past their hunting grounds, and which they called "Mechisipi," or "Mesissipi," meaning "Great River" or "Father of Waters." The information thus derived inspired the benevolent heart of the priest with an ardent desire to explore that mysterious river, and to promulgate the gospel to the pagan dwellers on its banks.

But in the summer of 1671, he was obliged to withdraw, with the Huron portion of his flock, from his station at the head of what is now called Ashland Bay, in consequence of the increasing hostility of the Sioux, a fierce and roving people, who inhabited the grassy plains to the southwest of Lake Superior. Returning eastward along the southern border of that great lake, Marquette next proceeded to found the mission and Indian school of St. Ignatius,* or Ignace, at the point or neck of land on the north side of the Straits of Michilimackinac, now called Mackinaw.† During the ensuing year, he appears to have visited, with Fathers Allouez and Dablon, the western shores of Lake Michigan, and to have proclaimed the Faith to the friendly tribes in that region.

It was on the 8th of December, 1672, that the Sieur Joliet arrived from Quebec at the palisaded mission-house of Point de St. Ignace, with instructions from Gov. Frontenac to take *Père* Marquette as a companion on his expedition for discovering the Mississippi. The Father's journal of the same opens with the following pious reference to Joliet's arrival:

"The day of the Immaculate Conception of the Holy Virgin; whom I had continually invoked, since coming to this country of the Ottawas, to obtain from God the favor of being enabled to visit the nations on the river Mississippi—this very day was precisely that on which M. Joliet arrived with orders from Count Frontenac, our governor, and M. Talon, our intendant, to go with him on this discovery. I was all the more delighted at this news, because I saw my plans about to be accomplished, and found myself in the happy necessity of exposing my life for the salvation of all those tribes, and especially the Illinois, who, when I was at St. Esprit, had begged me very earnestly to bring the word of God among them."

During the ensuing winter, Messieurs Joliet and Marquette made the necessary preparations for their journey. "We took all possible precautions," writes Marquette, "that if our enterprise was hazardous, it should not be fool-hardy. For this reason we gathered all possible information from the Indians who had frequented those

---

* So named after the father of the Jesuit order.

† Mackinac and Mackinaw are diminutives or contractions of the Indian word Missilimakinac, which, according to Lippincot's Gazetteer, should be pronounced *Mish-il-e-mak-e-naw*.

parts, and from their accounts traced a map of all the new
country, marking down the rivers on which we were to
sail, the names of the nations through which we were to
pass, the course of the great river, and what direction we
should take when we got to it." This rude map was afterward revised by the priest, who also entered all facts of
value in his note-book.

On the 17th of May, 1673, according to the Gregorian
calendar, the explorers set out from Saint Ignace on their
perilous voyage. They embarked in two light yet strong
and elastic bark canoes, with five French canoe-men and
men of all work, whose names we are unable to give. For
provisions, they carried a little Indian corn and some
jerked meat. They also took a suitable assortment of
goods for distribution as presents among the natives to be
met on the way. After coasting around the northern
curve of Lake Michigan—a wilderness region then, and
practically a wilderness still—they entered the little river
Menominee, which puts into Green Bay from the northwest, to visit a tribe called the Folle Avoine, from the wild
oats or rice found growing along that stream, and upon which
they largely subsisted. The Jesuit missionaries had preached
the Faith to these Indians for three or four years, so that they
were accounted "very good Christians." When informed
of Marquette's design of going to discover distant tribes, to
instruct them in the mysteries of his holy religion, they were
much surprised, and did all they could to dissuade him.

"They represented," according to his journal, "that he
would encounter those nations who never pardon strangers,
but kill without remorse and without cause; that the wars
which had broken out between different people, who
would be upon our route, would expose us to the manifest
danger of being carried off by some of the bands of warriors who are always in the field; that the great river is
very dangerous, when the channel is not known; that it is
full of hideous monsters, who devour altogether men and
canoes; that there was also a demon, whom they could see
from a great distance, who closed the passage of the river
and destroyed those who dared to approach him; and, in

conclusion, that the heats were so excessive that we should meet death inevitably."

In reply, Marquette thanked them for their good advice, but said that he could not follow it, since the salvation of souls influenced him, for which he would gladly give up his life. He ridiculed their pretended demon, and told them that he and his companions could protect themselves from the marine monsters, and would keep on their guard to avoid the other dangers threatened.

After praying with and giving these poor Indians some instructions, the good father and his French companions separated from them and crossed the bay to the mission of St. Francis Xavier, which had been principally founded by Father Allouez in 1669, and was located on that narrow tongue of land running up between Green Bay * and Lake Michigan. Quitting this missionary station early in June, the voyagers proceeded southward to the mouth of Fox River, at the head of the bay, and thence up that river, the rapids of which were surmounted with considerable difficulty. They next crossed Lake Winnebago, and shortly came to a village of the Miamis, Mascoutins, and Kickapoos, banded together, the first named of whom were the most civil and liberal. This village was pleasantly seated on an eminence in the open prairie. It was then the limit of French exploration in that quarter, and all beyond it was a *terra incognita*. Father Marquette was rejoiced to find standing in the village a handsome cross, adorned with skins, girdles, bows and arrows, which these simple natives had made as offerings to their Great Manitou,† "to thank him that he had had pity on them during the winter and given them a profitable hunt."

"We had no sooner arrived," says Marquette's journal, "than Mons. Joliet and I assembled the old men (of the village). I said to them that he had been sent on the part of Monsieur, our governor, to discover new countries, and

---

* The French first named this large arm of the lake *Baie des Puans*, or Stinking Bay, on account of the offensive vapors exhaled from its muddy and slimy shores.

† A word used by the Algonquin tribes to signify a spirit, good or evil, having control of their destinies.

I on the part of God to make clear to them the lights of the gospel, etc., . . . and that we had occasion for two guides to conduct us on our route. On asking them to accord this to us, we made them a present, which made them very civil, and at the same time they voluntarily answered us by a present in return, which was a mat to serve as a bed during our voyage. The next day, which was the 10th of June, the two Miamis they gave us for guides embarked with us in sight of all the inhabitants, who could not but be astonished to see seven Frenchmen, alone in two canoes, daring to undertake an expedition so extraordinary and so hazardous."

Taking a southwesterly course through the labyrinth of small lakes that intersected the flat surface of the country, the explorers soon reached the water-shed dividing the waters flowing to Lake Michigan from those falling into the Mississippi. On their arrival at the portage to the Mascousin, Ouisconsing, or Wisconsin River, the two Miamis guides helped them to transport their canoes and luggage across it (a distance of about two miles), and then left them to return to their own people. Having first invoked the protection of the Blessed Virgin, as the special patroness of their expedition, the Frenchmen re-entered their canoes and glided down the shallow channel of the Wisconsin, over shoals and through rapids, past islets covered with vines and underbrush, and along banks of alternating timber and prairie, where they saw many deer and buffaloes grazing.

After a navigation of forty or more French leagues,* our explorers arrived, without accident, at the discharge of the Wisconsin; and, on the 17th of June (1673), they entered the Mississippi,† "with a joy," writes Marquette, "I can not express." They were now embarked on that mysterious river, to which their thoughts had been so long

---

*The common French league is equal to only 2.76-100 English or statute miles.

†It was on the eastern bank of the Mississippi, about five miles above the mouth of the Wisconsin, that the village of Prairie du Chien was established a century later by some French traders. It owed its name to a band of the Fox Indians, called the "Dog Band," that long resided there.

turned, and which the pious priest named *Riviere de la Conception;* but they found it rather narrow at the point of emergence, and elsewhere of varying width. For the ensuing week, they somewhat leisurely descended the noble stream, attentively observing its high, bold and picturesque bluffs, its thickly wooded banks and islands, clothed in the full verdure of summer, and meeting with all manner of wild birds, beasts, fishes and creeping things, but seeing no human being. At night they went ashore and prepared their frugal repast, making but little fire, and then moored their canoes out in the water, and some one of the party was always on guard for fear of a surprise.

At length, on the 25th of June, having advanced over sixty leagues, and being in latitude below forty-one degrees north, the voyagers discovered the foot-prints of men in the sand on the western shore, and a well-beaten path leading up to a prairie beyond. Here Joliet and Marquette left their canoes in the care of their men, and started out to reconnoiter. Following the path for nearly two leagues, they came in sight of an Indian village, on the banks of a small river (supposed to be the Des Moines), and beyond it, upon a hill, two other villages. Approaching the first, they piously commended themselves to God, and uttered a loud cry; on hearing which the savages sallied out of their cabins, and, apparently recognizing the two Frenchmen by their dark robes, sent four of their elders to meet them. The inhabitants of these villages called themselves *Illiniwek,* or *Illini,* that is to say "men," or "superior men." They were otherwise known as Peouareas (Peorias), and Moingwenas, and belonged to a loose confederation of five or six tribes, who went under the general appellation of the Illini, or Illinois,* and whose principal residence was on the river of that name, east of the Mississippi. Marquette had before met representatives of this nation at the mission of St. Esprit on Lake Superior, and understood their language (a dialect of the Algonquin) sufficiently well to hold conversation with them.

---

*The French added the termination " ois " for the sake of euphony.

At the door of the wigwam, where he and Joliet were at first received, stood an old man, entirely naked, with his hands outstretched toward the sun, apparently to shade his eyes. When they drew near he greeted them with this friendly and fine salutation: "The sun is beautiful, Frenchmen, when thou comest to visit us; all our town awaits thee, and thou shalt enter in peace into all our cabins." And when they had entered therein, he softly said: "It is well, my brothers, that you visit us."

After exchanging civilities and smoking the peace calumet here, the visitors were conducted to the village of the principal chief or sachem, who, assisted by two of his nude dignitaries, extended to them a ceremonious yet cordial welcome. In this gathering of the chiefs and people, whose curiosity was greatly excited by the presence of the white men among them, Marquette after first making them four presents, announced the mission of Mons. Joliet and himself. He told them about the invisible God who created them, and who wished to reveal himself unto them. He then spoke of the great Chief of the French, who " would have them know that it was he who had produced peace throughout, and had subdued the Iroquois." Finally, he requested them to give him all the knowledge they possessed in regard to the sea, and of the nations through whose territories it would be necessary to pass before reaching it. In his reply, the Illinois chief could give his visitors but little information about the distant sea; but he besought them not to go any further, because of the great dangers to which they would be exposed, Always at war with the surrounding nations, these Indians could not understand how it was possible for the Frenchmen to travel in safety from one section of the country to another.

The council and speech-making were followed by a generous feast of four courses, viz: *Sagamittee*,* fish, boiled dog, and buffalo meat, served in large wooden platters. The boiled dog, although an Indian delicacy, was politely

---

*This was a common dish among the natives of the Mississippi Valley, and consisted of flour of maize, boiled in water and seasoned with grease.

declined by the two guests, and was removed from their presence. When the feast was ended, they were shown over the village, which was found to contain three hundred cabins. Before taking their departure, the head chief, as a special mark of consideration for Father Marquette, presented him with a mysterious calumet of peace, fancifully decorated with feathers, which was intended to serve him and his party as a safeguard on their voyage.

After spending a couple of days with these hospitable children of nature, the explorers re-embarked on the afternoon of the second day in sight of all the villagers, who, to the number of over five hundred, escorted them to their canoes, which they greatly admired, having never seen the like before. Being again afloat on the mysterious river, our Frenchmen were soon borne by its swift current to and through the slight rapids at the entrance of the Des Moines, and thence on to the mouth of the Illinois, putting in from the northeast. They next passed, on their left, that gigantic and craggy wall of lime and sandstone rock, which abuts the northern shore for twenty miles below the Illinois, and which rises at some points to the height of four hundred feet above the water.

"As we coasted along the rocks, frightful from their height and vastness," says Marquette's journal, " we saw upon one of them two monsters painted, (so) that we were alarmed at first sight, and upon which some of the most courageous savages dare not for a long time fasten their eyes. They are as large as a calf, have horns upon the head like a deer, a frightful look, red eyes, a beard like a tiger; the face something like a man's, the body covered with scales, and the tail so long that it made the circuit of the body, passing over the head and returning under the legs, terminating like the tail of a fish. The colors that composed it were green, red, and black."*

---

*The western Indians were not unacquainted with a rude kind of picture-writing. But it is supposed that these crude paintings, indistinctly representing men and beasts, though an object of idolatrous worship to the savages, and long the wonder of the curious, were little more than the exudation of colored matter from the rock itself. They were

This was near the mouth of Piasa Creek, and two miles above the modern city of Alton. A few miles farther on, while rowing in smooth water, and still conversing about the "monsters," the voyagers were unexpectedly caught in the muddy and impetuous current of the Pekitanoui (Missouri),* coming in from the northwest, and swept over to the Illinois side. Escaping this danger, they paused on their oars to view the outlet of that powerful stream which changes the character of the Mississippi, and doubtless took note of the fact that for several miles below the waters of the two rivers refused to coalesce. Continuing their course, they soon passed, on their right, the forest crowned site of St. Louis, and lower down, on their left, the mouth of the gentle Kaskaskia; and then they approached that roundish pile of rock, since known as Grand Tower, against which the whole current of the river seemed to set. This was the demon or evil Manitou of which the northern Indians had warned them, but it did not prevent their passage and safe arrival at the Ouabouskigou, the Ohio, or Ouabache of the French. "This river," says Marquette's journal, "comes from the lands of the rising sun, where there is a great number of people called Chaounons." † The explorers now entered the low country—the region of the reed cane, the cotton tree, and the cypress—where they experienced no little annoyance from musquitoes. Not far below the confluence of the Ohio, they perceived Indians on the eastern bank, who stopped and waited for them to approach. Marquette immediately showed his decorated calumet, which was accepted by the savages as a token of peace; and when the Frenchmen had put to shore, they

---

placed about fifty feet above the base of the cliff; but through the combined action of the elements, and the work of the quarryman, they are now totally obliterated.

*If we might credit the uncertain narrative of the Baron de la Honton, he first explored the Missouri River early in 1689, ascending it as far as the mouth of the Osage. See *La Honton's Voyages* (English ed., London, 1735), vol. I., p. 130.

† These were the Shawanoes, Shawanese, or Shawnees, who constituted one of the most restless and migratory of the Algonquin tribes, and are celebrated as the tribe of Tecumseh.

were feasted upon buffalo meat and bear's oil, with some white plums as a dessert. These Indians belonged to a tribe called the Monsoupelea, and were armed with fusees that had been procured from nations who traded with the English on the coast of Carolina. They told their visitors that the sea might be reached in ten days' sail, but this proved fallacious.

Continuing their rapid descent of the grand river, the voyagers next approached, on their right, a village of the Metchigamea,* who showed themselves very hostile, and made ready to attack them both by land and water. While his companions put themselves in an attitude of defense, Father Marquette resolutely displayed his grand calumet, and made signs that they had not come for war; "when," he tells us, "God touched suddenly the hearts of the old men who were on the shore, occasioned doubtless by the sight of our calumet, and they arrested the ardor of their young men." The Frenchmen then went ashore, though not without trepidation, and held a parley with the savages. This was carried on at first by signs and gestures, for they did not understand any of the six Indian dialects that Marquette spoke. Fortunately an old man was soon found who could speak a little Illinois, and he acted as interpreter. After presents had been distributed among these people, they became more civil, and offered their guests sagamittee and fish, but declined to give them any information about the nations or country to the southward.

Having passed the night in much uneasiness at this village, the voyagers re-embarked the next morning with their interpreter, and were piloted by a canoe carrying ten savages down the river, some eight leagues, to a large village of the Akamsea, or Akansea. When within half a league of the village, they perceived two canoes coming to meet them, in the first of which an Indian was standing up and holding in his hand a calumet, "with which he made many motions, according to the custom of the country."

---

* The Metchigamea, or Michigamies, were a warlike tribe, who appear to have subsequently fused with the Kaskaskias of Illinois.

He approached, "singing very agreeably, and presented it to them to smoke, after which he gave them sagamittee, and bread made of Indian corn, and then, taking the advance, made a sign to them to follow quietly after him."

Arrived at the village of the Akansea,* the Frenchmen were escorted to the platform, or scaffold of the war-chief, which was strongly built and covered with fine mats of rushes, upon which they were seated, having about them the old men next to whom stood the warriors, and after the latter a promiscuous crowd of squaws and children. Luckily, there was found here a young Indian who understood the Illinois language much better than the interpreter who had accompanied them from the Metchigamea. With his aid, Marquette talked to the whole assembly, at the same time making them some small presents, and told them about God and the mysteries of the Catholic faith and worship.

When asked what they knew about the sea and the nations who lived upon its shores, "they answered that we could be there in ten days; that it was possible for us to make the journey in five days, but that they were not acquainted with the nations who dwelt upon it, because their enemies prevented them from having any intercourse with the Europeans; that their tomahawks, knives, and glass beads, which we saw, had been sold to them in part by the nations to the east, and partly by a tribe of the Illinois living at the west, four days' journey from there; that the savages whom we saw with fusees were their enemies, who shut up their passage to the sea, and prevented them from having a knowledge of the Europeans and any trade with them. As for the rest, we should expose ourselves very much by passing further on, for the reason that their enemies were making continual irruptions upon the river, which they cruised upon continually." †

While this public talk was going on, the Indians brought to their guests, on platters or dishes of wood, sometimes sagamittee, then whole ears of corn, and then a

---
* It is conjectured that this was what was afterward known as the Kappa village of the Arkansas.

† Marquette's *Journal du Voyage.*

piece of dog-meat. The people of this tribe are described as being very liberal with what they possessed, but as living poorly in bark cabins, and not daring to go to hunt the wild cattle for fear of their enemies. They had, however, abundance of Indian corn, which they cooked in large earthen vessels, and plenty of watermelons. The men went naked, wearing their hair short, and boring the nose and ears to put in them rings of glass beads. The women were indifferently clad in skins, and wore their hair plaited in two braids, which fell behind the ears.

Messieurs Joliet and Marquette now conferrred together as to whether they should continue their voyage, or content themselves with the discoveries they had already made. Being persuaded that the Mississippi had its discharge in West Florida, at the Gulf of Mexico, and not to the east on the coast of Virginia, nor to the west in the Gulf of California, and being, moreover, apprehensive that if they went much farther south they might fall into the hands of the Spaniards, and thus lose the fruits of their long voyage, they discreetly decided to retrace their course.

Accordingly, on the 17th of July,* after a day's rest, the explorers turned their canoes up the great river, and had much difficulty in stemming its powerful current.

---

* Marquette's Journal here says: "After a month's navigation in descending the Mississippi, from the forty-second degree to the thirty-fourth and more, and after having published the Gospel to all the nations I had met, we left the village of the Akansea on the 17th of July to retrace our steps."

Making allowance for their incorrect latitude, which was about one degree too low, or near the equator, it seems that the explorers descended below the 35th parallel to a village in the vicinity of the present town of Helena. Nor is it incredible, as argued by some writers, that they should have sailed so far to the south in thirty days' time. It is apparent from Marquette's narrative that they were equipped with light canoes, oars, and sails for rapid traveling; that, after quitting the Illinois, their stoppages were few and of short duration; and that going with the current, and favored by the annual rise in the river, they could without difficulty have averaged thirty-six miles per day, including halts. This would have covered the distance of eleven hundred miles, by the windings of the river, from the mouth of the Wisconsin to that of the Arkansas. Charlevoix, in describing the birch-bark canoes, says that, " with a good wind, they can make twenty leagues in a

But few incidents are recorded of this tedious and toilsome homeward trip, which they made under the sweltering sun of midsummer, and exposed by night to the noxious exhalations from the bayous and morasses bordering the river. When they again approached the mouth of the Illinois, having been told by the Indians that this river afforded a more direct route to the great lakes than that of the Mississippi and Wisconsin, they entered and followed it to the northeast. As the voyagers ascended its sluggish channel, they were delighted with the stream and the varied aspect of the adjacent country.

"We had never seen any thing like this river," says the father in his journal, "for the richness of the soil, the prairies and woods, the buffaloes, the elks, the deer, the wild cats, the bustards, the swans (or wild geese), the ducks, the paroquets, and even the beavers. It is made up of little lakes and little rivers. That upon which we voyaged is wide, deep, and gentle for sixty-five leagues. During the spring and part of the summer, it is necessary to make a portage of half a league." †

In ascending the Illinois River, their first stop of any length was at a village of the Peorias, the location of which is not mentioned, though it was probably on or near Peoria Lake. "Here," says Marquette's narrative, "I preached for three days to them the mysteries of our faith, in all their cabins, after which, as we were about to embark, they brought to me, at the edge of the water, a dying infant, which I baptized a little while before it died, for the salvation of its innocent soul."

Higher up the stream, the voyagers found a village of the Illinois called Kachkaskia, containing seventy-four cab-

---

day, but, without sails, they must be good canoe-men to make twelve leagues in dead water."

It is true that La Salle, Tonty, St. Cosme, and others of the early *voyageurs* made no such quick time as that on the Mississippi. But their southern voyages were mostly undertaken in the winter or early spring, with heavier canoes and baggage, and they were otherwise encumbered or impeded in their progress by a following of Indians.

† This portage was from the Des Plaines branch of the Illinois to the Chicagou, which empties into Lake Michigan.

ins, where they were very kindly received by the inhabitants; so well pleased were the latter with the teachings of the good priest, that they made him promise to return and further instruct them. One of the chiefs and a young brave of the tribe conducted the Frenchmen thence to the *Lac des Illinois* (Lake Michigan), by which they at last returned to the mission of St. Francis Xavier on Green Bay, at the close of September. They had left this station four months before, and during that time had traveled a circuit of about twenty-seven hundred miles through regions hitherto unvisited by white men."*

The two explorers now shortly separated, never to meet again on earth. When Father Marquette reached the mission on Green Bay, his constitution was seriously impaired by the fatigues and hardships incident to his prolonged journey, and he was detained there by sickness during the ensuing year. In September, 1674, having partly regained his health, he completed his journal of the voyage down the Mississippi, and sent it to his superior at Quebec. An imperfect copy of this journal, it seems, soon found its way to Paris, and into the hands of Mons.Thevenot, an enterprising Parisian publisher. Appreciating the interest and importance of the narrative, he published it in 1681, in a volume styled *Recuil de Voyages* (Collection of Voyages), under the particular title of "*Voyage et découverte de qulque pays et nations de L'Amérique Septontrionale*," together with a rude map of the Mississippi Valley; several English translations of which are extant.

When this journal of Father Marquette first appeared

---

*The following table of the distances traveled over by M. Joliet and Father Marquette is taken from Sparks's Life of Marquette:

	Miles.
From the Mission of St. Ignace to Green Bay, about	218
From Green Bay (Puans) up Fox River to the portage	175
From the portage down the Wisconsin to the Mississippi	175
From the mouth of the Wisconsin to the mouth of the Arkansas	1,087
From the mouth of the Arkansas to the Illinois River	547
From the mouth of the Illinois to the Chicago (Creek)	305
From the Chicago to Green Bay, by the lake shore	260
Total	2,767

in print, its authenticity was denied, especially by the writers in La Salle's interest, who affected to treat it as a fiction, or narrative of a pretended voyage. "Indeed," writes Mr. Shea, "the services and narrative would hardly have escaped oblivion, had not Charlevoix brought them to light-in his great work on New France." But the opportune discovery in 1844 of the original manuscript of Marquette's journal and map,* in the keeping of the hospital nuns of the *Hotel-Dieu* at Quebec, to whose care it had been transferred, with other papers, from the old Jesuit College in that city shortly before the year 1800, has settled the question of its genuineness beyond dispute.†

The narrative itself has a peculiar value, owing to the loss of Joliet's original papers of the journey. It is also noteworthy for the terseness, simplicity, and charm of its style, particularly in the descriptive passages. Aside from some propensity on the part of its priestly author toward hyperbole,‡ and waiving the question as to how far he and Joliet actually went below the junction of the Ohio River, his journal may be accepted as a true and striking picture of the Mississippi Valley, and of its savage inhabitants, at that pristine period of the country's history. Marquette had an observant eye for the various phenomena of nature, and his brief explanation of the lake tides has not been greatly improved upon by the deductions of modern scientists.

Having at length received from the superior of his order at Quebec the requisite authority to establish a mission on the Illinois River, and his health now seeming to be restored, Father Marquette started for his new mission on the 25th of October, 1674. Leaving the station of St. Francis Xavier in a canoe, with two French attendants, he

---

* Now preserved among the old records in St. Mary's College, Montreal.
† Moses' History of Ill., vol. 1, p. 59.
‡ This tendency to exaggeration characterizes, in a greater or less degree, the writings of all the early explorers of America. It was doubtless natural to those men of impressible imaginations, in the continual presence of new and surprising objects; for their minds had not been trained to that accuracy of statement which is expected from reputable modern travelers.

coasted along the Green Bay Inlet to its southern terminus, and thence made a portage across the narrow peninsula to the western shore of Lake Michigan. En route, he overtook a party of the Pottawatomie and Illinois Indians, and journeyed with them up the lake. About the 23d of November, the missionary was again seized by his old malady, the dysentery, accompanied with hemorrhage, but pushed on, undaunted by disease and snowstorms, until the 4th of December, when he and his companions reached the mouth of Chicago Creek. Finding it bridged with ice, they moved up its frozen surface about two leagues, following the south branch, and there stopped and built a cabin, which is believed to have been the first white human habitation erected on the site of the metropolitan city of Chicago.

Being unable to proceed farther, the sick priest and his two attendants wintered in this dreary abode. He passed his waking hours in prayer and meditation, and said mass every day. In the latter part of January, he was visited by a deputation of three Illinois Indians, who brought him provisions and beaver skins, and wanted in return powder and merchandise; but he gave them only the latter. During the winter he also received a visit from a French trader or trapper, who was stationed some fifty miles away, and who had heard of his illness.

Again recovered somewhat, Father Marquette resumed his journey on the 29th of March, 1675, and, going by way of Mud Lake and the rivers Des Plaines and Illinois, he arrived at the village of the Kaskaskias on the 8th of April. It was here, near the site of the present town of Utica, that he began his mission, to which he gave the name of the "Immaculate Conception of the Blessed Virgin." But it was only for a little while that he was able to teach the benighted Indians; for "continued illness soon obliged him to set forth on that return voyage, which brought him to a lonely grave in the wilderness." On the 'eve of his departure from the village, he convened the inhabitants, to the number of two thousand, on a meadow hard by, and there on a rude altar, exhibited four pictures of the Virgin Mary, explained their significance, and exhorted the chiefs and people to embrace Christianity. It may be remarked, *en passant*, that the doctrine (now dogma) of the Immaculate Conception of the Virgin was a favorite tenet of the Jesuits, and that Father Marquette was especially devoted to it. Quitting the Indian village a few days after Easter, he was escorted by a band of the Kaskaskias to Lake Michigan, and, on taking final leave of them, he promised that either himself or some other missionary would return and resume his labors among them.

"He seems to have taken the way by the mouth of St. Joseph's River, and reached the eastern shore of Lake Michigan, along which he had not as yet sailed. His strength now gradually failed, and he was at last so weak that he had to be lifted in and out of his canoe, when they landed each night. Calmly and cheerfully he saw the approach of death, for which he prepared by assiduous prayer; his office he regularly recited to the last day of his life; a meditation on death, which he had long prepared, he also made the subject of his thoughts. And as his kind but simple companions seemed overwhelmed at the prospect of their approaching loss, he blessed some water with the usual ceremonies, gave them directions how to act in his last moments, how to arrange his body, and how to commit it to the earth. He now seemed but to seek a grave; at last, perceiving the mouth of a river, he pointed to an eminence as the place of his burial.

"His companions, Pierre Porteret and Jacques ———, still hoped to reach Mackinaw, but the wind drove them back, and they entered the river by the channel where it emptied then, for it has since changed. They erected a little bark cabin, and stretched the dying missionary beneath it, as comfortably as they could. Still a priest, rather than a man, he thought of his ministry, and, for the last time, he heard the confessions of his companions, and encouraged them to rely on the protection of God; then sent them to take the repose they so much needed. When he felt his agony approaching, he called them, and, taking his crucifix from around his neck, he placed it in their hands, and, pronouncing in a firm voice his profession of faith, thanked the Almighty for the favor of permitting him to die a Jesuit, a missionary, and alone. Then he relapsed into silence, interrupted by pious aspirations, till at last, with the names of Jesus and Mary on his lips, with his eyes raised as if in ecstacy above his crucifix, with his face all radiant with joy, he passed from the scene of his labors to the God who was to be his reward. Such was the edifying and holy death of the illustrious explorer of the Mississippi, on Saturday the 18th of May, 1675." *

Obedient to the instructions they had received, the two surviving attendants of the dead priest bore his body to the spot he had designated, committed it tenderly to the earth, and placed over it a rude cedar cross. Then, re-entering their canoe, they wended their way to Michilimackinac, to carry the sad tidings to the Jesuit Fathers at St. Ignace. The river, at the mouth of which Marquette died, is a small stream, in the western part of Michigan, which, according to Parkman, long wore his name, but it is now changed to a larger neighboring stream.

Two years later, in the spring of 1677, a party of Christianized Kiskakon Indians, from about Mackinac, who had been hunting in the vicinity of Marquette's grave, disinterred his remains, cleaned the bones after their custom, put them into a birch bark box, and transported them to St. Ignace. On the passage thither, they were joined by other Indians in canoes, and the convoy moved in procession, singing their doleful funeral songs, until they reached the landing at the mission-station. Here the revered relics of the missionary were received by Fathers Nouvel and Pierson, the priests then in charge, in presence of all the Frenchmen and natives of the place, and were deposited, with solemn religious rites, in a vault under the

---

*Life of Father Marquette, in Shea's "Discovery and Exploration of the Mississippi Valley," p. LXX, and seq.

Note.—The account of this eminent missionary-explorer's death by Charlevoix, formerly so generally received, is inaccurate in many particulars, because it was derived from tradition, and not from the contemporary narrative of Father Claude Dablon, and others.

5

floor of the log chapel. In process of time (the mission being afterward abandoned) their resting place was utterly forgotten, but it was discovered by a clergyman of Michigan, in 1877, two centuries after the event.

So lived and died, at the age of eight and thirty years, the meek and pious, yet fearless and self-sacrificing *Pere* Jacques Marquette. He was a model of the religious order to which he belonged, and deserved to have been beatified, if not canonized as a saint. His disposition was cheerful and happy, and his hold upon the hearts of those aborigines with whom he came in personal touch was something wonderful. This was doubtless owing to his uniform kindness toward them, to the purity of his private life, and to the grace and charm of his manner in the exercise of his priestly functions. Nor is it incredible, as related by a contemporary, that the Illinois Indians should have regarded him as a messenger sent to them from the Great Spirit. His name holds a conspicuous and honored place in the history of the Jesuit missionaries of North America, and is inseparably associated with the discovery of the Upper Mississippi. It is otherwise perpetuated in the appellations of several counties, towns and streams, in the different states of the northwest. Still, Illinois owes him a monument suitable to his character and services.

We must now resume and complete our skeleton sketch of Joliet's active and diversified career. After returning with Marquette to Green Bay, in September, 1673, he did not immediately proceed to Canada to report his discoveries, as is commonly supposed, but spent the following winter and spring in the upper lake country (engaged, no doubt, in the fur traffic), and during the next summer resumed his journey to Quebec. Passing down Lakes Huron, Erie and and Ontario, he made a brief halt at Fort Frontenac, which had been erected the year before, and was then commanded by LaSalle. The latter was probably among the first to learn the result of Joliet's voyage of exploration on the Mississippi, and may, perhaps, have seen his map and journal, which were soon afterward lost. The Sieur Joliet, had thus far been highly favored by fortune, and it was not until near the end of his long journey that he met with any serious mishap. But by the accidental upsetting of his canoe in the LaChine rapids, above Montreal, he lost his two canoe-men, and all of his valuable papers. In a letter penned shortly after to Governor Frontenac, he thus feelingly refers to his misfortune :

"I had escaped every peril of the Indians; I had passed forty-two rapids, and was on the point of disembarking, full of joy at the success of so long and difficult an enterprise, when my canoe capsized after all the danger seemed over. I lost my two men and box of papers within sight of the first French settlement, which I had left almost two years before. Nothing remains to me now but my life, and the ardent desire to employ it on any service you may direct." *

M. Joliet finally reached Quebec in August, 1674, and reported in person to the governor. Being separated at a great distance from Marquette, and deprived of his papers by casualty, he drew up a short account of his discovery from recollection, and also sketched out a map of the Mississippi. Gov. Frontenac transmitted these papers to France during the ensuing November, and in a dispatch of the 14th of that month to Minister Colbert (inserted at the close of this chapter), he wrote about the "great river" as an indubitable fact.† Father Dablon, in his writings, also gives an account of the voyage, "describing Joliet as one who had been where no European had ever set foot." ‡ No general publicity was given by the French government to the discovery of the Mississippi; nor was Joliet entrusted with any new commission to execute in the West. It is averred that in April, 1677, he petitioned Colbert for permission to settle with a colony in the country of the Illinois, but it

---
* This letter is inscribed on Joliet's map of his discoveries made in 1674.
† The papers have been preserved in the *Archives de la Marine* at Paris. It has been suggested that the map published by Thevenot, in connection with Marquette's Journal, was reproduced from the one made by Joliet and forwarded to Paris, as above stated. The latter shows the Mississippi to the Gulf, whereas Marquette's autograph map shows that river not quite to the Arkansas.
‡ Kingsford's History of Canada, I., p. 405.

was refused him on the specious ground that "Canada
ought first to be built up, strengthened, and maintained."*
In truth, his modest merit seems to have been thrown
into the shade by the rising pretensions of La Salle, who
had won Frontenac's favor.

On October 7, 1675, at the age of thirty, Louis Joliet
was united in marriage to Clairé Frances Bissot, daughter
of a wealthy Quebec merchant, who was extensively engaged in trade with the northern Indians. In 1679 he
made a journey of business and exploration to Hudson's
Bay, going by way of the Lower St. Lawrence and the river
Saguenay. During the next year, in tardy recognition of his
valuable services to the provincial government, he received
a grant of the large yet barren Isle of Anticosti, lying in
the Gulf of St. Lawrence. Taking possession of his island
domain in 1681, he erected a fortified house upon it, removed his family thither, and embarked in the fisheries.
But in 1690 his establishment was destroyed by a naval
force from New England, under the command of Sir William Phipps, who was on his way to attack Quebec; and
Joliet's wife and mother-in-law were made prisoners, and
held for some months. In 1693 he was appointed royal
pilot of the St. Lawrence River, and during the succeeding
year explored and mapped the bleak coast of Labrador, a
work involving great personal exposure. April 30, 1697,
he was invested with the "Seigneury of Joliette," a large
and since valuable estate, which lies on the north side of
the St. Lawrence below Montreal, in Beauce county, and
which is still possessed by some of his posterity.

Louis Joliet died comparatively poor in May, 1700,
being in his fifty-fifth year, and was buried, it is stated, on
one of the Mignan islands in the St. Lawrence. Without
possessing any very salient or brilliant qualities, he was an
intelligent, well-educated man, ambitious and enterprising,
undaunted by difficulty or danger, and faithful in the performance of every public duty. Few, if any, of his contemporaries contributed more than he did to the geograph-

---

* *Vide* Margry, I., p. 330.

ical knowledge of this continent. His surname has been fittingly preserved in the now flourishing city of Joliet, Illinois,* and in the nomenclature of other western localities. His descendants appear to have inherited his virtues and talents; and several of them hold positions of high trust and responsibility, civil and ecclesiastical, in the modern Dominion of Canada. Among the number may be mentioned the Hon. Bartholomew Joliet, and the eminent archbishops Tache and Tachereau.

We have nowhere met with any description of the persons of either Joliet or Marquette. Yet, in the absence of such word portraiture, we may well imagine the former to have been a man of medium stature, with a lithe, agile figure, black hair and eyes, sharply cut features, and a swarthy complexion—the same being physical characteristics of the average French-Canadian—while the latter (Marquette) was probably taller, and of a more dignified and commanding presence.

Following is a translation of Count Frontenac's dispatch to Minister Colbert in relation to the return of M. Joliet from his voyage to discover the Mississippi and the South Sea:

QUEBEC, 14th November, 1674.

The Sieur Joliet, whom M. Talon advised me when I arrived from France to send to discover the south sea, returned here three months since, and has discovered some admirable countries, and a navigation so easy by the fine rivers, that he found that from from Lake Ontario and Fort Frontenac they could go in barques to the Gulf of Mexico, having only to unload once, where Lake Erie falls into Lake Ontario.

These are some of the enterprises they could work upon when peace is established, and it shall please the king to push these discoveries.

He has been within ten days of the Gulf of Mexico, and believes that the rivers which from the west side empty into the great river which he has discovered, which runs north to south . . . , and that

---

*The name, in this instance, was taken more immediately from "Mount Joliet," a large natural mound in the valley of the Des Plaines, one and a half miles southwest of the city.

they will find some communication by waters which will lead to the Vermillion Sea and that of California.

I send you by my secretary the map which he has made and the remarks which he is able to remember, having lost all his memoirs and journals in the shipwreck which he suffered in sight of Montreal, where, after a voyage of twelve hundred leagues, he came near being drowned, and lost all his papers and a little Indian that he was bringing back with him.

He had left at Lake Superior, with the Fathers at Sault Ste. Marie, copies of his journals, which we can not obtain until next year; through these you will learn more of the particulars of that discovery in which he acquitted himself very creditably. FRONTENAC.

CHAPTER IV.

1666–1680.

LA SALLE AND HIS EARLY EXPLORATIONS.

While to Joliet and Marquette are rightly accorded the honor of having first brought to the knowledge of the civilized world the immense extent and grandeur of the Mississippi Valley, yet the fortunes of the French in this part of Northern America were greatly advanced by the energy, enterprise, perseverance, and endurance of the Sieur de la Salle. If the former had discovered and navigated the Mississippi River from the Wisconsin to the Arkansas, it was reserved for the latter and his coadjutors to extend and perfect that discovery from the Falls of St. Anthony to the Mexican Sea.

Robert Cavelier, Sieur de la Salle,* whose remarkable career now claims our attention, was born at Rouen in Normandy, France, November 22, 1643. His father, Jean Cavelier, and his uncle Henri, were opulent merchants and burghers of that ancient and still stately city. The son received a liberal education, commensurate with the means of his parents, and with those marked traits of intellect and character which he early exhibited. As a school-boy, he evinced an inclination for the exact sciences, and particularly the mathematics, in which he appears to have made great proficiency.

While still a minor, La Salle became a member of the Society of Jesus, and studied and taught for several years in their schools. But on attaining to man's estate, his growing ambition and love of independence impelled him to withdraw from that imperious and exacting order of religionists. It is told by one of his biographers that " he

---

* He is said to have been called La Salle from an estate of that name near Rouen, belonging to the Caveliers.

parted from them on good terms, and with an excellent reputation for scholarship and strict morals," yet it is certain that he never afterward cherished any liking for the order. In fact, his connection with the Jesuits caused him to forfeit, under the rigid French law, the inheritance to which he would otherwise have been entitled from his father, who died about that time. But an allowance was made to him of four hundred livres a year (about eighty dollars), the principal of which was advanced to him for the first year; and, with this insignificant sum, he quitted his paternal home and sailed for Canada in the spring of 1666.

We next find our young adventurer at Montreal, whither he had been preceded by his elder brother, the Abbé Jean Cavelier, who was a priest of the order of St. Sulpice, and whose presence there was an additional inducement for Robert to try his own fortune in this newly opened country. As before stated, the superior and priests of the Seminary of St. Sulpice had become feudal proprietors of the large Island of Montreal, and wished to have it settled and improved. They now made young La Salle a liberal offer, which, under the advice of his brother, he accepted. It was the grant, on easy conditions, of a large tract of wild land on the north side of the St. Lawrence, about ten miles above the then village of Montreal, but still on the island of that name. The locality was exposed to incursions from the hostile Iroquois, but it was very conveniently situated for the fur-traffic. Taking possession of his new domain in the fall of 1667, he marked out the boundaries of a village, and began to dispose of his lands in small parcels, after the French custom, to actual settlers, who were to pay him an annual rental therefor. The place subsequently took the name of La Chine, which was given to it in derision of its proprietor's early schemes for the discovery of a western passage to China. Meanwhile, to qualify himself for the stirring life before him, he commenced studying the Indian languages, and particularly the Iroquois, in which he made considerable proficiency.

From his frontier post on the banks of the noble St.

Lawrence, the thoughts of La Salle often wandered over the distant and untrodden regions toward the setting sun, and, like other inquisitive and speculative minds of that age, he dreamed of a western water-way to the Pacific Ocean. While thus working and musing, he was one day visited by a small band of Senecas,* from the south of Lake Ontario, who told him of a river called the Ohio, which took its rise in their country, and flowed off to the sea, but at so great a distance that it took eight months to reach its mouth. In this exaggerated statement, the Alleghany, Ohio, and Mississippi were all considered as one stream, and, with the geographical ideas then prevalent, it was supposed to fall into the Sea of Cortes, or Gulf of California. The story of these Indians so kindled La Salle's imagination that he determined to make an expedition to verify it, and repaired to Quebec to obtain Gov. Courcelles' approval of the project. Both the governor and intendant promptly gave him the desired letters of authority. In fact, they stood prepared to sanction any enterprise that cost them nothing, and yet promised an extension of French traffic and intercourse among the western Indians. As no pecuniary aid was proffered by the Canadian officials, La Salle was under the necessity of selling his " concession " at La Chine to raise funds for his exploration. He accordingly disposed of his improvements there to the superior of the Seminary of St. Sulpice, and with the proceeds of the sale, amounting to twenty-eight hundred livres, purchased four canoes and the requisite supplies for the expedition.

At the same time the Seminary was preparing for a similar undertaking. Emulating the example of the Jesuits, the priests of this association had already founded a mission at the Bay of Quinté † on Ontario Lake, and they now proposed to extend their operations to the tribes in the distant west. An expedition was therefore set on foot for this purpose, under the management of Fathers Dollier de

---
* One of the five tribes then composing the Iroquois Nation.
† This mission was established among the Cayugas in 1668, by the Abbé de Fénelon, a brother of the author of Telemachus, and Claude Trouvé, but it does not appear to have been very successful.

Casson and Réne de Galinée. But on going down to Quebec to procure the requisite outfit, they were advised by the governor to modify their plans so as to act with La Salle in exploring the unknown river to the southwest. In accordance with his suggestion the two expeditions were merged into one—an arrangement ill-suited to the temper of young La Salle, who was formed by nature for an untrammeled leader rather than a co-partner in any enterprise.

It was on the 6th of July, 1669, that the combined party, numbering some twenty-two men, with seven canoes, embarked upon the St. Lawrence. Accompanying them were two other canoes, carrying the party of Seneca Indians who had wintered at La Salle's settlement, and who were to act as guides and interpreters. On the 2d of August, after having stemmed the impetuous current of the St. Lawrence, and threaded the mazes of the Thousand Isles, the adventurous explorers emerged upon the broad and deep bosom of Lake Ontario. Passing thence to a small bay in the southern part of the lake, they were piloted by their guides to the village of the latter, near the Genesee River. Arrived there, they expected to find other guides to conduct them to the sources of the Ohio; but the Senecas refused to furnish a guide, and even burned before their eyes a young prisoner taken from one of the western tribes, he being the only person who could have served them in that capacity. This, with other unfriendly treatment experienced by the party of La Salle, caused them to suspect that the Jesuit priest at the village, who acted as their interpreter, was jealous of their enterprise, and had purposely misrepresented it to the Indians, in order to defeat it. After lingering at this place about a month, they had the good fortune to meet with an Indian from an Iroquois settlement near the head of the lake, who told them they could there find what they wanted, and offered to be their conductor.

Gladly accepting his proffered assistance, the explorers left the Senecas and coasted along up the southern shore of Lake Ontario, passing on their way the mouth of the Niagara, and on the 24th of September reached the village of Otinawatawa, near the present town of Hamilton. Here they were received by the natives in a friendly manner, and La Salle was presented with a Shawanoe prisoner, who assured him that the Ohio could be reached in six weeks' time, and that he would guide his party thither. Pleased with this proposal, they were about to set out on the journey, when they unexpectedly learned of the arrival of two other Frenchmen at a neighboring village. One of them proved to be Louis Joliet, who was returning to Quebec from a trip to Lake Superior. He gave to the Sulpitian priests a copy of a map that he had made, representing such parts of the upper lakes as he had visited, and, at the same time, told them of the Pottawatomies and other tribes in that region, who stood in great need of spiritual instruction.

On receiving this piece of information, the missionaries resolved that the Indians on those lakes must not sit in outer darkness, and that the discovery of the Mississippi might be effected as well by a northern route, as by going farther southward. La Salle remonstrated without avail against their determination, for it was in accordance with their original design. He had been troubled for some time with an intermittent fever, and finding his remonstrance unheeded, he informed them that his physical condition would not admit of his accompanying them farther. This plea of sickness was no doubt a ruse to bring about a separation, which was now agreed upon. After the solemnization of mass La Salle and his men fell back to Lake Ontario; while the Sulpitians descended Grand River to Lake Erie, and thence pursued their voyage up the lakes. On arriving among the Indians at Ste. Marie du Saut, they found, as La Salle had surmised, the Jesuit fathers already established in that western region, and that they wanted no assistance from the priests of St. Sulpice. The latter therefore retraced their lonely course, and reached Montreal on the 18th of June, 1670, without having begun any mission or converted any Indians.*

---

* But De Galinée, after his return, made the earliest map of the Upper Lakes known to exist.—Parkman's "La Salle and the Great West," p. 21.

The course pursued by La Salle, after his separation from the Sulpitian priests, is involved in obscurity. It is affirmed that some of his men now forsook him and returned to La Chine, which is not improbable. He is known to have kept private journals or records of his explorations at this period, which were in existence as late as 1756, but they never saw the light of print. The only contemporaneous and connected record of his movements is contained in a pamphlet bearing the title of "*Histoire de Monsieur de la Salle.*" It gives an account of his explorations and of the state of parties in Canada prior to the year 1678, and purports to have been derived by its unknown writer from La Salle himself, in the course of a dozen conversations had with him in Paris, whither he had gone from Canada in the autumn of 1677. According to this anonymous memoir, La Salle, after leaving the head of Lake Ontario, went to a village of the Onondagas, in what is now New York, where he obtained guides, and thence made his way southward to a tributary of the Ohio (probably the Alleghany), which he descended to the main river, and followed it "as far as to a rapid that obstructed it," at the site of what is now Louisville. It is asserted by some writers that he continued his descent of the Ohio from that point to its confluence with the Mississippi, but this is no doubt a fiction.*

This tour of exploration is supposed to have been made during the fall and winter of 1669-'70; for it appears that the celebrated *voyageur*, Nicholas Perrot, met La Salle in the early summer of 1670, hunting with a party of Iroquois on the Ottawa. That he discovered the Ohio, is a pretty well authenticated fact. He himself affirmed it,

---

* "Pierre Margry, a recent French writer, asserts that in 1670-'71 La Salle descended the Ohio to the Mississippi (Dussieux, Canada, p. 37); but the proof has not been given, and, not improbably, is a delusion, as no notice of the fact appears in any document of the time, and the friends of La Salle would not be likely to omit an expedition giving him a priority to the discovery of the Mississippi; nor would La Salle, having a post at Niagara, overlook the advantages of following the same course to the Mississippi."—Note by J. G. Shea to Washington's Diary of his tour to the Ohio in 1753, printed in New York, 1860.

in a memorial addressed to Count Frontenac in 1677. Moreover, his rival, Joliet, made two maps of the region of the Mississippi and great lakes, on both of which the Ohio is laid down, though not correctly, with inscriptions to the effect that it had been explored by La Salle. But his exploration of this noble river (which the French appropriately named *La Belle Rivière*, from the Iroquois word signifying beautiful), was not sufficiently extensive to reveal its true character, nor to disclose the fact that the Wabash was simply one of its tributaries.

With regard to La Salle's peregrinations during the years 1671 and 1672, we learn from the apocryphal memoir before cited, that he embarked with an exploring or trading party on Lake Erie, ascended the Detroit and St. Clair to Lake Huron, passed the Straits of Michilimackinac into Lake Michigan, and on to the southern extremity of this lake; that he thence crossed the country to a river (the Illinois) flowing to the southwest, which he followed to the Mississippi, and thence down that stream to the 36th parallel of latitude. Arrived thither, and being convinced that the great river had its discharge in the Gulf of Mexico, he returned on his course, intending at some future time to explore it to its mouth.

Little, if any, weight can be allowed to the above incredible story. La Salle was, at this period, leading the life of a *coureur de bois*. It is doubtless true that he was employed in some work of exploration. Indeed, it appears from an official despatch of M. Talon in 1671, that he had been "sent southward and westward to explore"; but this may have only referred to the region south of the lower lakes, and it is not unlikely that at this time he made the discovery of the Ohio. Mr. Parkman, in his "La Salle and the Discovery of the Great West," after learnedly discussing this obscure and controverted portion of La Salle's career, thus concludes: "La Salle discovered the Ohio, and in all probability the Illinois; but that he discovered the Mississippi has not been proved, nor, in the light of the evidence we have, is it likely to be." For our own part, we very much question if he ever saw the Illinois River, or any branch of it, prior to December, 1679, though, as suggested by Mr. Shea, he might have reached the mouth of the St. Joseph in Lake Michigan.

The expedition of Joliet and Marquette had well nigh demonstrated the fact that the Mississippi emptied its vast volume of waters into the Mexican Gulf; but this was far from satisfying the mind of La Salle, who wished to see and know for himself. He had read the published narratives of the Spanish adventurers in the southwest, and heard the vague stories of the Indians, and he seems to have entertained the idea (first put forth in Marquette's journal) that, by ascending the Missouri, or some other western affluent of the Mississippi, it would be found to interlock with another stream running southwest to the Vermilion, or Gulf of California, and thus afford the desired passage to the Pacific.* Nor was this theory so chimerical as it might first appear; for by mounting the Platte River to its source in the Rocky Mountains, one may thence readily pass to the headwaters of the Colorado, which flows off into the Gulf of California. But, above all, La Salle longed to trace the Mississippi itself to the sea, and thus acquire for himself the distinction he coveted, and for his sovereign an embryo empire. It was several years, however, before he could resume and carry out any of his bold schemes of exploration and discovery.

In the meantime, he sought and gained the patronage of Governor Frontenac. No sooner had that astute functionary been installed in office, than he eagerly scanned the resources of the colony, and prepared to bring them under his own control. Being advised that the Iroquois, at the instigation of the English, were intriguing with the Indians of the upper lakes to break their faith with the French, and transfer their trade in furs from Montreal to Albany

---

* The delusive idea of a water-way to the Pacific was partly derived by the French from the Spaniards, who, during the preceding century, had scoured the coasts of Mexico and Central America in the vain quest for a strait connecting the two oceans.

Founding of Fort Frontenac. 79

and New York, he determined to counteract that design by erecting a fort and depot near the outlet of Lake Ontario. Not wishing to excite the jealousy of the Canadian merchants and traders, he gave out that he only intended to make a tour of observation to the upper part of the colony. But, lacking means of his own for the enterprise, he required the principal merchants of Quebec and Montreal to each furnish him with a certain number of men and canoes. When the spring of 1673 had opened, he sent La Salle in advance from Montreal to Onondaga, to invite the Iroquois sachems to meet him in council at the foot of Lake Frontenac (Ontario), while he followed at his leisure up the St. Lawrence. In response to the invitation sent them, the Indians resorted in considerable numbers to the appointed place of meeting, and were well pleased with the attentions there shown them by the governor, who was the first Frenchman to address them by the name of "children," instead of "brothers." Cajoled by his blandishments and presents, and awed by his audacity and show of force, they acquiesced in the erection of a fort at the mouth of Cataraqui Creek, where Kingston now stands.

The building of this fort (which was begun in July of that year, and was called Frontenac after its founder), was in violation of the existing regulations of the king, which required the fur-dealers to carry on their trade with the natives within the borders of the French settlements. Still, in view of its importance as a means of overawing the restless Iroquois, all technical objections were waived, and provision was made for its maintenance. "With the aid of a vessel now building," writes Frontenac at this time, "we can command the lake, keep peace with the Iroquois, and cut off the fur-trade from the English. With another fort at Niagara, and a second vessel on the river above, we can control the entire chain of lakes." These extensive views accorded well with the schemes of La Salle, who, as we shall see, was soon employed in putting them into practice.

In November, 1674, LaSalle embarked for France,

with letters of recommendation from the governor* and others, and, on his arrival at Versailles, presented two petitions to the king (Louis XIV.); the one for a patent of *nobility, in consideration* of his valuable services as an explorer; and the other for a grant in seigniory of Fort Frontenac and the adjoining lands. He proposed to reimburse the king for the ten thousand livres which the new post had cost him; to maintain it at his own charge, with a garrison equal to that of Montreal, besides a score of laborers; to form a French colony around it; to build a church whenever the number of inhabitants should reach one hundred, and in the meantime to support one or more Recollet friars; and, finally, to form a settlement of domesticated Indians in the neighborhood. These liberal offers, on the part of LaSalle, were accepted by the crown; and by letters-patent of the 13th of May, 1675, he was raised to the rank of the untitled nobility.† At the same time he received a grant of Fort Frontenac, and the lands contiguous, to the extent of four and one-half leagues in front and one-half league in depth, besides the neighboring islands, and was also invested with the government of the fort and settlement, subject to the provincial governor.

After LaSalle's favorable reception at court, his more wealthy relations in Rouen advanced him considerable sums of money, which put him in position to fulfill the more important obligations annexed to his grant, and he now returned to Canada the proprietor of what promised to be one of the most valuable estates in the province.

---

*In a despatch to Minister Colbert, of the 14th of November, 1674, Frontenac thus commends his favorite: "I can not help, Monsieur, recommending to you the Sieur de la Salle, who is about to go to France, and who is a man of intelligence and ability—more capable than any body else I know here, to accomplish every kind of enterprise and discovery which may be entrusted to him, since he has the most perfect knowledge of the state of the country, as you will see if you are disposed to give him a few moments of audience."—Parkman's Discovery of the Great West, p. 89.

† This was an empty kind of honor, with which the Kings of France were wont to gratify the vanity and reward the services of their more deserving subjects.

During the two following years, while all New France was being rent and torn by civil and ecclesiastical feuds, he was busily occupied in clearing his lands, strengthening his fort, and developing his seigniory. In addition to furnishing the stipulated military and clerical forces, and erecting a chapel for the use of the latter, he built three or four decked boats, or brigantines, to carry freight on Lake Ontario,—to the head of which it was next proposed to advance. He was now on the high road to fortune, if riches had been his only object, and he consequently became a mark for the shafts of the envious and malevolent, or those whose opinions and interests conflicted with his own.

Meanwhile, he did not relinquish his favorite design of exploration. In the autumn of 1677, he again went to France, and laid his plans before Jean Baptiste Colbert, then minister for the colonies, and the great promoter of French industry and commerce. LaSalle dilated upon the immense extent of the western country, its endless natural resources, and the advantages that would accrue from colonizing it and opening trade with its numerous native tribes. For this purpose, he asked permission and authority to explore and build forts in the western valleys, with seigniorial rights over all lands, that he might discover and colonize within the period of twenty years. His petition was favorably considered by the minister, and Letters were accordingly issued to him by the crown. But he was required to complete his enterprise within five years instead of twenty, as desired. Following is an English copy of this curious and important state paper:

"*Louis, by the Grace of God, King of France and Navarre:*

"To our dear and well-beloved Robert Cavelier, Sieur de la Salle:

"We have received, with favor, the very humble petition which has been presented to us in your name, to permit you to endeavor to discover the western part of our country of New France, and we have consented to this proposal the more willingly, because there is nothing we have more at heart than the discovery of this country, through which it is probable that a passage may be found to Mexico; and because your diligence in clearing the lands which we granted to you by the decree of our council of the 13th of May, 1675, and by letters patent of the same date, to form habitations upon the said lands and to put Fort Frontenac in a good state of defense, the seigniory and government whereof we likewise granted to you, affords us every reason to hope that you will succeed to our satisfaction, and to our subjects of the said country. For these reasons and others thereunto moving us, we have permitted and do hereby permit you, by these presents, signed by our hand, to endeavor to discover the western part of our country of New France, and for the execution of this enterprise, to construct forts wherever you shall deem it necessary; which it is our will that you shall hold on the same terms and conditions as Fort Frontenac, agreeably and conformably to our said letters patent of the 13th of May, 1675, which we have confirmed, as far as is needful, and hereby confirm by these presents. And it is our pleasure that they be executed according to their form and tenor.

"To accomplish this, and every thing above mentioned, we give you full powers, on condition, however, that you shall finish this enterprise within five years, in default of which these presents shall be void and of none effect; that you carry on no trade whatever with the savages called *Outaouacs*,* and others who bring their beaver skins and other peltries to Montreal; and that the whole shall be done at your expense, and that of your company to which we have granted the privilege of the trade in buffalo skins; and we call on the Sieur de Frontenac, our governor and lieutenant-general, and on the Sieur de Chesneau,† intendant of justice, police and finance, and on the officers who compose the supreme council in the said country, to affix

---

* The Ottawas.

† Jacques de Chesneau had been appointed Intendant of New France in May, 1675. He was an enemy of both Frontenac and La Salle.

their signatures to these presents; for such is our pleasure.

"Given at St. Germain en Laye, this 12th of May, 1678, and of our reign the thirty-fifth.

"By the King,   Louis."*

" Colbert."

Inasmuch as no pecuniary aid was to be received from the government, La Salle had to look to his monopoly of the future trade in buffalo skins for the support of his expensive enterprise. Meantime, his relatives were induced to make him further advances of money, and some of them became shareholders in the venture. He also found a useful ally in La Motte de Lussiére, who became a partner in the company, and who joined him on the eve of his embarkation for Canada. La Salle sailed from Rochelle on his return the 14th of July, 1678, bringing with him about thirty men, besides an ample supply of stores, implements for building vessels, etc. After a two months sea voyage, he reached Quebec, and thence proceeded up the St. Lawrence to his seigniory of Frontenac. His new enterprise aroused jealousy and opposition from the start, among the old Canadian traders; but our resolute Norman was accustomed to grapple with obstacles and opposition, and he energetically proceeded to organize his expedition. Having laid aside as impracticable his scheme of a western passage to China and Japan, and convinced that the Mississippi emptied into the Gulf of Mexico, he had substituted a vast plan, which should eventually plant on the shores of the Gulf the national colors of France, and open to her the whole interior of this continent.

Of the men whose services La Salle had secured in France, and who were destined to win honor with him in his great explorations, the most useful and trusted was Henry de Tonty,† or Tonti, as it is written in Italian. He was a native of the Neapolitan town of Gaeta, Italy, where he first saw the light about the year 1650. His

---

* Frontenac's signature was affixed to this patent November 5, 1678.
† Tonty had been a *protégé* of the Prince de Conti, by whom he was recommended to La Salle.

father, Lorenzo di Tonti, was sometime governor of Gaeta, but fled to France to escape the political disturbances of his own country. He was an ingenious financier, and the inventor of the Tontine system of annuities, which he introduced into France during the latter part of the seventeenth century. Henry de Tonty entered the French military service in 1668, and served as a cadet two years. He next served four years as a midshipman, at Marseilles and Toulon, and made seven campaigns, four in ships and three in galleys. While at Messina, Sicily, he was made lieutenant and then captain of the first company of a regiment of horse. In assisting to repel an attack of the enemy on the post of Libisso, his right hand was shot off by a grenade, and he was taken prisoner and detained for six months, after which he was exchanged. He then repaired to France to obtain some favor of the king, who gave him three hundred livers. Returning to Sicily, he made a campaign as a volunteer in the galleys; and when the troops were discharged, being unable to obtain employment on account of the general peace, he enlisted under La Salle, in his expeditions of discovery.

Notwithstanding the loss of his right hand (which, however, was replaced by one of iron or copper), and a constitution apparently feeble, his indomitable energy made him the superior of most men in physical endurance. His experience, too, as a soldier, and his natural intrepidity, well fitted him for the life of a military explorer. Moreover, his fidelity was such that neither the frowns of adversity, nor the intrigues of secret or open enemies, could ever swerve him from the interest of his patron and employer. The Sieur La Motte, before named, was also a man of enterprise and integrity of character, but not so efficient or valuable an assistant to La Salle as the little veteran De Tonty.

The spiritual directors, who were selected by the chief for this memorable expedition, were expected to officiate as chaplains and missionaries at such forts and trading posts as might be established. Following are their names: Father Louis Hennepin, the first in respect to ability and enterprise; Gabriel de la Ribourde, venerable for his years, and his long and unselfish clerical labors; the amiable and devoted Zenobious Membre; and the pious Melithon Watteau, who was stationed at Niagara and made it his mission. All of these were Flemings, or natives of Flanders, and all were Recollet friars, of the mendicant order of St. Francis. It would doubtless have been more conducive to La Salle's interest if this had been otherwise, since the Jesuits already occupied the upper lake region, and had planted some missions in the northern part of the country of the Illinois. Under such circumstances, they were naturally jealous of any infringement upon their assumed territorial jurisdiction by members of another branch of the mother church, and were inclined to throw obstacles in the way of the latter.

Soon after his return from France to Fort Frontenac, La Salle dispatched fifteen men with merchandise to Mackinac and Lake Michigan, to barter for furs, and instructed them, after executing their commission, to repair to Green Bay, on the border of the Illinois, and there await his arrival. The first important step in his westward progress, one which had been long contemplated, was to establish a fort or block-house at the outlet of the Niagara channel. For this purpose, on November 18, 1678, La Motte and Hennepin embarked, with fifteen men, in one of the brigantines that lay at the landing of the fort, and started up Lake Ontario. Being retarded in their passage by rough weather, it was not until the 6th of December that they reached the mouth of the Niagara. Here, after several weeks, they were joined by La Salle and Tonty, who had been detained in procuring the necessary supplies. They, too, encountered adverse winds on the way, and the pilot to whom La Salle had intrusted one of his boats disregarded his instructions, and suffered her to be wrecked. The crew managed to escape, but the cargo was lost, excepting the ropes and anchors intended for use in constructing the new vessel.

The appearance of the French upon the lake excited the suspicions of the Seneca Indians, who inhabited its southern shores, and when it was proposed to erect a fort at the foot of the mountain ridge,* on the east side of the

---
* The block-house, which La Salle afterward built where Fort Niagara now stands, was called Fort Conti.

river, they made objection. In order to gain their consent, La Motte and La Salle both visited, in turn, the principal village of the Seneca's situated near the site of the present Rochester, New York, and distributed presents freely among their chiefs. Some diplomacy was also used by La Salle, and in lieu of a fort, it was finally agreed that the Frenchmen might erect a warehouse. This was now speedily completed and inclosed with a palisade. If was used as an abode by the men during the rest of that winter, and, subsequently, as a station and place of deposit for implements and merchandise.

The energies of La Salle were next directed to the construction of a sailing vessel, with which to navigate the upper great lakes. The spot chosen for this important experiment was at or near the mouth of Cayuga Creek,* on the eastern bank of the Niagara, and some five miles above the Falls. This difficult and tedious work (made doubly so by their want of proper facilities) was formally begun on the 22d of January, 1679, and was prosecuted under the personal supervision of the Sieur de Tonty, whose knowledge of marine architecture was thus brought into active requisition. The Senecas, it is averred, tried to burn the vessel while on the stocks, but she was launched by the middle of July, and was then towed farther up the river to be rigged. The builders celebrated her completion by firing cannon and singing songs in commemoration of the event. And well they might felicitate themselves upon their achievement; for she was the first sail-rigged and sea-going craft that ever spread canvas to the breeze on our inland seas. The little schooner was armed with five small cannon and three large muskets, and on her prow was carved the wooden figure of a griffin,† from which, in compliment to the armorial bearings of Count de Frontenac, she received her

---

*As usual in such cases, the place of the building of the "Griffin" is disputed. Some contend for a site known as the "Old Ship-yard," on the Little Niagara.

† Or *griffon*, according to the French orthography. The vessel was of sixty tons burden, and was estimated by Hennepin to have cost sixty thousand livres, or about $12,000; but this included a cargo of furs.

name. Every thing was now in readiness awaiting the return of the commander, who had gone to Fort Frontenac to replenish his stores, and was detained there by pecuniary difficulties. He arrived in the beginning of August, accompanied by Friars Ribourde and Membre, who were going to distribute the "bread of life" among the pagan tribes of the southwest.

At length, on the 7th of August, 1679, with the discharge of small artillery, and the chanting of the *Te Deum*, La Salle and his venturesome followers stepped aboard the new vessel, which was wafted by a gentle wind out upon the crystal surface of Lake Erie. Thus the Griffin, flying from her mast-head the pennon of France, went forth as a herald of civilization, and as the forerunner of that uncounted multitude of schooners, brigs, barks, propellers, and other smaller craft, which to-day ply the great lakes in every direction, in the peaceful and gainful pursuits of commerce. After a pleasant navigation of five days, the voyagers entered the noble channel of the Detroit, and found its forest-studded banks filled with different species of small game, of which they shot and killed enough for their needs. Ascending thence through Lake St. Clair and the connecting strait, they issued upon the sea-like expanse of Lake Huron, and in sailing over its dark and treacherous depths encountered a terrific storm, which threatened to speedily engulf their little bark, with all on board. In this extremity of peril, La Salle and the friars fell upon their knees to say their prayers, and invoked the aid of St. Anthony of Padua, as the patron saint of their expedition. It would seem that the saint heard and answered their prayers; for the Griffin weathered the gale, and, on the next day, rode unscathed into the Straits of Michilimackinac.

Approaching the roadstead at the mission of Saint Ignace, they fired an artillery salute to announce their arrival, and, immediately after landing, repaired to the mission chapel to return thanks to God for their recent deliverance from the fury of the elements. On this occasion La Salle wore a scarlet coat, trimmed with gold lace, which he kept by him for occasions of ceremony. He was received here by the Jesuit priests and traders with an outward show of respect and friendship, though they were privately antagonizing his enterprise. The neighboring Indians now swarmed in canoes about his armed vessel, viewing her with mingled feelings of wonder and terror. While anchored at this station, the commander found and took into custody four of his men, whom he had sent up the lakes with merchandise to exchange for pelts; they having disposed of the goods and pocketed the proceeds. At the same time he sent Tonty to Sault de Ste. Marie in pursuit of others, who were also caught.

Weighing anchor about the 2d of September, La Salle continued his westward voyage, and next arrived at one of the islands in the entrance to Green Bay, jutting out from Lake Michigan. Landing on the island, he was hospitably received by a Pottawatomie chief, who had visited in Canada, and here he was also met by the remainder of his advance traders, who had honestly disposed of his goods and collected in return a large quantity of furs. These were now conveyed on board the Griffin, and, with other pelts procured during her outward passage, were to be carried to Niagara for the benefit of his creditors. This transaction was in violation of the letter and spirit of La Salle's royal patent; but his pecuniary necessities were such at the time as to justify or excuse a liberal interpretation of the terms of that instrument. The pilot and five sailors, to whom he committed the charge of the Griffin, were instructed, after they had landed her valuable cargo, to return with the vessel to the southeastern part of Lake Michigan. The Griffin set sail from Green Bay on the 18th of September, but was never afterward heard of. It would have been better for the doomed vessel if she had never sailed on this return trip, and better still, perhaps, if La Salle had continued his own voyage in her to the head of the lake.

On the next day (the 19th), he embarked with his remaining men, fourteen in number, in four canoes, for the mouth of the river Miamis, afterward known as the St.

Joseph.* The canoes were heavily laden with a forge, implements, arms, etc., and their progress was retarded by tempestuous weather. After a perilous passage along the western and southern shores of the lake, in the course of which the voyagers suffered keenly from hunger and exposure, they reached their destination about the first of November. Here they were disappointed at not finding the Sieur de Tonty, who had started from Michilimackinac with a party of twenty men, and was slowly making his way up the eastern side of the lake; but he did not arrive until twenty days later. In the interval of waiting, La Salle, to keep his men from idleness, employed them in building a wooden fort, eighty feet long and forty wide, near the mouth of the river. It was completed by the end of November, and was named Fort Miami, after a neighboring tribe of Indians. Ample time had now elapsed for the return of the Griffin, and La Salle, being much troubled at her non-arrival, sent two men down the lake to look for the vessel, and pilot her to the entrance of the St. Joseph. Different opinions were entertained respecting the fate of the Griffin. Hennepin believed that she foundered in a storm in the north part of Lake Michigan, which is quite probable; others thought that the Indians might have boarded and burnt her; while La Salle himself long cherished the notion that her pilot and crew, after disposing of her valuable cargo, sunk her, and then ran away with their ill-gotten gains. Unfortunately, the loss of this much-prized vessel was irreparable, and it proved a serious blow to the success of his expedition.

But, without longer delay, on December 3, 1679, the reunited party, numbering some thirty-three persons, with eight canoes, began the ascent of the St. Joseph's River, en route to the Illinois. It was a miscellaneous and rather picturesque company, comprising soldiers, friars, artisans,

---

*At the mouth of this river, several years before, the Jesuit Father Allouez had collected some scattered bands of the Hurons and others, and established a missionary station, thereby making it a point known to these adventurers, and one which, knowing, they would endeavor to reach. See Breese's Early Hist. of Ill., p. 106.

laborers, *coureurs des bois*, and a few Indians. After a fatiguing journey southward of twenty-five leagues, in which they had often to drag their canoes against the shallow current of the river, they neared the site of the present city of South Bend, Ind. Thence a portage was made of two or three miles to the headwaters of the *Te-a-ki-ki* (Kankakee), which they reached with the assistance of a Mohegan Indian, whom La Salle had employed in the double capacity of guide and hunter for the expedition. The winter had now fully set in, the earth being thickly mantled with snow, and as the adventurers paddled their weary way down the narrow, torturous stream, flowing through reedy and frozen marshes, the whole landscape presented a most cheerless aspect. To increase their misery, they were distressed by the pangs of hunger until relieved by the fortunate capture of a large buffalo, which was found struggling in the mire of the river, and was soon slaughtered. Being thus regaled, they resumed their canoes and reached without accident the junction of the Kankakee and the Des Plaines, which unite to form the Illinois River.

Gliding rapidly down the channel of the latter, the voyagers shortly entered a region of bolder and more striking scenery. On the right they passed the elevation called Buffalo-Rock, standing out like an island in the valley, and farther down, on their left, appeared the tall cliff, since known as Starved Rock. A mile or more below it, on the north bank of the here expanded river (named by Hennepin the Illinois Lake), stood the principal town of the Illinois nation, in which were counted four hundred and sixty lodges. These were made in the shape of long arbors, with a frame-work of posts and poles, and covered with double mats of flat flags, so well sewed together that they were impervious to rain or snow. Each lodge had four or five fires, and each fire served one or two families. It was here, about the 25th of December, that La Salle and his hungry followers landed, in order to procure some maize, of which they stood sorely in need; but, as had been foreseen, they found the village deserted and silent, its inhabitants being away on their usual winter hunt. Some of the Frenchmen, however, discovered a supply of the desired grain stored in pits, and of it they took enough to supply their wants, intending to pay for the same when the owners should be met. After resting and refreshing themselves for a short time, they re-embarked and continued their course.

On New Year's day, 1680, the voyagers again landed to hear mass, which was solemnized by the friars, and the exercises were closed by Hennepin with an encouraging address to the men. Two days afterward, they entered that irregular expansion of the Illinois River (from seven to eight leagues in length) called Lac Pimiteoui, or Lake Peoria, meaning "the place of fat beasts." Moving on cautiously toward the south end of the lake, where the river resumes its ordinary width, they perceived smoke rising above the bare tree tops, denoting the presence of Indians, and on turning a sharp bend saw, on both sides of the stream, a number of pirogues, and about eighty cabins filled with people. This was on the morning of the fifth day after leaving the great village.* Having some reason to suspect an uncivil reception from the savages, La Salle now formed his small flotilla into a line across the river, so as to present as formidable an array as possible. As they thus swept down the stream to the village, some of the dismayed natives took to flight, and others seized their arms to make resistance; but, in the midst of their confusion, our little band of Frenchmen sprang ashore, armed and equipped for action. Awed by the bold and martial bearing of the latter, the Indians deputed two of their chiefs to present the peace calumet, which La Salle promptly recognized by showing one in turn, and thereupon a friendly intercourse was opened between them. This was succeeded by a feast, at which the more obsequious of the savages rubbed the uncovered feet of the friars with bear's oil, while others fed their guests with buffalo meat, putting the first three morsels into their mouths with much ceremony, as a mark of great civility.

When the feast was ended, M. de la Salle informed

---

* See Hennepin's *Description de la Louisiane;* Shea's translation (N. Y., 1880), p. 156.

Nicanope, and the other principal men of the tribe, that in descending the river he had stopped at their great town, and had taken some corn from their pits to supply the necessities of his men, but that he was prepared to make them full compensation. He then proceeded to explain the purpose of his visit, saying, in substance, that he had come to raise a fort in their neighborhood to protect them from the incursions of the Iroquois, and also to build a large canoe, in which to descend the "great river" to the sea and thence bring back goods to exchange for their peltry. He further told them that if his plans did not meet with their approval, he would pass on to the Osages and Missouris, and give them the benefit of his trade and protection. These Peoria Indians readily assented to what he said about his plans and purposes, and were profuse in their expressions of friendship and good will. Yet, despite all this, it soon became apparent to La Salle that secret enemies were striving to thwart his enterprise, and that the minds of the savages had been prejudiced against him in advance.

A few days afterward there arrived at this village a Mascoutin chief named Monso, or Monsoela, who came equipped with presents and accompanied by several Miamis braves, and who held nightly conclaves with the head men of the village. He professed to have been sent to warn the Illinois against the designs of La Salle, of whom he spoke as an intriguer and friend of the Iroquois, and that he had come among the Illinois only to open the way to their enemies, who were coming on all sides to destroy them.[*] Having thus re-aroused the distrust of the fickle-minded Peorias, the crafty chief and his party hastened away under the cover of night. In the altered and reserved demeanor of the natives, La Salle now met a fresh difficulty, which taxed all his address and knowledge of the Indian character to overcome. It was not without reason that he attributed the meddlesome visit of the Mascoutin chief to the machinations of the Jesuit Father Allouez, whose prin-

---

[*] Membre's Narrative in Le Clercq.

cipal station was among the Miamis, but who had been at the great town of the Illinois only a few months before.

To add to the commander's vexations, some of his own men, who had been discontented from the start, now became sullen and mutinous, and endeavored to stir up disaffection among the better disposed. Not succeeding in this to their satisfaction, they held private interviews with the Illinois to excite their ill-will against La Salle. As a last resort, the malcontents sought his life by secretly putting poison in his food. The effect of the poison, however, was neutralized by the timely taking of an antidote, and no ill-results followed. This was an age of poisoning, the practice having been introduced into France from Italy; and it appears that a similar attempt had been made against the life of La Salle, not very long before, at Fort Frontenac. Shortly after the departure of the Mascoutin chief, six of the Frenchmen, including some of the best workmen, basely deserted their employer, and set off on their return to Canada. To this dastardly course they were partly influenced by previous disaffection, and partly by the dangers of the expedition, which had been artfully magnified to their minds by the Indians. In order to stay further desertions, La Salle called the remaining men together, and told them that he did not intend to take with him any but those who would go willingly, and that he would leave the others at liberty in the spring to return to Canada, whither they might go without risk and by canoe; whereas, they could not then undertake it but with evident peril to their lives.*

It was now mid-winter, and the commander, wearied with his accumulating difficulties, and finding it impracticable to proceed farther to the south, resolved to erect a fort, which might afford shelter and security to his company until the opening of spring. The site chosen for this first European fortification in Illinois was a moderate sized hill, or termination of a ridge, on the eastern side of the river (as shown by Franquelin's, and Hennepin's old maps), and about half a league below the outlet of the lake where the

---

* Hennepin's "Description of Louisiana," p. 173.

explorers had first landed. The precise location of the fort, of which not a vestige remains, is clouded with doubt and controversy. Some would fix it at the village of Wesley City, four miles below the present city of Peoria; while others, with rather more show of reason, contend for a site higher up the river, and over against the northern suburbs of Peoria. Interest in the subject has revived from time to time, and the relative claims of these two different sites, were elaborately discussed through the Peoria press in January, 1890.*

La Salle's men worked with a "good grace" on the fort, and by the first of the ensuing March, 1680, it was nearly finished, and was occupied. It now received the significant name of *Crêve-cœur*, or Heart Break; not, as has been often stated (on the authority of a passage in Hennepin's "New Discovery"), because of the commander's dejection at the desertion of his men and his increasing difficulties, but after the fortress of Créve-cœur in Brabant of the Netherlands, which had recently been taken by the French arms and demolished. Such, more than two hundred and thirteen years ago, was the primal military occupation of Illinois by the French, though no continuous white settlement was established at Peoria Lake until nearly or quite a century later.†

---

*In La Salle's day, when the river carried a somewhat larger volume of water than at present, Lake Pimiteou, is described by him as consisting of "three small lakes, which intercommunicated with each other by so many straits." (See part of a letter by La Salle in vol. 2 of Pierre Margry's Collection). The chief difficulty now is to determine whether the explorer landed and encamped at the foot of the second, or of the third and lower sheet of water. As partly confirming La Salle, it may be as well to note what M. Joutel says in his journal about this chain of lakes. In describing the passage of his party up the Illinois River, in 1687, he writes: "The 9th (September), we came into a lake about half a league over, which we crossed and returned into the channel of the river, on the banks whereof we found several marks of the natives having been encamped. The 10th, we crossed another lake called l'imitehouy, and returned to the river."—*Journal Historique*.

† For a more circumstantial account of the building of Fort Crévecœur, see extracts from Hennepin's writings in the next succeeding chapter.

He Begins a New Vessel.

While the fort was building, La Salle put his best mechanics to work on a brigantine, which, when built, he proposed to freight with buffalo and other skins, to be collected in his descent of the Mississippi, and thence sail to St. Domingo or France, and dispose of the cargo. The keel of the new boat was laid, forty-two feet in length by twelve in breadth, and work on her hull was well advanced by the end of February. Being without rigging or sails for his vessel (they having been unluckily lost with the Griffin), the indomitable leader now formed the bold design of returning over-land to Fort Frontenac, to procure these and other appliances, leaving De Tonty in command at Créve-cœur, while Hennepin should meantime go up the Mississippi on a voyage of exploration,—La Salle promising to send men to meet him at the mouth of the Wisconsin, on his own return from the East.

CHAPTER V.

1675–1701.

FATHER LOUIS HENNEPIN.

The name of Father Hennepin having been already introduced in connection with La Salle's history, it is deemed proper to devote the present chapter to a delineation of his shifting and romantic career, since no more picturesque and interesting personage is to be found in the annals of French exploration and discovery in North America.

About the year of grace 1640, in the ancient town of Ath, in the interior province of Hainault, and in what was then a part of the Spanish Netherlands, but is now a part of the kingdom of Belgium, was born the celebrated Louis Hennepin. With respect to his early domestic life, we possess no definite information. In his writings he tells us much about himself, but very little concerning his family, from which it may be inferred that he came of obscure parentage. He appears to have been sent to school at a tender age, and he quaintly informs us that while prosecuting his early studies, "he felt a strong inclination to leave the world and to live in the rule of strict virtue." He accordingly entered the monastic order of Saint Francis,* to spend his days in a life of religious austerity. His novitiate was made in the Recollet convent at Bethune, in

---

* The Franciscans were an offshoot of the old Carmelite friars, of Mount Carmel, Palestine. The order was first established in Europe by St. Francis, of Assisi, Italy, in the year 1209. Through an excess of humility, he denominated the monks of his order "little brethren," or "friars minor"—a name by which they are still distinguished. They are also called "gray friars," from the color of their dress. "It was a mendicant order (says Breese's Hist. Ill., p. 102), vowed to the lowest poverty and the severest penance; gray coats and bare feet as badges of distinction, and an entire devotion to the precept, 'preach my gospel to

the province of Artois, France, and his master of Novices was Father Gabriel de la Ribourde, a man eminent in the order for his social position and exemplary life, who was destined, at a later day, to die for the Faith, while laboring as a missionary among the savages in America.

In order to learn Flemish, young Hennepin went from Bethune to Ghent, where a married sister of his resided, and where he stayed some time. As he approached the age of manhood, he manifested a strong propensity to travel in foreign parts, which occasioned his sister much anxiety. With the consent of the general of his order, he first set off to see Italy, and visited the principal Franciscan churches and convents in that country, as also in Germany. On returning home, he was sent to the convent of Halles in Hainault, where he discharged the duties of a preacher for a year, and then went to Artois. He was thence sent to Calais, and afterward to the convent of Biez at Dunkirk, in both of which places he appears to have been employed to solicit alms for the fraternity. During his sojourn at those seaport towns, the strange stories he heard related by old mariners stimulated anew his curiosity and desire to visit foreign lands; and with a view to further gratify his taste for travel, he went in the character of a missionary to the principal cities of Holland. While sojourning in that country, on August 11, 1674, he was present, as an assistant chaplain, at the obstinate and bloody battle of Séneffe, fought between the Prince of Orange and the Prince of Condé, and he there found abundant occupation in relieving and comforting the wounded and dying soldiers.

At about this time Canada again became a field of labor for the Recollet missionaries; and Louis XIV., yielding to the appeal of Governor Frontenac, ordered that five Recollet religious be sent to Canada, to reinforce the little

---

the heathen,' marked its members. From this and its kindred order, the Dominicans, has the Roman Church been supplied with many popes, cardinals, bishops, and other noted ecclesiastics, while in saints they have been most wonderfully fruitful."

community of that order already established there. Friar Hennepin was one of the number chosen to go upon this mission, which he readily undertook. Receiving the requisite authority from his superior, he repaired to the seaport of La Rochelle, and there, in the summer of 1675, embarked in the same ship with Francois de Laval, an eminent prelate, who had been recently appointed Bishop of Quebec. Among his other fellow passengers was La Salle, who was now returning from France to Canada, and with whose fortunes Hennepin was subsequently to become closely identified; but for whom, at their first meeting, he seems to have formed no admiration.

After a somewhat eventful voyage, they arrived in the month of September at Quebec, where Hennepin was shortly appointed priest to the cloister of the Hospital Nuns of St. Augustine. As the duties of this position were not onerous, he found time to make frequent excursions to the neighboring French and Indian settlements, and visited, in turn, the Three Rivers, St. Anne, Cape Tourmente, Bourg Royal, Point de Levi, and the Isle de St. Laurent. On these trips he went by canoe in the summer season, and in the winter his light luggage was drawn on the snow by a large dog, while he himself, on foot, was exposed to all the fury of the elements, with no covering save his cloak and hood, and with but very little to eat. In the fall of 1676, or the following spring, he was sent with Father Luke Buisset to Fort Frontenac, where they founded a small convent. Soon after this, Hennepin made a journey to the Jesuit missions among the Mohawks, and others of the Five Nations. Extending his tour to Albany (called Fort Orange by the early Dutch settlers), he was well received by the Catholic residents, who, if we may receive his own statement, entreated him to stay there and become their priest.

When the Sieur de la Salle undertook his first great expedition to the West, he solicited Father Hennepin, among other of the Recollet friars, to accompany him as a chaplain and missionary. The restless and inquisitive mind of Hennepin was fascinated by the very dangers of so bold an adventure, of which he was destined to become the principal chronicler. Accordingly, in November, 1678, he left Fort Frontenac with the advance party of the expedition under La Motte. Sailing slowly up Lake Ontario in a small brigantine, they reached the outlet of the Niagara River on the 6th of December, and, immediately after landing, chanted a *Te Deum* in gratitude for their safe arrival, which was listened to with silent wonder by a group of the natives from a neighboring village. Hennepin, with a few companions, then went in a canoe up the river seven miles to the foot of the high bluff or escarpment overlooking the lake, and, climbing the rocky heights above what is now Lewiston, soon came in sight of the great double cataract of Niagara, "thundering in its solitude." We should not assume that the friar and his party were the first Europeans to look upon these wonderful falls, since they had been known to the French from the time of Champlain; yet he is popularly credited with their discovery, probably from the circumstance that he wrote and published the first good description of them, barring his extravagant estimate of their height.* Proceeding with his companions along the bank of the river to the head of the rapids, opposite the modern Canadian town of Chippewa, he thence returned the next day, and was the first

* In his "Description of Louisiana" (1683), Hennepin writes: "The river (Niagara) plunges down a height of more than five hundred feet, and its fall is composed of two sheets of water and a cascade, with an island sloping down between." In his "New Discovery," he increases the height of the falls to six hundred feet, and La Houtan fixes it at about the same figure. Father Charlevoix (Travels in North America, pp. 152-3), in endeavoring to account for these gross exaggerations, remarks: "It is certain that if we measure its height by the three mountains (or ascents) which we must first pass over, there is not much to bate of the six hundred feet which the map of M. Delisle gives it; who, without doubt, did not advance this paradox but on the credit of the Baron de la Houtan and Father Hennepin. Charlevoix' own measurement of the cataract with a cord, in 1721, fell short of the present altitude of the American Fall, which is 165 feet.

In 1750, seventy years after the time of Hennepin, the Great Falls were visited and carefully described by Professor Kalm, the eminent Swedish traveler.

priest to offer mass at the Falls of Niagara. He then began the erection of a bark chapel on the eastern side of the river, near the Great Rock, where the Sieur la Motte and his men were building a fortified house. Shortly afterward he accompanied La Motte, and five other Frenchmen on a journey of thirty leagues through the snow-incumbered forests of western New York to the principal village of the Seneca nation, to negotiate with the sachems for permission to complete the house or fort at Niagara. Describing the elders of that village, Hennepin graphically says: "They are for the most part tall and well shaped, covered with a sort of robe made of beavers' and wolves' skins, or black squirrels, holding a pipe or calumet in their hands. The senators of Venice do not appear with a graver countenance, and perhaps do not speak with more majesty and solidity than those ancient Iroquois."

After the completion of the Griffin, Hennepin sailed in her, with La Salle and others, through Lakes Erie, St. Clair and Huron, and reached Michilimackinac on the 26th of August, 1769. Continuing his voyage in that vessel with the commander to Green Bay, and thence in canoes up Lake Michigan to the mouth of the Miamis, or St. Joseph, they shortly entered the country of the Illinois. On their way down the Illinois River, Hennepin observed indications of stone-coal, and other minerals, in the upper valley of that stream. The approach of the explorers to the outlet of Lake Pimiteoui, he thus narrates:

"Toward the end of the fourth day, while crossing a little lake, formed by the river, we observed smoke, which showed us that the Indians were cabined near there. In fact, on the fifth, about nine in the morning, we saw on both sides of the river a number of parakeets (pirogues), and about eighty cabins full of Indians, who did not perceive us until we had doubled a point behind which the Illinois were camped within half gunshot. We were in eight canoes abreast, all our men arms in hand, and allowing ourselves to go with the current of the river."*

---
* "Description of Louisiana," by Father Louis Hennepin; trans¹

Some two weeks after the landing of the French adventurers here, and when it was decided to erect a fort in the vicinity of their camp, Hennepin went with La Salle to choose a site for the same. Of the building of this fort the friar gives the following descriptive account:

"A great thaw having set in the 15th of January [1680], and rendered the river free below the village, the Sieur de la Salle begged me to accompany him, and we proceeded with one of our canoes to the place which we were going to select to work at this little fort. It was a little mound about two hundred paces distant from the bank of the river, which, in the season of the rains, extends to the foot of it; two broad, deep ravines protected two other sides and a part of the fourth, which we completely intrenched by a ditch which united the two ravines. Their exterior shape, which served as a counterscarp, was fortified with good *chevaux de friese*, and (we) cut this eminence down steep on all sides, and the earth was supported as much as was necessary with strong pieces of timber (and) with thick planks, and for fear of any surprise we planted a stockade around, the timbers of which were twenty-five feet long and a foot thick. The summit of the mound was left in its natural figure, which formed an irregular square, and we contented ourselves with putting on the edge a good parapet of earth capable of covering all our force, whose barracks were placed in two of the angles of this fort, in order that they might be always ready in case of an attack.

"Father Gabriel, Zenobe, and I lodged in a cabin covered with boards, which we adjusted with the help of our workmen, and in which we retired, after work, all our people for evening and morning prayer, and where, being unable any longer to say mass—the wine which we had made from the large grapes of the country having just failed us— we contented ourselves with singing vespers on holidays and Sundays, and preaching after morning prayers.

---

lated from the French edition of 1683, with notes, etc. By John G. Shea (New York, 1880), p. 156.

"The forge was set up along the curtain which faced the wood. The Sieur de la Salle posted himself in the middle, with the Sieur de Tonty; and wood was cut down to make charcoal for the blacksmith."*

On page 175 of the same work, Hennepin also tells us the fort " was called *Crève-cœur*," and that it was "situated four days' journey from the great village of the Illinois, descending toward the river Colbert" (Mississippi). By the phrase "great village," he undoubtedly referred to the one that stood in the vicinity of The Rock. In his second publication, entitled "New Discovery," etc. (English edition, London, 1698–1699, p. 103), Hennepin gives a shorter account of the construction of Fort Créve-cœur, containing, however, some further particulars, which we reproduce here.

"I must observe," he writes, "that the hardest winter lasts not above two months in this charming country; so, that on the 15th of January came a sudden thaw, which made the river navigable and the weather as mild as it is with us in the middle of the spring. M. la Salle, improving this fair season, desired me to go down the river with him to build our fort. After having viewed the country, we pitched upon an eminence on the bank of the river, defended on that side by the river, and on two others by two ditches (which) the rains had made very deep by succession of time, so that it was accessible only by one way; therefore, we cast a line to join these two natural ditches, and made the eminence steep on every side, supporting the earth with great pieces of timber. We made a hasty lodgment thereupon, to be ready to defend us in case the savages would obstruct the building of our fort; but nobody offering to disturb us, we went on diligently with our work. . . . The fort being half finished, M. la Salle lodged himself in the middle with M. Tonti, and everybody took his post. We placed our forge along the cur-

---

* Hennepin's "Description of Louisiana"; same edition as before cited, pp. 176–178.

tain, on the east side, and laid in a great quantity of coals for that use."

La Salle's own story of the building of Créve-cœur, as related in Pierre Margry's work (vol. II.), does not differ essentially from that of Hennepin, nor does he appear to fix its location with any more precision. The Indians continuing friendly, the fort was substantially completed and occupied before the first of March.

In the meantime, Father Membre devoted himself to missionary instruction among the Illinois, at their village or camp about half a league above the fort. La Salle, it is told, had made a present of three axes to one of their chiefs named Oumahouha (meaning the wolf), on condition that he should adopt Membre as his son and care for him. The good friar visited the Indians daily in their lodges, and in spite of his repugnance to their filthy habits and disgusting manners, labored earnestly, though with scant success, for their spiritual enlightenment. Marquette had previously described the Illinois as having "an air of humanity, which he did not observe in any of the other nations seen on his route." But Membre, after a familiar acquaintance with this people, has portrayed them more nearly as they really were, in all their ignorance and degradation.

"The greater part of these tribes," says he, "and especially the Illinois, with whom I have had most intercourse, make (the coverings of) their cabins of double mats of flat rushes, sewed together. Their villages are not inclosed with palisades, and being too cowardly to defend them, they take flight at the first news of a hostile army. They are tall of stature, strong and robust, and good archers. They had as yet no fire-arms—we gave some to a few. They are wandering, idle, fearful and desolate—almost without respect for their chiefs—irritable and thievish. The richness and fertility of the country gives them fields every-where. They have used iron implements and arms only since our arrival. Besides the bow, they use in war a kind of short pike and wooden maces. Hermaphrodites are numerous. They have many wives, and often take several

sisters that they may agree the better; and yet they are so
jealous that they cut off their noses on the slightest provo-
cation. They are lewd, and even unnaturally so, having
boys dressed as women, destined for infamous purposes.
. . . They are, moreover, very superstitious, although
they have no religious worship. They are, besides, much
given to play, like all the Indians in America that I am
able to know.*

Having come to the conclusion that Hennepin might
be more advantageously employed than in preaching homilies to the Frenchmen at Fort Créve-cœur, La Salle requested him to lead an exploring party down the Illinois
and up the Mississippi river. The worthy friar, according to his own subsequent account, was very averse to this
difficult and perilous undertaking, which yet was to make
him famous. He set up the plea of bodily infirmity, claiming that he had an abscess in his mouth, which had lasted
for more than a year, and which required his return to
Canada for medical treatment. His excuse, however, was
not held sufficient, since neither of his two missionary associates was so well qualified for the bold task as himself;
Father Ribourde being too old and Membre too young.
"Anybody but me," writes Hennepin, in his *New Discovery*,
"would have been much frightened with the dangers of
such a journey, and if I had not put all my trust in God, I
should not have been the dupe of La Salle."*

---

*See A Narrative of the adventures of La Salle's party at Fort Créve-
cœur, and in the Valley of the Illinois, by Zenobe Membre; printed in
LeClercq's "First Establishment of the Faith in New France." English translation, New York, 1881, vol. II, p. 134.

*With reference to this adventurous river voyage, the Margry Re-
lation has the following: "At the same time the Sieur de la Salle proposed to have the route he was to take to the river Mississippi explored
in advance, and the course of that river above and below the mouth of
the Divine river, or of the Illinois. Father Louis Hennepin offered to
take this voyage, in order to begin and make acquaintance with the
nations among whom he proposed to go and settle to preach the faith.
The Sieur de la Salle was reluctant to impose this task on him, but
seeing that he was resolute, he consented." See *note* in Shea's Hennepin, p. 179.

His compagnons de voyage were Michael Ako, or Accault, and Picard du Gay, a native of Picardy, whose real name was Anthony Augelle. Accault was tolerably versed in the language of the Illinois, and, for this reason, and because of his experience, he was made the business director of the party. Both of these men were robust and hardy, though physically, somewhat smaller than Hennepin. Besides being well clad and armed, they were supplied with a good canoe, a large peace calumet, and about one thousand livres worth of goods, to be used in trading with and conciliating the Indians who might be met on the river. The little party embarked near Fort Créve-cœur, on the evening* of the last day of February, 1680. La Salle and the rest of his men quietly escorted them to the bank of the river to see them off, and wish them a bon voyage. With a parting benediction from the good old Father Ribourde, who advanced to the waters' edge to bestow it, the voyagers plied their light paddles, and were soon lost to sight in the shadows and bend of the stream.

The Lower Illinois, on which they were now afloat, and which Hennepin called the Seignelay, is described by him as being as deep and broad as the river Seine, at Paris, and as widening out in several places to a quarter of a league. The first Indians met on the way were a party of the Peorias, who were returning up to their village, and who used every effort to induce the voyagers to turn back with them. Continuing to descend the river until the 7th of March, and having arrived within two leagues of its mouth, they found a tribe called the Maroas, or Tamaroas, numbering about two hundred families, who wished to take them to their village, which lay some distance below, on the bank of the "great river." Upon reaching the Mississippi it was discovered full of running ice, a sight well calculated to shake the strongest nerves. Being de-

---

*This was the time of their departure, as stated by La Salle, and it would seem to have been selected on purpose to avoid observation and annoyance by the neighboring Indians. See La Salle's letter of Aug. 22, 1682, in Margry, II., p. 245.

tained from this circumstance till the 12th of March our intrepid voyagers re-embarked, and, turning the prow of their canoe against the sweeping current of the unexplored river, continued to ascend it, slowly and with difficulty, for the succeeding four weeks.

On the 11th or 12th of April, having passed the mouth of the river Des Moines, they were surprised and captured by a war party of one hundred and twenty Sioux Indians, who were coming down the Mississippi in fifty canoes, in pursuit of a band of the Miamis. Having made this unexpected capture, the Sioux warriors held a council, and decided to return to their own country. Accordingly, on the next day, they began their homeward voyage, taking with them as prisoners Hennepin and his two companions. After a rapid navigation of nineteen days, and having passed through Lake Pepin, where the savages kept up a terrible howling, they landed in a cove of the river a few leagues below the Falls of St. Anthony. Here the Sioux warriors hid their own canoes in a clump of alders, and then broke up the canoe of the Frenchmen, lest the latter might return in it to their enemies. They next divided the property of their captives, including Hennepin's vestments and portable chapel, and distributed their persons to three separate heads of families, to take the place of their sons who had been killed in war. This being done, though not without sharp wrangling among themselves, the Indians started northward across the country for their homes, taking their captives with them. After a hurried march of five days, during which the friar and his companions had well nigh perished from cold, hunger and fatigue, they reached the Sioux villages near Mille Lacs, Minnesota, about the 5th of May.

The savage dwellers in these northern villages were called the Issati, or Isanati, and they formed one of the three divisions of the powerful Sioux Nation.* It was

---

* "The earliest record of the Siouan languages," says Professor J. W. Powell, " is that of Hennepin, compiled about 1680. The earliest printed vocabulary is that of the Naudowessie (*i. e.*, the Dakota) in Carver's Travels, first published in 1778." It is worthy of mention here,

with this uncouth people that Hennepin spent the ensuing summer and early autumn. He experienced some rather hard usage at first, but, upon the whole, was better treated than might have been expected. He was assigned to the care of a chief named Aquipaguetin, whom he did not like, but who adopted him as a son, and took him to his lodge and village. Here, in consequence of his enfeebled condition, the Indians made for him one of their sweating baths, in which he was immersed three times a week, and derived much benefit from the treatment. Regaining his health, he studied the language and manners of this barbarous race, and acted as physician to such of them as required his services. But he did not find among these wild men any encouragement for the exercise of his clerical functions. "I could gain nothing over them," he tells us, "in the way of their salvation, by reason of their natural stupidity." Yet, on one occasion, he baptized a sick child just before its death.

At the end of about two months, Hennepin and his associates in captivity were allowed to accompany a numerous hunting and fishing party of the Sioux down Rum River, from Mille Lac to the Mississippi. Arrived thither, the restless friar and Du Gay, after obtaining permission from the chief, Ouasicoude, set out in a birch canoe for the mouth of the Wisconsin, where they hoped to meet some Frenchmen whom La Salle was expected to send to meet them. Accault did not accompany them on the journey, as he preferred to stay with the Indians. Rapidly descending this hitherto unexplored part of the Mississippi, our two voyagers soon drew near the Falls of St. Anthony, so named by Hennepin in honor of his patron saint of Padua. He describes the falls as from forty to fifty feet high, with an island of pyramidal form lying nearly midway the stream.* Carrying their light canoe and luggage below

---

that some philologists have traced an apparent analogy between the language of the Sioux and that of the Tartars in northern Asia.

*As late as 1820, according to Schoolcraft (H. R.), the perpendicular height of the cataract, in its highest part, was about forty feet, its breadth being twelve hundred feet. But by the constant reaction of

the roaring cataract, they re-embarked, and held on their lonely way down the sinuous river to the confluence of the Wisconsin, a distance of sixty French leagues from the falls. Finding no Frenchmen there to receive them, they returned disappointed, and joined a large band of the Sioux who were hunting on the Chippewa, a stream which enters the Mississippi from the east at Lake Pepin, and leisurely followed them back up the river.

At length, after an irksome and anxious captivity of five and a half months, the friar and his associates were allowed to go free. Their release was effected through the opportune arrival of one of their own countrymen, Daniel Greysolon du L'hut,* who, with five armed Frenchmen, had penetrated into the Sioux country from Lake Superior, and made satisfactory terms with the savages.

Toward the end of September, Father Hennepin and his compatriots—eight Frenchmen in two canoes—left the Sioux villages on their return to the French settlements, and journeyed south and east, via the St. Francis, the Mississippi, the Wisconsin, and Fox Rivers, to Green Bay. Thence they coasted around the northern shore of Lake Michigan to Michilimackinac, where Hennepin spent the winter with the Jesuit Father Pierson, a former fellow-

---

the water against the underlying strata of soft sandstone, and the consequent breaking off of the upper and harder table rock, the height of the falls is now reduced to fifteen feet. Their natural beauty has also been marred and obscured by the erection of mills, and other works of civilized man.

*Some additional notice of the Sieur du L'hut, or Du Luth, may be acceptable to the general reader. He was a native of Lyons, France, and a cousin of the Sieur de Tonty, whom he more than once visited at Fort St. Louis of the Illinois. Having come to Canada as a young officer, he led the life of a military adventurer, and became noted for his enterprise and hardihood. In 1686 he was ordered by De Nonville, then governor of Canada, to fortify the Strait of Detroit. Proceeding thither with fifty men, he built a stockade called Fort St. Joseph, and occupied it till the summer of 1687, when he headed a force of French and Indians from the upper lakes in the war against the Senecas. In 1695 he was commandant at Fort Frontenac, and retained this position for some years. He died of chronic gout, in Canada, during the winter of 1709-'10. It was doubtless from this noted Frenchman, that the modern commercial city of Duluth derived its name.

townsman, at the mission of St. Ignace. On the 29th of the following March, 1681, before the ice had disappeared from the straits, our restless friar, with a few boatmen, resumed his journey eastward from Michilimackinac.* Dragging their canoes and provisions over the snow and ice until open water was reached, they then embarked and rowed along the western shore of Lake Huron to and through the St. Clair, and thence over Lake Erie to the Falls of Niagara. Making a portage round the falls, they next entered Lake Ontario and sailed along its southern side thirty league to a large village of the Senecas, where Hennepin stopped for a while and renewed his acquaintance with the chiefs of that nation. He thence proceeded to Fort Frontenac, and afterward descended the St. Lawrence to Montreal, where Governor Frontenac then was. Here he was very graciously received by the governor, to whom he gave a graphic recital of his river voyages and captivity among the wild tribes on the upper Mississippi, and showed him the advantages to be derived from their discovery.

Taking ship at Quebec for Old France, Father Hennepin reached that country again near the close of 1681, after an absence of six years. He then went to reside for a time at the Convent of St. Germain-en-Laye. After this he was

---

* Mackinac, or Michilimackinac, was then a place of much less consequence than in 1688 (seven years later), when the Baron de la Hontan was sent thither with a company of French troops. He gives us this quaint yet interesting description of the mission and settlement: "Missilimackinac is certainly a place of great importance. It lies in latitude of forty-five degrees and thirty minutes; but as to its longitude I have nothing to say, for reasons expressed in my second letter. 'T is not above half a league from the Illinois Lake (Michigan). Here the Hurons and Outaous have each a village; the one being severed from the other by a single palisade. . . . In this place the Jesuits have a little house or college, adjoining to a sort of church, and inclosed with pales that separate it from the village of the Hurons. These good Fathers lavish away all their divinity and patience in converting such ignorant infidels. . . . The *coureurs de Bois* have a very small settlement here, though 't is not inconsiderable, as being the staple (or mart) of all the goods that they truck with the south and west savages; for they can not avoid passing this way when they go to the seats of the Illinese and the Oumamis (Miamies), or to the Baye des Puant and the River Mississippi."—La Hontan's Voyages, English ed., vol. I., pp. 87, 88.

vicar and acting superior of the Recollets at Chateau Cambrésis, where he was visited by his former companion, Father Zenobe Membre, about 1683. Subsequently, he was Guardian for some three years of the Recollet convent at Rentz, in Artois. During this time he was requested by his superior to return to the mission in Canada, but he declined to comply; his excuse being that the "particular laws of his religious order did not oblige him to go beyond the sea against his will," and that the malice of his enemies there would expose him to perish among the savages.

At or before the year 1697, owing in part to his intriguing character, Hennepin was ordered by the Minister of War to quit the French realm; and, with the consent of his superior, withdrew into Holland, where he gained protection at the court of William III. In order to travel in that country without attracting particular notice, he laid aside his monastic garb, but did not renounce his vows, and continued to sign himself "Recollect and Notaire Apostolique." Becoming tired of Holland, we are told that he offered to return and again go as a missionary to America, but that he was not permitted to re-enter France for the purpose. With respect to his peregrinations in the last years of his erratic and checkered life, we have no authentic information. It is stated by some writers that he went on a pilgrimage to Rome, and was at the convent of Ara-celi in 1701, but that he returned thence, and died shortly after at Utrecht. He was then probably sixty-two years old.

During his extended travels in North America, Friar Hennepin had kept a diary or journal, and his first labor on returning to France was to prepare it for publication. His first and most valuable work, because written from personal observation, and without any special motive to prevaricate, was published at Paris early in January, 1683, and was dedicated to his Christian Majesty, Louis XIV. Its French title runs as follows: "*Description de la Louisiane, novellement découverte au sud-ouest de la Nouvelle France; Avec la Carté du Pays, les moeurs et la maniere de vie des Sauvages. Dediée à sa Majestie. Par le R. P. Hennepin, Missionaire Recollect et Notaire Apostolique.*"

His Writings. 111

This book became immediately popular, both in France and the adjacent countries, and translations of it soon appeared in the English, Dutch, and Italian languages. It contains a copious though desultory narrative of La Salle's first expedition to the West, and of Hennepin's own voyages and discoveries in connection therewith; and despite its author's egotism and propensity to magnify his individual exploits, the work is equally entertaining and instructive. The style is simple and natural, and the language perspicuous, though losing much of its originality in its English dress. He was an observant traveler, using his eyes wherever he went, and his pictures of the wild country and of savage life are very graphic. He had studied the Indians attentively, and portrays their manners vividly.

His second and more comprehensive, but less reliable, publication, did not see the light of print until fourteen years after the first. It is thus lengthily entitled in French:

" *Nouvelle Découverte d'un tres grand pays, situé dans L' Amerique, entre le Noveau Mexique et la Mer Glaciale; Avec les Cartes et les Figures necessaire, et de plus L'Histoire naturelle et morale, et les avantages qu' on peut tier par le etablissement des colonies. Le tout dediée á su Majesté Brittanique, Guillaume III., Par le Louis Hennepin,*" etc. A. *Utrecht* 1697, *Amsterdam* 1698, *and London* 1698-'99.*

In this book was first inserted the narrative of Hennepin's pretended descent of the Mississippi to the Gulf, and and in the preface thereto, by way of explanation, he says: " 'T is true I published part of it in the year 1684 (1683), in my account of Louisiana, printed at Paris by order of the French king; but I was then obliged to say nothing of the course of the river Meschasipi, from the mouth of the river Illinois down to the sea, for fear of disobliging M. la

---

*The English of this reads as follows: " New Discovery of a very Great Country, situated in America between New Mexico and the Icy Sea; with some necessary maps and illustrations, and, moreover, the history, natural and moral, and the advantages that may be had by the establishment there of some colonies. The whole dedicated to his Brittanic Majesty, William III. By Louis Hennepin," etc. Printed at Utrecht 1697, Amsterdam 1698, and London 1698-'99.

Salle, with whom I began my discovery. This gentleman would have the glory of having discovered the course of that river; but when he heard that I had done it two years before him, he would never forgive me, though, as I have said, I was so modest as to publish nothing of it."*

Hennepin's third and smaller work on America, bearing the title of "*Nouveau Voyage d' un pais plue grand que L'Europe; avec les reflexions des enterprises du Sieur de la Salle, fur les mines de St. Barbe,*" etc., was issued at Utrecht in 1698, and was also dedicated to the King of England and Holland, in that style of fulsome adulation then in vogue. In his prefatory note to this book, the friar speciously replies to those who had doubted the possibility of his having sailed down and up the Mississippi within the brief time mentioned in his "New Discovery." The story of his feigned descent of that river to the Gulf of Mexico obtained general credence in this country, notwithstanding the manifest difficulty of reconciling its dates and conflicting statements, until the appearance of Spark's Life of La Salle (in his series of "American Biographies," 1844–'47), since which time it has been rejected as a fiction. Hennepin would thus seem to have been guilty of deliberate falsehood, and in seeking to rob La Salle of his principal laurel, he only tarnished his own fame. La Salle, however, is not deserving of any especial commiseration; for it appears from the anonymous brochure or memoir put forth in his interest, in the year 1678, that he was not unwilling to have the world believe he had discovered the Mississippi, before the historic voyage thereon by Joliet and Marquette.

---

*"Before this publication, however, Tonty's Relation had been published, and, in 1691, a work entitled: 'The Establishment of the Faith in New France,' by the Recollet missionary, Father (Chrétien) Le Clercq, who had derived his materials relating to La Salle's expedition to the Gulf from the letters which the Father Zenobe Membre, who accompanied it, had written to the Bishop of Quebec. Parallel passages from Le Clercq and Hennepin have been examined, so closely resembling, in every important particular, as to compel the belief that Hennepin's publication of 1698 is a piracy upon it, and a wicked attempt to deprive La Salle of his hard-earned honor."—Breese's Early Hist. Ill., p. 128; Chicago, 1884.

Hennepin was, at this time, in the service or pay of the Dutch-English court; and it is affirmed that he was induced (perhaps required) to write a new account of his travels and discoveries in North America, comprising a narrative of his alleged voyage down the Mississippi to the sea, in order to favor the pretensions of King William III., who wished to set up for himself a claim to the country of Louisiana. This statement derives plausibility from the circumstance that, in 1699, two English vessels were sent to explore the passes of the Mississippi. There were also other motives that influenced and may help to explain the friar's dubious conduct. Among these was his inordinate vanity, which seems to have augmented with his years, and prompted him to air his personal grievances, and to pose before the reading world as a persecuted man. Then again, the prospective increase in the sale of his book, from the insertion of new and entertaining matter, must have exercised no little influence, particularly with his publishers.

Yet, apart from all this, there are reasons for suspecting that Hennepin himself was not responsible for all the fictions printed in his "New Discovery." The hand of an anonymous and careless editor is traceable in various parts of the book, which is said to have been altered even after its first printing. This charitable view of the matter, while it lessens Hennepin's culpability, does not exculpate him from censure. The whole truth about the origin and appearance of his last two publications, though inviting attention and inquiry, will probably never be known.*

But still, with all his faults and failings and caprices, Louis Hennepin was no ordinary man, and his was no ordinary destiny. Distinguished not only as a traveler and Recollet missionary, he was also the first popular writer on the French in North America. Moreover, his memory is lastingly linked with two, at least, of the great natural

---

* For a critical disquisition upon this curious and recondite subject, the inquring reader is referred to the late Dr. Shea's Notice of the Life and Writings of Father Hennepin, in his annotated edition of the "Description de la Louisiane," N. Y., 1880.

monuments of this country—the Falls of Niagara and the Falls of St. Anthony; and it was he who first publicly gave the name to that vast and magnificent territory, lying mostly on the west of the Mississippi, which is still worn by that portion of it incorporated into the sovereign State of Louisiana.

CHAPTER VI.

1680-1681.

LA SALLE AND TONTY.

It is now time to return to La Salle, the central figure in this important and difficult enterprise. On the second of March, two days after the departure of Father Hennepin from Créve-coeur, the resolute chief himself set forth on his return journey to Fort Frontenac. . He left Tonty, his trusted lieutenant, in command at the Illinois fort, with a company of fifteen men, and took with him four Frenchmen, besides his indispensable Mohegan hunter. The last month of the winter had been extremely cold, so that the passage of La Salle and his little party up the river and lakes was much obstructed by ice, either firm or drifting. At Peoria Lake his men had to make sledges for their two canoes, and drag them over the frozen surface. From thence they slowly and laboriously advanced, alternately by land and water, amid the chilling rains and melting snows of the opening spring.

Arriving at the great town of the Illinois on the 11th of March, they found it still a solitude, and the roofs of its lodges crested with snow, the copper-hued inhabitants not having as yet returned from their winter hunt. Encamping here, one of the hunters killed a stray buffalo, and while his men were smoking the meat of the animal, La Salle reconnoitered the adjacent country. Falling in with three Illinois Indians, he brought them to his camp, gave them food and presents, and secured from them a promise to send provisions to his men at the fort. During his short stay at this place, he attentively examined that rugged and precipitous cliff, designated by him as *Le Rocher* (The Rock), which had been passed without particular notice in his previous trip down the river. Being impressed with its rare capabilities as a defensive position, he soon afterward sent back word to Tonty to occupy and fortify it.

Quitting the vicinity of the Indian town on the 15th, the leader and his party continued their toilsome ascent of the Illinois and its Des Plaines branch until they approached the place where Joliet now stands, when further navigation was rendered impracticable by the firmness of the ice in the river. Here they hid their canoes, strapped their luggage on their shoulders, and started over-land for Lake Michigan, distant about fifty miles. The country all around was a flat and dreary waste, covered with half-melted snow and intersected by swollen streams, some of which they forded, and others they crossed on log rafts. On the 23d of March they were cheered by glimpses of the southern extremity of the lake, seen through the openings in the leafless forest trees; at night they encamped on its beach, and the next day followed its sandy shores east and northeast to Fort Miami. Here La Salle found the two men whom he had sent down the lake in the preceding November to look for the Griffin, they having gone to Mackinac and returned without getting any tidings of the missing vessel. He now ordered them to proceed to the fort on the Illinois, and gave them a letter to carry to De Tonty. In order to gain time, the dauntless chief, and his travel-worn companions, next turned their steps eastward across the southern peninsula of Michigan. Their journey through its gloomy and trackless forests was one of peculiar hardship, since they could keep no fire at night for fear of straggling parties of Indians. Coming to a tributary of the Detroit, they made a log canoe and descended in it to that river, and thence marched across the country some thirty miles to Lake Erie. Here they embarked in a canoe and coasted the northern shore of the lake as far east as the mouth of Grand River, and then proceeded overland to the post which La Salle had established below the Falls of Niagara. From thence, with a party of fresh men, he pushed down and across Lake Ontario to his seigniory of Fort Frontenac, whither he arrived on the 6th of May, 1680., Thus within the brief interval of sixty-five days, he had performed an arduous journey through the wilderness of over eight hundred miles, which, considering the season and circumstances under which made, was a most remarkable exhibition of pluck and physical endurance.

Arrived at his seigniory, La Salle found all of his affairs in confusion. Not only had the Griffin been lost, with her furs and pelts, but a vessel coming from France with a cargo for his company, valued at 2,200 livres, had been wrecked on St. Peter's Island, in the Gulf of St. Lawrence; and several canoes loaded with his merchandise had been swallowed up in the rapids of the St. Lawrence. Moreover, some of his agents had acted in bad faith with him, and his creditors were preparing to seize upon the residue of his property. But, in the presence of these accumulated misfortunes, which would have crushed any other man, he was neither disheartened nor swerved from his purpose. He at once hastened to Montreal to arrange matters with his principal creditors, and such was still his credit and influence there, that he was enabled to procure the requisite supplies for continuing his great enterprise. Returning from Montreal to Frontenac, he was met by two messengers just arrived with a letter from Tonty, stating that after his departure from Fort Créve-coeur, a majority of his men there had deserted the fort, and wasted or destroyed such stores as they could not carry away. Following his letter, came news by two traders on the lakes that the deserters had destroyed his fort at the mouth of the Miamis or St. Joseph, and plundered his warehouse at Niagara. Being further informed that twelve of the perfidious wretches were coming down the northern shore of Lake Ontario with evil intent, La Salle, with a party of nine trusty men, sallied out to meet them, and coming upon them unawares, killed two and captured seven of the number, whom he imprisoned at Frontenac, to await punishment by a civil tribunal.

One of the chief difficulties attending the enterprises of La Salle, and of other early French explorers in the West, was to secure the services of reliable men. The wilderness was in a measure full of vagabond hunters, known as *coureurs des bois*, who had fled from the restraints of civilization to lead lives of license and lawlessness, and whose consequent freedom from care and immunity from punishment for crime was a constant allurement to draw others from legitimate employment. The provincial government of Canada made stringent regulations from time to time for the suppression of this growing evil; but it was easier to enact such decrees than to enforce them.

On the 10th of August, having completed his outfit, and engaged the services of a lieutenant named La Forrest, with a company of twenty-five new men, La Salle again set out from his seigniory for the Illinois country, to "succor the forlorn hope under Tonty." Taking the most direct route, he passed up the river Humber or Trent, crossed Lake Simcoe, descended the Severn to the Georgian Bay of Lake Huron, followed its rugged eastern coast to the Manitoulin Islands, and thence moved westward to the French post on the straits of Mackinac. Finding it difficult to replenish his stock of provisions there on account of the enmity and jealousy of the French traders, and not wishing to be delayed, he pressed on up Lake Michigan with twelve men and four canoes, leaving La Forrest and the rest of the force to follow so soon as they could procure the needed supplies. On November 28th, the advance party under La Salle drew their boats ashore on the sandy beach close to the wrecked fort of Miami. Here, for the purpose of facilitating his progress, he left the bulk of his stores in charge of five men, and continued his journey with the remaining seven. Ascending the river St. Joseph to the portage, he thence crossed to the Kankakee, and rapidly descended its channel to the Illinois.

After entering the latter stream, our voyagers found the adjacent prairies dotted over with fat buffaloes, and being in want of fresh meat, they put to shore and soon shot a dozen or more of these favorite animals, the flesh of which they cut into thin strips and dried in the sun for future use. Resuming their canoes and passing the Rock, which La Salle had directed Tonty to occupy, they saw no sign there of any fortification, and heard no tidings of that trusted officer. Approaching the great town of the Illinois nation, a scene of havoc and ruin was presented to their astonished sight. A force of five hundred Iroquois warriors had then recently invaded the western country, driven away the Illinois, sacked their town, cut down their growing corn, and rifled their corn pits. Moreover, they had despoiled the sepulchers of the village dead,* scattered their bones over the adjoining plain, and stuck the skulls in derision on the charred poles of the burnt lodges.

Having carefully inspected the scene of these acts of savage barbarity and desecration, to ascertain whether Tonty and his band had fallen victims to the vengeance of the invaders, La Salle stationed three of his men here in concealment to keep a close watch, while he continued with the other four to descend the river. At different points on the way, he discovered the deserted camps of the opposing Indian forces, who had moved southward in compact bodies on both sides of the stream. Passing on through Peoria Lake, and coming to Fort Créve-coeur, he found it dismantled, but his unfinished boat was still on the stocks and but little injured. Some distance farther down, and a little way from the river, his eyes were met by the revolting spectacle of the half-charred bodies of some Indian women and children, who had been cruelly burned at the stake by the Iroquois. Still discerning no traces of his lost men, La Salle went on to the mouth of the Illinois, where for the first time, perhaps, he beheld that great and mysterious river, which he had long desired to trace to its unknown embouchure in the sea. It is said that those who were with him proposed to proceed without delay upon the projected voyage; but the prudent leader, having his men and resources dispersed, and being uneasy about the fate of Tonty, was compelled to wait a more propitious opportunity.

---

*According to the Jesuit Father Rasles, the custom of the Illinois was not to bury their dead, but to wrap them in skins, and expose them on scaffolds, or attach them by the head and feet to the boughs of trees. But it appears that this practice was not universal among them.

Returning expeditiously up the Illinois, he rejoined the three men who had been left in hiding near the ruined town, and, after procuring some half-burnt maize from the pillaged granaries, the united party re-entered their canoes and paddled up the river. When they reached the forks, and had gone a short distance up the Kankakee branch, they discovered on the bank a hut, containing a stick of wood that had been recently sawed, which was mistaken for an indication that Tonty and company had passed this way. Quitting the stream and concealing their canoes near this point, La Salle and his party made their way slowly, on foot, through blinding snow storms, to Fort Miami, whither they arrived late in January, 1681.* Here the weather-worn and exhausted travelers were warmly welcomed by La Forrest and his men, who, during the absence of the chief, had repaired the fort, cleared some land on which to raise a crop, and prepared material for a new vessel on the lake.

Leaving La Salle within the wooden walls of Fort Miami, to recuperate his energies and lay new plans for the unpromising future, we must now go back and relate the thrilling adventures of the Sieur de Tonty and his companions.

As before stated, he had been left in command of Fort Créve-coeur in March, 1680, with a garrison of fifteen men. Two-thirds of these were worthless knaves, who disliked La Salle, took no interest in his important enterprise, and were ripe for revolt whenever the occasion offered. His departure for the East, therefore, was the signal for the open manifestation of their disaffection. A month or more afterward, when the two men whom the chief had

---

*During this retrograde journey, the great comet of 1680–'81 appeared nightly in the heavens, with its brilliant and appalling train, covering an arc of from sixty to ninety degrees. According to Mr. Parkman, La Salle, in his correspondence, coolly referred to the comet as "an object of scientific curiosity;" whereas Increase Mather, the eminent Puritan divine of New England, spoke of it as "fraught with terrific portent to the nations of the earth."

sent from Fort Miami, with a letter to Tonty, arrived at Créve-coeur, they brought with them depressing intelligence. They told the already demoralized garrison, "that the Griffin was lost; that Fort Frontenac was in the hands of La Salle's creditors, and that he was without means to pay those in his employ." The belief now pervading the garrison that they would not be paid excited a spirit of mutiny and mischief among them, which shortly found the desired opportunity to ripen into action. No sooner had Tonty, with a few of the men, departed up the Illinois River to fortify the "Rock," as ordered by his chief, than those left behind proceeded to demolish the fort, and then fled, with such arms, ammunition and goods, as they could carry away. Two only of the number remained faithful, one of whom hastened to apprise Tonty of what had happened. Alarmed at this revolt and desertion, he dispatched four men, by two different routes, to carry the unwelcome news to La Salle, two of whom, as we have seen, reached their destination.

The Sieur de Tonty now had with him only five white men, namely: the young and spirited Francois de Boisrondet, L'Espérance (servant of La Salle), a Parisian youth named Etienne Rénault, and the two friars, Ribourde and Membre. With a part of this little band, the lieutenant repaired to the deserted fort, collected the tools, forge, etc., which had not been molested, and conveyed them up the river to the great town of the Illinois, where he temporarily fixed his quarters. But, as the sequel showed, it would have been better if the forge and tools had been left where they were. For the next five months the Frenchmen, while anxiously waiting the return of their leader, enjoyed the dubious hospitality of the savages. During this time Tonty endeavored to make himself useful by teaching them the construction of rude fortifications and the simpler arts of military strategy, and the friars labored faithfully to instruct them in the rudiments of Christianity.

In this way a fairly good understanding was maintained with the natives until about the first of September, when it was announced that an army of five hundred Iroquois and one hundred Miamis was swiftly marching into the country. It appears that a Shawnee Indian, on his way home from a visit to the Illinois, had first discovered the approach of the invaders, and returned to warn his friends of their impending danger. This intelligence created the utmost consternation among the inhabitants of the town; and Tonty, who had all along been an object of suspicion, was soon surrounded by a crowd of excited warriors, who brandished their weapons and accused him of being an emissary of the enemy. Owing to his imperfect knowledge of the Illinois language, he was unable to explain the situation to their satisfaction, and in their fury they seized upon the forge and implements, brought thither from Créve-cœur and threw them into the river. Doubting their ability to successfully defend themselves, since most of their young men were away on the warpath, they hurriedly sent their squaws and papooses down the river to an island, where they were left in charge of sixty old warriors. The remaining braves, to the number of about four hundred, now spent the night in preparing themselves for battle, painting their faces and greasing their bodies. Early the next day the scouts, whom they had previously sent out, returned and reported the Iroquois as near at hand, and armed with guns and swords obtained from the English. They further reported that they had seen a chief with the enemy arrayed in the French dress, and signified their belief that it was La Salle. This turned out to be simply an Iroquois warrior, wearing a European hat and waistcoat, yet it served to again make Tonty an object of dark suspicion. Being surrounded by a throng of infuriated savages, who threatened his life, he only saved himself from their uplifted weapons by promising that he and his men would go out with them to meet the common foe. Since no time was to be lost, the whole available force of the Illinois now hurried across the river and took position on the plain beyond, just as the enemy stealthily emerged from the timber that skirted the banks of the Big Vermillion. Thus the two Indian armies soon confronted each other, and, simultaneously raising the war-whoop, began to exchange shots and arrows, jumping from side to side to elude each other's shots. At this crisis, the Sieur de Tonty, knowing the Illinois warriors to be cowards, and seeing that they were outnumbered and likely to be defeated, determined to make an effort at negotiation, and thus stay the unequal fight. Relying on the treaty of peace then subsisting between the Iroquois nation and the French, he laid aside his gun for a necklace of wampum and started, at the imminent risk of his life, to meet the belligerent invaders. An Illinois Indian accompanied him part of the way, and they separated themselves from the main body of the Illinois, who were actively skirmishing with the enemy.

"When I was within gun-shot," writes Tonty, "the Iroquois shot at us, seized me, took the necklace from my hand, and one of them plunged a knife into my breast, wounding a rib near the heart.* However, having recognized me, they carried me into the midst of their camp, and asked me what I came for. I gave them to understand that the Illinois were under the protection of the King of France and the governor of the country, and that I was surprised that they wished to break with the French and not continue at peace. All this time skirmishing was going on, on both sides, and a warrior came to give notice that their left wing was giving away, and that they had recognized some Frenchmen among the Illinois, who shot at them. On (hearing) this they were greatly irritated at me, and held a council on what they should do with me. There was a man behind me with a knife in his hand, who every now and then lifted my hair. They were divided in opinion. Tegantouki, chief of the Tsonnouthouans, desired to have me burnt. Agoasto, chief of the Onnontagues,† wished to have me set at liberty, as a friend of M. de la Salle, and he carried his point. They agreed that, in order to deceive the Illinois, they should give me a necklace of porcelain beads to prove that they also were children of the gov-

---
* Membre tells us that " with his swarthy complexion and half-savage dress, they took him (Tonty) for an Indian."
† Onondagas.

ernor, and ought to unite and make a good peace. They
sent me to deliver this message to the Illinois. I had much
difficulty in reaching them, on account of the blood I had
lost. On my way I met the Fathers Gabriel de Ribourde
and Zenobe Membre, who were coming to look after me.
They expressed great joy that these barbarians had not put
me to death. We went together to the Illinois, to whom I
reported the sentiments of the Iroquois toward them, adding,
however, that they must not altogether trust them."*

Shortly afterward the Illinois returned to their village,
and many of the Iroquois, under different pretexts, also
crossed the river and disposed themselves in menacing
groups about the place. These hostile demonstrations, being
repeated the next day, caused the more timid Illinois
to seek safety in flight. Accordingly, at nightfall, they
set fire to their lodges, and while the attention of the
enemy was diverted by the flame and smoke of the burning,
they secretly betook themselves to their canoes, and
dropped down the river to join their women and children.
Tonty and his companions remained behind to deal as best
they might with the faithless Iroquois. The latter now
took possession of the village, and intrenched themselves
therein.

Two days later, when the Iroquois observed the scouts
of the Illinois on the neighboring hills, they thought that
Tonty had some communication with them, and obliged
him and his party to remove from their cabin into the fort,
or redoubt, of the former. They then requested Tonty to
repair to the Illinois, and induce them to make a treaty of
pacification, for their vaunted courage had subsided. He
accordingly proceeded, with Father Zenobe and a hostage,
to the camp of the Illinois. They gladly accepted the
peace proposal, and sent a hostage in return to the Iroquois.
But the inexperienced Illinois hostage soon disclosed to his
cunning interviewers the numerical weakness of his people,

---

* See M. de Tonty's Memoir of 1693, covering the period from 1678 to
1691. Friar Membre, in his account of this exciting episode, conveys
the idea that he himself went with Tonty into the Iroquois camp, but
this is not sustained by Tonty's Narrative.

and offered to give them, if they wished for peace, the beaver skins and some slaves which they had. The Iroquois chiefs were now enraged at the Sieur de Tonty, and loaded him with reproaches for having told them that the Illinois had twelve hundred warriors, and that there were sixty Frenchmen at the village. "I had much difficulty," writes Tonty, "in getting out of the scrape."

However, on the next day, a nominal peace was concluded between the representatives of the two nations, and the Iroquois made some presents of necklaces and merchandise to the Illinois. But, in utter disregard of the treaty, the Iroquois immediately began to construct canoes of elm bark, with which to descend the river and fall upon the Illinois. In the meantime Tonty apprised the latter of their danger, and advised them to retire to some distant nation.

Shortly after these events (on the 10th of September), Tonty and Father Membre were summoned to attend a council of the Iroquois. It seems that they still entertained a wholesome fear of Governor Frontenac, under whose protection the Illinois were, and did not want to renew their war upon the latter in presence of the Frenchmen. Their purpose, therefore, was to induce the French to leave the country. Accordingly, when Tonty and Membre appeared at the council, six parcels of beaver skins were brought into their presence. And the Iroquois spokesman, addressing Tonty, said, that the first two packages were to inform M. de Frontenac that they would not eat his children, and that he should not be angry at what they had done; the third was a plaster to heal the wounds of Tonty; the fourth was oil to anoint him and Membre, that they might not be fatigued in traveling; the fifth proclaimed that the sun was bright; and the sixth, and last, required them to depart for the French settlements.*

These proffered gifts were scornfully rejected by Tonty, who, in imitation of the Indian mode of expressing contempt, indignantly kicked them away, and thus rebuked

---

* Tonty's Memoir of 1693.

the savages for their insolence and perfidy. The council ended in recrimination and disorder, and on the next day the exasperated chiefs ordered the Frenchmen to quit the country forthwith. The Sieur de Tonty had now, at the repeated risk of his life, tried every expedient to save the Illinois 'from the fury of the invaders of their soil and homes, and since by remaining longer he would imperil the lives of his own men, he made a virtue of necessity, and speedily departed.

On the morning of the 11th, he and his five companions embarked in a wretched bark canoe, with but scanty supplies, and made haste up the river. The same day, about noon, the canoe broke, and they landed to repair it and dry their peltry. While some of the men were thus employed, Father Ribourde imprudently retired into an adjacent grove for the purpose of saying his breviary. As he did not return when expected, Tonty became alarmed for his safety, and started out with a companion to hunt him. With the quick eyes of woodmen, they soon discovered the tracks of Indians, by whom it was thought the friar had been seized, and they fired guns to direct his return, if still alive. Not seeing or hearing any thing of him that afternoon, in the evening they built fires along the river bank, and then withdrew to the opposite shore, to observe who might approach them. Toward midnight several Indians were seen flitting about the fires, and then vanished in the darkness. It was afterward learned that they belonged to a band of young Kickapoo warriors, who had been hovering for some days about the Iroquois camp in quest of scalps. By chance, it would seem, they had fallen in with the innocent old friar, whom they killed and scalped, hiding his body in a sink, and carrying away his breviary, which subsequently came into the hands of one of the Jesuit fathers. Thus perished by the war-club of the merciless savage, in the sixty-sixth year of his age, the Recollet father, Gabriel de la Ribourde. He was the only son and heir of a gentleman of Burgundy, and had not only renounced his inheritance and the world, to enroll himself among the lowly children of St. Francis, but even when advanced in life and honored with the first dignities of his order, had sought (in 1670) the new and toilsome mission of Canada.*

While this painful tragedy was being enacted, the Iroquois invaders, unrestrained by the presence of Frenchmen, were brutally desecrating the sepulchers of the dead at the great town of the Illinois, and preparing to further wreak their vengeance upon the living. Starting down the river in pursuit of the retreating Illinois, they steadily followed them day after day; but as both of the opposing armies moved in close array, neither was able to gain any material advantage over the other. At length, the Iroquois chiefs attained by strategy what their vaunted prowess and arms had failed to achieve. They publicly gave out that their object was not to destroy the Illinois, but simply to drive them from the country. Deceived by this artifice, the Illinois separated, some of them descending the Mississippi River, and others fleeing across and beyond it. But the Tamaroas tribe, more stupid or credulous than the rest, lingered at their village, not far below the mouth of the Illinois, until they were suddenly attacked by a superior force of the enemy. The pusillanimous men are said to have fled at the first onset, leaving their defenseless women and children, numbering several hundred, to fall into the hands of the merciless foe. Then followed those savage butcheries and burnings, the horrible evidences of which were seen by La Salle only a few weeks afterward. Having scattered the timorous Illinois in every direction, and satiated their greed for carnage, the rapacious horde of Iroquois now set off on a forced march to their own country, taking with them a number of captive squaws and papooses, whom they had reserved to grace their triumph on returning to their eastern homes.

After the melancholy end of Father Ribourde, and the ineffectual search for his body, Tonty and his men resumed their toilsome ascent of the Illinois River. On reaching the forks of that stream, they neglected to leave there any

---

† Shea's Hist. of the Discov. and Explo. of the Miss. Val., page 159, *note*.

mark or trace indicating their course, which might have
served as a guide to La Salle, and saved him no little
trouble. But evidently afraid of encountering some hostile band of Indians, they turned up the Des Plaines*
branch of the Illinois, and made their way by short journeys to Lake Michigan. Their aim was to find an asylum
among the friendly Pottawatomies. After coasting the
lake shore for a considerable distance, their canoe became
disabled, and their provisions failed them. Leaving one
man in charge of their canoe and other articles, the Sieur
de Tonty and the rest of the party set off by land for the
nearest Pottawatomie village, which lay some twenty leagues
to the north. But as Tonty had a fever at the time, and his
limbs were swollen, he did not reach the village until the
11th of November. During this hard journey the travelers
lived on wild garlic, which they grubbed from under the
snow, and when they came to the village they found it deserted, for the Indians had gone to their winter quarters.
They, however, discovered a little maize and some frozen
gourds, with which to appease their hunger.

Returning to the lake shore, the Frenchmen re-embarked and continued their voyage. Being again obliged
to land, they found a fresh trail, and, following it, made a
portage of a league across the peninsula to Green Bay.
Entering an estuary of the bay, called Sturgeon Cove, they
appear to have ascended it several leagues, when they were
stopped by a high wind, which continued for a week. During this time they consumed all their little stock of provisions, and were in despair of being able to overtake the
savages. Their shoes having worn out, they now made
coverings for their feet of the late Father Gabriel's cloak.
The stream had meantime frozen up, so that they could not
proceed farther in their canoe. When they were preparing
to set out on foot, two Ottawa Indians chanced to arrive at
their camp, and conducted them to a village of the Pottawatomies. Here the famished travelers met a kind reception, and had their wants liberally supplied.

---

* Called by the Indians the Checagou.

According to the narrative of Father Membre, Onanghisse, the head chief of the Pottawatomies, was a great admirer of the French, whom he had before befriended. And he was accustomed to say that "he knew of only three great captains, Frontenac, La Salle, and himself."*

After recruiting somewhat from the extreme hardships of the journey, Father Membre went to spend the winter at the mission-house of the Jesuits on Green Bay, while Tonty and the other four members of the party remained with the Pottawatomies. In the following spring, they all proceeded to old Mackinac, and there awaited the arrival of their leader.

---

* Both Tonty and Membre have left accounts of this journey of retreat from the Illinois to the Pottawatomies, but, for the most part, we have followed the relation of the former.

CHAPTER VII.

1681-1683.

LA SALLE'S EXPLOITS CONTINUED.

Reverting to La Salle, who was left at Fort Miami to recruit his powers and resources, we again resume the account of his stirring career. During the winter of 1680–81, while his fortunes seemed at the lowest ebb, he was never more active, or more determined upon achieving ultimate success. Believing that the then recent foray of the Iroquois into the country of the Illinois, was mainly for the purpose of extending their territorial possessions, whence to draw fresh supplies of furs, and that those fierce warriors were also being used by his white adversaries to put an end to his own operations in this wide and attractive region, he evolved from his busy brain a plan to counteract their designs. His scheme was to unite all the different and often warring tribes of the West into a defensive league; to colonize such of them as would consent about a fort to be erected and maintained by him on the Illinois River, and thus oppose an effectual barrier to the further incursions of the Iroquois and their adherents. This extensive plan exemplifies La Salle's fertility of resource in emergency, and its success in execution was answerable to his expectations.

After the close of the bloody and desolating war of Philip, of Pokanoket, with the New England colonists, in 1676, some of his vanquished allies quitted their eastern homes, and sought a refuge in the forests on the southeastern borders of Lake Michigan. These were mostly Abenakis and Mohegans, or Mohicans—the latter tribe having furnished the reliable hunter and servant, who had already rendered such useful service to La Salle. It was to these small bands of Eastern exiles that our explorer first addressed himself in the trial of his new expedient for the furtherance of his general plans. He found them very willing to join their lot with his in any undertaking he might propose, asking only the privilege of calling him their chief. His next move was to effect a reconciliation between the Miamis and Illinois, who, though kindred tribes, had been long estranged. Desiring to first confer with the Illinois, many of whom had returned since the evacuation of their country by the Iroquois, La Salle set out with a party from Fort Miami on a journey thither. On entering the prairies, which were still white with snow, he and several of the men became snow-blind, so that they were obliged to go into camp on the edge of a grove until they could recover their sight. Resuming his journey, he met with a band of the Outagamies (Foxes), whose chiefs he drew over to his interest by means of presents. From them it was learned that Tonty and his party were safe among the Pottawatomies, and that Hennepin had passed through their country (Wisconsin) on his way to Canada. This was welcome intelligence to La Salle, who, for several months, had been very anxious about their safety. Following down the Kankakee River, he fell in with a party of the Illinois, who were stalking the prairies in quest of game, and who related to him the unhappy occurrences of the preceding year. La Salle expressed his regret at what had happened, and advised them to form an alliance with the Miamis, in order to prevent the recurrence of like disasters in the future. He told them that he and his men would come back to reside among them, furnish them with fire-arms and goods, and help them in repelling the hostile incursions of the Iroquois. Well pleased with this proposition, they gave him some maize, and promised to confer with other members of their tribe and report to him the result.

Returning now to Fort Miami, La Salle sent La Forrest down Lake Michigan to Mackinac, whither it was expected that Tonty would go, and where both were to stay until he should follow them. It still remained for him to confer with the Miamis, and he accordingly started with

ten men to visit their principal village, situated near the
portage between the St. Joseph and Kankakee. Here he
found a small party of Iroquois warriors, who had for some
time demeaned themselves with great insolence toward the
villagers, and had spoken with contempt of himself and men.
On being informed of this, he sternly rebuked them for
their arrogance and calumnies, and such was the fear his
presence inspired among them that at night they fled from
the village.

"The next day the Miamis were gathered in council,
and La Salle made known to them the objects he wished to
accomplish. From long intercourse with the Indians, he
had become an expert in forest diplomacy and eloquence,
and on this occasion he had come well provided with presents
to give efficacy to his proceedings. He began his address,
which consisted of metaphorical allusions to the dead, by
distributing gifts among the living. Presenting them with
cloth, he told them it was to cover their dead; giving them
hatchets, he informed them that they were to build a scaffold in their honor; distributing among them beads and
bells, he stated they were to decorate their persons. The
living, while appropriating these presents, were greatly
pleased at the compliments paid to their departed friends,
and thus placed in a suitable state of mind for that which
was to follow. . . . Lastly, to convince them of the
sincerity of his intentions, he gave them six guns, a number of hatchets, and (then) threw into their midst a huge
pile of clothing, causing the entire assemblage to explode
with yelps of extravagant delight. After this, La Salle thus
closed his harangue:

"'He who is my master, and the master of all this
country, is a mighty chief, feared by the whole world; but
he loves peace, and his words are for good alone. He is
called the King of France, and is the mightiest among the
chiefs beyond the great water. His goodness reaches even
to your dead, and his subjects come among you to raise
them up to life. But it is his will to preserve the life he has
given. It is his will that you should obey his laws, and
make no war without the leave of Frontenac, who com-

mands in his name at Quebec, and who loves all the nations alike, because such is the will of the great king. You ought, then, to live at peace with your neighbors, and above all with the Illinois. You have had cause of quarrel with them; but their defeat has avenged you. Though they are still strong, they wish to make peace with you. Be content with the glory of having compelled them to ask for it. You have an interest in preserving them, since, if the Iroquois destroy them, they will next destroy you. Let us all obey the great king, and live in peace under his protection. Be of my mind, and use these guns I have given you, not to make war, but only to hunt and to defend yourselves.'" *

Having ended his mission to the Miamis nation, La Salle sent two of his men, with two of the Abenakis, to announce the result to the Illinois, in order to prevent further acts of hostility, and to recall the dispersed tribes. Moreover, he dispatched men with presents to the Shawnees, to invite them to come and join the Illinois against the Iroquois. All this being done to his satisfaction, he left Fort Miami on the 22d of May, 1681, and, after a pleasant canoe voyage, arrived at the post of Mackinac about the middle of June. Here he had the happiness of meeting Tonty, Father Zenobe, and others of his men, from whom he had been separated for more than a year. " The Sieur de la Salle (says Membre's Narrative, before cited,) related to us all his hardships and voyages, as well as his misfortunes, and learned from us as many regarding him; yet never did I remark in him the least alteration, always maintaining his ordinary coolness and self-possession. Any one but he would have renounced and abandoned the enterprise; but, far from that, by a firmness of mind and an almost unequaled constancy, I saw him more resolute than ever to continue his work, and to carry out his discovery."

Before La Salle could resume and push forward his great enterprise to a successful issue, it was necessary for him to return to Canada, collect his scattered resources, and

---

* Davidson & Stuve's Hist. of Ill., 1st ed., p. 93. See *Relations des Découvertes*, compiled for the government from La Salle's letters.

make terms with his creditors. The whole party, therefore, embarked for Fort Frontenac. The long and watery way was measured without any noteworthy incident, and by the end of July our untiring chief had reached Montreal, and was consulting with the capitalists and merchants who had been furnishing him with money and goods. His seigniory of Frontenac was already mortgaged for a large sum, much of which had been expended in profitless explorations; yet by surrendering some of his monopolies, by the aid of a rich relative named Plét,* and by the continued favor and support of Governor Frontenac, he found means to appease his more pressing creditors, and obtained advances for another respectable outfit.

The season was well advanced before La Salle could complete his preparations, and again begin to move through the great lakes. He started upon this third and crowning

---

*In order to secure this relative from loss in case of his death, La Salle executed an instrument in the nature of a will, of which the following is a copy:

[Will of La Salle.]

"Robert Cavelier, Esq., Sieur de la Salle, seignior and governor of Fort Frontenac, in New France, considering the great dangers and continual perils in which the voyages I undertake engage me, and wishing to acknowledge as much as I am able, the great obligations which I owe to M. Francois Plét, my cousin, for the signal services which he has rendered me in my most pressing necessities, and because it is through his assistance that I have preserved to this time Fort Frontenac against the efforts which were made to deprive me of it, I have given, granted, and transferred, and give, grant, and transfer, by these presents, to the said M. Plét, in case of my death, the seigniory and property of the ground and limits of the said Fort Frontenac and its depending lands, and all my rights in the country of the Miamis, Illinois, and others to the south, together with the establishment which is in the country of the Miamis, in the condition which it shall be at the time of my death; that of Niagara and all the others which I may have founded there, together with all the barges, boats, great boats, movables and immovables, rights, privileges, rents, lands, buildings, and other things belonging to me, which shall be found there; willing that these presents be and serve for my testament and declaration in the manner in which I ought to make it, such being my last will as above written by my hand, and signed by my hand, after having read it and again read it (*lu et relu*).

"Made at Montreal the 11th of August, 1681.

[Signed.] "CAVELIER DE LA SALLE."

expedition with a company of thirty men (some of whom, however, quit his service before reaching Mackinac), and ten or twelve heavily-laden canoes. Passing up Ontario Lake to the vicinity of the present Toronto, he thence made a long portage to Lake Simcoe. It was October when he entered the Georgian Bay of Lake Huron, and it was not until the close of that month that his little flotilla was pushed out upon the northern waters of Lake Michigan. As the voyagers crept slowly along the dreary eastern shore of the lake, skirted by high and, for the most part, barren sand-hills, we may conjecture some of the melancholy thoughts of their chief: "A past of unrequited toil and sad disappointment, a present embittered by the tongue of slander and hate, and the future clouded with uncertainty, must have intruded themselves into his mind, but could not for a moment divert him from the great purpose which, for years, had been the guiding star of his destiny." After a monotonous and toilsome trip, the leader and his men reached the well-known mouth of the Miami in the latter part of November, and drew their canoes ashore under the shelter of the palisaded fort.

Here La Salle found his poor Mohegan and Abenaki allies, in their squalid wigwams, patiently waiting his return, and from among them he chose eighteen men to accompany him on his southern exploration. These, being added to his twenty-three French and Canadians, made a force of forty-one men. The Indians insisted upon taking with them ten of their squaws to cook for them, and three children, thus making a total of fifty-four persons. Some of these supernumeraries were useless and others a burden; but there seemed no help for it, and they all went. Abandoning the old route via the St. Joseph and Kankakee for one more direct, the advance party of the expedition, under the conduct of the faithful Tonty and Membre, set out from Fort Miami on the 21st of December, in six canoes, and coasted around the southern bend of the lake to the mouth of the little river Chicago. La Salle himself followed a few days later, with the rest of his men (the Indian contingent going by land), and rejoined the others on the 4th of January, 1682. It was now the middle of winter in this latitude; the earth was thickly carpeted with snow, and the streams were all bridged over with ice. Tonty had caused sledges to be constructed, on which the explorers conveyed their canoes, baggage, and provisions up the congealed surface of the Chicago, and thence over the portage to the Des Plaines, or northern fork of the Illinois, which was also found sheeted with ice. Filing down its smooth surface, in long and picturesque procession, to the head of the Illinois proper, and thence down that river, they passed on their wintry way the great town of the Illinois, now partly rebuilt, but temporarily deserted of its inhabitants, and at length came to open water at the foot of Peoria Lake. Here were found encamped and spending the winter a large number of Indians belonging to the great town above. Having relinquished for the time his project of building a sailing vessel for navigating the Lower Mississippi, La Salle made no attempt to complete the one previously begun at Fort Créve-cœur;* but, after obtaining a supply of maize from the natives, and leaving some orders with them, he and his Frenchmen resumed their canoes and held on their course to the mouth of the river.

Arrived thither the 6th of February, they were obliged to wait on account of the floating ice in the Mississippi, and also for their Eastern Indians, who had fallen behind. By the 13th, however, these laggards had all arrived; the navigation was open, and the adventurous leader launched his small flotilla on the current of the majestic river which was to bear him southward to the sea. The voyagers traveled rather tardily, since they carried no provisions except Indian corn, and were compelled to hunt and fish almost daily.

About seven leagues below the mouth of the Illinois they found the Missouri River (called the Osage by Father Membre) putting in from the west, and pouring its yellow and turbulent flood into the clearer and more placid waters

---

*On their return voyage the next summer (1682), the French explorers are said to have found this unfinished bark burnt.

of the Mississippi. On the 14th, they passed, on their left, the village of the Tamaroas, containing one hundred cabins. The Indians were away on the chase, but the voyagers left there some marks to indicate their presence and the course they had taken. After several more days of rowing and sailing down the impetuous river they reached the confluence of the Ouabache (Ohio), where they stopped a short time to replenish their stock of provisions. Re-entering their canoes, they advanced about sixty leagues without stopping to encamp, because the banks on both sides were low and swampy and full of rushes and underbrush.

On the 24th of February, the commander landed at the Third Chickasaw Bluffs, not far above the future site of Memphis, and the hunters were immediately sent out to scour the woods for game. All of them returned in good time except one Pierre Prudhomme. Fearing that he had been seized by some prowling band of the Chickasaws, who frequented that region, La Salle put several Frenchmen and Indians on his trail, and, in the meantime, threw up an intrenchment and stockade. After nine days of active search Prudhomme, who had lost his way in the forest, was found and brought into camp in a famished condition. To console the unfortunate hunter, La Salle named the newly built fort for him, and left him with a few others in charge of it.

Again the explorers embarked; and with every day of their adventurous progress, the mystery of this unknown region was more and more unveiled. The hazy sunlight, the mild and balmy air, the tender foliage, the opening flowers, the cheery notes of the birds, all betokened the revival of Nature, and that they had entered the realms of spring.*

On the 12th of March, having advanced some forty leagues, and passed the village of the Mitchigameas, they were astonished to hear on their right the beating of Indian drums and war cries, emanating from a war-dance at a village of the Akansas (Arkansas). Apprehending an attack, La Salle, under cover of a fog, immediately with-

---

* Parkman's Discovery of the Great West.

drew his flotilla to the opposite shore, and there, on a projecting point or cape, threw up an intrenchment and felled trees to prevent a surprise. He then directed some of his men to go along the bank of the river, and by signs, invite the Indians to come over to them. This being observed by some chiefs of the Akansas, they sent several of their young men in a pirogue, which approached within gunshot of the French camp. Here the calumet of peace was displayed, and two of the savages, standing up in their canoe, made signs for the Frenchmen to come to them. At this invitation La Salle sent one of his Canadians and six Abenakis, who were received with manifestations of friendship, and were escorted back by six of the Akansas. La Salle thereupon made presents to them of tobacco and some goods, and they, in turn, invited him to visit their village. Being thus assured, he crossed the river with his entire force to the village called Kappa, where he stayed three days, and was feasted throughout with corn, beans, dried fruit, and fish. On the day after his arrival La Salle took formal possession of the country by planting a cross and setting up the arms of France; whereat the villagers, not knowing the purport of the ceremony, showed signs of great joy. The explorers were surprised to find here many domestic fowls, and some tamed bustards, which were probably kept for ornamental purposes. They took their departure on the 17th, and six leagues farther down the river, came to another village of the same nation, called Toninga, and three leagues beyond that still another,* the inhabitants of which all received them hospitably. These Arkansas Indians called themselves Oguappas, or Quappas, and are said to have formerly dwelt higher up the Mississippi. It was observed that they were much less morose and severe in their manners, and more open-hearted and generous than the tribes of the north, which was doubtless partly owing to climatic influences.

Having been furnished with the requisite guides, the

---

* Joutel, who visited the Arkansas five years later, makes mention of only two villages on the Mississippi; but there was a third on the Arkansas, just above its mouth.

explorers thence continued their voyage, and on the 22d, after passing the hilly site of Vicksburg, reached the territory of a tribe called the Taensas, who dwelt around a little lake or bayou, formed by the Mississippi. Being fatigued, La Salle sent Tonty and Membre thither with presents. Arrived at the main village of the Taensas, they were agreeably surprised at the evidences presented of Indian civilization. The houses were built of earth mixed with straw, and roofed with cane mats in the form of a dome, and were arranged around a square or quadrangle. The house of the head chief was a single room forty feet square, and fifteen feet high to the top of the roof. It was entered and lighted by one large door, in which the chief sat in state, waiting the approach of his visitors. Around him were grouped some sixty old men, dressed in white robes made of the under bark of the mulberry tree, and near him sat three of his wives clothed in like manner, who, to do him honor when he spoke to them, indulged in guttural cries. After paying their respects to these dignitaries, the Frenchmen were conducted to the temple near by, which was oval-shaped and somewhat larger than the royal residence. Within it were deposited the bones of defunct chiefs, and in the middle stood an altar, at the foot of which a fire was kept burning day and night by two old *prêtres*, or priests, who were the directors of their worship. The top of the temple was surmounted by three roughly carved eagles, facing toward the rising sun; and, surrounding it, was a mud or adobe wall studded with sharp pointed stakes, on which were hung the skulls of their enemies who had been sacrificed to the sun. The district around the village was planted with different kinds of fruit and nut bearing trees and wild vines, which furnished a considerable part of the subsistence of the people.

The chief of the Taensas sent provisions to La Salle, and the next day paid him a formal visit at his camp. He came with wooden canoes, attended by the officers of his household, to the sound of the tambour and the wild music of the women. The chief was clothed in a fine white blanket, and was preceded by two attendants carrying fans of white feathers. La Salle received him with great politeness, made him a few presents, and received in return provisions, and some of their robes or blankets. During this interview the Indian potentate maintained a grave demeanor, not unmixed with curiosity and marks of friendship toward the Frenchmen.

Re-embarking on the strange river, and having advanced twelve leagues farther, the explorers (on the 26th) fell in with some fishermen of the Natchies (Natchez) nation, who were enemies of the Taensas, though a kindred people. With his usual precaution, La Salle passed over to the opposite bank, and then sent Tonty to them with the peace calumet. The Indians were found well disposed, and some of them crossed the river with Tonty to the French camp. Although their village lay some three leagues inland, La Salle did not hesitate to go thither, with Membre and a part of his men; and on their arrival, they met a kindly welcome. The chief of this village was a brother of the great chief or Sun of the whole nation, whose village lay several leagues down the river, and about one league from the present city of Natchez. After spending the night at the first village, La Salle and his party proceeded the next day to the town of the Sun-chief, where they were handsomely entertained, and, by permission, erected a cross bearing the king's arms. This proceeding was viewed with great satisfaction by the inhabitants, but it would have been otherwise if they had understood its real significance. As with the Taensas, so here among the Natchez, the French visitors saw substantially built houses, a royal residence, a rude temple of the sun, with its altar of perpetual fire, and an established form of religious worship. The friar Membre, in his Narrative, speaks of both tribes as being half-civilized, and as presenting a good field for missionary effort.

On the way back to their camp, La Salle and party were accompanied by several of the head men of the Natchez, and also by a chief of the Koroas, or Coroas. This chief now conducted the explorers to his village, which was situated ten leagues below on a pleasant eminence. Arrived at the village, the usual Indian feast was made, and the customary presents were given and received. Here the voyagers were told that they still had ten days' sail to the sea.* Leaving the Koroas on Easter Sunday, the 29th of March, they passed the mouth of Red River two days afterward, and still keeping on their course for a distance of nearly forty leagues, they discovered some Indian fishermen on the bank of the river, and immediately heard the beating of drums and war-cries. Four Frenchmen were sent forward to offer them the calumet, but they had to return in haste, because the natives let fly at them a shower of arrows. These Indians belonged to the Quinipissa tribe, and in consequence of their hostility La Salle continued his voyage two leagues lower down, when he landed at a small village of the Tangibaos, which had been recently pillaged, and contained dead bodies.

At length, on the 6th of April, after nearly two months of navigation, the explorers arrived at a point where the river divides itself into three principal channels or passes, which branch off to the Gulf. They landed and encamped on the bank of the most westerly. The next day (the 7th), La Salle divided his company into three bands, to go and explore the different passes. He himself took the southwestern, Tonty and Membre the middle one, and D'Autray † the eastern. As the adventurous leader now drifted down the narrow channel, between low alluvial banks, "the brackish water gradually changed to brine, and the breeze grew fresh with the salt breath of the sea." Then, lo! the broad, heaving bosom of the great Gulf itself opened to his enraptured gaze, with its light-green waves foaming and breaking upon the marshy shore; "without a sail, without a sign of human life."

The three passes or outlets of the river were found to be large and deep, and quite salt two leagues below their head. With an astrolabe, which La Salle always carried

---

*An ordinary day's sail with the Indians was from ten to twelve leagues.

† The Sieur D'Autray was a son of M. Bourdon d'Autray, then lately deceased, but formerly procurator general of Quebec.

with him, he took the latitude of the mouth, and ascertained it to be about 28° 30' north, but kept this to himself. The Mississippi was roughly estimated by the explorers at eight hundred leagues in length, and it was reckoned that they had traveled at least three hundred and fifty French leagues from the confluence of the Illinois, which was considerably less than the actual distance by the river. After coasting the spongy and reed-fringed beach for a short distance, La Salle retraced his course to his camp; and on the 8th the reunited party mounted to a spot of dry ground on the bank of the main river. Here, on the 9th of April, with all possible solemnity, they performed the ceremony of taking possession of the country. A column had been prepared, to which was affixed the arms of France, with this inscription: "*Louis Le Grand, Roi de France et de Navarre, regne; Le Neuvieme Avril,* 1682."

The Frenchmen were all mustered under arms, and, while the New England Indians of the party looked on in wondering silence, the former, led by Father Zenobe, chanted the *Te Deum,* the *Exaudiat,* and other hymns in praise to God for their great discovery. Then, amid discharges of musketry and shouts of *Vive le Roi,* the column was planted by the Sieur de la Salle, who, standing near it, recited, in a loud voice, the following declaration, which had been drawn up at his dictation by Jacques de la Metairie, a Canadian notary, who accompanied the expedition from Fort Frontenac:

"In the name of the most high, mighty, invincible, and victorious Prince, Louis, the Great King of France and Navarre, Fourteenth of that name, this ninth day of April, 1682, I, in virtue of the commission of his Majesty, which I hold in my hand, and which may be seen by all whom it may concern, have taken, and do now take, in the name of his majesty, and of his successors to the crown, possession of this country of Louisiana, the seas, harbors, ports, bays, adjacent straits, and all the nations, peoples, provinces, towns, villages, mines, minerals, fisheries, streams, and rivers, comprised in the extent of said Louisiana, from the mouth of the great river St. Louis, on the eastern side, otherwise called Ohio, Alighin, or Chukagona, and this with the consent of the Chaouanons, Chicachas, and other people dwelling therein, with whom we have made alliance; as also along the river Colbert, or Mississippi, and rivers which discharge themselves therein, from its source beyond the country of the Kious, or Nadouessious, and this with their consent, and with the consent of the Motantees, Illinois, Mesigameas, Natches, Koroas, which are the most considerable nations dwelling therein, with whom also we have made alliance, either by ourselves or by others in our behalf;* as far as its mouth at the sea, or Gulf of Mexico, about the 27th degree of the elevation of the North Pole, and also to the mouth of the river of Palms; upon the assurance we have received from all these nations, that we are the first Europeans who have descended or ascended the said river Colbert; hereby protesting against all those who may in future undertake to invade any or all of these countries, people, or lands above described, to the prejudice of the right of his majesty, acquired by consent of the nations herein named. Of which, and of all that can be needed, I hereby take to witness those who hear me, and demand an act of the notary, as required by law."

" To which the whole assembly responded with shouts of *Vive le Roi*, and with salutes of fire-arms. Moreover, the Sieur de la Salle caused to be buried at the foot of the tree to which the cross was attached a leaden plate, on one side of which were engraved the arms of France, and, on the opposite, the following Latin inscription: '*Ludovicus Magnus Regnat, Nono Aprilis, M. D. C. LXXXII.,*' etc. . . .

"After which the Sieur de la Salle said, that his majesty, as eldest son of the church, would annex no country to his crown without making it his chief care to establish the Christian religion therein, and that its symbol must now be planted; which was accordingly done at once by erecting

---

*There is some obscurity in this enumeration of places and Indian nations, arising from ignorance of the geography of the country, and the consent of the aborigines is, of course, assumed; but it appears to have been La Salle's design to take possession of the whole territory watered by the Mississippi and its numerous tributaries.

a cross, before which the *Vexilla* and the *Domine salvum fac Regem* were sung. Whereupon the ceremony was concluded with cries of *Vive le Roi*.

"Of all and every of the above, the said Sieur de la Salle having required of us an instrument, we have delivered to him the same, signed by us, and by the undersigned witnesses, this ninth day of April, one thousand six hundred and eighty-two.

"LA METAIRIE, *Notary*.

"*Witnesses:* De la Salle, P. Zenobe (Recollect Missionary), Henri de Tonty, Francois de Boisrondet, Jean Bourdon, Sieur d'Autray, Jacques Cauchois, Pierre You, Gilles Meucret, Jean Michel (Surgeon), Jean Mas, Jean Dulignon, Nicolas de la Salle."*

These formal acts, attesting La Salle's important geographical discovery, gave to Louis XIV. a territory far more extensive than his hereditary European possessions, though not destined in the sequence of events to become a permanent appendage of the French crown.

Having thus achieved the great object of the expedition, our explorers began their return voyage on the 10th of April. As they laboriously ascended the current of the deep river, they were half famished, having nothing to eat but some potatoes and tough alligator meat. The adjacent banks were so low, and covered with thickets of canes and undergrowth, that they could not stop to hunt without making a long halt. On the night of the 12th, they slept at the village of the Tangibaos,† and the next day reached the district of the Quinipissas. Determined to have some maize at any cost, La Salle now sent out a party of his Abenakis to reconnoiter. They returned on the morning of the 14th, bringing with them four of the Quinipissas women whom they had captured, and thereupon La Salle went and encamped opposite their village. The day after he sent one

---
* See Historical Coll's of La., Part I., pp. 48–50. An authenticated copy of these proceedings was afterward sent to Paris, and deposited in the Department of the Marine and Colonies.
† Supposed to have been near the site of New Orleans.

of the women back with presents of merchandise to indicate his good will, and the savages brought him in return a little corn. Being invited to cross the river to the vicinity of their village, the Frenchmen did so, but kept strictly on their guard. Before daybreak the next morning, they were attacked in their camp by the Quinipissas, whom they easily repulsed, killing ten and wounding others, besides burning their canoes. This is the only recorded instance of the sacrifice of human life during the course of the expedition.

Re-embarking on the evening of that day (the 18th), La Salle and his followers reached the village of the Koroas, about the first of May, but found them no longer friendly and obliging as before. Arrived at the district of the Natchez, they landed and went out to their village, but, seeing no women there, suspected some evil design. The Natchez gave them food to eat, but the Frenchmen ate it with their guns in their hands, fearing an attack from the great number of warriors by whom they were surrounded. Returning hastily to their canoes, they held on their way up the river, stopping at the Taensas and the Arkansas, where they were well received.

Leaving the Arkansas villages about the middle of May, La Salle pushed ahead with two canoes of his Mohegans, but falling sick on the river, he stopped at Fort Prudhomme, and was there joined by the rest of his company on the first of June. His sickness being protracted and dangerous, the Friar Membre remained with him to nurse him. Meantime, Tonty was sent forward with a few companions to Mackinac, to arrange his affairs. It was not until the first of July that La Salle recovered sufficiently to travel. He then resumed his voyage, and advanced by short stages to Fort Miami, and thence to Mackinac, whither he arrived early in September.*

The Sieur de la Salle had at length triumphed over

---

* For fuller details concerning this memorable and successful expedition, see the Narratives of Membre and Tonty, and the *Procès Verbal* of La Metaire.

every opposing obstacle, and though not finding the
long-sought passage to the Pacific Ocean, he had followed
the Mississippi River to its entrance into the Mexican Gulf,
and written his name high in the list of American dis-
coverers. It remained for him to extend and utilize his
discovery to the best advantage for himself and his
sovereign. As the country of the Illinois formed the center
of his operations, he now resolved to abandon the tedious
and difficult line of access to it through Canada and the
lakes, beset by so many enemies, and to open a passage to
his western domain by way of the Gulf and Lower Mississippi. He proposed to build a fort on the head waters of
the Illinois, and found there a French and Indian colony, which might serve the twofold purpose of a bulwark
against the inroads of the Iroquois, and a central point for
the fur-trade of the western tribes. And he hoped, before
the close of the ensuing year, to establish another fort and
colony at the embouchure of the Mississippi, thus placing
the trade of the whole great valley under his control. This
new enterprise was not unworthy of the genius of La Salle.
It was his intention on his arrival at Mackinac to have
gone at once to Canada, and thence to France, to procure
aid from the king in the execution of his plan; but his
health and circumstances not permitting, he sent Father
Membre with dispatches, making known the extent and
importance of his discovery.

Soon after this a report reached La Salle, that the
Iroquois—those fierce Romans of the wilderness—were
about to renew their raid upon the western tribes. As
such a hostile movement might be fatal to his projected
colony, he deemed it the part of prudence to follow Tonty,
whom he had already sent to the Illinois, and joined him
at the great Indian town. This celebrated village stood
on the northern side of the Illinois River (which here runs
from east to west), about one mile from the modern town
of Utica, in what is now La Salle county.* It thus occupied a part of the wide strip of bottom land lying between

---

* So named in memory of the great explorer.

the river and the bluffs to the north. The large quantities of human bones and implements of savage life that have been turned up here, from time to time, by the plough-share of the husbandman, form the only vestiges of the populous tribes, who once made this attractive locality their principal abode. Along the southern border of the stream extends a range of irregular sandstone bluffs, which culminates a mile above the old village in a natural abutment, known to the early French explorers as *Le Rocher*, but, at a later period, as the "Starved Rock." Several miles below this, on the same side, occurs a canyon in the hills and bluffs, through which the waters of the Big Vermilion, or Aramoni of the French, find their way to those of the Illinois. Of the Starved Rock and its surroundings, Breese thus enthusiastically writes:

"It is a most romantic spot. I have stood upon the 'Starved Rock' and gazed for hours upon the beautiful landscape spread out beneath me. The undulating plains rich in their verdure, the rounded hills beyond clad in their forest livery, and the gentle river pursuing its noiseless way to the Mississippi and the Gulf, all in harmonious association, make up a picture over which the eye delights to wander; and when to these are added the recollection of the heroic adventurers who first occupied it—that here the banner of France so many years floated freely in the winds, that here was civilization, whilst all around them was barbaric darkness—the most intense and varied emotions can not fail to be awakened." *

From the river which washes its base, the huge cliff rises perpendicularly to an altitude of one hundred and twenty-six feet; and only on one side, that next to the land, can it be climbed with difficulty.

To the summit of this natural citadel, embracing an area of half an acre, La Salle and Tonty repaired in December, 1682, and commenced the work of fortification. With the assistance of their men, they felled the stunted growth of pines and deciduous trees that crowned the

* "Early History of Illinois," p. 121.

Rock, and with these built a rude storehouse. Then they cut and dragged timbers, with great labor, up the rugged ascent of the cliff, and inclosed the top with a stout palisade. The fort was practically finished during that winter, and was named by La Salle *Fort de St. Louis*, in honor to the reigning monarch of France. It was intended as the nucleus of a permanent settlement, and was continuously occupied by the French until the year 1700, and occasionally afterward.*

With the completion of the fortress (in the spring of 1683) the Illinois Indians began to gather about it, looking upon La Salle as the great chief who was to protect them from the Iroquois; and the surrounding country soon again became animated with the wild concourse of savage life. Besides the Illinois, there were also scattered along the river valley, and among the neighboring hills and prairies, the fragments of at least half a dozen other tribes, namely: Miamis from the sources of the Kankakee, Piankashaws and Weas from the Wabash, Shawnees from the Ohio valley, and some Abenakuis and Mohicans from New England. La Salle's dexterous diplomacy had thus been crowned with unexpected success, a result largely due to the general terror inspired by the ferocious Iroquois. In a memorial addressed to the French Minister of Marine, he reported the whole number of warriors around Fort St. Louis at four thousand, which would represent a population of twenty thousand persons. But this exaggerated number could only have been possible at particular seasons of the year, since those nomadic people went and came according as the fish, game, and wild fruits were more or less abundant.

By virtue of the authority conferred in his patent, La Salle ruled his broad domain as a seigniory, and went through the form of parceling out portions of the land to

---

* The outline of another fort or earthwork, which might have been a work of the early French, is yet to be seen on the rocky bluff about half a mile south of Fort St. Louis, near the edge of the prairie. See Baldwin's Hist. of La Salle Co., Ill., p. 55.

his French followers. The latter, however, were too indolent and profligate to improve or derive any benefit from such grants, thinking more of their Indian concubines than of cultivating wild lands. To maintain his new colony, the chief found it necessary to furnish its members with military protection, and merchandise to barter for furs and pelts—no easy task in his 'situation. While he was concerting and endeavoring to execute measures for the maintenance and development of his colony, his rivals and enemies in Canada, from envy or short-sighted policy, were doing all they could to defeat him. Unfortunately, his friend and patron, Count Frontenac, had been removed from office, and Le Febvre de la Barre, a headstrong and avaricious old naval officer, governed in his stead. From the outset of his administration, La Barre showed himself a bitter enemy to La Salle. Yet the latter, busy with his own affairs, and not knowing or assuming to know the jealousy with which he was regarded, wrote to the new governor from Fort St. Louis, under date April 2, 1683, expressing the hope that he would have from him the same support that he had received from his predecessor. After saying that his enemies would try to influence the governor against him, he went on to give some account of his explorations. He stated that, with only twenty-two Frenchmen, he had formed amicable relations with the different tribes along the Mississippi River, and that his royal patent authorized him to establish posts in the newly discovered country, and to make grants around them, as at Fort Frontenac, and then added :

"The losses in my enterprise have exceeded 40,000 crowns. I am now going four hundred leagues south-west of this place to induce the Chicasas to follow the Shawanoes and other tribes, and settle like them at Fort St. Louis. It remained only to settle French colonists here, and this I have already done. I hope you will not detain them as *coureurs des bois* when they come down to Montreal to make necessary purchases. I am aware that I have no right to trade with the tribes who descend to Montreal, and I shall not permit such trade to my men; nor have I ever issued licenses to that effect, as my enemies say that I have done."

Despite this reasonable request on the part of La Salle, the men whom he had sent to Montreal on business were detained there, and on the 4th of June he again wrote to Governor La Barre, in a more urgent strain, as follows:

"The Iroquois are again invading the country. Last year the Miamis were so alarmed by them that they abandoned their town and fled, but on my return they came back, and have been induced to settle with the Illinois at my fort of St. Louis. The Iroquois have lately murdered some families of their nation, and they are all in terror again. I am afraid they will take flight, and so prevent the Missouris and neighboring tribes from coming to settle at St. Louis, as they are about to do. Some of the Hurons and French tell the Miamis that I am keeping them here for the Iroquois to destroy. I pray that you will let me hear from you, that I may give these people some assurance of protection before they are destroyed in my sight. Do not suffer my men, who have come down to the settlements, to be longer prevented from returning. There is great need here of reinforcements. I have postponed going to Mackinac, because, if the Iroquois strike any blow in my absence, the Miamis will think I am in league with them; whereas if I and the French stay among them, they will regard us as protectors.

"But, monsieur, it is in vain that we risk our lives here, and that I exhaust my means in order to fulfill the intention of his majesty, if all my measures are crossed in the settlements below, and if those who go down to bring munitions, without which we can not defend ourselves, are detained under pretexts trumped up for the occasion. If I am prevented from bringing up my men and supplies, as I am allowed to do by the permit of Count Frontenac, then my patent from the king is useless. It would be very hard for us, after having done what was required, even before the time prescribed, and after suffering severe losses, to have our efforts frustrated by obstacles got up designedly. I trust that, as it lies with you alone to prevent or permit the return of the men whom I have sent down, you will not so act as to thwart my plans, as part of the goods which I have sent by them belongs not to me, but the Sieur de Tonty, and are a part of his pay. Others are to buy munitions indispensable to our defense. Do not let my creditors seize them. It is for their advantage that my fort, full as it is of goods, should be held against the enemy. I have only twenty men, with scarcely one hundred pounds of powder. I can not long hold the country without more. The Illinois are very capricious and uncertain. . . . If I had men enough to send out to reconnoiter the enemy, I would have done so before this; but I have not enough. I trust that you will put it in my power to obtain more, that this important colony may be saved."

(Dated at) "Portage de Chicagou, 4 Juni, 1683."*

It was in vain, however, that La Salle appealed to Governor La Barre for favor or support in his enterprise. That functionary, on the contrary, was meantime writing letters to the Minister of Marine and Colonies, disparaging La Salle's discoveries, and pretending to doubt their reality; saying, that, " with a score of vagabonds he had pillaged his countrymen and put them to ransom, and was about to set himself up as king, and that the imprudence of the man was likely to involve Canada in a war with the Iroquois." These calumnies, being repeated, at length reached the ear of the French monarch, who, under a mistaken notion of the true state of affairs, wrote La Barre to this effect: "I am convinced like you, that the discovery of the Sieur de la Salle is very useless, and that such enterprises ought to be prevented in the future, as they tend only to debauch the inhabitants by the hope of gain, and to diminish the revenue from beaver skins."†

Apparently emboldened by the king's letter, the governor seized upon Fort Frontenac, under pretext that La Salle had not fulfilled the conditions of his grant by maintaining there a sufficient garrison; and, against the remonstrances

---

* Parkman's La Salle and the Great West, pp. 299–301.
† *Lettre du Roy á La Barre, 5th Aout*, 1683, in Margry.

of the mortgagees of the fort and seigniory, he ejected La Salle's lieutenant, La Forrest, and put two of his own minions, La Chesnaye and La Ber, in charge of the fort. No sooner were these appointees installed in office, than they began living off of La Salle's stores, and they were afterward accused of selling what had been provided them by the government for their own benefit. But not content with this arbitrary stretch of power, and bent upon the ruin of La Salle, Gov. La Barre next sent the Sieur de Baugis, an officer of the king's dragoons, to Fort St. Louis, and made him the bearer of a letter to La Salle, requiring his presence at Quebec. The position of the latter had now become intolerable, and he resolved to proceed to France, in order to obtain relief from the crown. Giving the command at Fort St. Louis to M. de Tonty, and bidding adieu to his French and Indian retainers, La Salle departed for Canada about the first of October. Enroute, he met De Baugis, who informed him of the nature of his errand. The former submitted to the indignity with as good a grace as possible under the circumstances, and sent a letter to Tonty to receive the new commandant with due courtesy. Arrived at Fort St. Louis, De Baugis and Tonty passed the winter there together, though not very harmoniously—the one commanding in the name of La Barre, and the other representing the interests of La Salle.

In the following spring they both had enough to do. The threatened incursion of the Iroquois had been postponed, yet not abandoned. In the last of March, 1684, those restless and enterprising warriors, to the number of three hundred—taking advantage of La Salle's absence, and incited thereto by certain of the provincial authorities of New York, who wished to divert the fur-trade of the western Indians from Montreal to Albany—again invaded the country of the Illinois, and laid siege to the rock-seated fort of St. Louis. But it proved too strong for their unskillful and unsteady assault, and after six days effort they retreated with loss.

CHAPTER VIII.

1684–1687.

LAST GREAT ENTERPRISE OF LA SALLE.

The Sieur de la Salle arrived from the west at Quebec early in November, 1683, and there embarked for Old France. He thus, unwittingly, took a last leave of the wide and wild theater of Canada, where, for sixteen years, he had played so conspicuous a part as an explorer and negotiator with the Indians, sometimes achieving signal triumphs, but, more often, experiencing severe reverses of fortune. After an uneventful ocean passage, he landed at Rochelle on the 23d of December, and thence traveled by diligence to Paris; then and still the *eye* of France, and the gay capital of Europe. Here he was joined by his lieutenant, La Forrest, and later on, by Zenobe Membre, both of whom had preceded him from Canada. Here, too, he found influential friends, who appreciated his merits and services to the crown. Among the number was his former patron, Count Frontenac, who, though in retirement for the time, gave him the benefit of his influence, still considerable, at court.

La Salle now prepared and laid before the Marquis de Seignelay,* Minister of Marine and Colonies, two memorials (including a petition for the redress of his grievances), setting forth his discoveries and plans for the colonization of Louisiana. He proposed to establish a fortified colony on the river Colbert, or Mississippi, some sixty leagues above its mouth, and to make it the principal depot for the trade of the great river valley. To accomplish this design, he asked for one war vessel of thirty guns, a few cannon for the forts, and authority to raise, in France, two hundred men, who were to be armed and maintained at the

---

* Seignelay was a son and successor of the great Colbert, who died September 6, 1683.

king's charge for one year. He further proposed, with this force, and an army of Indian warriors, to be afterward raised by himself, to undertake the conquest of New Biscay (Durango), the most northerly intendency of Mexico, where there were not more than five hundred Spaniards. La Salle accompanied his memorials with a map, indicating his discoveries in the country called Louisiana, which, however, showed that he still had but an imperfect knowledge of the geography of that region.

In the beginning of April, 1684, La Salle was granted an interview with his majesty, Louis XIV., to whom he unfolded his fascinating scheme. The time was opportune for his application. The grand monarch had been long incensed at Spain (with which kingdom he was now again at war) because of her jealous exclusion of French ships from her American ports, and he was anxious to gain a permanent footing on the shores of the Mexican Gulf, within easy reach of his West India possessions. It was, therefore, not difficult to obtain the royal assent and patronage to an enterprise which accorded so well with his own ambition. Our explorer had asked for the use of only one vessel, but the king, in his generosity, gave him four. At the same time, as an act of simple justice to La Salle, he wrote a letter to Governor La Barre, at Quebec, directing him to restore to the former possession of Forts Frontenac and St. Louis; and La Forrest was shortly sent back to Canada, empowered to re-occupy both forts in La Salle's name.

Active preparations were now begun for the colonizing expedition, and agents were sent to Rochelle and Rochefort to collect recruits. About one hundred and fifty ex-soldiers were enrolled, most of whom, unfortunately, belonged to the beggar and vagabond class. There was, however, one volunteer soldier, named Henri Joutel, who came from La Salle's own town of Rouen, and whose father had been a gardener to the Cavaliers. He proved a trusty and useful officer, and subsequently became the principal historian of the expedition. La Salle had given orders to engage three or four mechanics in each of the principal trades; but the selection was so poor that when they reached their destination it was found that they were very indifferent workmen. Eight or ten families of respectable people, and some young women, attracted by the prospect of matrimony, offered to go and help found the new colony. Their offers were accepted, and considerable advances were made to them, as well as to the artisans and soldiers. Several adventurous young gentlemen, of good families, also joined the expedition as volunteers. Among them were two nephews of La Salle, the Sieur de Moranget, and the Sieur Cavelier, the latter being only fourteen years of age.

One of the first cares of the leader had been to provide for the ecclesiastical part of his enterprise, in which it became necessary to procure a special dispensation from the Pope. Applying to the superior-general of the Seminary of St. Sulpice, the latter appointed three priests to accompany him and found a new mission. They were Jean Cavelier, brother of La Salle, M. Chefdeville, his relative, and M. de Maiulle, called Dainmaville by Joutel. As the Recollets had for a number of years actively seconded the designs of La Salle, he made it a point to take as many as three of those fathers with him also. He accordingly applied to the superior of that order, who granted him the *religious* he desired, namely: Father Zenobious Membre, superior of the mission, Anastasius Donay, and Maximus Le Clercq.

Such was the *personnel* of the soldiers, artisans, emigrants, priests, and adventurers, who were to plant the standard of France and the cross on the wilderness shores of far-away Louisiana. It were needless to observe that, for the most part, they were ill-adapted by discipline or experience for the stern task set before them.

The fleet, which was furnished by the king, consisted of four vessels, namely: The Joly, a royal ship or frigate, carrying thirty-six guns; the Belle, a small frigate of six guns; the Aimable, a store-ship; and the St. Francois, a ketch of two masts. La Salle had asked to be given sole command of the expedition, with a subordinate officer and two or three pilots to navigate the ships, as he might direct. But the Marquis de Seignelay gave the command to Capt.

Beaujeu, of the royal navy, whose authority was restricted to the management of the vessels at sea, while La Salle was to prescribe the route they were to take and command on shore. This division of authority displeased both men, and caused chafing and bickering between them from the start. Yet it was perhaps the best that Minister Seignelay could do under the circumstances, as La Salle himself was without nautical skill or experience. Beaujeu was a Franco-Norman, and an officer of approved valor and experience, but envious, self-willed, irascible, and utterly wanting in the qualifications requisite to the founding of a distant colony. Moreover, his wife is said to have been dominated by the Jesuits, a circumstance that excited La Salle's suspicion. Amid the hurry and bustle of the embarkation, La Salle did not forget to write to his aged mother a farewell letter, which has been preserved among the family papers of the Caveliers.

All things having been provided necessary for the voyage, the little fleet, bearing about two hundred and eighty persons, including the crews of the vessels, sailed from Rochelle on the 24th of July, 1684. When two or three days out, the bowsprit of the frigate Joly broke, which compelled Capt. Beaujeu to return to the port of Chef de Bois to procure a new one. This accomplished, the fleet again put to sea on the first day of August, steering to the south, southwest. After weathering the Island of Madeira, they entered the region of the trade winds, and encountered two separate storms, the second of which dispersed the vessels. The Joly, in which La Salle himself had taken passage, being a faster sailer than the others, reached Petit Goave, on the west coast of St. Domingo, on the 27th of September, and was soon after joined by the Aimable and the Belle. The St. Francois, laden with provisions, ammunition, and tools for the new colony, lagged behind, and put in at Port de Paix, whence she sailed to join the rest of the fleet; but during the night, while her captain and crew thought themselves safe, they were surprised by two Spanish piraguas, which captured the ketch and her cargo. The loss of this vessel was primarily due to the negligence of Beaujeu, who had refused to stop at Port de Paix, although requested to do so by La Salle. This was the first of the series of disasters that befell the expedition. It depressed the hopes of the colonists and distressed the mind of La Salle, who, shortly before his arrival in St. Domingo, had been seized by a violent fever, which afterward affected his brain, and brought him to the verge of the grave.

Owing to the continued illness of La Salle and other causes, the remaining vessels of his expedition were detained at the port of Petit Goave, for over six weeks. During this time they laid in fresh provisions, a store of Indian corn, and all kinds of domestic fowls to stock the new colony. The French governor-general of the Isles, and the governor and intendant of St. Domingo, favored the enterprise in every way, and endeavored to restore a good understanding between La Salle and Beaujeu, so necessary to the success of the undertaking. Meanwhile, the soldiers and most of the crews plunged into every kind of debauchery and intemperance, so common in the West Indies, and thus contracted various diseases, of which some died in the island, and others never recovered.

At length, on the 25th of November, the squadron, now consisting of three vessels, weighed anchor and again put to sea, La Salle and his trustiest followers sailing in the store-ship Aimable. They pursued their way past the Cayman Isles, touched at the Isle of Pines to take in water, and thence sailed to Cape San Antonio at the western extremity of Cuba, where they anchored. Attracted by the beauty of the spot, the French landed and rested here for two days, and appropriated to their use some wine which had been left by the Spaniards. For fear of injury by northerly winds, said to be prevalent at the entrance to the Gulf of Mexico, on approaching it, they twice lay to, but happily entered on the first of January, 1685, when a solemn mass of thanksgiving was celebrated by Father Anastase Douay. The voyagers were now upon that great southern sea, over which no French vessel, carrying the national colors, had ever before sailed. Steering northward, they arrived on the 15th in sight of the Florida coast, when a violent wind compelled the Joly to stand off, but the Aimable and Belle followed close to the shore.

La Salle had been told in St. Domingo that the Gulf Stream ran with incredible velocity toward the Bahama channel. This false information, together with the incorrect sailing directions he had received, set him entirely estray; for thinking himself much farther north than he really was, he not only passed Appalache Bay without recognizing it, but followed the coast westward far beyond the outlet of the Mississippi, and would have continued to follow it, if he and his fellow voyagers had not perceived by its turning south, and by the latitude, that they had passed the hidden river. It will be remembered that when La Salle was at the mouth of the Mississippi three years before, he had obtained its latitude, approximately, but not the longitude. Indeed, the mariners of that day knew little or nothing about longitude.

The Aimable and the Belle at last came to anchor, about the middle of February, at Espiritu Santo Bay, on the coast of Texas, and there awaited the arrival of Capt. Beaujeu, who joined them a few days later with the Joly. A conference was now held by the commanders, which resulted in their resolving to retrace their course, and they returned ten or twelve leagues to a bay, which they named St. Louis, since known as St. Bernard, or Matagorda. As provisions began to fail, Beaujeu declined to further continue the search on that exposed coast, unless his crew was provisioned from the stores of the colonists; to which La Salle objected. Finally, the Sieur La Salle, impatient of further delay, anxious to get rid of his disagreeable colleague and command alone, and thinking that the lagoons of the coast might connect with the most westerly arm or outlet of the Mississippi, decided to disembark his troops and colonists on the western shore of Matagorda Bay. To this purpose, boats were sent to sound and buoy the inlet to the bay. This being done, the little frigate Belle was taken in without accident on the 18th of February. On the 20th the Aimable weighed anchor and started through the narrow channel leading into the bay; but her captain, M.

d'Aigron, being on ill terms with La Salle, disregarded his orders, and either through gross negligence or design drove the vessel on the shoals, where she stranded, so that she could not be got off.

La Salle was some little distance from the seashore when this deplorable disaster happened, and was on the point of returning to remedy it, when he saw a large party of wild Indians approaching. This necessitated his putting his men under arms, and the roll of their drums put the savages temporarily to flight, but he had trouble with them afterward. The storeship remained stranded for three weeks or more, without going to pieces, though full of water. The men saved all they could from her in boats, including a quantity of flour and powder, but could only reach her in fair weather. At length a gale arose, which completely wrecked the ship, and scattered the residue of her cargo on the waters of the bay.

After the landing had been eventually effected, which included eight iron cannon from the hold of the Aimable, Beaujeu prepared to depart for France. Although he and La Salle had been at variance throughout the long voyage, their official relations became more amicable at its close. He seems, at heart, to have wished La Salle and his enterprise well, and was no doubt anxious to have it appear that he had discharged his duty as naval conductor of the expedition, so as to avoid censure from the Minister of Marine. Before quitting this low and dangerous coast, it is stated that he offered to go to Martinique and return with additional provisions for the colony, but that La Salle, from motives of pride and over self-reliance, declined the offer.*
On the 12th or 14th of March, after a polite leave-taking, Beaujeu sailed away in the Joly, taking with him several of the better class of the colonists, who had lost heart in the enterprise.

The remaining adventurers, to the number of about one hundred and eighty, now found themselves stranded

---

* See the correspondence between Beaujeu and La Salle, printed in Vol. II of Margry's Publications.

upon the borders of an unknown wilderness, nearly five hundred miles from the place of their original destination, and most of them were suffering, more or less, from dysentery and other diseases contracted during their long sea-voyage. The first labor of the commander was to throw up an intrenchment on the sandy beach, and to erect therein a temporary building in which to shelter his people and goods, and to protect them from the depredations of the neighboring savages. The house was constructed of driftwood, cast up by the sea, and of the timbers and plank from their wrecked ship. Leaving Joutel and Moranget with a hundred men at this naval camp, La Salle next set out with some fifty others, including his brother and the Fathers Zenobe and Maxime, to explore the interior of the bay, and seek a proper place to locate his colony. The captain or pilot of the Belle had orders to sound the bay and take his vessel in as far as he safely could. He accordingly advanced along the shore about twelve leagues, and anchored opposite a point which took the name of Hurier, from the officer who was appointed to command there. This post served as a station between the camp on the seashore and the fort, which La Salle and his party went (on the 2d of April) to establish at the western head of the bay. The site of the latter was fixed on a rising ground, two leagues up a small river called La Vache, now La Vaca, and in latitude about twenty-seven degrees north. The building of the fort was a work of severe and protracted labor, since there was no wood within a league, and all the timbers had to be cut and transported from a distance, many of them being brought from the wreck of the Aimable.

By the 21st of April (Easter eve) the fort was so far advanced as to be ready for partial occupancy, and the Sieur de La Salle returned to the main camp. The succeeding three or four days were devoted to celebrating with all possible solemnity, under the circumstances, the festivals of the church, after which preparations were made for removing the women and children, and such of the sick as could be moved, to the new establishment. Meanwhile, however, a few of the soldiers had deserted, and others had died of the diseases contracted at St. Domingo, notwithstanding all the care they received, and the relief afforded by the use of broths, preserves, and wine.*

When the fort was completed, La Salle gave to it his favorite name of St. Louis. The naval camp at the mouth of the bay was then abandoned, and Joutel and his command rejoined the main body of the colonists. The fort was mounted with eight pieces of rusty old cannon, and had a sort of magazine under ground for the safe deposit of the more valuable effects, in the event of fire. Here, then, in this lone spot on the Texan coast, the ensign of France was flung to the winds of heaven; here a rude chapel was raised, in which masses were said and vespers chanted by the missionary priests and friars; and here, too, in the grassy prairie hard by, a common field was opened, planted, and tilled for the maturing of crops. By this early yet transient occupation, the King of France gained a color of claim to the country which, though contested by Spain, was never finally relinquished until the vast and indefinitely defined territory of Louisiana was ceded to the government of the United States.

The scenery environing Fort St. Louis was not without its charms, and served in a measure to relieve that feeling of despondency arising in the minds of the colonists from their isolation and misfortunes. At the foot of the stockade inclosure flowed the river, swarming with fish and water-fowl, and beyond that the bay, bordered by reedy marshes, stretched away to the south-east; while to the south-west lay two large ponds, with a forest in the distance. To the north and west rolled a sea of grassy prairie, dotted at certain seasons with grazing buffalo and wild goats,

---

* See Le Clercq's (Father Chrétien) "First Establishment of the Faith in New France" (Vol. II), for an account of La Salle's attempt to reach the Mississippi by sea, and of the establishment of a French colony at St. Louis or Matagorda Bay. It is, in some respects, the best contemporaneous narrative extant of that historical voyage. The discreet father only hints at the unfortunate disagreement between La Salle and Beaujeu, but this matter is set forth in detail by Joutel and others.

and decked with the beautiful wild flowers for which Texas is still remarkable. It was, in truth, as since demonstrated, a goodly land for the habitation of civilized man. But the degraded aborigines, with such uncouth names as Guoaquis, Guinets, Bahamos, and Quealomouches, who then roamed the coast of this southern country, had no thought of cultivating the soil, or of any other useful labor, beyond the requirements of a most meager subsistence.

Having provided as well as he could for the comfort and safety of his people, La Salle now prepared to renew his search for the hidden river. But he first found it necessary to make open war on the neighboring tribes of Indians, whose repeated acts of hostility gave him no peace; and he accordingly set out for this purpose on the 13th of October, with sixty soldiers, wearing wooden corslets to protect them against the arrows of the savages. In different engagements with them he killed some, wounded others, and put others still to flight. The execution thus done among the natives inspired them with terror, and rendered the colony somewhat more secure than before.

About the 31st of October, 1685, putting Joutel in command at the fort, with provisions for several months, La Salle and his brother, with some fifty well-armed men, started ostensibly to seek the mouth of the Mississippi. The accounts we have of this long and rambling journey are rather vague and contradictory. The leader himself was reticent as to his plans and purposes, and the story told by the elder Cavelier is not very intelligible. They first passed eastward along the northern shore of the bay, and examined the outlets of the rivers emptying into it, none of which seemed large enough to form an arm of the Mississippi. La Salle thence turned northward and westward and traveled the country a long distance, in the hope, it would seem, of reaching the borders of Mexico. At length, on the 13th of February, 1686, having come to a large river, he built a small fort on its banks, in which he left a part of his men, and with the others continued to explore the country in the direction of Mexico. Still advancing, he visited several villages and tribes, who treated him kindly, and from whom he gained considerable information in regard to the Spaniards, who were generally hated by the Indians in Texas. Under other circumstances, it would have been no very difficult task to have gathered an army of native warriors and led them across the Rio del Norte; but La Salle was without horses and a sufficiency of men to prosecute his contemplated invasion of New Biscay.* He was away on this expedition longer than he had expected, owing to delays in rafting over so many rivers, and the necessity, wherever he went into camp, of throwing up intrenchments to guard against Indian assaults. Retracing their tortuous course, the leader and his followers reached Fort St. Louis in the latter part of March, tattered, weather-beaten, and worn out by long marchings and vigils, but bringing with them a welcome supply of fresh meat for the other colonists.

Shortly before this the Belle, the only remaining vessel of the colony, was lost on the farther side of the bay, though it was some weeks before particulars of the accident were received at the fort. Through a lack of precaution on the part of those in charge of her, she was wrecked with all her stores, consisting of thirty-six barrels of flour, a quantity of powder, some tools, and a lot of the clothing and personal effects belonging to La Salle. The priest Chéfdeville, the pilot, and four of the crew escaped with difficulty in a canoe, but managed to save some of the papers and luggage of their chief. Meantime, La Salle himself fell seriously ill, the fatigues, of his great journey, and the tidings of this last misfortune, having overcome his physical strength. " In truth (says the priest Cavelier, in his *Relation du Voyage*), after the loss of the vessel, which deprived us of our only means of returning to France, we had no resource but in the firm guidance of my brother, whose death each of us would have regarded as his own." So long as the little frigate remained, La Salle had the means of following along the coast and finding the mouth of the Mississippi,

---

*According to Mr. Shea, La Salle was lured by Penaloso, a renegade Spanish governor of New Mexico, to undertake the conquest of the rich mines in northern Mexico.

and he might also have sailed to St. Domingo and obtained succor for his colony. But now, all his plans being disconcerted and his affairs brought to a crisis, he resolved to try and reach Canada by land.

This resolution was the result of dire necessity, and he must have anticipated the difficulties and hazards likely to attend its execution. Preparations were speedily made for the journey; and on April 22, 1686, after celebrating the divine mysteries in the little chapel, La Salle issued from the gate of the fort, accompanied by his brother, his nephew Moranget, the friar Douay, the younger Duhaut, a German from Wittemburg named Hiens,* and others to the number of twenty in all. They traveled on foot, each man carrying his pack and weapons on his shoulders, and shaped their general course to the north-east. Crossing the Colorado on a raft, they journeyed through a pleasant country of alternate prairie and woodland, decked with wild flowers, and clothed in the fresh green livery of spring. After passing the Brazos and Trinity, and other smaller rivers, they reached the habitations of the Cenis Indians (then a powerful tribe, but now long since extinct), where they experienced a friendly reception. Here the travelers were surprised to see saddles, bridles, clothing, and various other articles of Spanish manufacture, which these Indians had obtained from their allies, the Comanches, who inhabited the country bordering New Mexico. After quitting the Cenis village, La Salle and his company advanced eastward as far as the river Neches,† in the vicinity of which both himself and nephew were attacked by malarial fever. This mishap caused a delay of some two months, and proved fatal to the success of the expedition. When the sick leader was sufficiently convalescent to travel, he found that his ammunition was well nigh spent, and that four of his men had

---

*Hiens was an ex-buccaneer, who had joined La Salle's expedition at Petit Goave, in St. Domingo.

†The name Tejas or Texas was first applied (by the Spaniards) as a local designation to a spot on the river Neches, in the Cenis territory, whence it extended to the whole country.—Yoakum's History of Texas, p. 52.

deserted to the Assonis Indians. Under these untoward circumstances, no better alternative presented itself than to return to Fort St. Louis. Their return march was greatly facilitated by the use of some horses, which La Salle had bought of the Cenis, and they met with no serious accident on the way, excepting the loss of one of their men, who was seized by an alligator while attempting to cross a large river, supposed to have been the Colorado.

The temporary excitement produced in the little band of colonists by the return of their chief soon gave way to a feeling of dejection akin to despair, and La Salle had a hard task to sustain their drooping spirits. But the journey to Canada, by way of the Illinois, was their only hope; and the chief, after a brief rest, prepared to renew the attempt. In the month of November, while thus occupied, he was again taken sick with a flux, which prostrated him for four or five weeks. At the end of this time he was once more able to travel, and all hands at the fort were busied in making from their scanty stores an outfit for his traveling party. Christmas day again came, and was solemnly observed. " There was a midnight mass in the chapel, where Membre, Douay, Cavelier, and their priestly brethren, stood in vestments strangely contrasting with the rude temple and ruder garb of the worshipers. And as Membre elevated the consecrated wafer, and the lamps burned dim through the clouds of incense, the kneeling group drew from the daily miracle such consolation as true Catholics alone can know." *

It was on the morning of the 7th of January, 1687, that La Salle mustered his small company of adventurers for this his last journey. The five horses purchased from the Cenis Indians were brought into the inclosed area of the fort, and loaded for the march. Assembled here was the poor remnant of the colony—those who were to go, and those who were to stay behind. The latter numbered something over twenty persons. There was the Sieur Barbier, who was to command in place of Joutel; the Marquis

---

* Parkman's La Salle and the Great West, p. 373.

de Sablonniere, a dissolute young nobleman; the two friars, Membre and Le Clercq, and the young priest Chéfdeville; also a surgeon, some few soldiers and laborers, seven women and girls, and a few children—all of whom were "doomed in this deadly exile to wait the issues of the journey, and the possible arrival of a tardy succor." La Salle had previously caused an earthwork to be thrown up around the habitations of the colonists adjoining the fort, and had taken other precautions for their safety. He now made them a farewell address, full of touching pathos, and delivered with that engaging air which this unhappy man sometimes assumed, and which moved them all to tears. Then followed the painful parting scene. "We separated from each other," says Joutel, "in a manner so tender and so sad, that it seemed we all had the presentiment that we should never meet again."* At length, equipped and armed for the journey, the adventurers filed from the gate, crossed the little river La Vache, and held their slow march over the prairie to the north-east, "till intervening woods shut Fort St. Louis forever from their sight."

La Salle's traveling party was made up of some good and several bad men, and was perhaps not wholly of his own selection. It comprised his brother and their two nephews, Moranget, and the boy Cavelier, now aged about seventeen; the friar, Anastase Douay; the trusty soldier, Joutel; Duhaut, a man of reputed respectable birth and education; Liotot, the surgeon of the company; Hiens, the German and ex-buccaneer; the Sieur de Marle; Teissier, a pilot; L'Archeveque, a servant of Duhaut, and a few others, numbering in all seventeen. Besides these, there was Nika, La Salle's Shawanoe hunter, who, together with another Indian, "had twice crossed the ocean with him, and still followed his fortunes with an admiring though undemonstrative fidelity." †

Pursuing the same route as before, the travelers advanced over a level country of grassy prairies and wooded

---

* Joutel's Journal Historique.
† Parkman's La Salle and the Great West, p. 397.

river bottoms, meeting on the way a war party of the Bahamos, and several other bands of Indians, more or less friendly. They successively crossed the Colorado and the Brazos in a portable canoe covered with bullocks' hides, and, after passing several other smaller streams, encamped near a western tributary of the Trinity, on the 15th of March.

La Salle was now in the vicinity of some corn and beans, which he had concealed in a pit during his former expedition, and he sent seven of his men to find it. They were Duhaut, Liotot, Hiens, Teissier, L'Archeveque, Nika, the Indian hunter, and Saget, a servant of the chief. They found and opened the *cache*, but its contents were unfit for use. In returning, however, they killed two buffaloes, and sent Saget back to the main camp for horses to bring in the meat. The next day La Salle ordered Moranget and De Marle to go with his servant and the horses to the hunters' camp. Proceeding on their errand, the latter found the carcasses of the buffaloes cut up and placed upon a scaffold to dry. In accordance with a custom among hunters, Duhaut and his companions had put aside the marrow bones and other choice bits of the game for their own use. Seeing this, the hot-headed Moranget, whose quarrelsome temper had before involved him in difficulties, fell into a rage and abused and menaced Duhaut and his friends, and ended by appropriating both the smoked meat and the bones to himself. This outburst of passion seems to have kindled into an avenging flame an old grudge which Duhaut had cherished toward Moranget, as well as his uncle.

Duhaut thereupon withdrew, and privately conspired with Liotot, Hiens, and others of their party, upon a bloody revenge. Waiting until night, when the Sieur Moranget, their principal victim, after taking his turn at watch, had fallen asleep, the conspirators silently approached the spot where he lay, and while the others stood by with their guns cocked, Liotot brained him with an ax. Nika, the Indian, and Saget, La Salle's footman, were dispatched in the same manner. The last two died without a struggle, but it appears to have been otherwise with Moranget. The sacrifice of the unoffending Nika and Saget shows the deep-seated villany of the assassins; but it was no doubt made in order to cut off all communication with the chief, whom they had singled out as their next and main victim. And so it often happens that the commission of one bloody crime leads on to another, and still another, until at last the perpetrator expiates his offenses with his own life.

Meanwhile, La Salle himself was at the main camp, six miles or more away, impatiently waiting the return of his nephew and party. Two days were thus passed in painful suspense, when, on the morning of the 19th of March, he started out in search of his missing relative and servant, accompanied only by Father Douay and an Indian guide. Joutel, whom he had at first intended to take with him, was left in charge of the camp, with instructions to keep a strict watch; for it seems that La Salle, always more or less suspicious, had observed the mutinous spirit of some of his men.

"All the way," writes Father Douay, "he conversed with me of matters of piety, grace, and predestination; expatiating on all his obligations to God for having saved him from so many dangers during the last twenty years that he had traversed America. . . . Suddenly, I saw him plunged into a deep melancholy, for which he himself could not account; he was so troubled that I did not know him any longer; (and) as this state was far from being natural to him, I roused him from his lethargy. Two leagues after, we found the bloody cravat of his lackey; he perceived two eagles flying over his head, and at the same time discovered some of his people on the edge of the river, which he approached, asking for his nephew. They answered in broken words, showing us where we should find him. We proceeded some steps along the bank to the fatal spot, where two of these murderers were hidden in the grass, one on each side with guns cocked; one missed Monsieur de la Salle, the other firing at the same time shot him in the head; he died an hour after, on the 9th of March, 1687.

"I expected the same fate, but this danger did not occupy my thoughts; penetrated with grief at so cruel a spectacle, I saw him fall a step from me, with his face all full of blood; I watered it with my tears, exhorting him to the best of my power to die well. He had confessed and fulfilled his devotion just before we started; he had still time to recapitulate a part of his life, and I gave him absolution. . . . Meanwhile his murderers, as much alarmed as I, began to strike their breasts and detest their blindness. I could not leave the spot where he had expired without having buried him, as well as I could, after which I raised a cross over his grave."*

Such is the simple and pathetic narrative of the only eye-witness, who has given us an account of La Salle's unhappy death. So much of this narration as relates to the alleged manifestation of remorse by his murderers, to the burial of his body and the erection of a cross over it, is expressly contradicted by Joutel, and is not sustained by any writing of the elder Cavelier. Indeed, it is affirmed that Douay told a different story at the time; and it would seem that he invented these fictions to soften the atrocity of the crime itself, as also to support his own character as a priest and man of resolution. As supplementary to the above, we here give M. Joutel's account of the catastrophe:

"He (La Salle) seemed to have some presage of his misfortune, inquiring of some whether the Sieurs Liotot, Hiens, and Duhaut had not expressed some discontent. And not hearing any thing of it, he could not forbear setting out the 20th, with Father Anastasius (Douay) and an Indian, leaving me the command in his absence, and charging me to go the rounds about our camp, to prevent being surprised, and to make a smoke for him to direct his way in case of need. When he came near the dwelling (camp) of the murderers, looking out sharp to discover something, he observed eagles fluttering about a spot not far from them, which made him believe they had found some carrion, and he fired a shot, which was the signal of his death and forwarded it.

---

* See Douay's Narrative, in Shea's Discov. and Explo. of the Miss. Val., pp. 213-14.

"The conspirators, hearing the shot, concluded it was M. de la Salle, who was come to seek them. They made ready their arms, and provided to surprise him. Duhaut passed the river, with Larcheveque. The first of them spying M. de la Salle at a distance, as he was coming toward them, advanced and hid themselves among the high weeds, to wait his passing by; so that M. de la Salle, suspecting nothing, and having not so much as charged his piece again, saw the aforesaid Larcheveque at a good distance from him, and immediately asked for his nephew, Moranget, to which Larcheveque answered that he was along the river. At the same time the traitor, Duhaut, fired his piece and shot M. de la Salle through the head, so that he dropped down dead on the spot, without speaking one word. . . . This is the exact relation of that murder, as it was presently after told me by Father Anastasius.

"The shot which had killed M. de la Salle was also a signal of the murder to the (other) assassins for them to draw near. They all repaired to the place where the wretched dead corpse lay, which they barbarously stripped to the shirt, and vented their malice in vile and opprobrious language. The surgeon, Liotot,* said several times, in scorn and derision: 'There thou liest, great bashaw! There thou liest!' In conclusion, they dragged it naked among the bushes, and left it exposed to the ravenous wild beasts."†

The precise locality of this gloomy tragedy, or succession of tragedies, can not now be determined. It is said (correctly, we think) to have occurred on a small tributary of the Trinity, since it was only about three days slow journey from thence to the main trunk of that river. But Mr. Sparks, in his Life of La Salle, says, "the place was probably on one of the streams flowing into the Brazos from the

---

* According to Tonty's Relation, Liotot's grievance against La Salle was, that in the journey along the sea-coast, he had compelled the brother of Liotot, who, could not keep up, to return to the camp, and that in returning alone he was killed by the savages; but this is not confirmed by Joutel.

† See Joutel's Journal, printed in the Hist. Coll's of La., edited by B. F. French, N. Y., 1846, Part I., pp. 143, 144.

east,—perhaps forty or fifty miles north of the present town of Washington, Texas."

Thus violently ended, at the age of forty-three years and four months, the extraordinary career of Robert Cavelier, Sieur de la Salle; a man celebrated alike for his daring and discoveries, his merits and misfortunes. We could have wished that his life had been longer spared, so that he might have found means to extricate the remnant of his Texan colony from impending destruction. The character of La Salle has been drawn by many different pens, yet, in general, they have found it easier to sum up his defects and failures than to set in a proper light his transcendent virtues. His reputation as a successful explorer and colonizer would probably have stood higher with his contemporaries and posterity, if he had never embarked from France on his last expedition to the Mississippi; but then his name would be divested of much of that dramatic and tragic interest with which it is enshrouded.

Hennepin, in the preface to his "New Discovery," written chiefly for Dutch and English readers, uses this harsh language in regard to La Salle's melancholy fate: "God knows that I am sorry for his unfortunate death; but the judgments of the Almighty are just, for that gentleman was killed by one of his own men, who were at last sensible that he exposed them to visible dangers without any necessity, and for his private design."

Again, in his "Nouveau Voyage," or continuation of his "New Discovery,"* he writes in a different strain, as follows: "Thus fell the Sieur Robert Cavelier de la Salle, a man of considerable merit, constant in adversities, fearless, generous, courteous, ingenious, and capable of everything. He labored for twenty years together to civilize the savage humors of a great number of barbarous people among whom he traveled, and had the ill-hap to be massacred by his own servants, whom he had enriched. He died in the vigor of his age, in the midddle of his course,

---

* English edition, London, 1699, p. 34.

before he could execute the design he had formed on New Mexico." Elsewhere, in the same work, Hennepin further says: "La Salle was a person qualified for the greatest undertakings, and may be justly ranked amongst the most famous travelers that ever were."

Henri Joutel, the fullest and most reliable historian of La Salle's Texas expedition, has drawn the character of his commander in these measured words:

"He had a capacity and talent to make his enterprises successful; his constancy and courage, and extraordinary knowledge in the arts and sciences, which rendered him fit for anything, together with an indefatigable habit of body, which made him surmount all difficulties, would have procured a glorious issue to his undertaking, had not all these excellent qualities been counterbalanced by too haughty a behavior, which sometimes made him insupportable, and by a rigidness to those under him, which at last drew on him their implacable hatred, and was the occasion of his death.*

This careful estimate seems just and impartial, though Joutel did not know La Salle at his best, but rather when his constitution was broken by disease, and his temper soured by misfortunes. Moreover, he lived too near him to fully appreciate the magnitude and significance of his services as a pioneer of civilization in North America. From the charge of harshness and tyranny toward his men, La Salle, in a letter written to a business correspondent some five years before his death, thus defends himself:

" The facility I am said to want is out of place with this people, who are libertines for the most part; and to indulge them means to tolerate blasphemy, drunkenness, lewdness, and license, incompatible with any kind of order. It will not be found that I have, in any case whatever, treated any man harshly, except for blasphemies and other such crimes openly committed. . . . I am a Christian, and do not want to bear the burden of their crimes."

---

* Joutel's *Journal Historique*.

Although proud, shy, cold, and austere in his general deportment, La Salle was not incapable of inspiring strong attachments among those to whom he gave his confidence, and who had the penetration to discern the lofty bearing of his genius. He required every sacrifice at the hands of the men in his employ, but he himself led the way in every difficulty and every danger. He was something of an enthusiast, and about his various schemes and enterprises there was much that appeared visionary and impracticable; yet such was his persevering energy that he succeeded in many things where others would have faltered and failed, and his failure to found a colony at the outlet of the Mississippi was largely due to circumstances beyond his personal control.

In no one particular was his superiority over contemporary explorers more manifest than in his intercourse with the aborigines of the country, whom he every-where made subservient to his designs. He was greatly respected by the Indians throughout the Mississippi Valley. This was attributable not only to his liberal and conciliatory policy in dealing with them, but to his grave and taciturn manner, which comported well with their own ideas of dignity and decorum. It is worthy of remark, in passing, that he nearly always traveled with a train of ecclesiastics, showing a preference for the Recollets. They went not merely as missionaries to convert the heathen, but to assist him in his enterprises and write up his doings, and were among his most efficient and faithful coadjutors. He was not a prudent or successful business man; his transactions as an Indian trader and fur-dealer, though on a large scale, were usually attended with loss, and he died hopelessly insolvent. His ambition was fame—fame as a discoverer and explorer of new and unknown lands. For the gratification of this passion he sacrificed his means, his comfort, his health, and finally life itself. His plans were too extensive and complex for his resources or credit, and even his uncommon energy and fortitude could not always cope with the enmities and jealousies that were constantly arrayed against him. Nevertheless, he stands in the history of the period as the foremost pioneer in North America. Moreover, he was the first chartered owner and occupant of Illinois, and the first to establish a European settlement on her soil.

Physically as well as intellectually, La Salle seemed born to command. He was of a tall and martial figure, and appears to have inherited a vigorous constitution, which, however, was considerably impaired by sickness and hardships in his later years. His picture represents him with a fine oval face, and a high open forehead. From his Norman lineage he derived his pluck and tenacity of purpose, qualities that nearly allied him to the ruling class of England. He was never married, and left no offspring to perpetuate his name and fame. He held his lease of life by the same fragile thread as the meanest camp-follower in his train. He died a martyr to his own ambition and the glory of France. He was one of those great actors on the stage of our earlier continental history, about whom men write and converse while he sleeps the sleep that knows no waking. It has been felicitously observed of him, that "he was as brave as the bravest, as pure as the purest, and as unfortunate as the most unfortunate."

In Masson's "Abridgment of Guizot's History of France," p. 490, is the following condensed yet graphic, recital of La Salle's achievements: "La Salle, in his intrepid expeditions, discovered the Ohio and Illinois, navigated the great lakes, crossed (descended) the Mississippi, which the Jesuits had been the first to reach, and pushed on as far as Texas. Constructing forts in the midst of savage districts, taking possession of Louisiana in the name of Louis XIV., abandoned by (some of) his comrades, and losing the most faithful of them by death, attacked by savages, betrayed by his own men, thwarted in his prospects by his enemies, this indefatigable man fell at last beneath the blows of a few mutineers in 1687, just as he was trying to get back to New France. He left the field open after him to innumerable travelers (and adventurers) of every nation and tongue, who were one day to leave their mark on those measureless tracts. It is the glory and misfortune of France to always lead the van in the march of civilization, without having the wit to profit by the discoveries and the sagacious boldness of her children."

CHAPTER IX.

1687-1689.

SURVIVORS OF LA SALLE'S TEXAN COLONY.

The surviving members of La Salle's traveling party, who were not in sympathy with his murder, refrained from openly expressing their indignation through fear of their own lives, and uneasily awaited the issue of events. Meanwhile, Duhaut and Liotot seized upon every thing in the camp belonging to the late commander, and arrogated to themselves the command in his stead.

On the 20th of March, the day following the catastrophe, the combined party broke camp and recommenced their journey, as if anxious to get away from the gloomy locality. Impeded in their advance by heavy rains they were three days in reaching the main stream of the Trinity, which they crossed in a boat made of raw hides, swimming their horses. Continuing their slow march through the timbered valley to the vicinity of another and smaller river,* the travelers halted and held a council in regard to their future movements. Being short of provisions, it was decided that Liotot, Hiens, Teissier, and Joutel should proceed to the villages of the Cenis Indians, about ten leagues away to the north-east, and there barter for a supply of maize and beans. Joutel was thus assigned to the companionship of three villains whom he detested, and at the same time suspected of contriving an opportunity to take his life, because of his fidelity to their late commander. But having no choice in the matter, he dissembled his fears and set off with his sinister associates. A day's ride brought them to the nearest Cenis village, which consisted of a scattered group of large, grass-thatched lodges, resembling huge hay ricks. The Frenchmen were received with much ceremony

---

* Probably an eastern arm of the Trinity.

by the painted and tattooed elders of the village, and were assigned a cottage in which to lodge. But these Indian hosts, while feeding their visitors by day, did not hesitate to pilfer from them by night as opportunity offered. They had no religion worth considering, and, in common with the surrounding tribes, were more or less addicted to cannibalism.

After a few days stay at the village, the companions of Joutel returned to the French camp, leaving him to continue the traffic alone. During his sojourn there he met with two French sailors named Ruter and Grollet (Jacques), who had forsaken La Salle on the occasion of his journey to this region in the preceding year, and who were now domesticated among the Cenis. When apprised of the murder of his late commander, Ruter expressed both surprise and regret.

Some days afterward, Joutel was ordered to return with the provisions he had purchased to Duhaut's camp, and upon his arrival thither found a miserable state of affairs. The elder Cavelier and Friar Douay had been treated with harshness and contempt by Duhaut and Liotot, and were constrained to prepare their meals apart to themselves. Joutel now joined them, and around their own camp-fire they talked of nothing else but how to escape from the company of the miscreants in which circumstances had placed them. No other feasible expedient presented itself except to continue their journey to the Mississippi, and thence to the Illinois and Canada, as originally undertaken by La Salle himself. In carrying out this plan, the first and principal difficulty was to get the consent of Duhaut and Liotot; for they had already announced their intention to return to Fort St. Louis on the bay, and there build a vessel with which to sail to the West Indies. The announcement of this impracticable purpose—impracticable because their carpenters were all dead, and they were without suitable appliances and material for the work—showed that those desperate men had no mind to peril their personal safety by going to Canada. In pursuance of that resolution Hiens and three other members of the party were sent to the village of the Cenis to barter for additional horses.

In this critical posture of affairs, the elder Cavelier, with whom a sacrifice of truth cost no particular effort, opened negotiations with the Sieur Duhaut. The old priest represented that he and his friends were too much fatigued by travel to undertake a journey back to the fort, preferring to remain among the Cenis Indians, and requested a share of the goods, for which he offered to give his note of hand. To this preposition Duhaut, after consulting with his companions, unexpectedly assented, but soon afterward changed his mind on being told that it was the secret intention of Cavelier and party to proceed to the Illinois and Canada. He then gave out that he would go with them to execute their design, which disconcerted and troubled the latter.

Duhaut and the others appear to have remained at the same camp, east of the Trinity, through April and until the first week in May, only advancing a little nearer to the river which lay between them and the village of the Cenis. Iliens and his three French companions were still at the village, being detained partly by the overflow in the river, but principally by the attractions of the Cenis women. During his stay there he heard of Duhaut's new plan of going to find the Mississippi, and declared to those with him that he was not of that mind, and refused his consent.

"After we had been some days longer in the same place," writes Joutel, " Iliens arrived with the two half-savage Frenchmen (Ruter and Grollet), and about twenty natives. He went immediately to Duhaut, and after some (heated) discourse, told him he was not for going toward the Mississippi, because it would be of dangerous consequence for them, and therefore demanded his share of the effects he had seized. Duhaut refusing to comply, and affirming that all the axes were his own, Hiens, who it is likely had laid the design before to kill him, immediately drew his pistol and fired it upon Duhaut, who staggered about four paces from the place, and fell down dead. At the same time Ruter, who had been with Hiens, fired his piece upon Liotot, the surgeon, and shot him through with three balls.

"These murders committed before us, put me in a terrible consternation; for, believing the same was designed for me, I laid hold of my firelock to defend myself. But Hiens cried out to me to fear nothing, to lay down my arms, and assured me he had no design against me; but that he had revenged his master's death. He also satisfied M. Cavelier and Father Anastase, who were as much frightened as myself, declaring he meant them no harm, and that though he had been in the conspiracy, yet had he been present at the time when M. de la Salle was killed, he would not have consented, but rather obstructed it.

"Liotot lived some hours after, and had the good fortune to make his confession; after which the same Ruter put him out of his pain with a pistol shot.* We dug a hole in the earth, and buried him in it with Duhaut, doing them more honor than they had done to M. de la Salle and his nephew, Moranget, whom they left to be devoured by the wild beasts. Thus those murderers met with what they had deserved, dying the same death they had put others to."†

The Indian spectators looked with astonishment and terror upon these brutal homicides, which put to shame even their own thirst for blood. The Frenchmen present, however, excused the deed to the savages by telling them that those two men had been killed, "because they had all the powder and ball, and would not give any to the rest." Jean L'Archeveque, who had been entirely devoted to Duhaut, was absent hunting at the time, and Hiens was for shooting him on his return to camp, but was dissuaded therefrom by Joutel and the two priests.

The only excuse or apology Duhaut and Liotot had offered for their own atrocious crimes, was that they had been driven thereto by despair at their ill-usage. If they

---

* It is related by Father Douay, in his account of these murders, that the flash of Ruter's pistol set fire to Liotot's hair and clothing, which were burned on his body, and that in this torment he died. This happened nearly two months after the death of La Salle.

† See Joutel's Journal in "Historical Collections of Louisiana," Part I., pp. 157, 158.

had remained at home in France, and not been subjected to any great temptations, they might have passed through life as respectable citizens; but, as it was and is, their names must be consigned to merited execration and ignominy.

These latter tragedies came like a thunderbolt from a cloudless sky, and cleared the way for the escape of the innocent members of the party. Prior to this, however, Hiens and his associate outlaws had promised the chiefs of the Cenis to accompany them on a foray against a tribe called the Kanoatinos, who dwelt some distance off to the northwest, and with whom the former were at feud. To facilitate this purpose the surviving Frenchmen now decamped and removed their head-quarters to the Cenis village. The two Caveliers, Joutel, Douay, and two others were lodged in a cabin by themselves, where they were watched by the villagers, while Hiens and his six followers, armed and mounted, went with the native warriors on their raid. After an absence of less than a fortnight, the war party returned, bringing with them several Indian prisoners, and a number of scalps, as trophies of their victory over the enemy.

When the savage feasting and rejoicing thereat, which lasted several days, had come to an end, M. Cavelier and Joutel took occasion to inform Hiens of their proposed journey to and up the Mississippi. The latter at first stoutly opposed the project, as he had no thought of going thither himself, but finally consented on condition that Cavelier should give him a writing certifying to his innocence of La Salle's murder, which the priest did not scruple to do. For the rest, Hiens treated his departing fellow-travelers with the liberality of a successful freebooter, giving them a fair proportion of the booty he had acquired by his recent villanous crimes. "Before our departure," says Joutel's Journal, "it was a sensible affliction to us to see that villain walk about the camp in a scarlet coat, with gold *galons* (lace), which had belonged to the late Monsieur de la Salle, and which he had seized."

The escaping party was composed of seven persons, viz.: the two Caveliers (uncle and nephew), Joutel, Douay,

De Marle, Teissier, and a Parisian youth named Barthélemy. Teissier was an accomplice in the death of both Moranget and La Salle, but had received a *pro forma* pardon from the elder Cavelier. They had six indifferent horses, a quantity of powder and ball, and some axes, knives, and beads, for use in barter with the natives on the route. They left the Cenis village without regret, late in May, and were attended by three guides. Hiens embraced them at parting, as did the other half-dozen ruffians who stayed with him. The general course of the travelers was to the north-east, in the direction of the Lower Arkansas, which was more than three hundred miles distant. After several days travel through an open country, passing hamlets and villages on the way, they reached the nation of the Assonis, or Nassouis, dwelling near the river Neches, where they were fairly well received. Here they were detained by continued rain until about the 13th of June, when they again set forward, with fresh guides, on their journey.

The travelers next approached the village of a tribe called by Joutel the Nathosos, who inhabited the country between the Sabine and Red River. The dusky dwellers in this village had hitherto known the Europeans only by report, and coming out to meet their visitors, regarded them with great curiosity. Desirous of doing the Frenchmen special honor, they took them on their backs and carried them into the village; but Joutel, being a large and heavy man, bore down his carrier so much that two other Indians had to assist him, one on either side. Arrived at the chief's cottage, their horses were unloaded, and one of the elders of the village proceeded to wash the faces of the visitors with warm water from an earthen vessel. Then they were invited to mount a scaffolding of canes, covered with white mats, where they sat in the burning sun and listened to several speeches of welcome, of which they did not understand a single word.

Taking leave of this hospitable people, our travelers next came to a village of the Cadodaquis, where they experienced a similar reception. Crossing Red River and approaching the Washita, they arrived at the village of another nation, who gave them a still more oppressive welcome. As the leader of the party the elder Cavelier became the principal victim of the Indian attentions. They danced the calumet before him, singing as loud as they could roar, beat upon their calabashes, stuck feathers in his hair, and performed various other antics. The old priest endured the irksome ceremony as long as he well could, and then, pretending that it made him ill, he was assisted to his lodge; but they continued to sing, howl, and dance all through the night. The meaning of all this Indian ceremony was that their visitors should make them a present, which was accordingly done to their satisfaction.

At length, after a wearisome journey of nearly two months from the Cenis, during which time they had the misfortune to lose one of their number (De Marle), who was accidentally drowned, the travelers drew near to the Arkansas River, at a place some fifty miles above its junction with the Mississippi. Conducted thither by their native guides, they at last stood upon the banks of the Arkansas, and, looking across to the farther side, beheld an Indian village, and below and near it on a small eminence was a cabin built of cedar logs, and a tall wooden cross, evidently the work of French hands. Overwhelmed with emotions of gratitude at their deliverance, they all knelt down and, lifting up their hands, gave thanks to the Divine Goodness for having directed their footsteps to this little outpost of civilization. Presently, two white men emerged from the door of the cabin and fired their guns as a salute to the wanderers, who answered it with a volley from their own. Then two canoes crossed from the opposite shore and ferried them over to the village, where they were heartily greeted in their own tongue by Messrs. Couture and De Launay, two of six men whom Henri de Tonty had stationed there during the preceding year.* The whole distance from Fort St. Louis of Texas, to the Ar-

---

* This station was afterward known to the French as *Poste aux Arkansas*, and later, to the Americans, as Arkansas Post. The Arkansas Indians had two villages on this river, the second one being near its mouth.

kansas, following the route of the traveling party, was computed by Father Douay at two hundred and fifty leagues.

It may be remembered that in the spring of 1685, by an order of the King of France, M. de Tonty had been reinstated in command at Fort St. Louis of the Illinois, with the title of captain and governor. In the autumn of that year, he made a special journey to Mackinac to seek intelligence of his absent chief. Arrived thither, he learned that a letter had been received from Governor Denonville, then lately arrived from France, stating that La Salle had landed on the coast of the Gulf of Mexico, and that he had lost one of his vessels there. Upon hearing this news, Tonty returned to the Illinois, and organized an expedition on his own responsibility, and at his own expense, to go to La Salle's assistance. Accordingly, on the 16th of February, 1686, he departed from Fort St. Louis, with thirty Frenchmen and five Indians, in log canoes, and descended the Illinois and the Mississippi to the Gulf, which he reached in Holy Week. Finding no traces of the French colony there, he sent some of his canoes to scour the coast for thirty leagues on either side of the diverging outlet of the river. But all this search was futile, for La Salle was then rambling in the distant wilds of southern Texas. Disappointed yet not disheartened at his failure, Tonty wrote a letter to his commander, informing him of this trip in quest of him, which he committed to the keeping of an Indian chief of the Quinipissas tribe, to be delivered so soon as an opportunity should offer. He then returned with his force up the Mississippi to the mouth of the Arkansas, which he entered and ascended some distance to a village of that nation. Here, on lands which had been previously granted to him by La Salle, the Sieur de Tonty stationed six of his men, who volunteered to remain, and who were to report to him any information they might gather from the natives or otherwise concerning his chief.

But to go back to the party of Cavelier and Joutel. They tarried for several days at the French outpost on the

Arkansas, resting from the fatigues and anxieties of their extraordinary journey. As chief spokesman of the party, the elder Cavelier related to M. Couture and De Launay the history of their long sea-voyage, and subsequent wanderings and sufferings in the southern wilderness, including an account of La Salle's dismal end, which drew tears from their eyes. For various prudential reasons, this last bit of information was kept from the Arkansas Indians, who held him in great respect, and impatiently expected his return.

The travelers departed from the house of the Frenchmen about the 28th of July, leaving behind them their horses and young Barthélemy, the Parisian, who afterward told slanderous stories about La Salle's alleged cruelty to his men. They embarked with a number of the natives in a pirogue forty feet long, belonging to one of the chiefs of the village, and were accompanied part of the way by M. Couture. Descending the Arkansas to the next village (called Torriman) of that nation, they tarried there until the following day, when they went in two canoes to cross and ascend the Mississippi, which had been so long the object of their search, and which Joutel terms, in his journal, the "fatal river." After stopping to visit the third village of the Arkansas, which was seated on the banks of the Mississippi, they thence proceeded up the river eight leagues to Kappa, the fourth and last village of that people. On the 2nd of August our five travelers took leave of M. Couture at the Kappa village, and re-embarked in a single canoe with four Arkansas guides. In their north-bound voyage, they found it requisite to often cross the river, and sometimes to carry their canoe and luggage, on account of the rapidity of the current, and at night, for greater safety, encamped on some one of the smaller islands. On the 19th they reached the mouth of the Ohio, to which their Indians made a sacrifice of some tobacco and buffalo steaks. Leaving that behind them, and still ascending, they passed the confluence of the turbid Missouri on the first of September, and the next day turned from the "Father of Waters",into the quiet channel of the Illinois.

In navigating this central part of the Mississippi,

neither Joutel nor Douay observed any thing very remarkable in the painted rocks of the Piasa, as described by Marquette. "The 2nd" (of September), writes Joutel, "we arrived at the place where the figure is of the pretended monster spoken of by Father Marquette. That monster consists of two scurvy figures drawn in red, on the flat side of a rock, about ten or twelve feet high, which wants very much the extraordinary height that relation mentions. However, our Indians paid homage, by offering sacrifice to that stone."*

Father Douay saw, and briefly describes in his narrative, certain rude figures on another rock, some forty leagues below the mouth of the Missouri, which, on Thevenot's reproduction of Marquette's map, is marked as the evil Manitou of the Illinois Indians. Douay goes on to state, that "about midway between the river Ouabache (Ohio) and that of the Massourites, is Cape St. Anthony; it was to this place, and not farther, that the Sieur Joliet descended in 1673." But in the above unsupported and improbable statement, the Recollet father simply displays his own ignorance and jealousy of the prior discoveries made by Joliet and Marquette; for it is morally certain that they went a long distance below the confluence of the Ohio.

But to return from this digression. After entering the Illinois River, it required ten days more of hard rowing and pushing to bring the travelers to the rock-seated fort of St. Louis, whither they arrived on the 14th of September, and were once more among friends and countrymen. The Sieur de Tonty was away in the east, fighting the Iroquois; but his lieutenant, Belle Fontaine, was in charge of the fort, and his little garrison received the way-worn voyagers with a salvo of musketry, which was supplemented by the whooping of the Indian occupants of the Rock, who ran down to the river to meet them. As the season was growing late, our travelers were eager to press forward to Quebec, in order to take shipping there for France. After a few days of repose, therefore, they took leave of Belle Fon-

---

* Joutel's *Journal Historique.* See *ante*, Chap. III. of this work.

taine and his men (from whom they had studiously withheld any knowledge of La Salle's death), and proceeded on their way up the river to Lake Michigan. On arriving at the mouth of Chicago rivulet, they embarked on the waters of the lake in a canoe, which had been procured for that purpose at the fort; but being driven back by stress of weather, they abandoned their design, buried a part of their effects on the lake shore, and returned to Fort St. Louis to spend the winter.

At the close of the month of October, Captain Tonty returned from the Seneca war, accompanied by several of his French friends, and he now listened with profound interest to the long and sad narrative of his travel-worn guests from the south-west. With the connivance of his party, the elder Cavelier did not scruple to practice on Tonty the same deceit he had used with his lieutenant. He told him that La Salle had been with them nearly to the Cenis villages, and that when they parted from him he was in good health, which was technically true so far as a majority of the old priest's party was concerned. The main purpose of this studied deception was to derive all the pecuniary advantage he could from his character of representative of his brother. Besides, both he and his associates were still not without some apprehension from the accomplices of La Salle's murderers, should any of them return to Canada or France. If the elder Cavelier had been frank and candid with Tonty, the expedition which the latter subsequently undertook for the relief of the Texan colonists might have been attended with better results. Friar Douay tells us that the presence of Tonty made their stay at the fort much more agreeable, and speaks of him, as "this brave gentleman, always inseparably attached to the interests of the Sieur de la Salle, whose lamentable fate we concealed from him, it being our duty to give the first news to the court."*

The elder Cavelier carried a letter of credit from La Salle—whether genuine or not, it were needless to inquire—

---

* Narrative of Father Anastase Douay, in Le Clercq's *Etablissement de la Foi*, vol. II.

requesting Tonty to furnish him with supplies, and pay him 2,652 livres in beaver skins. On the strength of this and his verbal representations, Cavelier drew upon Tonty to the amount, it is averred, of four thousand livres in furs,* besides a canoe and a quantity of other goods, all of which were delivered to him on his quitting the fort, and for which in return he gave his promissory note. The only excuse for this deliberate deception and fraud was the destitution of the old priest and his companions, and the further fact that he had a claim against his brother's estate, which, however, he must have known was insolvent. It seems hardly credible that during all this time, the Sieur de Tonty should not have received a hint of, or even suspected, the death of his former commander.

After living upon Tonty's generous hospitality for six months, the Cavelier party finally departed from Fort St. Louis the 20th of March, 1688. Seven days of travel up the Illinois River and its northern fork brought them to the Chicagou, whence they again embarked on Lake Michigan, and, after many perils, reached Michilimackinac on the 6th of May.† Here the elder Cavelier disposed of a portion of his ill-gotten furs to a trader, and received in exchange an order on a Montreal house. Being thus supplied with funds for the rest of the journey our travelers left Mackinac about the 5th of June, and proceeded by way of northern Lake Huron, French River, Lake Nipissing, and the Ottawa River to Montreal. Here, after converting the remainder of their furs into money, they provided themselves with much

---

* Tonty's Memoir does not make it so much.

† The Baron de la Hontan, who was then at Mackinac with a small detachment of French soldiers, in a letter dated the 26th of May, thus speaks of Cavelier and his party: " M. Cavelier arrived here May 6th, accompanied by his nephew, Father Anastase, the Recollect, a pilot, one of the savages. and some few Frenchmen, which made a sort of party-colored retinue. These Frenchmen were some of those that M. de la Salle conducted upon the discovery of Mississippi. They give out that they are sent to Canada, in order to go to France, with some dispatches from M. de la Salle to the King. But we suspect that he is dead, because he does not return along with them."—La Hontan's Voyages, vol. 1, p. 87.

needed clothing and other necessaries, and then went down the St. Lawrence to Quebec, whither they arrived the 29th of July. Taking passage on the 20th of August for Old France, they arrived in safety at Rochelle on the 9th of October, 1688, and thence proceeded to Rouen. The wanderers had been absent from home something over four years, and during that period had performed one of the most adventurous and remarkable journeys on record.

It was not until their return to France, that the gloomy secret of La Salle's tragic death was disclosed. When it was told to Louis XIV., he gave orders for the arrest of all persons concerned in the murder who might appear in New France, but no one was ever arrested. M. Joutel had hoped that a royal ship-of-the-line would be sent out for the rescue of the surviving colonists on the coast of Texas; yet this was not done. Being occupied with other and, to him, weightier matters, the king left the miserable little band to their fate. In fact, it was probably too late then to have saved them from destruction.

The priest, Jean Cavelier, made a written report of La Salle's expedition to Seignelay, the Minister of Marine and Colonies, and also wrote a journal of the sea-voyage to the Gulf, which is in print, but was not brought down to the time of his brother's death. It is stated that he afterward inherited a large estate from a relative in France, and " died rich and very old." Apart from his natural prudence and self-command, he had most of the defects without any of the redeeming and ennobling traits of La Salle; and the correspondence of the latter shows that he entertained but little affection for this elder brother, who was " always interfering with or crossing his plans."

" Joutel," writes Parkman, " must have been a young man at the time of the Mississippi expedition, for Charlevoix saw him at Rouen thirty-five years after. He speaks of him in terms of emphatic praise; but it must be admitted that his connivance in the deception practiced upon Tonty leaves a shade on his character, as well as on that of Douay." Joutel's Historical Journal of that expedition did not appear in print until the year 1713. As he was only

an ordinary scholar, it is fair to presume that he had the
assistance of a competent scribe in preparing his work for
publication. Its general accuracy and impartiality are
unquestioned, though in the matter of dates it is perhaps
inferior to Douay's Narrative. It contains the best description extant of the country of Texas at that early day.

We now return to M. de Tonty. In September, 1688,
he was visited at his fort in the Illinois by M. Couture,*
and two Indians from the Arkansas, who danced the calumet. It was then, for the first time, we are told, that he
learned with sorrow and indignation of the lamentable
fate of his chief, and of the deceit that had been practiced
upon him by the elder Cavelier and party. The opinion of
this *Fidus Achates* of M. de la Salle is epitomized in his
observation, that "he was one of the greatest men of the
age." The leader whom he had so long followed was, indeed, beyond any human aid; but the still surviving colonists, languishing on the distant shores of the Gulf, might
yet be saved from extermination. He therefore resolved
upon an expedition for their relief, and furthermore, if it
were found practicable, to make them the nucleus of a war
party to cross the Rio del Norte into Mexico. Tonty's
means or resources were utterly inadequate to the accomplishment of so bold and difficult an undertaking; nevertheless, he made the attempt.

After some little preparation, this impulsive and chivalrous man set off from his fortified rock early in December of that year (1688),† in a large canoe, with five
Frenchmen, two Indian slaves, and a Shawnee hunter.
Passing down the Illinois and the Mississippi to the mouth
of Red River, and thence up the latter stream, he reached
the Natchitoches on the 17th of the ensuing February, and
the Cadodaquis on the 28th of March. The Cadodaquis
were allied with the Nachitoches and the Nassoui. All

---

* Couture was a native of Rouen, and a carpenter by trade.

† Parkman's "La Salle and the Great West," p. 439.

Tonty's own Memoir says that he set out on this journey in October, 1689; but as he probably wrote from recollection, his dates can not always be relied upon.

three of these nations dwelt in the Red River Valley, and all spoke substantially the same language. Upon his arrival at the Cadodaquis village, Tonty was told that Hiens and his French confederates were at a village of the Naouadiches, some eighty leagues to the south-west. But when he was preparing to go there, all of his men refused to follow him, excepting one Frenchman and the Shawnee Indian. Not being able to compel the attendance of the others, he set forward on the 6th of April, with the two men who were faithful, and five native guides. A few days afterward, in crossing a stream, his French companion lost his bag containing the most of their powder. But, undeterred by this accident he pressed on to the Naouadiche village, lying east of the Cenis, where the criminals were said to be. Arrived thither on the 23d, he found no traces of Hiens and his associates. When he inquired for them of the head men of the village, they told him different stories, and when he charged them with having killed the Frenchmen, the women began to cry, from which he inferred that his charge was true. These villagers refused Tonty guides to further continue his journey, although, as he tells us, it was only three days' travel from thence to where La Salle had been murdered. Owing, therefore, to his lack of guides, and the shortness of his ammunition, he was obliged to relinquish his purpose of endeavoring to reach the fort on Matagorda Bay. While at this Texan village, he seems to have heard rumors in regard to the breaking up and destruction of the French colony on the coast by the Indians.

In retracing their winding track, Tonty and his companions found the country flooded by the heavy vernal rains, and experienced incredible hardships in threading the Red River wilderness. They had to construct a raft and paddle through the water, sleep on logs laid one upon another, build fires on the trunks of trees, and subsist on a little bear and dog meat. He says, in his memoir, that he never suffered so much in his life as during this journey back to the Mississippi, which was reached on the 11th of July. Making his way thence to the village of the Coroas,

Tonty stayed there several days to recuperate, after which he went up to his post on the Arkansas. Here he fell sick of a fever, brought on by exposure, which detained him till the 11th of August. He then resumed his river voyage homeward, and arrived at Fort St. Louis, of the Illinois, late in September, 1689. Ten months were consumed in this extraordinary journey, which was one of the longest and hardest he ever made.

This unavailing attempt was the last that was made to rescue the unhappy colonists from the savage immensity which shut them out from home and civilization. Their final extirpation by the Texas Indians was subsequently learned from the Spaniards in Mexico. By priority of discovery and occupation, Spain claimed all the country surrounding the Mexican Gulf, and the viceroys of Mexico had been active and energetic in enforcing this claim. The capture of one of La Salle's vessels off the coast of St. Domingo had first made known his designs to the Spanish authorities, and during the succeeding three years as many as four expeditions were sent out from Vera Cruz to find and destroy his colony. They scoured the entire coast, and even found the wrecks of his vessels, but owing to the secluded, inland position of the French fort, it had eluded their search. The Spaniards therefore rested for a time in the belief that the intruders upon their territory had perished, when fresh advices from the frontier province of New Leon caused the viceroy to order a renewal of the search.

Accordingly, in January, 1689, Don Alonzo de Leon started with a strong body of horsemen from a military post in the province of Quagila (Coahuila), and marched northward over the barren mountains until he came to the Spanish-Mexican town of Calhuila. He then turned to his right, and, crossing the Rio Bravo del Norte, entered the territory of the Bahamos Indians. Guided thence by a French prisoner (supposed to have been a deserter from La Salle), he traversed the country to the north-east, crossing in turn the Nueces, the San Antonia, and the Guadalupe, and at length reached the Bay of St. Bernard, called by the Spaniards Espiritu Santo.* Arrived at the French fort of St. Louis on the 22d of April, the Spanish leader and his cavalcade proceeded to reconnoiter the place. They found the dead bodies of several of the colonists, who had been killed by blows or pierced by arrows; also a lot of old French books (mostly religious works) scattered around, and a number of iron cannon mounted upon navy gun carriages; but no living thing was there, and no explanation of the mystery was obtainable from the stolid savages dwelling on the shores of the bay. After an interval of several days, however, there arrived at the Spanish camp two strangers, whose faces were painted, and who were otherwise attired as Indians. They were James Grollet and Jean L'Archeveque, the latter having been one of the principal accomplices in the murder of La Salle. Finding life insupportable among the savages, these two Frenchmen had come, under pledges of good treatment, to surrender themselves to the Spanish commander. From them was obtained about all that is definitely known in regard to the melancholy end of the occupants of the fort.

The neighboring Indians, as we have seen, had been from the first on ill terms with the French colonists; and it appears that some three months before a band of the savages had stealthily approached the fort, the inmates of which had been suffering from the small-pox, to take them by surprise. Fearing treachery, the French refused their visitors admittance, but received them at a house without the palisade, where the savages made a pretense of trade. Suddenly, at a preconcerted signal, the larger part of this band of warriors, who had been in hiding under the river bank, rushed from their cover, entered the gate, and massacred nearly all of the French inmates. L'Archeveque and Grollet stated that they, with some others of their companions, came hither from the Cenis villages and buried fourteen corpes of the slain. The four

---

* See manuscript map of the route of the Spaniards in Margry's Collection.

children of a Canadian named Talon, together with an
Italian and a young Frenchman named Eustache de Bremen,
were saved by some Indian women who had been
domesticated at the fort, and who hurried them away,
carrying the children on their backs. These young captives
were all soon after surrendered to the Spaniards.

Conspicuous among those who are believed to have
thus perished under the war clubs and scalping-knives of
the vengeful savages were the two friars, Maxime le Clercq
and Zenobe Membre. And here it may be as well to collate
the known facts in the adventurous life of the latter,
who died at about the age of forty-four. Agreeably to a
statement of Hennepin, Membre was born at Bapaume, a
small fortified town in the south part of Artois, France,
about 1645. His name of Zenobius was probably assumed
on entering the Recollet convent in Artois. He appears
to have been a cousin of Father Chrétien le Clercq, who
published an abridgment of his letters and journals in
L'Etablissement de la Foi. With this cousin, he was first
sent out to Canada as a missionary in the year 1675. In
1682, after returning from the memorable expedition down
the Mississippi, he was sent by La Salle to lay the result
of that expedition before the government of France.
Having fulfilled his mission at court, he went to Bapaume,
and there held the position of Warden to the Recollets
until 1684, when, at La Salle's request, he was appointed
superior of the Recollet missionaries who were to accompany
his expedition by sea to the Mississippi. After the
stranding of the "Aimable" at the entrance to Matagorda
Bay, he came near being drowned while passing that vessel
in a boat, which was driven by the force of the waves
against the wreck and dashed to pieces. In January,
1687, when La Salle finally left Fort St. Louis of Texas,
Membre was intending, as soon as possible, with the aid
of Father Maxime le Clercq, to establish a mission among
the friendly Cenis Indians; but this project was never
carried out.

Father Membre was not a man of superior parts or
learning. His letters and journals are often involved and

obscure, yet they bear intrinsic marks of fidelity, and show him to have been a less prejudiced observer of men and things than some of his clerical companions. Neither his natal year, nor the month nor day of his martyrdom, is definitely determined; but, surely, this amiable man and devoted missionary merited a better and happier destiny.

"L'Archeveque and Grollet were sent to Spain, where, in spite of the pledge given them, they were thrown into prison, with the intention of sending them back (to Mexico) to work in the mines. The Italian was imprisoned at Vera Cruz. The fate of Bremen is unknown. Pierre and Jean Baptiste Talon, who were now old enough to bear arms, were enrolled in the Spanish navy, and being captured in 1696 by a French ship of war, regained their liberty; while their younger brother and sister were carried by the viceroy to Spain. With respect to the ruffian companions of Heins, the conviction of Tonty that they had been put to death by the Indians may have been correct; but the buccaneer himself is said to have been killed by Ruter, the white savage. And thus, in ignominy and darkness, expired the last embers of the doomed colony of La Salle."*

Here ends the wild, lurid, and most tragical story of the first Gallic explorers and colonists of Texas; a story which exemplifies the familiar adage that truth is often stranger than fiction. Such was the dismal fate of others of the earlier European settlements in America, until the colonists became sufficiently numerous and powerful to cope with the ravages of disease and the hostility of the savages.

---

* Parkman's "La Salle and the Great West," p. 445.

CHAPTER X.

1689–1712.

ILLINOIS AS A DEPENDENCY OF CANADA.

After La Salle's ineffectual attempt to plant a colony in the delta district of the Mississippi, it was over twelve years before the government of France essayed another experiment in that quarter. Busily engaged in a great war with William of Orange and the German princes for European supremacy, the French monarch had neither the time nor the inclination to indulge in projects of distant and expensive colonization. During this long interval there was but little immigration into the Mississippi Valley, nor were any steps taken by kingly authority for the government of the newly-acquired territory. Meantime, however, the Jesuit missionaries and fur-traders from Canada were both active and enterprising; the one in disseminating the Catholic faith among the aborigines, and the other in bartering cheap goods and "fire-water" for their furs and pelts.

Fort St. Louis continued for some years to be the seat of French power in the Illinois, with Henri de Tonty as commandant and governor, whose authority extended about as far in every direction as his French-Italian imagination chose to stretch it. In 1690, or 1691, the company of Foot, in which he had held the rank of captain since 1684, but without receiving any regular pay, was ordered to be disbanded. Being thus thrown out of employment in the line of his profession, he made a trip down the lakes to Quebec, and there prepared and forwarded to the French Minister, Count de Pontchartrain, a petition setting forth his military and other service to his king and country, and praying that a new command might be assigned to him. The truth of Tonty's statements was certified to by the then aged

Count Frontenac, who had been reinstated in the governorship of Canada in 1689, and who remained in office until his death at Quebec. In answer apparently to this petition, the proprietorship of Fort St. Louis of the Illinois was granted to Tonty, conjointly with La Forrest, another former lieutenant of La Salle. Here they carried on for some years a limited trade in furs with the Indians. In 1696 a royal decree was issued against the *coureurs des bois*, who had long been a source of disquietude to the Canadian government; but an express provision was made in the decree in favor of Messrs. Tonty and Forrest, who were empowered to send up the country, annually, two canoes laden with goods, with twelve men, for the maintenance of the fort. Again, in 1702, a provincial order was made to the effect that La Forrest should henceforth reside in Canada, and Tonty on the Mississippi, and the establishment on the Illinois was discontinued. Some two years prior to this, however, as the sequel will more fully disclose, Tonty joined D'Iberville's colony in Lower Louisiana. He thus finally passed from the country of the Illinois, where he had been a conspicuous and honorable figure for twenty years, and had achieved for himself a name which will outlast the effacing fingers of time.

The decline of Fort St. Louis was partly due to the dispersion of the surrounding native tribes, but chiefly, perhaps, to a change in the main route of French travel and transit from the great lakes to the Mississippi; the *voyageurs* and fur-traders having found the portage shorter and less difficult by way of the Fox and Wisconsin Rivers, than the Illinois. In 1718, the fort was temporarily reoccupied by some French traders, but, three years later, it was again deserted; and when Charlevoix passed by the Rock in 1721, he saw only the remains of its palisade and rude buildings.

The founding of Kaskaskia has been variously ascribed to members of La Salle's party, on returning from their exploring expedition to the mouth of the Mississippi in 1682; to Father Jacques Gravier about 1685; to Henri de Tonty in 1686, and to others still, explorers or missionaries, at different dates, in the last quarter of the seventeenth century. But the Kaskaskia of our time is not so old as was formerly supposed.

The original site of this Indian settlement has been identified with that of the tribe of the same name, first found on the banks of the Illinois River, at or near the wide bottom lying immediately to the south of the modern town of Utica, in La Salle county. It will be remembered that when Father Marquette and his companions returned from their voyage of discovery down the Mississippi (in 1673), they stopped at a village of the Kaskaskias,* on the Upper Illinois, which then comprised seventy-four lodges. Being very hospitably entertained by the villagers, the good priest, at their request, returned thither in April, 1675, and began a mission among them called "The Immaculate Conception of the Blessed Virgin." After the departure and death of Marquette, as already related, Father Claude Allouez was appointed to succeed him by the superior general of the Jesuits at Quebec.

Father Allouez came to America from Toulouse, France, in July, 1658, and had been actively and zealously employed, with other priests, in planting Jesuit missions among the Indians of the upper lake region. Having established the mission on Green Bay, in 1669, he was assigned to its charge, including the neighboring tribes. During October, 1676, he set out from that station, with a few French attendants, on a voyage to his new mission at the Illinois, and on the way skirted the western and southern shores of Lake Michigan. In his narrative of this roundabout voyage (printed in Shea's "Discovery and Exploration of the Mississippi"), the Father says:

"In spite of all our efforts to hasten on, it was the 27th of April (1677), before I could reach Kachkachkia, a large Illinois town. I immediately entered the cabin where Father Marquette had lodged, and the sachems, with

---

* On Thevenot's reproduction of Father Marquette's map, the name of this tribe is printed *Cachouachouia*, but on his original map, as preserved at St. Mary's College, Montreal, it is written *Kachkaskia*.

all the people, being assembled, I told them the object of my coming among them, namely, to preach the true, living and immortal God, and his son Jesus Christ. They listened very attentively to my whole discourse, and thanked me for the trouble I took for their salvation.

"I found this village much increased since last year (meaning probably 1675). It was before composed of only one nation, the Kachkachkia. There are now eight; the first having called the others, who dwelt in the neighborhood of the Mississippi. You can (readily) form an idea of the number of Indians who compose this town; they are lodged in three hundred and fifty-one cabins, easily counted. They are mostly ranged on the banks of the river. The place which they have selected for their abode is situate at 40° 42'; it has on one side a prairie of vast extent, and on the other an expanse of marsh, which makes the air unhealthy, and often loaded with mists; this causes much sickness and frequent thunder. They, however, like this post, because from it they can easily discern their enemies."

This description corresponds in the main with that of Father Hennepin,* who says that the village was "situated at forty degrees of latitude, in a somewhat marshy plain, on the right bank of the river," which was "as broad as the Seine before Paris." But some allowance must be made for the old latitude, which was too low, and, with the French explorers, was never more than approximately correct. That this Illinois village stood in the vicinity of bluffs or high ground is evidenced by the remark of Al-

---

* The population of this great village had still further increased in 1680, when Hennepin computed the number of lodges at four hundred and sixty, with several fires to each lodge. The Recollet Father Membre, writing in the same-year, fixes the number of cabins at between four and five hundred, and estimates the entire Indian population at from seven to eight thousand. This large estimate probably included the "Cascaskias," whose village he locates south-west of the "bottom of Lake Dauphin (Michigan), at about latitude 41° north." In Margry's publication (vol. II., pp. 128, 175), as cited by Shea, we are also told that the village of the Kaskaskia proper, was two leagues below the mouth of the Pestegouki, or Fox (of Illinois), and six leagues below the confluence of the Checagou (Des Plaines) and Teakiki, and that both it and the great village were destroyed by the Iroquois.

louez, that, "from it they could easily discern their enemies."

In his journal, just quoted, Father Allouez relates that he relaid the foundation of the Illinois mission by the baptism of thirty-five children, and a sick adult, who soon after died. He further states that on the 3d of May, 1677, the anniversary of the Feast of the Holy Cross, he erected in the village a cross twenty-five feet high, and chanted the *Vexilla* in the presence of " a great number of the Illinois of all tribes." In 1679 he revisited this mission, and remained until the approach of La Salle's expedition of that year, when he withdrew to the north. In 1684 he again repaired to the Illinois, accompanied by M. Durantaye, who then commanded at Mackinac. He was there sick in 1687, when the Cavelier-Joutel party reached Fort St. Louis from Texas, but left shortly after, on hearing that La Salle was still alive. Although chiefly a missionary to the Miamis, Allouez still clung to his Illinois mission, which he probably visited once more in 1689. He died at Fort Miami, in 1690. He is described as the ablest of all the Jesuit Fathers sent to the Illinois. A man of cold yet persevering temper, he seems to have ruled his extensive charge principally by the sheer force of intellect.

The immediate successor of Father Allouez, in the Illinois mission, was Sebastian Rasles,* who embarked in a canoe at Quebec in August, 1691, and completed his lengthened voyage in the spring of 1692. After laboring with the Illinois for a year or more, he was recalled to his original charge among the Abenakis on the Kennebec, in Maine. Here, after long years of laborious service, he was barbarously slain by a party of New England soldiers in August, 1724.

Father Jacques Gravier, who had visited the Illinois mission as early as 1687, received it from Father Rasles. With the permission of Captain de Tonty, he erected a chapel within the palisade of Fort St. Louis, which overlooked the Indian village across the river. His relation of

---

* Otherwise written Sebastien Rasle, or Ralé.

occurrences at the "Mission of the Immaculate Conception" of the Illinois, from March 20, 1693, to February 15, 1694, presents an interesting view of his toils and trials with these Indians. He remained in general charge of the mission until 1697, when he was recalled to his former station at Mackinac. In 1700, he made a canoe voyage, by way of the Illinois and Mississippi, to the French establishment at Biloxi. Remaining there some time, he returned to the Illinois and resumed his labors among the Peorias. Here, in an assault upon him, instigated by the medicine-men of the tribe, he received a serious wound, from the effects of which he subsequently died at the Mobile, about the year 1708.

Father Gravier was among the first of the Jesuit missionaries to investigate the principles of the Illinois language, and to reduce them to grammatical rules. He was an earnest, able, and faithful missionary priest.

Gravier was succeeded in 1697 by the Fathers Julian Binneteau and Jacques (or Francois) Pinet, the latter of whom went to labor among the Tamaroas. Of Binneteau it is recorded by Bancroft, that, having followed the Illinois in one of their annual hunts on the prairies bordering the Mississippi, he was there seized with a mortal fever, "and his bones were left to bleach on the wilderness range of the buffalo." His death occurred in December, 1699.

In 1698, came Gabriel Marest, or Marêt, who, four years before, had accompanied D'Iberville on a voyage to Hudson's Bay, and had chanted *aves* to the benighted Esquimaux on its frozen shores. Father Marest was especially associated with the Kaskaskias, whose language he easily mastered, and in which he compiled a catechism. It was under his immediate guidance, in the year 1700, that the mission to the Kaskaskias was removed from the Illinois River to the Mississippi. The subjoined account of the transfer and migration of the tribe is extracted from an exhaustive article upon the subject by Hon. E. G. Mason, of Chicago, printed in the "Magazine of American History," for March, 1881 (Vol. VI):

"But the evidence," says Mr. Mason, "that this mission remained upon the Illinois River until the year 1700, and that there was no settlement before that time upon the site of the Kaskaskia we now know, appears to be well nigh conclusive. A letter written to the Bishop of Quebec by John Francis Buisson de St. Cosme, a missionary priest, describes the journey of his party from Michillimackinac to the mouth of the Arkansas, by the Illinois and Mississippi Rivers, in the year 1699. They stayed at the house of the Jesuit Fathers at Chicago, and set out from there about November 1st, on what one of their predecessors calls the divine * river, named by the Indians Checagou, and made the portage to the river of the Illinois. Passing the Illinois village before referred to, they learned that most of the Indians had gone to Peoria Lake to hunt. Arriving there, they met the Fathers Pinet and Marest, with their flock, of which St. Cosme gives a good account, and he speaks of their work as the Illinois mission.

"The party journeyed onward under the guidance of La Salle's trusty lieutenant, Tonti. While on the Illinois River, certain Indians attempted to prevent their going to the Mississippi, and intimated that they would be killed if they did so. Tonti replied that he did not fear men; that they had seen him meet the Iroquois, and knew that he could kill men; and the Indians offered no further opposition. They reached the Mississippi the 6th of December, 1699, and the next day reached the village of the Tamarois, who had never seen any 'black gown,' except for a few days, when the Reverend Father Gravier paid them a visit. A week later, they ascended a rock on the right, going down the river, and erected a beautiful cross, which their escort saluted with a volley of musketry, and St. Cosme prayed that God might grant that the cross, which had never been known in those regions, might triumph there. From the context of this letter, it is evident that this ceremony took place not far below the site of the present Kaskaskia, which St. Cosme must have passed to reach this

---

* The term *divine* was applied to the river Des Plaines, which was variously called *Checagou*, *Chekagou*, *Chicagou* and *Chigagou*, by the early explorers.

rock, but he makes no mention of such a village. Furthermore, within fifteen miles or so of Kaskaskia, there is a rocky bluff on the Mississippi side of the river, then known as the Cape of the Five men, or *Cap Cinq Hommes*. This is doubtless a corruption of the name of the good Father St. Cosme, as appears from a map made a little more than one hundred years ago, which gives both names, *Cinq Hommes* and St. Cosme, to this very bluff. It probably is the identical one he ascended, and he could not have spoken of the cross as unknown in those regions, had there been any settlement so near the spot as the Kaskaskia we now know. Tonti, who was the leader of this party, is thought by some to have founded Kaskaskia in 1686. Nobler founder could no town have had than this faithful and fearless soldier, but the facts just narrated make such a theory impossible.

"Again in the early part of the year 1700, a bold voyager, Le Sueur (on his way to the copper mines in the Sioux country), whose journal is in print, pushed up the Mississippi from its mouth, where D'Iberville had just planted the banner of France, and passed the site of Kaskaskia without notice of such a place. He speaks of the village of the Tamarois, where by this time, St. Cosme had taken up his abode on his return from the south.* About July 15th, going northward, Le Sueur arrived at the mouth of the Illinois, and there met three Canadian *voyageurs* coming to join his party, and received by them a letter from the Jesuit Marest,

---

* It is doubtful if Father St. Cosme ever returned from the South as above stated, unless for a brief season. He was born in France about the year 1658, and ordained a Jesuit priest in 1683. We next find him engaged as a missionary in Canada, from whence, in the autumn of 1699, he was sent to establish a mission among the Natchez Indians on the Lower Mississippi. Arrived thither, he soon gained the confidence of the Sun Chief and the esteem of his nation, but did not succeed very well in converting those sun-worshipers to the Roman Catholic faith. In 1707, being obliged to make a journey to Mobile, St. Cosme embarked in a canoe with three other Frenchmen, and while sailing down the river, they were set upon and killed by a band of the Chetimacha Indians. The Natchez, it is said, avenged his death by the slaughter of a great part of the offending tribe.—See Appleton's Encyclo. of Amer. Biog., vol. 5, p. 369.

dated July 10, 1700, at the 'Mission of the Immaculate Conception of the Blessed Virgin at the Illinois.' The letter of St. Cosme and the journal of Le Sueur seem to show clearly enough that down to the middle of the year 1700, the present Kaskaskia had not been settled, and that the mission was still on the Illinois River.

"And, lastly, we have the journal of the voyage of Father James Gravier, in 1700,* from the country of the Illinois to the mouth of the Mississippi; from which we learn that he returned from Michilimackinac, and set out from Chicago on the 8th of September, 1700. He says he arrived too late at the Illinois, of whom Father Marest had charge, to prevent the transmigration of the village of the Kaskaskias, which was too precipitately made, on vague news of the establishment on the Mississippi, evidently referring to the landing of D'Iberville the year before. He did not believe that the Kaskaskias, whom Marest accompanied, would have separated from the Peorias and other Illinois, had he arrived sooner, and he obtained a promise from the Peorias to await his return from the Mississippi. After having marched four days with the Kaskaskias, Gravier went forward with Marest, whom he left sick at the Tamarois village, and departed from there October 9, 1700, to go to the lower part of the Mississippi, accompanied only by some Frenchmen. The Indians, with Marest, we may presume, halted between the Kaskaskia and Mississippi Rivers, where we soon after find them; and thus doubtless was accomplished the transfer of the mission to its final location. The eagerness of the Illinois tribes to be in closer communication with the French was probably intensified by their desire to escape any further assaults from their dreaded enemies, and to rear their wigwams where they would never hear the war-cry of the Iroquois. Both motives would operate more powerfully with the Kaskaskias than with any others, because they had been longer

---

* *Relation, ou Journal du Voyage du R. P. Jacques Gravier, de la Compagnie de Jésus, en* 1700, *depuis le pays de Illinois jusqu' a L' embouchure des Mississippi,* p. 68. Cramoisy Series of *Relations,* N. Y., 1859.

under the influence of the French, and because, in their old location, they were the first to receive the onslaughts of the relentless foemen of the Illinois. Hence they set out to go to the Lower Mississippi, but Gravier's influence, and perhaps Marest's illness as well, led them to pause at the first suitable resting-place. And when we consider that, a few years later, this same Marest, who accompanied these Indians on their migration, was stationed at the present Kaskaskia, in charge of the Mission of the Immaculate Conception, as appears from his letters; that he died and was buried there, as is shown by the parish records, and that we hear nothing further of a mission of this name on the Illinois River, we may reasonably conclude that the Kaskaskia of our time should date its origin from the fall of the year 1700, and should honor James Gravier and Gabriel Marest as its founders."

Shortly after the transfer of the mission had been effected, the site of the new settlement was fixed on the right bank of the Kaskaskia or Okaw River, six miles above its confluence with the Mississippi, and nearly two miles east of the latter river. It is not improbable that an Indian settlement had previously existed here, though this is a matter of conjecture. The village was christened by the missionaries "*Le Village d' Immaculée Conception de Cascasquias;*" but no regularity of design was observed by its founders, nor was any attempt made to profit by the natural advantages of its position.

At that pristine period, the scenery about Kaskaskia was well calculated to attract and please the eye of such of the French missionaries as had a taste for the beautiful in nature. " The velvet verdure of the plain, the glassy surface of the idle river, the lofty hill* (on the east), with its stately forest, the air scented with the fragrance of its wild flowers, the little springs gushing from its side in sparkling beauty, all reposing in the sleep of nature, with their virgin

---

* The river at Kaskaskia was three hundred and fifty feet wide, and the bluffs opposite the town rise to the height of about two hundred feet.

freshness upon them,—there was a landscape to charm her most capricious lover." *

For the first few years of her existence, Kaskaskia is little noticed in contemporaneous records, except as a mission station. The early history of the place is mostly drawn from the parish records, and the letters and journals of the missionary priests. Some of these records are in the custody of the priest of the parish, and others are in the keeping of the bishop of the diocese. The oldest record of the church at Kaskaskia is the "Register of Baptisms of the Mission of the Illinois, of the title of the Immaculate Conception of the Blessed Virgin." The first entry in it, according to Breese, bears date March 20, 1695. Retaining the French spelling of the names, it reads as follows:

"In the year 1695, March 20th, I, Jacques Gravier, of the Society of Jesus, baptized Pierre Aco, newly-born of P. Michael Aco. Godfather was De Hautchy, godmother Maria Aramipinchicoue; Maria Joanna, grandmother of the child."†

This entry is claimed to be a copy of the original record, which was made before the removal of the mission from the Upper Illinois River. The register was continued until June 1719, when the mission of Kaskaskia was changed into a parish. A new baptismal register was then opened, which bears this French title: "*Registre des Baptems faits dans L'Eglisse de la Mission et Paroisse de la Conception de Notre Dame, commence le* 18 *Juin*, 1719."

Marriage and burial registers were likewise kept from quite an early date, and were continued down, with varying regularity, until toward the middle of the present century. On these venerable records appear the signatures of many men of note and influence in the early French history of Illinois.

In 1707, Father Marest was joined at Kaskaskia by

---

* Breese's Early Hist. of Ill., p. 153.

† It is affirmed that Michael Aco's wife was the daughter of a Kaskaskia chief, and that he was the identical Ako, or Accault, who accompanied Friar Hennepin in his voyage of exploration up the Mississippi in 1680.

Father Jean Mermet, who had previously attempted a mission among the Mascoutins and others on the Lower Ohio, and had also labored at the great village of the Illinois. Mr. Bancroft, in the third volume of his History of the United States, gives us the following distinct picture of Father Mermet's labors and success at Kaskaskia:

"The gentle virtues and fervid eloquence of Mermet made him the soul of the mission of Kaskaskia. At early dawn his pupils came to church, dressed neatly and modestly, each in a deerskin, or a robe sewn together from several skins. After receiving lessons, they chanted canticles; mass was then said in presence of all the Christians, the French, and the converts, the women on the one side and the men on the other. From prayers and instructions, the missionaries proceeded to visit the sick and administer medicine, and their skill as physicians did more than all the rest to win confidence. In the afternoon the catechism was taught in the presence of the young and the old, when every one, without distinction of rank or age, answered the questions of the missionary. At evening all would assemble at the chapel for instruction, for prayer, and to chant the hymns of the church. On Sundays and festivals, even after vespers, a homily was pronounced; at the close of the day parties would meet in houses to recite the chaplets in alternate choirs, and sing psalms until late at night. These psalms were often homilies, with words set to familiar tunes. Saturday and Sunday were the days appointed for confession and communion, and every convert confessed once in a fortnight."*

This description by Bancroft is chiefly drawn from a narrative letter written by Father Marest to Father Germon, dated November 9, 1712, and published in the *Lettres Edifiantes*, at Paris. In the course of that letter, Marest remarks: "The Illinois are much less barbarous than the other Indians. Christianity and their intercourse with the French have somewhat civilized them. . . . It would be difficult to

---

*Father Mermet continued to labor at the Kaskaskia mission until his death in 1718.

say what is their religion. It consists entirely in some superstitions with which their credulity is amused."

These missionary priests were truly a heroic and self-devoted class of men. Of their hard and trying manner of life, the same father gives us some glimpses in his printed correspondence. On Good Friday, in the year 1711, he set out on a trip across the country to the Peorias, who wanted a new mission opened among them. Concerning this journey on foot through the wilderness, he thus vividly writes:

"I departed, having nothing about me but my crucifix and breviary, and being accompanied by only two savages, who might abandon me from levity, or might fly through fear of enemies. The terror of these vast, uninhabited regions, in which for twelve days not a single soul was seen, almost took away my courage. This was a journey wherein there was no village, no bridge, no ferry-boat, no house, no beaten path, and over boundless prairies, intersected by rivulets and rivers, through forests and thickets filled with briars and thorns, through marshes in which we sometimes plunged to the girdle. At night repose was sought on the grass or leaves, exposed to the winds and rains, happy if by the side of some rivulet, whose waters might quench our thirst. Meals were prepared from such game as might be killed on the way, or by roasting ears of corn."

Father Marest was longer in missionary service with the Illinois Indians than any of his predecessors. He died, it is said, near Peoria, September 17, 1715.

It has been a mooted question among Illinois antiquarians as to which is the more ancient of the two villages, Kaskaskia or Cahokia. Pittman, in his account of the French Settlements, says that Cahokia "was the first settlement on the Mississippi;" and in the "Annals of the West" it is stated that "Cahokia appears to have been a trading post and missionary station earlier than Kaskaskia." These statements are supported by the weight of probability, though the difference in age between the two can hardly exceed one year. According to Breese's History, the Jesuit Fathers Pinet and Binneteau established the mission at

Founding of Cahokia. 207

Cahokia, and christened the little community which grew up around it by the name of *St. Famille de Caoquias*. It is doubtful, however, if Father Binneteau ever labored at this mission.

"The credit of establishing the mission of Cahokia, at first called Tamaroa, belongs to Rev. Jacques Pinet, but at what date has been a matter of dispute. Up to the time of St. Cosme's visit to the Tamaroas in 1699, it appears that no 'black gown' had been seen there, except Father Gravier for a few days. The following year, however, when Le Sueur had reached this village (where he remained seventeen days), he found three French missionaries, viz.: Rev. J. Bergier, and Fathers Pinet and Joseph de Limoges, and also a number of Canadian traders, who were purchasing furs and skins. In October of the same year (1700), Father Gravier mentions the fact in his journal that, on his way down the Mississippi, he stopped at the village of the Tamaroas, and found Father Pinet there, 'peaceably discharging the functions of a missionary, and Rev. M. Bergier, also,' who had care only of the French. Father Bergier remained at Cahokia until his death, July 16, 1710." *

Father Pinet met with unusual success in his mission at Cahokia, and soon found his chapel too small to accommodate the crowds that resorted thither to the mass. The Indians under his spiritual charge were the Tamaroas and Cahokias, the latter being an allied tribe or branch of the former. The imposing rites of the Roman Church were well calculated to awe the senses of these ignorant and superstitious savages, but the religious impressions made upon their minds were feeble and transient, and when away from the influence and guidance of the priests, they were prone to relapse into the excesses of barbarism.

When the village of Cahokia was originally established (say in 1699), it stood upon the immediate bank of the Mississippi; but in the course of a few years the river

---

* "Illinois, Historical and Statistical." By John Moses, Chicago, 1889, Vol. I., p. 85.

shifted its bed to the west, so as to leave the village some distance inland. It long remained a place of considerable importance for trade, though there was never any thing attractive in its situation or environs. At present it is a straggling, decayed, and antiquated little village, seated on a sandy ridge in the American Bottom, opposite Carondolet, and about one mile east from the Mississippi River.

Besides Kaskaskia and Cahokia, other French villages afterward sprang up in that vicinity, which will be noticed hereafter. Other and branch missions were also established among the Illinois Indians by the zeal and enterprise of the Jesuit clergy; who, prior to the introduction of any form of civil government in the country, officiated in the double capacity of spiritual directors and temporal rulers of the people.

Although anticipating somewhat the chronological order of events in our history, we make space here for the following extracts from Father Charlevoix' interesting and instructive description of the Illinois country, through which he traveled with an armed escort in the autumn of 1721. Of Peoria, then still an Indian village, he says:

"The two following days, we traveled a charming country; and the 3d of October, about noon, we found ourselves at the entrance of Lake Pimiteouy. It is the river which grows wider here, and which for three leagues is one league in breadth. At the end of these three leagues, we find on the right a second village of the Illinois, distant about fifteen leagues from that at the Rock.* Nothing can be more pleasant than the situation; it has over against it, as in perspective, a very fine forest, which was then of all colors, and behind it a plain of immense extent, bordered with woods. The lake and the river swarm with fish, and their sides with wild fowl. I met also in this village four French-Canadians, who informed me that I was between four parties of enemies, and that it was unsafe for me either to go forward or return."

---

* By the course of the river, the distance was nearer thirty than fifteen leagues.

Accompanied by two of the Canadians from Peoria as guides, Charlevoix and party resumed their journey, and next stopped at Cahokia, concerning which village, and the missionaries stationed there, he thus writes:

"The same day (10th of October), we went to lay in a village of the Caoquias and Tamarouas. These are two nations of the Illinois which are united, and who do not together make a very numerous village. It is situated on a little river which comes from the east, and which has no water but in the spring season; so that we were forced to walk a good half league to the cabins. I was surprised that they had chosen such an inconvenient situation, as they might have found a much better; but they told me that the Mississippi washed the foot of the village when it was built, and that in three years it (the river) had lost half a league of ground, and that they were thinking of looking out for another settlement. I passed the night in the house of the missionaries, who are two ecclesiastics of the Seminary of Quebec, formerly my disciples, but who might now be my masters. The oldest of the two (Dominique A. Thaumer) was absent. I found the youngest (Francois le Mercier) such as he has been reported to me, severe to himself, full of charity for others, and making virtue amiable in his own person But he has so little health, that I think he can not long support the way of life which they are obliged to lead in these missions."

Of Kaskaskia and its environs, the same traveler writes : "I arrived next day (the 12th) at the Kaskasquias, at nine in the morning. The Jesuits had here a very flourishing mission, which has lately been divided into two, because it was thought proper to form two villages of savages instead of one. The most populous is on the side of the Mississippi; two Jesuits* have the government of it in spiritual affairs. Half a league lower is Fort Chartres, about a musket-shot from the river. M. Duquet de Boisbriant, a Canadian gentleman, commands here for the Com-

---
* Fathers Boulanger and Kereben.

pany, to which the place belongs; and all the space between the two places begins to be peopled by the French. Four leagues further, and two leagues from the river, there is a large village of French, who are almost all Canadians, and have a Jesuit for their priest. The second village of the Illinois is two leagues distant from it and farther up the country, and is under the charge of a priest.

"The French here are pretty much at their ease. A Fleming, who was a servant of the Jesuits, has taught them how to sow wheat, and it thrives very well. They have some horned cattle and fowls. The Illinois cultivate the lands after their fashion, and are very laborious. They likewise breed poultry, which they sell to the French. Their women are sufficiently dexterous; they spin the buffalo's wool, and make it as fine as that of the English sheep. Sometimes one would even take it for silk. They make stuffs of it, which they dye black, yellow and dark red; they make gowns of it, which they sew with thread made of the sinews of the roebuck. They expose these to the sun for three days, and when dry beat them, and without difficulty draw out threads of great fineness.

"All this country is open. It consists of vast meadows (prairies) which extend for twenty-five leagues, and are separated by little groves that are all of good wood."

Remaining at Kaskaskia for a month, Charlevoix resumed his way down the Mississippi, and reached the confluence of the Ohio about the 15th of November, 1721. With regard to this river (then still called the Ouabache), and the advantage of having a settlement at its mouth, his journal says:

"Immediately after this reach, we passed on the left by the fine river Ouabache, by which one can go quite up to the Iroquois, when the waters are high. Its entrance into the Mississippi is a little less than a quarter of a league wide. There is no place in Louisiana more fit, in my opinion, for a settlement than this, nor where it is of more consequence to have one."*

---

* *Vide* "An Historical Journal of Travels in North America, under-

taken by order of the King of France." By Father Charlevoix (English Translation, London, 1763), pp. 284-291, and 303.

Pierre Francois Xavier de Charlevoix, an eminent Jesuit scholar, historian, and traveler, was born at St. Quentin, in the North of France, October 29, 1682. At the age of sixteen he entered the Society of Jesus, and while still a student of divinity was sent to Canada in 1705. During the succeeding four years he taught in the Jesuit College at Quebec, and afterward returned to France, where he was made a professor of *belles-lettres* in one of the Jesuit universities. In 1720 he again came to Canada, and during the next year ascended the river St. Lawrence, and the great lakes to the head of Lake Michigan, from whence he entered and traversed the Illinois country. Descending the Mississippi to New Orleans, he thence visited the French establishments at Biloxi and on the Mobile, and afterward sailed via St. Domingo to France, whither he arrived (1722) after an absence of two years.

Charlevoix was author of several learned and valuable works. He first published a history of the Catholic Missions in Japan, which was followed by a history of Saint Domingo; and in 1744 his *Histoire de Nouvelle France*, which had been withheld for nearly twenty years, appeared in three large volumes. Although quoted and praised by scholars, no translation of it was made from the French until somewhat recently, when an edition in English, with copious notes, was published by Dr. John G. Shea (N. Y., 1865-72), in six volumes.

About the year 1744, Charlevoix also published his Journal of Travels in North America, in the form of letters addressed to the Duchesse de Lesdiguiere. It is averred that, from this work the British Ministry first gained a correct notion of Canada and its dependencies, and of the great advantages to be derived from the possession of that country. The last literary performance of our author was his History of Paraguay, which contains a full account of the operations of the Jesuits in that southern quarter of the globe.

Charlevoix died in La Flêche, France, on February 1, 1761, at a green old age.

CHAPTER XI.

1698–1711.

PERMANENT SETTLEMENT OF LOWER LOUISIANA.

By the treaty concluded at Ryswick, in 1697, Louis XIV. relinquished nearly all of his European conquests, and recognized the Prince of Orange as King of England, Temporary tranquillity being thus restored in Western Europe, Louis had some leisure to devote to his American possessions, and to the renewal of his former endeavor to establish a colony at or near the embouchure of the Mississippi River. This monarch was obviously ambitious to enhance the glories of his reign by creating for France a colonial dominion on the sunny shores of the Gulf of Mexico, which might rival the flourishing English settlements on the Atlantic coast. Accordingly, in the beginning of the year 1698, he gave orders for the fitting out of a suitable expedition to colonize Louisiana. The command of this royal enterprise was entrusted to Captain d'Iberville, a distinguished young naval officer, whose energy, tact, administrative ability, and varied experience peculiarly qualified him for so arduous and important an undertaking.

Pierre le Moyne,* Sieur d'Iberville, was a native of Canada, having been born in Montreal, July 16, 1661. He was, it is said, the third son of Charles le Moyne, himself a gallant soldier, and was one of eleven brothers, seven of whom died naval officers. When but a boy of fourteen, Pierre entered the French navy as a midshipman, and by meritorious service rose rapidly in his profession. In 1692 he became captain of a frigate, and, ten years later, captain of a line-of-battle-ship. During this period of active

---

* By some authors, this family name is written *Lemoine*.

service, he acquitted himself not only as a brave and skillful naval officer, but as an efficient agent of the French government in settling colonies in Acadia and Cape Breton Island. In 1697 he made a cruise with his ship, the Pelican, into the misty and frigid waters of Hudson's Bay, where he engaged and sunk an English man-of-war, captured her two consorts, and reduced Fort Nelson, or Fort Bourbon, as it was called by the French. Returning to France from this brilliant cruise, he sought and obtained command of the new colonizing expedition to the Mississippi.

On the 24th of September, 1698, Captain d'Iberville set sail from Rochelle upon his distant and uncertain enterprise, taking with him M. de Sauvolle,* and his young brother, Bienville. His squadron consisted of two frigates, the Badine and Marin, of thirty guns each (the former was commanded by himself, and the latter by the Comte de Surgéres) and two smaller ships, bearing a company of marines and about two hundred colonists. A majority of the latter were ex-soldiers, who had served in the armies of France, some of whom were accompanied by their wives and children. The other colonists were made up of artisans, laborers, and needy adventurers. They were all supplied with the necessary clothing, provisions and implements for beginning a settlement in the remote solitudes of Louisiana. Stopping at Brest to complete his outfit, the commander sailed from that port on the 24th of October, shaping his general course to the south-west. After an auspicious passage, he dropped anchor in the haven of Cape Francois, now Cape Haytien, St. Domingo, late in the following December.

On arriving thither, his fleet was joined by the war ship Le Francois, of fifty guns, commanded by the Marquis de Chateaumorant, who had received orders to escort the expedition to its destination. Being thus reinforced,

---

*It is doubtful if Sauvolle belonged to the Le Moyne family of brothers, though Mr. Gayarre treats him as a full brother, and tells us that he inherited a fortune from his godfather.

D'Iberville again put to sea on the 1st of January, 1699, taking the route via Cape San Antonio, at the western end of Cuba. Having doubled that cape on the 15th of January, he steered northward over the Mexican Gulf, and reached the southern shore of Florida on the 24th. Anchoring his ships securely off the Island of Santa Rosa, he then proceeded to reconnoiter the Bay of Pensacola (called by the Spaniards Santa Maria de Galva), where he found two Spanish war vessels, and a small fort and garrison. Upon sending in a boat with two officers, the Spanish commander received them politely, but refused the French permission to enter with their vessels. The Spaniards had long been in possession of East Florida, but it was not until they had learned that a French armament was fitting out for the western coast of the peninsula, that they made haste to establish this military post on Pensacola Bay. The new erection, therefore, was an obvious indication of their intention to anticipate, and, if possible, frustrate the designs of the French in these waters.

Leaving Pensacola Bay and standing along the low coast to the west, D'Iberville, on the 31st of the month, cast anchor off Dauphin Island, lying on the west and near the entrance of Mobile Bay. This Island was first named by the French *Isle de Massacre*, from the circumstance that on its level surface was found a mound composed of earth and the bones of long dead Indians, who had fallen there in combat with their enemies. Sailing still farther westward, the French commander next discovered a group of small islands, to which was given the name of *Isles des Chandeleur*. Anchoring his frigates near them, he went to examine the channel between Cat Island and Ship Island, and, having landed his colonists on the latter, he caused temporary huts to be erected there for their shelter from the weather. The Marquis de Chateaumorant, having now fulfilled his mission, and finding the waters on this coast too shallow to remain long in safety with his large frigate, sailed away on his return to St. Domingo.

About the 11th of February, Iberville sent his brother Bienville, with a felucca and canoe, to the mainland, which lay about four leagues to the north of his anchorage. Having entered a little bay, the exploring party discovered several piroques filled with half-naked savages, who fled with consternation at the approach of the Frenchmen. On the next day, however, the latter contrived to intercept a woman of the Indians, by whom they were enabled to open an intercourse with her tribe, which was the Bilocci, or Biloxi—a name given by the French to the bay itself. On the evening of the same day there arrived at this bay a war party of some eighty Bayagoulas, so called, who were then at war with the Indians on the Mobile. From the former it was learned, by the language of signs (for there was no interpreter,) that they dwelt off to the south-west, on the shores of a large and deep river, called by them the *Malabouchia*. Having ascertained by further inquiry among the natives the probable distance and course of the unknown river, Iberville prepared to go in quest of it.

Accordingly, on the 27th of February, he set off from Isle de Vaisseau (Ship Island) with two shallops, carrying twenty-four men each—one of which was commanded by Bienville—and took with him as a guide Father Anastase Douay, who had been a companion of La Salle in his last Mississippi expedition. Sailing cautiously southward along the low and marshy coast, at the end of three days the voyagers happily discovered the outlet of the "hidden river," which it was believed no European vessel had as yet penetrated from the sea. On the 2d of March they entered one of its principal passes, which Father Anastase* thought he recognized as the Mississippi, from its turbid and seething waters. On the 3d they began to ascend the river, and, after seven days of sailing and rowing, had attained a dis-

---

* Father Douay, as Hennepin informs us, was a native of Quesnoy in Hainault, and, subsequent to his return from America in 1688, had been appointed vicar of the Recollet convent at Cambray. Remaining there until summoned to join D'Iberville's colonizing expedition, he probably returned with the latter to France in 1699, since we find no further mention of him in Louisiana. We were pleased to have met with Pére Anastase once more; and now that he disappears from the historic page, we can only say, hail! and farewell.

tance of forty leagues from the Gulf. Here our explorers
came upon three pirogues filled with naked savages, who
hastily fled at their advance. One of the natives, however,
was overtaken in his flight, and by making him some trifling
presents, which gained his good will, he was induced to
bring back his companions. They belonged to the tribe
of the Bayagoulas, and readily undertook to conduct the
Frenchmen to their village, further up the river, which was
reached on the 14th of March. It was found to contain
between four and five hundred inhabitants, and mustered
about one hundred warriors. Among the villagers were
found stuffs of European fabric, said to have been given
them by La Salle or Tonty. The chiefs of the Bayagoulas
received their French visitors in a very civil manner, and
gave to them, among other things, a few domestic fowls,
which they claimed to have reared from some they had obtained from nations to the west of the Mississippi, near
the seashore. Such fowls were not uncommon among the
southern Indians at this time, though it seems that they
were kept more as pets than for use as an article of food.
They were doubtless originally brought to the country by
the Spaniards.

M. d'Iberville was still in doubt whether the river he
was ascending was the Mississippi or not; for he had not
as yet seen or heard of the Tangibaos, of whom La Salle
had made mention. Upon inquiry, however, it was ascertained that this small tribe had been destroyed by another
called the Mongoulachas, or Bayagoulas, the Quinipissas of
La Salle and Tonty. Soon afterward, Bienville found in
the possession of one of these natives a letter which Tonty
had penned to La Salle, and left in the keeping of a chief
of the Quinipissas tribe, on the occasion of his trip to the
Gulf in the spring of 1686.* This opportune discovery

---

*This letter of Tonty's, to which we have previously alluded, or so much of it as was published, reads as follows:

"VILLAGE OF THE QUINIPISSAS, *April* 20, 1685 (1686).

"*Sir:* Having found the posts on which you had set up the King's arms thrown down by driftwood, I have planted another further in, about seven leagues from the sea, where I left a letter in a tree be-

dissipated all doubts in the minds of Iberville and his associates as to what river they were navigating, and inspired them with fresh confidence to continue their upward voyage. Among the Indians of this delta region, they also found part of an old suit of Spanish armor, which was supposed to have belonged to De Soto's army.

On the 18th, still cautiously ascending, our voyagers passed on their right the Baton Rouge, the first high bank* they had seen since entering the river. Here was established the northern limit of the hunting grounds of the Bayagoulas. Some distance above that they came to a point where the river made a long détour or circuit, and, to save time, the commander caused the trees to be felled, and transported his boats to the opposite side of the peninsula. The Mississippi afterward cut itself a channel through this point, which has ever since been known as "*Point Coupée.*" On the 20th the explorers arrived at a large village of the Oumas, containing over three hundred braves, who welcomed them with music and dances, and acquainted them with the Indian ceremony of smoking the calumet of peace. At this village they saw many domestic fowls, which were mostly kept for ornamental purposes.

Here the Sieur d'Iberville, learning that there was a river or bayou to the eastward, which he could reach by a short portage, and down which he might descend through lakes to the sea, left the Mississippi, with two canoes and a guide, sending Bienville down the main river with the large boats, under instructions to meet him at the Isle de

side. . . . All the nations have sung the calumet to me; they fear us excessively since you defeated this village. I conclude by saying, that it is a great disappointment to me that we should return without the good fortune of meeting you, after two canoes have coasted toward Mexico for thirty leagues, and toward Florida for twenty-five, etc." See Charlevoix' New France, V., p. 123.

* On this bluff, twenty-five feet above high water, and one hundred and twenty-nine miles by the river above New Orleans, the French subsequently established a fortlet and village (now city), which received the name of *Baton Rouge*, or Red Post. This name, according to Le Page du Pratz's early History of Louisiana, is derived from the large cypress trees that formerly grew there, the wood of which is red.

Vaisseau. Proceeding on his return course, Bienville reached the island, without accident, about the first of April. Here he was met by Iberville, who had arrived before him, having come down through the bayou Manshac or Iberville, and the two connecting lakes or arms of the Gulf, which he severally named Maurepas and Pontchartrain.

On the 12th of April, M. d'Iberville went to examine a small bay, lying several leagues north of Isle de Vaisseau, to which he gave the name of St. Louis. Pleased with the situation and appearance of this bay, he would have removed his colony thither forthwith, but for the fact that the water at its entrance was too shallow for his vessels of heavy draft. Finally, he decided to locate his establishment on the eastern side of the mouth of Biloxi Bay, a northern arm of Mississippi Sound. The spot thus chosen was tolerably healthy, yet sandy and unproductive in the extreme. Its sterility, however, was not particularly objected to by the colonists, who thought nothing about agriculture, but only of trading with the Indians, and scouring the country for its supposed mineral wealth.

In his official report, D'Iberville thus describes the first settlement ever made by white men upon the soil of what is now the State of Mississippi:

"After having visited several places well adapted for forming settlements, our provisions falling short, we thought best to commence operations at the Bay of Biloxi, four leagues north-west of the place where the ships were anchored, and which could be approached at a distance of two leagues. We made choice of this place merely on account of the road, where the small vessels can go and come at all times, and where we could assist, without fear, with a portion of the crew, in building the fort which I ordered to be constructed there; whilst, in the meantime, the place most convenient for the colony can be selected at leisure.

"This fort is built of wood, with four bastions; two are made of hewn timber placed together, one foot and a half thick, and nine feet high; the other two of double palisades. It is mounted with fifty-four pieces of cannon,* with a plentiful supply of ammunition." He left M. de Sauvolle in command; DeBienville, as king's lieutenant; LeVasseur, major; DeBordenac, chaplain; M. Caré, surgeon; two captains, two cannoniers, four sailors, eighteen filibusters, thirteen Canadians, ten mechanics, six masons, and thirty sub-officers and soldiers (ninety in all).

M. d'Iberville named this fort for Count Maurepas, who was then Secretary of Foreign Affairs. After causing a group of log huts to be built around the fort for the use of the colonists, and having them to plant a quantity of beans and Indian corn, he distributed provisions for four or five months, and, on the 3d of May, re-embarked for France. Sailing through the old Bahama Channel, and touching at St. Domingo, he arrived in safety at the port of Rochefort on July 2, 1699.†

On the 22d of May, after the departure of Capt. d' Iberville, Lieutenant Bienville set out with a small party on an excursion into the interior of the country. During the course of this trip, he was informed that a band of two hundred Chickasaws, headed by two white men (supposed to be Englishman from the colony in Carolina), had fallen upon and destroyed a village of the Colapissas, situated on the northern shore of Lake Pontchartrain. He, however, met with no enemy. Returning to Fort Biloxi, he again set off, on the 9th of June, with two canoes, to explore the coast on the east. Having passed the mouth of Pascagoula River and Mobile Point, he approached so near to Fort Pensacola that he perceived it was still occupied by the Spaniards.

About the first of July the colonists at Biloxi Bay were cheered by the unexpected arrival of two bark canoes, carrying several Canadians and two Jesuit priests, Father Anthony Davion and Father Montigny. They came

---

*This is manifestly an error or misprint. The real number of cannon mounted upon the fort, as stated by Bancroft, Gayarré and other historians, was twelve.

†See M. d'Iberville's brief official narrative of this expedition, printed in "Historical Collections of Louisiana and Florida," edited by B. F. French. (New Series, N. Y., 1869), pp. 30-32.

by way of the Illinois and the Mississippi, and having learned from the Oumas that the French were establishing a colony near the Gulf, had come down to see them. After a pleasant visit here of ten days, the two priests departed to begin a mission among the Tonicas on the Mississippi, near the Yazoo.

In September of the same year (1699), while Lieutenant Bienville was descending the Lower Mississippi, and when at a point some twenty-eight leagues from the sea, he discovered in the river an English ship of sixteen guns, commanded by one Captain Barr, who had left a consort in waiting at the mouth. The English captain was not certain that he was actually upon the Mississippi, and Bienville gladly availed himself of the opportunity to assure him that it was not the Mississippi; that the river he sought ran much farther to the west, and that the stream on which he was sailing was within the limits of a country that had been taken possession of in the name of his majesty, the King of France. By this deception the wily Frenchman induced the English mariner to face about and return to the sea; and from this circumstance the place has ever since borne the name of *Détour des Anglais*, or "English Turn."

It is related as a fact, that on board Captain Barr's ship was a Protestant Frenchman, who secretly handed to Bienville a letter addressed to the King of France, in which his majesty was assured that if he would accord liberty of conscience to a Protestant colony in Louisiana, more than four hundred Huguenot families, already inured to exile and hardships, would immigrate hither from the Carolinas. The letter was afterward transmitted to Count Pontchartrain, the French Minister of Colonies, who, with the harshness and bigotry of that age, returned for answer, that his " Christian majesty had not expelled heretics from his kingdom in order to establish them in America."

On the 6th of January, 1700, M. d'Iberville re-appeared in the waters of the Gulf off Fort Biloxi, with two large ships of war—the Renomme rating fifty guns, and the Gironde forty-six—bringing with him sixty Canadian immigrants, and a fresh supply of provisions and stores for the needy colonists. He also brought royal commissions, appointing Sauvolle governor, or commandant of the colony; Bienville lieutenant, and Boisbriant major. By the same vessels arrived Pierre le Sueur and thirty miners, who had been sent by M. de Huillier, of Quebec, to open and work a copper mine which had been discovered on the St. Peter's (now Minnesota) River, one of the affluents of the Upper Mississippi. Le Sueur, moreover, had instructions from the governor of Canada to erect a fort on the St. Peter's, to hold in awe the Sioux or Dakotas. He departed in April on his mission to the far north.*

When the vigilant D'Iberville was informed by his brother Bienville that two English ships had appeared in the mouth of the Mississippi, he determined to forthwith construct a fort on that river, so as to anticipate any future attempt of the English to gain a foot-hold on its shores. Having dispatched Bienville through the lakes and bayous to the Bayagoulas, to procure guides to some suitable spot on the lower part of the river, the commander himself left Isle de Vaisseau, or Ship Island, on the 15th of January, taking with him sixty men, two shallops, and two smaller vessels loaded with the necessary provisions, implements, etc. After entering and ascending the Mississippi about eighteen leagues, he was met by Bienville, and they selected a position secure from inundation, and there begun the construction of a log and earth fort, which received the name of Iberville.

Toward the middle of February, while still engaged upon the fort, M. d'Iberville was joined by the veteran De Tonty, who arrived with a party of twenty Canadians from the Illinois, and who is said to have come in response to an invitation that had been sent him from Sauvolle. Tonty was now past his prime, yet his long and varied experience

---

* "Stoddard, in his Sketches of Louisiana, on the authority of a MS. narrative of La Harpe, says that Le Sueur ascended the St. Peter's River to the mouth of Blue Earth River, where he erected a fort called L'Huillier, which was abandoned the next year on account of the hostility of the Sioux."—Monette's Val. of the Miss., I., p. 206.

with La Salle, and his intimate knowledge of the principal Indian nations of the Mississippi Valley, rendered him a valuable acquisition to the southern colony. Availing himself of Tonty's presence and assistance, D'Iberville decided to ascend the river as far as the Natchez, and establish amicable relations with the natives on the way. Hastily organizing an expedition for this purpose, he set out with Bienville and Tonty, proceeding in boats and canoes. They first stopped at the Bayagoulas, where they remained till the first week in March, when they proceeded to the Oumas.* Continuing their upward voyage, they next reached the Natchez, whose villages lay about three hundred and seventy-five miles from the Gulf, by the windings of the river.

When the great Sun-chief heard of the approach of the French, he came forth from his village to meet them, borne upon a litter, and attended by a large and picturesque procession of his people. This nation, formerly very numerous and powerful, was now reduced to about twelve hundred warriors. The missionary St. Cosme, already referred to, had arrived the year before, and taken up his residence among them. The better class of these Indians appeared to D'Iberville much more civilized than any others he had met with in the country. During his brief stay here, one of their temples was struck and set on fire by lightning. The keepers of the temple thereupon solicited the squaws to throw their infants into the fire, in order to appease the anger of the divinity; and a number of children were thus sacrificed before the Frenchmen could prevail upon them to desist.† Delighted with the beauty of the Natchez country, and especially with the high, bold bluff, which commands an extensive prospect up and down the river, D'Iberville selected it for the future capital of Louisiana, and suggested the name of Rosalie, which was given to the fort afterward built here by the French.

On the 22d of March, Bienville and St. Denis, attended by twenty Canadians and a number of Indians, set off

* The village of the Oumas, or Houmas, was situated two and one-half leagues east of the river.
* Martin's History of Louisiana, vol. I., p. 152.

from the Natchez on a tour of exploration to the westward, which extended to Red River, and occupied them nearly two months. At the same time, D'Iberville, accompanied, perhaps, by De Tonty,* returned to his fort above the outlet of the Mississippi, and thence to the anchorage of his ships at Isle de Vaisseau. Upon his arrival, he was surprised to learn that the Spanish governor of Pensacola had been there with a twenty-four gun ship, manned by one hundred and forty marines, and some armed shallops, intending to drive the French from the coast. But finding his force insufficient for this purpose, he had left a written protest against the French occupation of the country, claiming that it was within the limits of his Catholic majesty's dominions in Mexico. The French, however, had come to stay, and paid little heed to the protest of Spain, whose power and prestige as a nation were on the decline. Having put his colony in as good a state of defense as possible, and given Bienville command of the fort on the Mississippi, M. d'Iberville sailed for France on the 28th of May, 1701.

About the middle of May, and before the sailing of D'Iberville, Bienville returned from his western expedition. He had ascended the Ouachita (Washita) a considerable distance, thence traversed the country westward to Red River, and returned down the latter stream and the Mississippi, having passed through a fertile region and visited several Indian tribes, particularly the Yatasses and Natchitoches. The main object of this expedition was to search for mines of the precious metals, and another was to ascertain the probable distance to the nearest Spanish establishments on the west. On the 22d of July in that year (1701), M. de Sauvolle died, an early victim to bilious fever, leaving the sole direction of affairs in the colony to Lieutenant Bienville.

On the 18th of the ensuing December, D'Iberville

---

* As Tonty still retained some interest in Fort St. Louis of Illinois, it is not improbable that he returned there on business during that year (1700), though we find no reliable record of such a journey.

again appeared in these southern waters with a French armament, consisting of the Renomme, a fifty gun ship, the Palmier, of forty-four guns, and a large brigantine. His arrival was very opportune for the starving colonists, whose number had been diminished by disease and casualties to about one hundred and fifty persons, and who had been driven to such straits as to have subsisted for some time wholly upon maize. Considering the unfavorable condition and prospects of the colony, the commander now ordered the removal of the principal establishment from Biloxi to the Mobile.

Accordingly, in the first week of January, 1702, Bienville set out to execute the orders of his chief, leaving only twenty men as a garrison at Biloxi. The site of the new establishment was fixed on the west side of the Mobile River, about eighteen leagues from the sea. Here a depot was formed and a fort soon built, which received the name of *Fort Louis de la Mobile*. By the 20th of March, the colonists had become settled in their new quarters, to which were transported such of their munitions and stores as had been kept on Dauphin Island. This removal brought the French into somewhat closer relations with the Choctaws, who inhabited the country to the north of Mobile Bay, and who were then at war with the Chickasaws. But M. d'Iberville, before his departure for France, was enabled to effect a truce between those puissant tribes.

On the 24th of June (1702), a Spanish shallop arrived from Pensacola, bringing a letter from Don Francisco Martin, governor of that post, stating that his garrison was in a state of famine, and requesting a supply of provisions, which was sent to him by Bienville. Again, on the 11th of November, Don Martin himself arrived at Fort Louis from Pensacola, with the intelligence that France and Spain were at war with England. He asked for provisions and munitions, and in view of the alliance of the two former powers, his request was granted. In the meantime, on the first of October, Father Davion visited the fort, with two Canadians from the Yazoo River. They were accompanied by Father Limoges, who was stationed among the Natchez, and who informed Bienville that the Coroas Indians had killed his missionary colleague, Foucault, and three other Frenchmen.

On the 28th of November two Spanish officers arrived at the French head-quarters from St. Augustine, Florida, with a letter from the governor of that town, stating that he was besieged by an English force from Charleston, with a fleet of seventeen vessels, and some two thousand savages. In response to the appeal of the Spaniards for aid, M. de Bienville gave them a liberal supply of munitions of war, and also dispatched a force of one hundred men to their assistance. It thus appears that, notwithstanding the jealousies of the rival colonies, situated so near each other, with conflicting territorial claims, the French generously assisted their neighbors on different occasions with both provisions and ammunition. At this period the Spaniards found great difficulty in maintaining their establishments in Florida. This was principally due to the inveterate animosity of the Indians of the country, who were encouraged in their hostilities, and sometimes materially aided, by the English colonists of South Carolina.

In the summer of 1703, M. d'Iberville sent his brother, Anthony le Moyne de Chateaugué, to Louisiana, with seventeen Canadian colonists, who carried with them implements of husbandry, etc. About the 1st of May, 1704, the Pelican, a fifty-gun ship, arrived from France at Dauphin Island, loaded with provisions and military stores for the colony. She brought out two companies of troops to reinforce the garrisons, four priests, two nuns, and twenty poor young women, who were shortly afterward married to the bachelor colonists. This was the first shipment of unmarried women to Louisiana, and was followed by others at intervals.

During the autumn of that year there was much sickness and mortality in the French colony, and the horrors of famine were averted only by relief received from the Spanish governor of Pensacola. On the 27th of October,

15

intelligence was received that the Spanish fort of Pensacola had been destroyed by fire, together with a large quantity of provisions, clothing, and stores; and at the same time a request came that the French would send them a schooner to carry the tidings of their disaster to Vera Cruz. On the 11th of December news came that the English were fitting out an armament at Charleston, to operate against the French establishments at Biloxi and on the Mobile, but this fortunately proved to be incorrect. In January, 1705, a trader named De Lambert arrived at the Mobile from a small French post on the Wabash (probably the Lower Ohio), which he had abandoned in consequence of the hostile disposition of the savages in that interior region. During this year war again broke out between the Choctaws and Chickasaws, which was characterized by more than the usual Indian barbarities. A temporary peace, however, was at length effected through the active mediation of the French under Bienville, though at considerable personal risk to the latter.

On the 9th of July, 1706, Pierre le Moyne, Sieur d'Iberville, died at sea, near St. Domingo, aged forty-five years. He had been previously attacked with yellow fever, and barely escaped with his life. Unable to sustain the enervating influence of a tropical climate, he had retired to France to recuperate his broken health. After a year or more he again sailed to the West Indies, and was there stricken by a severe disease which terminated his earthly existence.* He thus fell a lamented victim to his sense of official duty, and of devotion to the service of his king and country. We have already passed in review the chief incidents in his active and fortunate career, and need only add here a brief estimate of his character. He was a man of great energy and determination of purpose, and, as a naval commander, was quick and judicious to decide, and prompt and bold in the execution of his plans. Less learned, brilliant, and fanciful than La Salle, he was better balanced, more practical, and therefore more

---

* Monette's "Valley of the Mississippi," Vol. I, p. 207.

successful as a colonizer. The idol of his Canadian countrymen, he was justly recognized as one of the ablest captains in the French navy. His premature decease cast a gloom over the infant colony of Louisiana, of which he had been both the persevering founder and constant benefactor. His name is fitly perpetuated in one of the rivers, as well as in a parish, of the Pelican State of Louisiana.

After the death of D'Iberville, contention and trouble arose in the colony. Bienville was charged with sundry acts of misconduct and mismanagement, and was dismissed from office, but his successor dying on the way from France, he still retained the command. In January, 1707, intelligence was brought to the fort on the Mobile that St. Cosme, the Jesuit missionary among the Natchez, and three other Frenchmen, had been slain by the Chetimachas, as they were descending the river to the sea.* Presents were thereupon sent by the French to the surrounding nations, to induce them to wage war upon that treacherous tribe.

In September, 1710, an English corsair, with an armed party, made a descent upon Dauphin Island, and pillaged it of property said to have been worth sixty thousand livres. During the years 1709 and 1710, the Louisiana colonists suffered severely from sickness and famine; and in March, 1709, there was a great flood in the Mobile and other rivers, which inundated the houses of Fort Louis. For this reason the French abandoned the fort, and built another at or near the mouth of Mobile River, where the city now stands.

Such, in imperfect outline, are the principal occurrences in the history of the colony of Lower Louisiana during the first twelve years of it precarious existence. In the French colonial annals of the period, nothing is more astonishing than the number of canoe and boat voyages made by them to every part of the wilderness Valley of the Mississippi. The comparative ease and safety with which these long and difficult journeys were performed indicated great tact

---

*See *note* in the preceding chapter, page 201.

and facility on the part of the French in adapting themselves to the primitive modes of life and locomotion of the aborigines, and in gaining and retaining their good will. What has been remarked by the brilliant historian, Prescott, of the Spanish conquerors of Mexico, may apply with equal pertinence to the French explorers of the Mississippi Valley:

"The mere excitement of exploring the strange and the unknown was a sufficient compensation to the Spanish adventurer for all his toils and trials. It seems to have been ordered by Providence that such a race of men should exist contemporaneously with the discovery of the New World, that those regions should be brought to light which were beset with dangers and difficulties so appalling as might have tended to overawe and discourage the ordinary spirit of adventure." *

Recurring once more to Henri de Tonty, it may now be proper to relate what little is known in regard to his last years, and to sum up his character and career. In 1702 he was sent by Captain d'Iberville on a mission to secure the Chickasaws in the French interest. The route taken by him from Mobile is laid down on some of the old French maps, but of the incidents of his trip, or the measure of success that attended it, we have no knowledge. After this we find no further special mention of his name, save that he died in September, 1704, at Fort Louis on the Mobile.† That was a sickly season with the colony, and marked by more than the ordinary mortality; and it seems probable that no kind friend or priest was with our hero to chronicle the particulars of his last hours, or if so the record thereof has perished. At the time of his singularly quiet exit from the scenes of busy life, Tonty must have been aged about fifty-four. Though not an old man in point of years, he was old in experience and knowledge of the world, and especially

---

* Prescott's "History of the Conquest of Mexico," vol. 3, book vii., chap. iii.

† See Charlevoix' History of New France, vol. III, p. 201, *note* by the editor.

in the number and variety of exciting adventures through which he had passed, as well in Europe as in America.

He could hardly be classed as a great captain or leader, though he was not incapable of devising and executing the boldest enterprises. As a first lieutenant, he rendered invaluable services to La Salle, and next to his chief, contributed most toward the exploration of the Mississippi Valley. His courage and address were strikingly exhibited in his intercourse with the Indians, both in war and in peace; but his acts were mostly performed where there were few to observe, and fewer still to record them. He was "honest, sincere, generous, faithful, and brave"—the *beau ideal* of a true soldier. These admirable qualities endeared him to all his compatriots in life, and have made him a prime favorite with all of La Salle's biographers.

"Very few names in French-American history," writes Parkman, "are mentioned with such unanimity of praise as that of Henri de Tonty. Hennepin finds some fault with him; but his censure is commendation.* The dispatches of the governor, Denonville, speak in strong terms of his services in the Iroquois war, praise his character, and declare that he is fit for any bold enterprise, adding that he deserves reward from the king. The missionary St. Cosme, who traveled under his escort in 1699, says of him: 'He is beloved by all the *voyageurs*. It was with deep regret that we parted from him; he is the man who best knows the country; he is loved and feared everywhere.'" Parkman himself adds: "He seems never to have received the reward his great merit deserved."† La Salle, however, had done what he could for Tonty, and, as already noticed, made him a grant of lands on the Arkansas River.

He had a younger brother named Alphonse de Tonty, a captain in the French service, who long held command at the post of Detroit, and against whom charges of pecu-

---

* When the "Griffin" was building at Niagara, Hennepin says that Tonty took some offense at his keeping a journal, and tried to seize it.

† "Discovery of the Great West," *note*, p. 441.

lation were preferred; but no stain tarnishes the fair escutcheon of the little, copper-handed *Henri*. Around his name more than that of any other of the French explorers, is wreathed a halo of chivalry and romance, and only a few years since, he was made the hero in a popular historical fiction, entitled "The Story of Tonty." He is sometimes referred to as the Chevalier de Tonty, but, though a true knight, it does not appear that he ever received the honor of knighthood. He did not share La Salle's antipathy to the Jesuits, but rather courted their favor, and in return for his considerate attentions, they heralded his praises and helped to embalm his memory.

As early as 1697, a book, purporting to be a Memoir of the Sieur de Tonty, was published in France under this title: "*Dernières Découvertes dans L'Amerique Septentrionale, de M. de la Salle, par Chevalier de Tonti, Gouverneur du Fort St. Louis aux Illinois. Paris, 1697.*"* Copies of the same having found their way to New France, Tonty disavowed to M. d'Iberville and Father Marest all responsibility for the work, which he characterized as full of errors and exaggerations. But then he had written a memoir, and sent it to Paris in 1693, which formed the basis of the above spurious publication.

The real or admitted memoirs of Henri de Tonty are embraced in the valuable collection of Pierre Margry, director of the Archives of the Marine and Colonies at Paris, under this general title: "*Découvertes et Établissements des Francais dans L'Ouest et Sud de L'Amerique Septentrionale* (1614–1754), *Memoirs et Documents originaux*"—Paris, France, 1877–78. Volume I of this publication contains "*Voyages et état des Francais sur les lacs et le Mississippi, sous les ordres de M. de la Salle et de Tonty, du 1678 à 1684.*" Volume II contains "*Lettres of Henri de Tonty sur ce qu' il a appris de M. de la Salle, le voyage qu' il a fait pour l' aller chercher, et son depart prochein pour marcher contre les Iroquois, 1686–1689.*"

---

* An English translation of this memoir, or relation, was printed in London in 1698, entitled an "Account of M. de la Salle's Last Expedition and Discoveries in North America," which was republished in New York in 1814.

Petition of M. de Tonty. 231

Besides the above, Tonty wrote and addressed to Count de Pontchartrain a short memoir of himself (before noticed), which is also printed in Margry's collection, as well as elsewhere. It is without date, but is supposed to have been written in the year 1690 or 1691. Following is an English version of this curious and interesting autobiographical paper:

Petition of the Chevalier de Tonty to Count de Pontchartrain, Minister of Marine.

Monseigneur—Henri de Tonty humbly represents to your highness, that he entered the military service as a cadet, and was employed in that capacity in the years 1668 and 1669, and that he afterward served as midshipman four years at Marseilles and Toulon, and made seven campaigns, that is, four on board ships of war, and three in galleys. While at Messina he was made captain, and in the interval lieutenant, of the first company of a regiment of horse. When the enemy attacked the post of Libisso, his right hand was shot away by a grenade, and he was taken prisoner and conducted to Metasse, where he was detained six months, and then exchanged for the son of the governor of that place. He then went to France to obtain some favor of his majesty, and the king granted him three hundred livres. He returned to the service in Sicily, made the campaign as a volunteer in the galleys, and when the troops were discharged, being unable to obtain the employment he solicited at court on account of the general peace, he decided, in 1678, to join the late Monsieur de la Salle, in order to accompany him in the discoveries of Mexico, during which, until 1682, he was the only officer who did not desert him.

These discoveries being finished, he remained, in 1683, commandant of Fort St. Louis of the Illinois; and in 1684 he was there attacked by two hundred Iroquois, whom he repulsed with great loss on their side. During the same year, he repaired to Quebec, under the orders of M. de la Barre. In 1685, he returned to the Illinois, according to the orders which he had received from the court, and from M. de la Salle, as a captain of foot in a marine detachment and governor of Fort St. Louis. In 1686, he went with forty men in canoes, at his own expense, as far as the Gulf of Mexico, to seek for M. de la Salle. Not being able to find him there, he returned to Montreal, and put himself under the orders of Monsieur Denonville,* to engage in the war with the Iroquois.

At the head of a band of Indians, in 1687, he proceeded two hundred leagues by land, and as far in canoes, and joined the army, when, with these Indians and a company of Canadians, he forced the ambuscade of the Tsonnonthouans.† The campaign being over, he returned

---
* Jacques Réne de Brisay Denonville superseded La Barre, in 1685, as governor of Canada, and served about four years.

† Or Senecas.

to the Illinois, whence he departed, in 1689, to go in search of the remains of M. de la Salle's colony; but being deserted by his men, and unable to execute his design, he was compelled to relinquish it when he had arrived within seven days' march of the Spaniards. Ten months were spent in going and returning. As he now finds himself without employment, he prays that, in consideration of his voyages and heavy expenses, and considering, also, that during his service of seven years as captain, he has not received any pay, your highness will be pleased to obtain for him from his majesty a company, with which he may continue his services in this country, where he has not ceased to harass the Iroquois by enlisting the Illinois against them in his majesty's cause.

And he will continue his prayers for the health of your highness.

HENRI DE TONTY.

Nothing can be more true than the account given by the Sieur de Tonty in this petition; and should his majesty reinstate the seven companies which have been disbanded in this country, there will be justice in granting one of them to him, or some other recompense for the services which he has rendered, and which he is now returning to render at Fort St. Louis of the Illinois. FRONTENAC.

CHAPTER XII.

1712-1717.

LOUISIANA UNDER M. CROZAT—DEMISE OF LOUIS XIV.

Hitherto the small, isolated French settlements in the Illinois, and those founded by D'Iberville and Bienville on the shores of the Gulf of Mexico, had been separate and unorganized dependencies of Canada, or New France. But they were now soon to be united in one large province, under the designation of Louisiana, with a government dependent upon and subordinate to that of New France. This immense wilderness territory extended from Lake Michigan and the Wisconsin river on the north to the Mexican Gulf at the south, and from the Ohio Valley on the east to the base of the Rocky Mountains and New Mexico in the west. It was already known to possess a temperate and salubrious climate, a rich and very productive soil, and to abound in fur-bearing animals; and it was also believed to contain metallic ores of untold value.

In 1711 the government of Louisiana was committed by the French king to a governor, or commandant-general, with other subordinate officers. The chief head-quarters of this colonial government was established, as before, on the Mobile, and a new fort was completed near the site of the present city of Mobile. The Sieur de Muys, who had been commissioned governor, died on the outward passage from France; but M. Diron d'Artaguette, the *commissiaire ordonnateur*, who had arrived in Louisiana in 1708, entered upon his official duties.* This, however, was provisional.

In order to the more speedy and systematic development of the commercial and mineral resources of the

* Bancroft's History, III., p. 343; and Monette's Hist. of Miss. Valley, I., 209.

country, Louis XIV., by letters patent, bearing date at Fontainbleau, September 14, 1712, and registered in the Parliament of Paris on the 24th of September, granted a monopoly of the commerce, and sole direction of the affairs of the new province (for the term of fifteen years) to M. Antoine Crozat, Marquis de Chatel, a man of great wealth, one of his majesty's councillors, and secretary of his household, crown and revenue. This royal patent constituted the first regular charter of government for Louisiana. It is a lengthy and elaborately drawn paper, the introductory portion whereof reads as follows :

"*Louis, by the grace of God, King of France and Navarre,*

" *To all who shall see these present letters, greeting:*

" The care we have always had to procure the welfare and advantage of our subjects, having induced us, notwithstanding the almost continual wars which we have been obliged to support from the beginning of our reign, to seek for all possible opportunities of enlarging and extending the trade of our American colonies; we did, in the year 1683 (1684), give our orders to undertake a discovery of the countries and lands which are situated in the northern part of America, between New France and New Mexico, and the Sieur de la Salle, to whom we committed that enterprise, having had success enough to confirm a belief that a communication might be settled (opened) from New France to the Gulf of Mexico, by means of large rivers, this obliged us immediately after the peace of Ryswick to give orders for the establishing a colony there, and maintaining a garrison which has kept and preserved the possession, we had taken in the year 1683, of the lands, coasts and islands, which are situated in the Gulf of Mexico, between Carolina on the east and Old and New Mexico on the west.

"But a new war having broke out in Europe shortly after, there was no possibility till now of reaping from that colony the advantages that might have been expected from thence, because the private men, who are concerned in the sea-trade, were all under engagements with other colonies, which they have been obliged to follow. And, whereas, upon the information we have received concerning the disposition and situation of the said countries known at present by the name of the Province of Louisiana, we are of opinion that there may be established therein a considerable commerce, so much the more advantageous to our kingdom in that there has hitherto been a necessity of fetching from foreigners the greater part of the commodities which may be brought from thence, and because in exchange thereof, we need carry thither nothing but commodities of the growth and manufacture of our own kingdom.

" We have resolved to grant the commerce of the country of Louisiana to the Sieur Anthony Crozat, our councillor, secretary of the household, crown, and revenue, to whom we intrust the execution of this project. We are the more readily inclined hereunto, because his zeal and the singular knowledge he has acquired in maritime commerce encourage us to hope for as good success as he has hitherto had in the divers and sundry enterprises he has gone upon, and which have procured to our kingdom great quantities of gold and silver in such conjunctures as have rendered them very welcome to us.

"For these reasons, being desirous to show our favor to him, and to regulate the conditions upon which we mean to grant him the said commerce, after having deliberated this affair in our council, of our certain knowledge, full power and royal authority, we, by these presents, signed by our hand, have appointed, and do appoint, the said Sieur Crozat, solely to carry on a trade in all the lands possessed by us, and bounded by New Mexico, and by the English of Carolina, all the establishment, ports, havens, rivers, and principally the port and haven of the Isle Dauphine, heretofore called Massacre, the river of St. Louis, heretofore called Mississippi, from the edge of the sea as far as the Illinois, together with the river of Saint Philip, heretofore called the Missoury's, and of Saint Jerome, heretofore called Ouabache, with all the countries, territories, lakes, within land, and the rivers which fall directly or indirectly into that part of the river St. Louis."

The kind of government to be established under this patent, and the powers, duties, and restrictions imposed by it upon M. Crozat, are specifically defined in the *Articles*, the first of which is thus worded:

I. "Our pleasure is that all the aforesaid lands, countries, streams, rivers, and islands be and remain comprised under the name of the government of Louisiana, which shall be dependent upon the general government in New France, to which it is subordinate; and, further, that all the lands which we possess from the Illinois be united, so far as occasion requires, to the general government of New France, and become part thereof,* reserving, however, the liberty of enlarging, as we shall think fit, the extent of the government of the said country of Louisiana."

Article II. granted "to the said Sieur Crozat, for fifteen successive years, to be reckoned from the day of enrolling these presents, a right and power to transport all sorts of goods and merchandise from France into the said country of Louisiana, and to traffic thither as he shall think fit." And all other persons or companies were herein forbidden to trade thither, under any pretense whatever, under penalty of confiscation of goods and ships, and other more severe punishments, as occasion should require.

Article III. permitted him "to search for, open, and dig all sorts of mines, veins, and minerals throughout the whole extent of the said country of Louisiana, and to transport the profits thereof into any part of France during the said fifteen years." By this article there was also granted to Crozat, in perpetuity, his heirs and others claiming under him or them, the property of and in said mines, veins, and minerals, which he should bring to bear, paying the king, in lieu of all claim, the fifth part of all the gold and silver, to be transported to France at Crozat's own expense (not including the risk of sea and war), and the tenth part of what effects he might draw from the other mines, veins, and minerals, which tenth was to be conveyed to the

---

*This provision was doubtless intended to apply to the northern part of the Illinois country.

king's magazine in Louisiana. He was also permitted to search for precious stones and pearls, paying the one-fifth part of the same to his majesty, in like manner as directed for the gold and silver.

It was further herein provided, that the said Crozat, his heirs, or those claiming under him or them the perpetual right aforesaid, should forfeit the property in the said mines, veins, and minerals, if they discontinued the work during three years, and that in such case, the said mines, veins, and minerals should be fully re-united to the king's domain, without the formality of any process of law, but only by an ordinance of reunion from the sub-delegate of the intendant of New France, who should be in the said country.

Articles IV., V., and VI. relate to and regulate the trade to be carried on by said Crozat with the French and Indians in Louisiana, and also to the mills and manufactories he was authorized to set up in the said country.

Article VII. provides, that the royal "edicts, ordinances and customs, the usages of the mayoralty and shrievealty of Paris, shall be observed for laws and customs in the said country of Louisiana."

The next succeeding six articles specify the minimum number of ships to be sent out annually by the said Crozat to said Louisiana, and oblige him to transport thither at his own charge such of the king's troops as may be needed for garrison duty; exempt from all duties the goods and merchandise by him exported from or imported to the said country, but require the same to be deposited in and delivered from the government custom and warehouses; and, further, grant him the use of the felluccas and canoes belonging to the king in said Louisiana, on condition that at the expiration of his patent, he shall restore them, or an equal number in their place, to the governor of the province.

The three concluding articles of the patent are worded as follows:

XIV. "If, for the cultures and plantations which the Sieur Crozat is minded to make, he finds it proper to have blacks in the said country of Louisiana, he may send a ship every year to trade directly upon the coast of Guinea, taking permission from the Guinea Company so to do, (and) he may sell those blacks to the inhabitants of the colony of Louisiana; and we forbid all other companies and persons whatsoever, under any pretense whatsoever, to introduce blacks or traffic for them in the said country, nor shall the said Sieur Crozat carry blacks elsewhere.

XV. "He shall not send any ships into the said country of Louisiana, but directly from France, and he shall cause the said ships to return thither again, the whole under pain of confiscation and forfeiture of the present privilege.

XVI. "The said Sieur Crozat shall be obliged, after the expiration of the first nine years of this grant, to pay the officers and the garrison which shall be in the said country during the six last years of the continuance of the present privilege.

"The said Sieur Crozat may in that time propose and nominate the officers, as vacancies shall fall, and such officers shall be confirmed by us, if we approve them." *

Such are the material provisions of the ample charter granted by the king to M. Antoine Crozat, in the hope of receiving thereby rich monetary returns to replenish his depleted exchequer. We have given the more space to the exposition of this patent, because under it was instituted the first civil government for the Province of Louisiana, including the Illinois.

To effectuate the main purpose of his grant, Crozat sent out from France the necessary miners and mining tools, with other artisans and laborers, and some slaves from St. Domingo, to begin prospecting for the precious metals.

On May 17, 1713, a large French ship arrived in the waters of Louisiana, having on board Antoine de la Mothe Cadillac,† the newly appointed governor of the colony, his

---

* For the full text of Crozat's Letters Patent, see "Historical Collections of Louisiana," vol. III.

† La Mothe, or La Motte, Cadillac was born of noble parentage in Gascony, France, about the year 1666. Sailing thence to America, he

family, and M. Duclos, intendant commissary. By the same vessel was also brought a commission naming Bienville as lieutenant-governor. The coming of Cadillac and his associates would have had a more salutary influence on the future of the colony, if he and Bienville had acted in concert; but they were mutually jealous of each other from the outset, and each had his party of followers, which proved detrimental to the interests of both.

At this early and unpromising stage of her history as a colony, although over two thousand persons had been transported thither, Southern Louisiana contained not more than four hundred whites, twenty negro slaves, and about three hundred head of horned cattle, which latter had mostly been imported from St. Domingo.

The Sieur Crozat expected to realize handsome profits from the fur-trade with the Indians, and if he had confined himself to that alone, he would have succeeded better in the end; but the possibility of sudden wealth from the discovery of rich mines of gold and silver was what chiefly engaged the attention of his agents, and induced them to the most lavish outlay of capital. To accomplish this object, prospecting parties were sent out to various parts of the country, and small posts were established on the upper waters of Red River, the Washita, the Yazoo, the Coosa,* the Cumberland (near Nashville), and on other southern rivers. Indeed, to such a degree were Crozat and his partners affected by this mania for the precious metals, that they often magnified insignificant findings into supposed realities of great value. But though gold and silver were not to be found, either by washing, digging or boring, large deposits of the less valuable ores of lead and iron were found in what is now south-eastern Missouri. The mining adventurers in this wild region drew their principal subsistence from the French settlements of Kaskaskia and Ca-

---

served as a captain in Acadia, and in 1694 was sent by Frontenac to command at Mackinac; after which, in 1701, he founded the military post of Detroit. During his five years' stay in Louisiana, he not only officiated as governor, but was a partner in Crozat's commercial ventures. His name is perpetuated in a thriving lumber city of Michigan.

* That on the Coosa was called Fort Toulouse.

hokia, to which they added such of their number as preferred to cultivate the soil and a fixed abode to the more precarious pursuit of mining. Hence, from this source, the Illinois colony derived a considerable accession of European bone and muscle.*

Under the auspices of M. Crozat an attempt was made to open trade with the Spaniards at Vera Cruz, by sending thither a vessel laden with a valuable cargo of merchandise, but it was not allowed to land either there or at any other Mexican port. The occupancy of Louisiana by the French had been regarded by Spain from the first as an encroachment upon her territory, and a menace to her supremacy in the Gulf; and, therefore, after three years of ineffectual negotiations with the viceroy of Mexico, Crozat was obliged to relinquish his scheme of commercial relations with the Spanish ports. Another project was to establish trade overland with the interior provinces of Mexico, but in this case, after repeated efforts, he also failed, his goods being seized and confiscated and his agents imprisoned. Nor did the fur-trade with the Indians prove so remunerative as had been anticipated. English agents from Carolina were active in their efforts to incite the Choctaws and Chickasaws against the French, and, wherever it was practicable, they controlled the fur-traffic by furnishing goods to the Indians at reduced prices. Agriculture, the only source of permanent prosperity, was of course neglected. At the end of four years, he had expended about 425,000 livres and realized only 300,000,† and he found himself unable to meet his liabilities or pay his men.

On the 23d of August, 1717, M. Crozat, despairing of any better success in the future, surrendered his vested rights and privileges to the young king, Louis XV., who then occupied the throne of France under the regency of the Duke of Orleans, and thereupon the government of Louisiana reverted solely to the officers appointed by the crown.

---

*At a later period the French opened and worked lead mines, to some extent, on the Upper Mississippi, about Galena and Dubuque.

† Davidson and Stuve's Hist. Ill., p. 114.

During the five years of his connection with the province, although it was widely explored, the growth of the French settlements therein was inconsiderable, and but little was accomplished for their real benefit. The principal prosperity they enjoyed grew out of the enterprise of individual merchants and traders, who, despite the restrictions of Crozat's monopoly, managed to carry on a limited trade with the natives and with some of the neighboring European colonies. At the close of this epoch the colonists and adventurers in Upper and Lower Louisiana, including the king's troops sent thither to protect them, did not exceed fifteen hundred souls.

From the foregoing review of the Parisian Crozat's operations in Louisiana, we turn to chronicle certain civil and military events which transpired in the province during that period. In February, 1716, Lieut. Bienville departed up the Mississippi, under the orders of Governor Cadillac, on an expedition to the Natchez nation, where some French hunters and traders had already found a lodgment. Having learned that five Frenchmen had been slain, and that six more were still prisoners in the hands of the Natchez, Bienville dissembled his knowledge of the matter until he had induced the war-chiefs to meet him in council, when they gave up their six prisoners. He then reproached them with the murder of the other Frenchmen, and refused to treat with them until the guilty authors should be surrendered up to him. They replied that it was not possible for sun-chiefs and men of valor to thus give up their people. Upon this they were immediately put in irons and imprisoned under guard. On the next day the prisoner chiefs requested permission to send a deputation to their grand chief, desiring him to send the head of the chief Whitehead, who was the principal murderer. Bienville having given his consent, the deputation was sent, and returned, not with the head of that chief, but with another who was willing to devote himself to death in place of Whitehead. This and other similar offers the French commander firmly declined.

16

In the meantime he received a letter from a Canadian among the Natchez, informing him that six pirogues of his countrymen were on their way down the river, and that, ignorant of this rupture with the Indians, they would fall into the hands of the latter. Bienville promptly dispatched a canoe from his camp, which passed the Natchez village unperceived, and, meeting the Canadian *voyageurs*, apprised them of their danger. Not wishing to resort to extreme measures against the Natchez, Bienville finally proposed peace to them on condition that they should put to death Big-beard, one of the murderers, and help to build a fort for the French; which terms they complied with. The fort was erected on an elevated bluff overlooking the river, and on the site that had been previously selected by M. d'Iberville. It was named Rosalie in compliment to the wife of Count Pontchartrain, formerly Secretary of State for the Colonies. Thus was laid the military foundation of the present city of Natchez,—the oldest permanent white settlement on the Lower Mississippi, save that of Arkansas Post, which was never a place of much importance. Having re-established peaceful relations with the Natchez nation, Bienville stationed a garrison at Fort Rosalie to maintain it, and returned down the river with the rest of his men to the French head-quarters.

Late in August, 1716, Louis Juchereau de St. Denis returned to Fort Louis on the Mobile from an extraordinary journey overland to Mexico, or New Spain. Two years before, in 1714, he had been sent by Governor Cadillac to the middle provinces of Mexico for the double purpose of finding a market for Crozat's goods, and of forestalling the action of the Spaniards, who were supposed to be meditating an establishment at the Natchitoches. Having been supplied by the governor with ten thousand livres worth of merchantable goods, St. Denis, with twenty-four Canadians, and an equal number of southern Indians, ascended the Mississippi and Red River to the village of the Natchitoches, located on an island in the latter stream. Arrived thither, he at first employed his men in building some log cabins for the use of those whom he intended to leave behind. Then, taking with him twelve picked Canadians, and a few active young Indians, all well armed and mounted, he quit the low valley of Red River, and boldly struck across the far-spreading plains to the westward. After twenty days' march, he reached a tribe of the Cenis nation, in the vicinity of Trinity River. Being furnished by them with fresh guides, the leader and his troop traveled thence about one hundred and fifty leagues to the south-west, when they arrived at the Spanish settlement of San Juan Bautista, or Presidio del Norte, situate some two leagues beyond the Rio Grande. Here St. Denis was well received by the Spanish commandant, Don Pedro de Vilescas, who took him and the principal men of his party to his own quarters, and assigned lodgings for the remainder.

It was now near the close of the year 1714, and, after a few days' rest, St. Denis began negotiations with Don Pedro for the opening of a regulated trade with the French colonists of Louisiana. But the Spanish officer informed him that he could do nothing without the permission of his immediate superior, the governor of Caouis (Coahuila), to whom he sent a courier for orders. The governor decided that St. Denis would have to go to the capital and see the viceroy in person. To this he assented, but was in no hurry about starting, having meantime become enamored of Dona Maria, the handsome daughter of Don Pedro. At length, on setting out from Caouis, he wrote to the Frenchmen-at-arms whom he had left at Presidio del Norte to return to the Natchitoches. He made the journey southward to the city of Mexico (distant over two hundred leagues) with M. Jallot, one of his French companions, and was escorted by a body of twenty-five Spanish horsemen. Upon his arrival at the capital, St. Denis presented his credentials to the viceroy, who, after perusing them, sent him to prison, where he was detained for three months, and might have been kept in "durance vile" much longer, if it had not been for the personal intercession of some French officers in the service of New Spain. After his liberation he was generously treated by the viceroy, who spared no effort to induce him to enter the military service of Spain.

Among other arguments used for this purpose, the viceroy told him that he was already a half Spaniard, since he sought the hand of the daughter of Don Pedro de Vilescas, and was to marry her upon his return to San Juan.

Prior to his departure from the city of Mexico, St. Denis is said to have concerted a plan with the viceroy for the planting of Roman Catholic missions among the Indian nations in Texas. Quitting the Mexican capital about the 26th of October, 1715, he journeyed, with a small escort, back to Presidio del Norte. Here he performed a valuable service to the Spanish commandant, by preventing the removal of certain dissatisfied tribes from the Rio Grande, whose trade and friendship was of importance to the Spaniards. Soon after this he married Don Pedro's daughter, with whom he lived happily for six months, when it became necessary for him to return to Louisiana. But no sooner had he arrived at the French head-quarters, and reported to Governor Cadillac the result of his lengthened mission, than he made haste to join another land expedition to Mexico. Arrived thither, he repeated some of his former experiences, and was again imprisoned by the Spanish authorities, but managed to effect his escape.

Returning to Louisiana, in 1719, St. Denis was afterward appointed commandant of the post of Natchitoches, where he was joined by his wife and family, and where we shall find him taking part in the Natches war. He was, indeed, one of the most remarkable personages of his time in the province, and the narrative of his Mexican adventures reads more like the story of a paladin of romance than sober reality. It is true that he accomplished little or nothing in the way of establishing commercial intercourse with the arrogant and exclusive hidalgos of Mexico, yet his long journeys back and forth across the country added greatly to the geographical knowledge of the French, and enabled them to extend and confirm their alliances with the principal aboriginal tribes of Texas.*

---

*From Charlevoix' History of New France (vol. vi., p. 12 and note), we glean some further particulars in regard to the checkered life

In January, 1717, soon after the return of St. Denis from his first overland journey to Mexico, the governor sent a sergeant with a few soldiers to take possession of the before-mentioned island of Natchitoches, and to establish a military post there; it being regarded by the French authorities not only as a place of strategic importance, but as a good location for interior trade with the natives of that region. This was the commencement of the still existing town of Natchitoches.

On the 9th of March, in that year, M. de la Mothe Cadillac, having served almost four years as governor of Louisiana, and failing to give satisfaction, was relieved by M. de L'Epinay, who arrived with three ships, bringing out some fifty immigrants, and three companies of infantry to fill the depleted garrisons of the province. The retiring executive returned by the same vessels to France, where he died in the following year. Bienville, however, still retained the position of lieutenant-governor, and, about this time received the decoration of the Cross of St. Louis.

Heretofore the business of agriculture had been almost totally neglected by the colonists, and they had often experienced a partial famine in consequence of such neglect. It was now proposed to form an agricultural settlement on the banks of the Mississippi River, and to raise necessary provisions for the consumption of the settlers. The growing of articles for export, such as rice, indigo and tobacco, was also contemplated, for which the soil was found well adapted.

It was during the year 1717, while looking for a suita-

of Louis Juchereau de St. Denis. Born in Quebec, Canada, September 18, 1676, he was a son of Nicholas Juchereau Sieur de St. Denis, or Denys, and an uncle of the wife of M. d'Iberville. In 1720, after his second expedition to Mexico, the Chevalier de St. Denis received the brevet of captain, and the insignia of the Cross of St. Louis—a military order instituted by Louis XIV., in 1693, for the encouragement of the officers of the army and navy. In 1721, he was sent with a detachment of regular troops to Natchitoches, and remained there in command of that post. The date of his death is not determined, though it was subsequent to the year 1731. It is told that he died much regretted by the Indians of the Red River Valley, with whose language and customs he was entirely familiar, and over whom he wielded an extensive influence.

ble location on the Mississippi, to become the nucleus of the projected agricultural and commercial settlement, that Bienville selected the tract whereon New Orleans now stands, lying on the north bank of the river, where it makes a great curve to the east, and distant one hundred and five miles from its mouth. The situation was low and swampy, and by no means inviting to the superficial observer; but with its proximity to the waters of Lakes Borgne and Pontchartrain, and with a deep river channel to the sea, it promised ultimately to become a commercial mart,—considerations which no doubt influenced its choice. Having fixed upon the site, Bienville afterward caused it to be surveyed, and sent a party of woodmen there to make a clearing. Such appears to have been the origin of that great southern emporium, of whose gradual rise into prominence and importance, we shall have occasion to further speak in the sequel.

As a not inappropriate conclusion to the present chapter, some general notice may here be taken of the demise and character of Louis XIV., the *Grand Monarque*, under whose authority all the discoveries, explorations, and settlements by the French in the Mississippi Valley had hitherto been effected. On September 1, 1715, after a short illness, the great king breathed his last in his palace at Versailles, having reached the advanced age of seventy-seven, and reigned seventy-two years. During the three preceding years, he had been severely tried by domestic afflictions. His ambitious second wife, Madame de Maintenon, whom he had privately married, went into voluntary retirement. He lost by death his son and heir apparent, his grandson and eldest great-grandson; so that his youngest great-grandson succeeded to the crown under the title of Louis XV.

Louis the Fourteenth had fallen heir to the throne of France in 1643, when less than six years old, and during his minority his mother was regent of the kingdom, with Cardinal Mazarin as her chief councilor. The reign of this Louis was the longest and, in many respects, the most illustrious in the annals of France. Among the princes of his time, he stood pre-eminent in commanding presence, in regal dignity, and in absolute power. After the death of Mazarin, in 1661, he had no prime minister, but he wisely chose great men for his assistants and ministers of government. Under him Colbert and Louvois long filled the first offices of state; the former being the great promoter of French industry and manufactures, while the latter was his able and successful minister of war. His foremost generals were Turenne, Condé, and Luxembourg, while Vauban was his chief military engineer. The younger Mansard was made head architect and superintendent of the royal buildings.

During his reign, Paris and its environs were adorned with parks and public edifices to an extent previously unknown. The most noted of these were the *Observatoire*, the Church of *Val de Grace*, the Colonnade of the *Louvre*, the *Hotel des Invalides*, the completion of the *Palais Royal*, the *Place des Victoires*, the *Place Vendome*, and additions to the palace of the *Tuileries;* but, above all others in extent and magnificence, is the palace and garden of Versailles.* The architecture of these various buildings, like the dress of that age, is profusely ornate, and wanting in pure taste.

Louis XIV. was a munificent patron of literature, science and the arts, and some of the most celebrated writers of France flourished under his reign. The French tongue was then cultivated and polished to such a degree that it became the language of court and diplomatic circles throughout Europe. He made his capital the gayest and most luxurious in Europe. He caused the court of Versailles to be every-where admired and imitated as a model of taste and elegance, and of a princely and refined style

---

* "It was on this splendid palace that Louis XIV. lavished the wealth of his people, to give expression to his own grandeur and selfish ambition. It was built on the site of the hunting lodge of Louis XIII., ten miles from Paris, which city Louis disliked, because he saw there only the edifices and monuments of other kings. The buildings constituting the palace, undertaken in 1661, were committed in 1670 to the architect Mansard, and their construction was continued to the end of the reign."— *Anderson's History of France.*

of living. But as he sought only the gratification of his pride and vanity, his love of pageantry and pleasure, and his thirst for dominion and renown, his personal rule extinguished all civil freedom, sound morals and manly sentiments among his subjects. Court favor, therefore, became the aim and end of all individual effort, and adroit flattery was the surest way to attain it. A venal age, virtue and merit were but lightly esteemed. In fine, such were the baneful effects of his policy and example, that from his reign has been dated the decline of the great French monarchy, though it was accelerated by the incapacity of his successors.

The latter years of Louis' imperial sway were clouded by reverses to his armies in the field, and by a spirit of bigoted intolerance in his civil administration. His revocation of the Edict of Nantes* was as impolitic as it was unjustifiable, and his stern persecution of the Protestant Huguenots drove from his kingdom nearly half a million of his most industrious and useful subjects. But religious toleration, as now generally understood and approved, was in that age little known, and still less practiced, on the continent of Europe. The king believed and acted upon the theory that unity of religious faith was essential to the stability of his throne. His ruling principle of government was embodied in the famous aphorism ascribed to him—*Le etat c' est moi,* or, "I am the state." †

To the readers of English history Louis XIV. is remembered as the generous friend and supporter of James II., the dethroned Catholic king of England.

Among the best known French works on this great prince's reign are Voltaire's *Siècle de Louis XIV.,* St. Simon's *Memoirs,* and *Louis XIV. et son Siècle,* by Alexander Dumas.

---

* This famous edict had been enacted by Henry IV., in April, 1598, and being in the nature of a compromise, it was deemed irrevocable. The order for its revocation was issued October 22, 1685.

† The great king may never have uttered these words, though they perfectly express his sentiments; for, in 1666, he wrote: "It is God's will that whoever is born a subject should not reason, but obey."—Parkman's *Old Régime in Canada,* p. 172.

CHAPTER XIII.

1717-1723.

FRENCH FINANCES, AND LAW'S MISSISSIPPI COMPANY.

The long wars and general extravagance of Louis XIV. had exhausted France, and entailed upon her a debt estimated at not less than two billions of livres, or about four hundred millions of dollars. The people were oppressively taxed, but still the surplus revenues of the kingdom were wholly inadequate to meet the annual interest on the indebtedness. The consequence was that the government stocks sank to a merely nominal value, and its credit was depressed to the lowest ebb. In this dilemma, while the regency was casting about for some means of financial relief, John Law, the famous financier-adventurer, appeared at the Court of Versailles with his " magnificent credit system."

John Law, eldest son of a Scotch silversmith and banker, was born in Edinburgh in April, 1671. He received a liberal education, and at an early age discovered a strong bent for finance. After the death of his father, and before attaining to his majority, he became notorious as a gambler and debauchee. Having unhappily killed an antagonist named Wilson, in a duel, he fled to France to avoid arrest. From thence he passed into Holland, where he made a special study of banking in the great banking house at Amsterdam. After perfecting his theory he returned to Edinburg in 1700, and shortly published a work advocating the establishment of a bank which should hold all the sources of revenue of the state in its own hands, and, treating them as capital, should issue notes thereon, and at the same time make a profit by discounting bills and notes. His plan of banking was ridiculed by the British wits of the day, and was discarded by the Scottish

Parliament. He then went with his scheme to Paris,
where it attracted considerable attention, but was utterly rejected by the old king and his comptroller-general of finance.
Law sojourned for awhile in Paris, leading a gay and
luxurious existence, playing high and winning large sums
of money. But his prosperous career was interrupted by
a message from the chief of police, ordering him to quit
Paris, on the ground that he "was rather too skillful at
the game which he had introduced." For several years
succeeding he shifted his abode from one state to another
in Italy and Germany, offering his scheme of finance to
every court that he visited, though without success. The
Duke of Savoy, afterward King of Sardinia, was much
impressed with his project, but, after considering it for a
time, remarked: "I am not sufficiently powerful to ruin
myself."

Upon the decease of the great Louis, in 1715, John
Law returned to Paris with a fortune of half a million of
dollars, which he had acquired by gambling. Louis XV.
was then but a child, and during his non-age the government was administered by Philippe, Duc d' Orleans,* as
regent. The finances of France being at this time in a
bankrupt condition, Law soon gained a hearing at court
for his favorite banking project. The regent had before
been favorably impressed with the scheme, which suited his
bold and reckless spirit, and his taste for profligate extravagance. Accordingly, on the 2d of May, 1716, despite
the opposition of his ministers and the Parliament of Paris,
he granted letters patent to Law, authorizing him and his
brother William to establish a bank of deposit, discount
and circulation, under the firm name of "Law and Company," to continue for twenty years. The capital of this
institution was fixed at six millions of livres, divided into
shares of five hundred livres each, which were to be sold
for twenty-five per cent of coin, and seventy-five per cent.
of the public securities. The coin, which had been already
debased by an arbitrary edict of the regent, was held in

---

* He was a cousin or second cousin of the young king.

the bank for the redemption of its notes. Inasmuch as the bank accepted at par government securities, on which there was a discount of seventy-eight per cent., and as there was a general lack of private credit, its stock was soon taken, and a very lucrative business was established. Thus, while the bank was limited in its operations, and while its paper really represented the specie in its vaults, it seemed to realize all that had been promised for it. It speedily acquired public confidence, and produced an activity in commerce that was unknown under the preceding reign. Moreover, the bills of the bank bore an interest, and as it was stipulated that they would be of invariable value, and as hints had been adroitly circulated that coin would experience successive diminution in value, every body hastened to the bank to exchange gold and silver for the paper money. In a few months the bank shares arose enormously, and the amount of its notes in circulation exceeded one hundred and ten millions of livres.

Hitherto all had gone on well enough, and all might have continued to go well, if the paper system had not been further expanded. But Law had yet to develop the grandest part of his scheme. He had yet to disclose his ideal world of speculation, his El Dorado of unlimited wealth. His financial theory was, that the currency of a country is simply the representative of its moving wealth, and that this representative need not possess any intrinsic value, as in the case of gold and silver, but might consist of paper, or any other substance which can be conveniently handled. He held that while there was no standard of prices or money, credit was every thing, and that a state might safely treat even possible future profits as the basis of a paper currency. The English had brought the vast imaginary commerce of the South Seas in aid of their banking operations; and Law sought to bring, as a powerful auxiliary of his bank, the whole trade of the Mississippi Valley. To this end he now produced his Mississippi scheme, which was to make him a conspicuous figure in the colonial annals of Louisiana and Illinois. The prolific resources and possibilities of Louisiana still filled the imaginations of the

French people with visions of boundless riches. The ill-success that had there attended the operations of Crozat and his partners was not sufficient to dispel the illusion from the public mind, or to beget therein more rational views. The stories of its vast mineral deposits were artfully revived; ingots of gold, the products of its supposed mines, were exhibited at the Paris mint; and the sanguine court saw in the future of that province an empire, with its fruitful valleys, growing cities, busy wharves, and exhaustless mines of gold and silver, pouring its precious freights into the channels of French commerce.

As soon, therefore, as the charter of the Sieur Crozat was annulled, Law proceeded, under letters patent from the regent, to organize the *Compagnie d'Occident*, or Company of the West, which was based upon the plan of colonizing and drawing profits from the French possessions in North America. The charter of the company was registered in the Parliament of Paris on the 6th of September, 1717; and all of the king's subjects, including corporate bodies, and even aliens, were allowed to take stock in it. The capital was fixed at about one hundred millions of livres, divided into shares of five hundred livres each, bearing interest at four per cent., which were subscribed for in the public securities. As the bank was to co-operate with the company, the regent issued an order that its bills should be received the same as coin in all payments of the public revenue. Law was made chief director of the company, which was copied after the Earl of Oxford's South Sea Company, originated in 1711, and which distracted all England with the frenzy of speculation.

Among the more important privileges conferred on this company by the government, was the exclusive control of the commerce of Louisiana for twenty-five years, to begin the 1st of January, 1718. All other subjects of his majesty were prohibited from trading hither, under penalty of confiscation of their merchandise and vessels; but this was not intended to prevent the colonists from trading with each other, or with the Indians. Power and authority were also given the company to make treaties with the Indian nations, and to wage war against them in case of aggression or insult; to import negro slaves into the province; to open and work all mines, free of duty; to grant lands, even allodially; to cast cannon, build ships of war, raise and equip troops, and to nominate the provincial officers, who were to be commissioned by the crown. In addition to the above, the regent promised the company protection against foreign powers, and presented it with all the forts, guns, ammunition, boats, and stores in Louisiana, that had been surrendered by the Sieur Crozat. Nor was this all. During the continuance of its charter, the goods of the company were to be exempt from duty, and the white inhabitants ot the province from the payment of any state tax.*

The paper system of Law, and his scheme of colonization, were earnestly opposed by D'Anguesseau, the chancellor, and by the Duke de Noailles, Minister of Finance, who foresaw the evils that the system was calculated to produce. Finding that they seriously interfered with his plans, the regent dismissed them from office; but the opposition of the Parliament of Paris was not so easily managed, since that body aspired to an equal authority with the regent in the administration of affairs. The chief hostility of the parliament was directed against Law, a foreigner, a heretic, and an adventurer. So far was this hostility carried, that secret measures were taken to investigate his malversations, and to collect evidence against him; and it was resolved in parliament that should the testimony collected justify their suspicions, they would have him seized and arraigned for trial, and, if convicted, would hang him in the court-yard of the palace. Receiving intimation of his threatened danger, Law took refuge in the Palais Royal, the residence of the regent, and implored his protection. The regent himself was embarrassed by the sturdy opposition of the parliament, which contemplated nothing less than a decree reversing his own measures of finance. However, by assembling a board of justice, and bringing to bear the absolute

---

*History of Louisiana, by Francois Xavier Martin (New Orleans, 1827), vol. 1, pp. 198, 201.

authority of the king, he triumphed over parliament and relieved Law from the dread of being hanged.

The credit system now went on with full sail. The Company of the West, being identified with the bank, rapidly increased in power and privileges. One monopoly after another was granted to it; the trade of the Indian seas, the slave trade with Senegal and Guinea, the farming of tobacco, the royal coinage, etc. Each new privilege was made a pretext for emitting more bills, and caused a proportionate advance in the prices of stock. At length, on the 4th of December, 1718, the regent gave the institution the imposing title of the Royal Bank of France, and proclaimed that he had effected the purchase of all the shares, the proceeds of which were added to its capital. Arbitrary measures were now begun to force the bills of the bank into artificial circulation. On the 27th of December an order was made in council, forbidding, under severe penalties, the payment of any sum above six hundred livres in gold or silver. This decree rendered bank bills necessary in all considerable transactions of purchase and sale, and called for a new emission. The prohibition was occasionally evaded or opposed, but confiscations were the consequence.

The worst effect of this illusive system was the mania for gain, or for gambling in stocks, that now seized upon the French nation. Under the stimulus of lying reports, and the compulsory effects of government decrees, the shares of the company went on rising until they reached thirteen hundred per cent. Nothing was talked of but the prices of shares, and the immense fortunes suddenly made by lucky speculators. The most extravagant dreams were indulged concerning the wealth that was to flow in upon the company from its colonies, its trade, and its various monopolies. To doubt of these things was to excite anger, or incur ridicule. And in a time of public infatuation, it requires no small exercise of courage to doubt a popular fallacy.

Paris now became the center of attraction for the adventurous and avaricious, who flocked thither not only

The Mania for Speculation. 255

from the provinces, but from the neighboring countries. A stock exchange was established in a hotel on one of the principal streets,* and immediately became the resort of stock jobbers and speculators. Guards were stationed at either end of the avenue to maintain order, and to exclude horses and carriages. The whole street swarmed throughout the day like a bee-hive. Bargains of all kinds were struck with avidity. Shares of stock passed from hand to hand, mounting in value, one knew not why. Fortunes were made in a moment, as if by magic, and every lucky bargain prompted those around to a more desperate throw of the die.

To ingulf all classes in this ruinous vortex, Law divided the shares of fifty millions of stock into one hundred shares each, thus accommodating the venture to the humblest purse. Society was thus stirred to its very dregs, and people of the lowest order hurried to the stock market to invest their small savings. All honest, industrious pursuits, and moderate gains were now despised. The upper classes were as base in their venality as the lower. The highest nobles, abandoning all generous pursuits and lofty aims, engaged in the vile scuffle for gain. Even prelates and ecclesiastical bodies, forgetting their true objects of devotion, mingled among the votaries of Mammon. The female sex likewise participated in the sordid frenzy. Princesses of the blood, and ladies of the first nobility were among the most rapacious of stock-jobbers. Meanwhile, luxury and extravagance kept pace with this sudden inflation of fancied wealth, and a general laxity of morals was diffused throughout society.

Law went about with a countenance beaming with satisfaction, and apparently dispensing wealth on every hand. Even his domestics were enriched by the crumbs that fell from his table. Wherever he went his path was beset by a base throng, who waited to see him pass, and sought the favor of a word or a smile, as if a mere glance from him would bestow a fortune. The same venal atten-

---

* It was afterward removed to the Place Vendome.

tion was paid by all classes to his family. The highest born ladies of the court vied with each other in meanness to secure the lucrative friendship of Mrs. Law and her daughter. The wealth of the banker rapidly increased with the expansion of the bubble. In the course of a few months he purchased some fourteen titled estates, paying for them in paper money; and the unthinking public hailed these vast acquisitions of landed property as so many proofs of the soundness of his system.

The illusory credit continued its course triumphantly for eighteen months. Law had nearly fulfilled one of his promises, viz., to pay off the public debt; but it was paid in bank shares; which had been inflated several hundred per cent above their real value, and which were shortly to vanish like smoke in the hands of the holders.

Toward the close of the year 1719, the Mississippi scheme had reached its culmination. Nearly half a million of strangers had crowded into Paris, in quest of fortune. The hotels and boarding houses were overflowing; lodgings were procured with great difficulty; granaries were turned into bed-rooms; splendid houses were multiplying on every side; and the streets were thronged with new and costly equipages.

On the 11th of December, Law obtained another prohibitory decree, for the purpose of drawing all the remaining specie in circulation into the bank. By this it was forbidden to make any payment in silver above ten livres, or in gold above three hundred. The repetition of decrees of this nature, the object of which was to depreciate the value of coin and increase that of paper, awakened distrust of a system which required such bolstering. Sound financiers conferred together, and agreed to make common cause against this continual expansion of the paper system. The shares of the bank and of the company began to decline in value. Wary speculators took the alarm, and began to *realize;* a term now first brought into use, it is said, to signify the conversion of ideal property into something real.

The regent, discerning these signs of decay in the system, sought to sustain it by bestowing office upon its author. Accordingly, in January, 1720, he appointed Law to be comptroller-general of the finances. But before his appointment, the banker had to abjure his Protestant faith and take out letters of naturalization,—a feat of no great difficulty with him.

In February following, a decree was published in the king's name uniting the Royal Bank to the India Company, by which last appellation the whole establishment was subsequently known. By this time, the bank is said to have issued notes to the amount of one thousand millions of livres; being more paper than all the other banks of Europe were able to circulate. Various compulsory measures were now adopted, which gave a temporary credit to the bank; but with all these props and stays, the system continued to totter. On the 22d of May a royal edict was issued, in which, under pretense of having reduced the value of his coin, it was deemed necessary to reduce the value of his bank notes one-half, and of the India shares from nine thousand to five thousand livres. On the 27th this oppressive edict was revoked, and bank bills were restored to their former value. But the fatal blow had at length been struck; the delusion was at an end; and specie payments, except in small sums, were suspended by the bank.

To avert popular odium from himself, the regent, on on the 29th of May, dismissed Law from the office of comptroller-general, and stationed a Swiss guard in his house to protect him from the anger of the populace. But he continued, in private, to co-operate with him in his financial schemes. A general confusion now took place in all financial affairs; and execrations were poured out on all sides against the unfortunate banker.

About the middle of July the last grand effort was made by Law and the regent to keep up the system, and provide for the enormous issue of paper. A decree was formulated, giving the India Company the entire monopoly of commerce, on condition that it would in the course of a year reimburse six hundred millions of livres of its bills,

17

at a fixed rate per month. On the 17th, when this decree was sent to Parliament to be registered, it raised a storm of opposition in that assembly, and a vehement discussion ensued. In the forenoon of that day, several. persons were stifled in the crowd at the door of the bank, where they had gone to change ten franc notes for specie to buy provisions in the market. During the same day Law ventured to go in his carriage to the Palais Royal. But as he passed along the streets, he was saluted with cries and curses, and reached the palace in a terrible fright. The regent, whose nerves were stronger, amused himself with his fears, but kept him there and sent away his carriage, which was assailed by the mob and pelted with stones until its glasses were shivered.

In December, 1720, John Law finally quit Paris and France, traveling in a private conveyance of the regent. When he was fairly out of the way, a council of the regency was summoned to deliberate on the state of the finances and the affairs of the India Company. It was then ascertained that bank bills were in circulation to the enormous amount of two milliards and seven hundred millions of livres, while the specie remaining in the kingdom was estimated at not more than thirteen hundred millions of livres.

When Law left Paris, he took with him only eight hundred *louis d'or*, and a few personal effects. The chief relic of his immense fortune was a big diamond, which, it it is said, he was often obliged to pawn. His furniture and library were sold by auction at a low price, and his landed estates were confiscated to the government. In October, 1721, he went to England, and was presented at court to his majesty George I. Returning again to the continent, he led an adventurous life, shifting about from place to place. He received from France an annual pension of twenty thousand livres until the death of the Duke of Orleans in 1723, and down to that time entertained hopes of arranging a settlement of his accounts with the French India Company, to which he was heavily indebted. By degrees, however, he sank into obscurity, and finally died in poverty in Venice, March 21, 1729, at the age of fifty-eight years.

It is now generally conceded that John Law was a very ingenious calculator, a sincere believer in his own monetary theory, and the founder to some extent of the modern system of banking. The evil genius of his system appears to have been the regent, who in a manner forced him on to an expansion of his paper currency far beyond what he had originally contemplated. "Law was like a poor conjuror in the hands of a potent spirit that he had evoked. He only thought at the outset to raise the wind, but the regent compelled him to raise the whirlwind." *

" Works on Law and his system are numerous," says the American Encylopedia (X., p. 218); "but it is only within the present century that justice has, to any degree, been done to the extraordinary talents of which he was really possessed."

The unsound financiering and mania for speculation, originating with and fostered by the great "projector," proved most disastrous to the material and moral welfare of France; yet a great impetus was given to the settlement of Louisiana through the agency of his Company of the West, which, under different names and auspices, was continued for fifteen years. The first efforts of the company at colonizing the new province were upon a large scale; indeed, extraordinary measures were adopted for this purpose. A royal edict was issued, authorizing the collection and transportation of settlers to the Mississippi, under which the streets and prisons of Paris and other cities were swept of their mendicants and vagabonds. These unwilling colonists were conveyed to the seaport of Rochelle, and, with implements of all kinds for the working of mines, were crowded on board of ships, and sent to Louisiana.

---

* See the admirable essay, entitled *The Mississippi Bubble*, in the "Crayon Papers," by Washington Irving, from which the foregoing sketch of Law's personal career is chiefly condensed.

On the 9th February, 1718, three ships, of the Western Company—the Dauphine, the Vigilante and the Neptune—arrived at Dauphin Island to take possession of Louisiana. After discharging their cargoes, these vessels sailed on their return to France; and on the 8th of March two frigates, the Duchesse de Noailles and the Victoire, cast anchor at Ship Island.* By the first named frigate came Pierre Duqué de Boisbriant, a French-Canadian, who had received the appointment of king's lieutenant† of the province, and who was the bearer of a commission appointing his cousin, Bienville, governor and commandant-general, in place of M. L'Epinay removed. Besides the of-officers and the soldiers belonging to the company, these different vessels brought out about six hundred colonists, who were intended to settle the various concessions or land grants that had been made to persons of prominence, as inducements to immigration. The new colonists were of different ages, sexes and conditions, but mostly belonged to the poor and ignorant class. Some of them perished from the lack of thrift and enterprise; some from imprudence and the diseases incident to the climate; while others lived and prospered by their own energy and industry.

In October, of that year (1718), Bernard de la Harpe, one of the leading spirits of the province, at this period, started to take possession of a grant or concession of land that had been made to him on the upper waters of Red River. With a party of fifty Frenchmen, in two boats and three pirogues, he pushed up that stream to the Natchitoches, where he found M. Blondel in command of the French fort, then recently erected there, and on the island near by were about two hundred Indians, belonging to the Natchitoches, Dulcinoes and Yatasse tribes. LaHarpe thence continued to ascend the river until he reached the nation of the Nassonis, whose villages were located from seventy to eighty leagues above the Natchitoches. Upon

---

* French's "Historical Collections of La." New Series (N. Y., 1869), p. 140; also vol. II, First Series, p. 66.

† That is *lieutenant du roi*, or lieutenant-governor.

his arrival thither, he at first employed his men in constructing a block-house for their use and the storage of his goods, in which labor they had the friendly assistance of the Nassonis. From this point of vantage, he afterward attempted to open a trade with the Spaniards in New Mexico, and also explored the wide range of country between Red River and the Upper Arkansas. Agreeably to his own narrative, he ascended the Arkansas, or one of its constituent branches, to the base of the Rocky Mountains, and there found several tribes living together in one large village. In pursuance of the usual French policy, he made himself well acquainted with the different Indian nations inhabiting those wild and hitherto unvisited regions, and formed amicable relations with several of them. His printed journal of his voyage and discoveries is characterized by simplicity of style and easy credulity, but it is none the less entertaining, and contains, withal, much useful information respecting the aborigines whom he visited.* It was not until the end of the year 1719 that La Harpe returned to the head-quarters of Governor Bienville.

From the beginning of operations by the Western Company in Louisiana, the directors thereof had evinced much anxiety, for the occupation of the Gulf coast, west of the river Sabine, with a colony. But Governor Bienville, believing in the policy of concentrating the settlements near the Mississippi, had declined sending colonists to that remote quarter, where they would be exposed to the attacks of both the Indians and Spaniards. At length, in August, 1721, under special instructions from the directors, he issued the following official order, addressed to La Harpe, for the establishment of a post near the Bay of St. Bernard, or Matagorda:

"We, Jean Baptiste de Bienville, chevalier of the mil-

---

* Vide " *Journal du voyage de la Louisiane, fait par le S'r Bernard de la Harpe, et des découvertes qu' il a faites dan la partie de L' ouest de cette colonie,*" from the year 1718 to 1722, inclusive; printed in the "Historical Collections" of Louisiana.

itary order of St. Louis, and commandant-general for the king in the Province of Louisiana:

"It is hereby decreed that M. de la Harpe, commandant of the Bay of St. Bernard, shall embark in the packet, 'Subtile,' commanded by Beranger, with a detachment of twenty soldiers, under Belile, and shall proceed forthwith to the Bay of St. Bernard, belonging to this province, and take possession in the name of the king and the Western Company; shall plant the arms of the king in the ground, and build a fort upon whatsoever spot appears most advantageous for the defense of the place.

"If the Spaniards or any other nation have taken possession, M. de la Harpe will signify to them that they have no right to the country, it being known that possession was taken in 1685 by M. de la Salle, in the name of the King of France, etc. "BIENVILLE."
"August 10, 1721." *

Pursuant to this order, La Harpe sailed shortly after upon his doubtful enterprise; but on arriving at the bay he found no safe harbor, and owing to the opposition manifested by the natives on its shores (who were partly influenced by the Spaniards in Mexico), he built no fort there. Mindful, indeed of the fate of La Salle's colony, and unwilling to expose his own men to savage massacre, he returned to Dauphin Island early in the following October,† and the enterprise was thereafter abandoned.

In 1719 the directors of the company sent out for publication in the province of Louisiana a proclamation and schedule, fixing the prices at which goods and merchandise were to be obtained in the company's stores at Dauphin Island, Mobile, and Biloxi. To these prices an advance of five per centum was to be added to goods delivered at New Orleans; ten per cent. at Natchez; thirteen at Yazous; twenty at Natchitoches, and fifty at the Illinois and on the

---
* Monette's "Valley of the Mississippi," vol. 1, p. 235.

† The town of La Harpe, in Hancock County, Ill., appears to have been so named in memory of this noted Frenchman.

Missouri. The commodities of the country were to be received at the company's warehouses in Mobile, Biloxi, Ship Island, and New Orleans, at the rates following, viz: Silk, of which very little was produced, from one dollar and fifty cents to two dollars the pound; tobacco, of the best kind, five dollars the hundred; rice, four dollars; superfine flour three dollars; wheat, two dollars; barley and oats ninety cents the hundred; deer-skins from fifteen to twenty-five cents; dressed, without head or tail, thirty cents; hides eight cents per pound.*

No sooner had M. de Bienville superseded L'Epinay as governor of Louisiana, in 1718, than he revived his scheme for transferring the seat of government of the province from the sterile sands of the Gulf coast to the alluvial banks of the Mississippi. Having already selected a site for the new capital, he now sent the Sieur de la Tour, chief engineer of the colony, with a force of eighty convicts (lately arrived from the prisons of France), to clear a strip of land along the river, and trace out the plan of the town. The settlement thus begun here was named *Nouveau Orleans*, in honor to the Duke of Orleans, then prince regent of France. But M. Hubert, commissary of the colony and Company of the West, refused to transfer the offices and warehouses of the company from Mobile and Dauphin Island, which were more accessible to vessels from the sea. For this reason, New Orleans was maintained for several years only as a small military and trading post. In 1720 La Tour surveyed the mouths or passes of the Mississippi, and reported that New Orleans might be made a commercial port. At this time it was a collection of less than one hundred palisade cabins, built of cypress wood on low, malarious ground, subject to inundations, and surrounded by a forest or thicket of willows, canes, and dwarf palmettos. In January, 1722, the town was visited by Father Charlevoix, who thus recorded his impressions of the place:

"The environs of New Orlans have nothing very re-

---

† Martin's History of Louisiana, vol. 1, page. 219.

markable. I did not find this city so well situated as I had been told; others are not of the same opinion." Again, he writes: "I have nothing to add to what I said in the beginning of my former letter concerning the present state of New Orleans. The truest idea that you can form of it is to represent to yourself two hundred persons that are sent to build a city, and who are encamped on the side of a great river, where they have thought of nothing but to shelter themselves from the air, while they wait for a plan, and have built themselves some houses. M. de Paugér,* whom I have still the honor to accompany, has just shown me one of his drawings. It is very fine and very regular, but it will not be so easy to execute it as to trace it on paper." †

The Mobile and Alabama Rivers had formed a favorite line of communication with the northern interior, and from its closer connection with the sea, Fort Louis on the Mobile remained a principal post; but in August, 1723, the official quarters of Bienville were removed to New Orleans, and its destiny was fixed. Thus the central point of French power in Louisiana, after hovering for over twenty years round Ship and Dauphin Islands, and the bays of Biloxi and Mobile, was at last permanently established on the banks of the Mississippi, and the southern colonists began to gather in settlements along that great river, so as to be within easy reach of the rising capital. Although many of the French doubted the wisdom or propriety of Bienville's conduct in thus changing the seat of government, yet time has amply demonstrated the clearness of his foresight, and the soundness of his judgment in this important action.

From a mere provincial head-quarters and central depot for the commercial transactions of a single company, New Orleans has since progressively grown to be the great emporium of the Lower Mississippi Valley, the recipient of the trade of some fifteen thousand miles of river navigation, to say nothing of her extensive railway connections,

---

* De Paugér was second or assistant engineer of the colony; and in 1722 he established the little post called Balize, at the south pass of the Mississippi.

† "Journal of Travels in North America," pp. 332, 334.

and the busy port where the ships and merchants of all nations do congregate.

Even at that early day her rare commercial advantages, present and prospective, were well understood on the Paris Bourse. Yet, all around the nascent city, was then a matted and marshy forest, "calculated by its dreariness and solitude to inspire far other thoughts than those of commerce, empire, wealth, and power."

At or before this time (1723), the Province of Louisiana was divided for civil and military purposes into nine districts, each of which was placed under the jurisdiction of a separate commandant. These military districts were named as follows: (1) Alibamons,* (2) Mobile, (3) Biloxi, (4) New Orleans, (5) Natchez, (6) Yazoux, (7) Illinois and Wabash, (8) Arkansas, (9) Natchitoches. The province was also divided into three ecclesiastical districts.

We must now revert to the war which broke out in 1719 between France and Spain, and which extended to their American colonies. On the 19th of April in that year two ships arrived from France, bringing out some colonists, and an abundant supply of provisions and ammunition. By these vessels, Governor Bienville received letters from the court informing him that war had been declared in Europe between France and Spain. The governor thereupon called a council of his officers, at which it was determined to make an attack on Fort Pensacola, before the Spanish garrison there could be reinforced. For this expedition he assembled his regular troops, together with some Canadians and Indians, and put them under the command of Captain de Chateaugué, his brother, and Captain de Richebourg. Embarking his little army in three vessels, the commander sailed early in May to Santa Rosa Island, where the Spaniards had an outpost. This the French seized without opposition, and then advanced upon Pensacola, which they invested and took by surprise; for the Spanish commandant claimed that he was not aware of the exist-

---

*The district of the Alibamons lay between the rivers Alabama and Tombigbee.

ence of war between the two nations. Having made himself master of Pensacola, Bienville sent the prisoners he had taken in a vessel with some troops, commanded by Captain de Richebourg, to Havana. He then left his brother, Chateaugué, in command of Fort Pensacola, with a garrison of sixty men, and returned to Dauphin Island.

The French, however, were soon compelled to relinquish their conquest. On the 5th of August two Spanish vessels arrived from Havana before Pensacola, and summoned the commandant to surrender. This being refused, a brisk cannonade began on both sides, and was continued until night. On the next day the Spaniards again sent a summons to Chateaugué to surrender. He asked four days time to consider the matter, and was allowed two, during which he sent by land to Dauphin Island for assistance. Unfortunately, Bienville was not then in a position to afford him any aid, and the attack was renewed. Captain Chateaugué defended the fort as long as he could, but being deserted by a part of his garrison, he was obliged to capitulate, when he was sent a prisoner to Havana. The Spanish commandant was now reinstated, and immediately set to work to repair the injuries done by the cannonading; and in order to strengthen the defenses of the place, he erected a little fort on the Isle of Santa Rosa.

Soon after this the Spanish commander of Pensacola dispatched a large bateau, armed with six pieces of cannon, to harass the French establishment on Dauphin Island. The bateau being joined by another armed vessel, they opened a sharp fire upon the island, which was stoutly returned by the French ship, Philip, and a battery on shore. After bombarding the island several days, and making various ineffectual attempts to land their forces, the Spanish vessels were compelled to withdraw, their departure being hastened by the unexpected appearance of a French squadron of five vessels, commanded by M. de Champmeslin.

This fleet arrived before Dauphin Island on the 1st of September, 1719, and brought out about eight hundred people, comprising officers, soldiers, and colonists, for Louisiana. A council of war being held, it was decided to retake Pensacola, and rescue the French soldiers who had been taken prisoners by the Spaniards. Accordingly, on the 7th of September, the entire fleet, with the exception of one vessel, set sail for Pensacola. The French and Canadian troops, from Dauphin Island, who formed a little army by themselves, commanded by the Sieur de St. Denis, were debarked near the mouth of the river Perdido, to attack the large fort by land, while the squadron held on its way. No sooner had the French ships of war entered and come to anchor within the harbor at Pensacola, than they opened fire upon the Spanish forts and vessels. After a fierce cannonade of two or three hours, the Spaniards, numbering about twelve hundred, surrendered, and were made prisoners of war. Among them were found forty French deserters, twenty of whom were hung at the yard-arm of the admiral's ship, and the remainder condemned to ten years' labor as galley slaves. On the next day a Spanish vessel, laden with provisions and stores, entered the port of Pensacola, not knowing that it had changed masters, and was immediately captured by the French.

After the re-taking of Pensacola, the two forts were demolished, and all the houses were destroyed save four, which were kept for the use of the small garrison left there. The captured munitions and stores were transported to Dauphin Island.*

But the operations of this inter-colonial war, which lasted two years, were not wholly confined to the fringe of European settlements on the coast of Florida and Louisiana. Adventurous white traders and explorers had already found a route across the wide and barren plains of the west, from the Missouri River to New Mexico; and during the year 1720 a Spanish expedition was organized at Santa Fé† to operate against the French in Northern

---

* Dumont's Historical Memoir of Louisiana.

Note.—It was during the autumn and winter of that year (1719), that Governor Bienville removed the main body of the colony from Dauphin Island to Old Biloxi, and thence to New Biloxi, on the west side of the bay of that name.

† Santa Fé was settled by the Spaniards as early as 1582–'83.

Louisiana, while, at the same time, it was expected that a fleet would assail the posts of the latter on the Gulf.

Accordingly a force of three hundred Spanish cavalry, together with some traders, women, and a few priests, set out from Santa Fé on their eastward march across the country, guided by a band of Padouca, or Comanche, Indians. The intention of the leaders of the expedition was to proceed by way of the Upper Arkansas, and to secure the co-operation of the Osage Indians in a combined attack upon the Missouris, who were friends or allies of the French. Seventy only of the Spaniards appear to have persevered in this dangerous enterprise, and they were conducted by their ignorant guides so far to the north that they struck the Kansas, instead of the Arkansas River, at a point not far above its junction with the Missouri. Here they unwittingly found themselves among the Missouri Indians, who spoke the same language as the Osages. The wily chiefs of the Missouris dissembled their own intentions until they had ascertained the purpose of the invaders, and received a supply of arms from them. They then assembled their young warriors, and, falling suddenly upon the Spaniards, put them all to death, save the commander, who is said to have escaped by the fleetness of his horse.

Such, in substance, is the story of the invasion and attempted occupation of the country of the Missouris by the Spaniards from New Mexico, whose objective point was the Illinois.—(Martin's Hist. of La., pp. 234–5.)

The account of this Spanish expedition, as given in Bossu's Letters of Travel, agrees in essential points with the above, but varies from and is fuller in its details. He writes:

"In 1720 the Spaniards formed the design of settling at the Missouris, who are near the Illinois, in order to confine us (the French) more on the westward; the Missouris are far distant from New Mexico, which is the most northerly province the Spaniards have.

"They believed that in order to put their colony in safety, it was necessary they should entirely destroy the Missouris; but concluding that it would be impossible to subdue them with their own forces alone, they resolved to make an alliance with the Osages, a people who were the neighbors of the Missouris, and at the same time their mortal enemies. With that view, they formed a caravan at Santa Fé, consisting of men, women and soldiers, having a Jacobine (Dominican) priest for their chaplain, and an engineer captain for their chief and conductor, with the horses and cattle necessary for a permanent settlement. The caravan being set out mistook its road, and arrived at the Missouris, taking them to be the Osages. Immediately the conductor of the caravan ordered his interpreter to speak to the chief of the Missouris, as if he had been that of the Osages, and tell him that they were come to make an alliance with him, in order to destroy together the Missouris, their enemies.

"The great chief of the Missouris concealed his thoughts upon this expedition, showed the Spaniards signs of great joy, and promised to execute a design with them which gave him much pleasure. To that purpose, he invited them to rest for a few days after their tiresome journey, till he had assembled his warriors, and held council with the old men; but the result of that council was, that they should entertain their guests very well, and affect the sincerest friendship for them.

"They agreed together to set out in three days. The Spanish captain immediately distributed fifteen (five) hundred muskets, with an equal number of pistols, sabers and hatchets; but the very morning after this agreement, the Missouris came by break of day into the Spanish camp, and killed them all except the Jacobin priest, whose singular dress did not seem to belong to a warrior. . . .

"All these transactions the Missouris themselves related, when they brought the ornaments of the chapel hither—(to the Illinois). These people, not knowing the respect due the sacred utensils, hung the chalice to a horse's neck, as if it had been a bell. They were dressed out in these ornaments; the chief having on the naked skin the chasuble, with the paten suspended from his neck.

"The Missouris told him (Boisbriant) that the Spaniards intended to have destroyed them; that they had brought him all these things as being of no use to them, and that if he would, he might give them such goods in return as were more to their liking. Accordingly, he gave them some goods, and sent the ornaments to M. de Bienville, who was then the governor of the Province of Louisiana. As the Indians had got a great number of Spanish horses from the caravan, the chief of the Missouris gave the finest of them to M. de Boisbriant. They had likewise brought with them the map which had conducted the Spaniards so ill; who came to surrender themselves, confessing their intention to their enemies."—*Nouveau Voyages aux Indies Occidentales, Par M. Bossu, Capitaine dans les Troupes de la Marine. A Paris*, 1768. English edition, London, 1771, Part I., pp. 150-155.

CHAPTER XIV.

1718–1732.

LIEUTENANT BOISBRIANT'S RULE IN THE ILLINOIS—THE NATCHEZ WAR.

Early in the month of October, 1718, Pierre Duqué de Boisbriant, as king's lieutenant for Louisiana, departed from the Mobile up the Mississippi, with a considerable detachment of regular troops, to regulate affairs in the Illinois, and to establish a permanent military post for the better protection of the French inhabitants in that important part of the province. Arrived at Kaskaskia, he temporarily located his head-quarters there, which was the first military occupation of the village; but it was only for about fifteen months that he made it his residence. Selecting a convenient site for a post, some sixteen miles above and to the north-west of Kaskaskia, he sent a number of artisans and laborers to work there, and by the spring of 1720 they had built and completed the fort, which was thenceforth the head-quarters of the commandant and the seat of authority in the district. It was erected at the expense of the Company of the West, and was named Fort Chartres, or Fort de Chartres, probably in compliment to the then Regent of France, from the title of his son, the Duc de Chartres.* The fort stood less than one mile from the Mississippi, and a little to the east of an older fortlet that had been raised by the adventurers under Crozat. This second fort was not a place of much military strength, being constructed principally of wood; but it subserved the purpose of its builders and occupants, and in time was supplanted by that extensive stone erection, at the same place, which figures so prominently in the later French history of Illinois.

---

* It might also have been so called from a city of that name in France.

Upon the building of Fort Chartres, a village began to grow on the bottom between it and the river. The "company" erected its warehouses here, and the Jesuits built the church of St. Anne de Fort Chartres. Under the jurisdiction of the priest of this church, chapels were subsequently erected at Prairie du Rocher and St. Philippe's. After the rebuilding of the fort in 1756, the village took the name of New Chartres; and, a few years later, it is said to have contained forty families. Part of the ancient records of the parish of St. Anne have been preserved to this day.*

Shortly after the occupation of Fort Chartres, all the French villages in Illinois became extended and received considerable accessions to their population. In 1719, a parish was formed of the mission at Kaskaskia, of which, in the succeeding year, Father Nicholas Ignatius de Beaubois had charge. In 1721 the Jesuits established a monastery and college (so called) at Kaskaskia, and in 1725 the village became incorporated as a town. At Cahokia, the Sulpitians erected a water-mill for grinding corn and sawing lumber, and also improved and stocked a fine plantation.

As the transactions of the Western Company were multiplied and extended in Lower Louisiana, the district of the Illinois was likewise benefited; for they furnished a market for its surplus agricultural productions, already considerable, and to the furs and pelts gathered in traffic with the Indians, as well as to the lead dug from the mines of Missouri. But this was not all. The colonists could now obtain from the company titles to their landed possessions, and thus be quieted in any uneasiness they might otherwise have felt in regard to them. The only tenure by which they had hitherto held their village lots and parcels of land was by verbal grant or mere acquiescence of the Indians, with no reference to the king, "the lord paramount of the soil according to French law."

The "company" had succeeded to the rights of the crown in the land, and, though extensive domains were

---

* History of Randolph Co., Ill., etc., p. 376.

granted by it to some favored or influential persons in the southern part of Louisiana, there were but few in the northern part who sought to secure more than those small parcels or tracts, the cultivation of which had inspired them with a feeling of home. Moreover, it was important to the managers of the company that the soil should be cultivated, as a ready and certain source of subsistence to those attached to it, and for the success of all their operations. Disappointed in the eager search for mineral wealth, many of the adventurers betook themselves from necessity to the pursuits of agriculture. Grants of land were therefore made, for the purposes of settlement and cultivation, to all who applied for them. The earliest recorded private grants date back to 1722, and were mostly executed by M. de Boisbriant, commandant in the Illinois, representing the king, and Marc Antoine de la Loire des Ursins, on behalf of the Royal Indian Company, successor to the Company of the West. The following is one of the earliest of record:

"Pierre Duquet de Boisbriant, Knight of the Military Order of St. Louis, and first King's Lieutenant of the Province of Louisiana, commanding at the Illinois, and Mons. Antoine de la Loire des Ursins, principal Commissary for the Royal India Company, on the demand of Charles Danie, to grant him a piece of land of five arpents in front on the side of the Mitchigamia River, running north and south, joining to Michael Philip on one side, and on the other to Meleque, and in depth, east and west to the Mississippi. In consequence, they do grant to the said Charles Danie, *in socage*, the said land, whereon he may from this date commence working, clearing and sawing, in expectation of a formal concession,* which shall be sent from France by Messrs. the Directors of the Royal India Company, and the said land shall revert to the domain of the

---

* This more "formal concession" seems to have been neglected by the company.

said company if the said Charles Danie does not work thereon within a year and a day.

" Given this 10th day of May, 1722.
    (Signed,) " BOISBRIANT,
      "   " DES URSINS."*

Remarking upon the above and similar grants, Judge Breese writes: "Incipient titles were only granted by these officers, but almost all of them ripened into a right without the formality of a concession from the company in France, and became allodial, though granted *in socage*, for the simple reason that they were considered of so little value as property that the agents of the company did not trouble themselves to see whether the conditions and services were performed or not.

" The manner in which the settlers cultivated is peculiar, I believe, to the French, and deserves a passing notice. They had not, as we have, separate fields, nor did they reside on the cultivated lands in general. They dwelt in villages, on lots of ground containing generally an arpent square (less than the English acre), which they inclosed with pickets of cedar or other durable wood, sharpened at the top, and appropriated it to the purpose of a garden, reserving a small part only for a barn, stable, and other outhouses. Their farming lands were adjacent to the village in the neighboring prairie, divided into strips, sometimes not more than half an arpent in width, extending originally west from the Kaskaskia to the Mississippi River, a mile or more in length, and uninclosed by any fence whatever. These farming strips, thus lying contiguous to each other, embraced what was long known as the 'common field.'" †

It appears from a petition presented by the inhabitants of Kaskaskia to the district commandant of the Illinois, early in 1727, that in the year 1719 Major Boisbriant had caused to be drawn the lines of the grand square in the

---
* He was afterward killed in the massacre at Fort Rosalie.
† " Early History of Illinois," p. 173.

prairie which they then tilled, and designated to each inhabitant his respective parcel of land. He then established a "common" for stock, lying outside of the lines of the cultivated fields, and extending south to the mouth of the Kaskaskia River, and also including the adjacent islands in the Mississippi, and a strip of bottom land on the east side of the former river, for their cattle, horses, and swine to range upon. But the written instruments of concession were not delivered to them by the Superior Council of Louisiana.

Under this arrangement, it was necessary to watch their live stock while grazing on the common adjacent to the cultivated lands, the idea not having occurred to them until Boisbriant gave them the hint, that a fence would protect them from their ravages and render watching useless. It was not, however, until 1727 that they did inclose these lands by planting pickets upon the lines marked out by Boisbriant, thus making a large field of several thousand acres. The "commons" afforded a rich pasturage for their cattle and horses, and much of it was covered with a luxuriant growth of walnut, oak, and hickory, the mast from which, added to the hazel-nuts, served to fatten their numerous swine.

On the 22d of June, 1722, Messieurs Boisbriant and Des Ursins granted to the inhabitants of Cahokia their "commons," situated on the alluvial bottom between that village and the Mississippi, and near to the present great city of St. Louis. The same officials also confirmed to them their "common field," which extended from the bluffs that line the American Bottom on the east to the Rigolet or creek of Cahokia.*

In the following year, on June 14, 1723, Boisbriant and Des Ursins granted to Philip Francois de Renault, director-general of the mining operations of the company, one league square of land in the south-west part of what is now Monroe county, Illinois, and also a tract of land of more than fourteen thousand acres at Peoria. Renault was

---

* Breese's History, pp. 174 to 176.

a man of fortune and enterprise, who had left *La Belle France* in the spring of 1719, with two hundred miners and laborers, and every thing needful to prosecute the business pertaining to his office. On the voyage to Louisiana, he purchased at St. Domingo five hundred Guinea negroes to work in the mines. Arriving on the Lower Mississippi, he thence ascended the river in canoes to the Illinois and Missouri, where gold and silver were supposed to exist in abundance. Sanguine hopes were entertained by the stockholders of the "company" at his anticipated success, but they all eventually ended in disappointment. Prospecting and mining parties were sent out into various parts of the country. Diligent search was made for minerals on Drewry's Creek, in what is now Jackson county; about St. Mary's, in Randolph county; along Silver Creek, in Monroe county; at several points in St. Clair county, and in other parts of Southern Illinois, as well as in Missouri. But, after expending a large amount of money and four years of valuable time, Renault had to content himself with the gift of the before mentioned wild lands, and with dull lead instead of the glittering ores.*

On the concession made to him in Monroe county, he laid out a little village, which he honored with his own baptismal appellation of "St. Philippe." It stood on the plain, about one mile east of the Mississippi, and five miles from old Fort Chartres. Like all the other French villages, it had its "common field," the allotments being made by the founder, and also its "commons," embracing a large scope of the unappropriated domain. It contained at one time sixteen houses, besides a small chapel, but in 1765 nearly all the inhabitants deserted it, and went to reside on the western bank of the Mississippi. Not a vestige of either this or Charte Village now remain to tell the story of their rise, progress, or decline. The name of the worthy Renault, however, is still perpetuated in that of a precinct and post-office of Monroe county.

---

* Later geological investigation has shown that silver is combined with the lead mined in this region, but in hardly sufficient quantities to pay for its separation.

To Boisbriant himself, the Company of the Indies, before the surrender of its vast privileges to the crown, granted what in Europe would have been considered a handsome principality, embracing several thousand acres of rich bottom land, extending from the bluffs on the east to the Mississippi. In 1733, he transferred this fine tract to his nephew, Jean St. Therese Langlois, an officer of the king's troops then quartered in the Illinois. Imitating Renault's example, Langlois established upon his estate the village of Prairie du Rocher, reserving to himself certain seignorial rights recognized by the feudal law and the customs of Paris. He divided the land set apart for the village into small, narrow allotments, with a "common field," as usual, to actual settlers, some of whose descendants continue to cultivate it in a primitive way to the present time. This village took its name from the rocky bluff that bounds it on the east, and runs parallel with the river at the distance of a league therefrom. It is situated about three miles east of Fort Chartres, and, at the close of the French dominion, comprised twenty-two dwelling-houses and a chapel.

Aside from those we have mentioned, but few grants of any magnitude were made by the Royal India Company to persons in Illinois. Good lands were far too abundant in those days to be much cared for, or considered of any particular value; otherwise, many of the French settlers might have possessed dukedoms. At this period, the presence of the commandant, and of the local officers of the "company," together with a detachment of his majesty's troops, at Fort Chartres, made it the focus of whatever of wealth, culture, and fashion there was in the district of the Illinois.

In 1725, Governor Bienville, owing to the jealousy and opposition of his enemies, was recalled to France, and his brother, Chateaugué, was also deposed from his office of lieutenant-governor in the colony. M. de Boisbriant, as first king's lieutenant, now became governor *ad interim* of Louisiana, with head-quarters at New Orleans, and his position of major-commandant at the Illinois was filled by the Sieur de Liette, a captain in the royal army. Boisbriant was an amiable and benevolently inclined gentleman, and his administration of affairs was deservedly popular, both in Upper and Lower Louisiana. In August, 1726, he was relieved of his duties as commandant-general of the province by M. de Périer, an officer of the marines, and a knight of St. Louis, who had been appointed to succeed Bienville.

Shortly after his arrival and installation in office, Governor Périer's attention was called to the Natchez and Chickasaw Indians, and to the insincerity of their professions of friendship for the French. He thereupon addressed the directors of the India Company, and urged upon them, as his predecessor had done before, to provide more effective protection for the white settlers exposed to the hostility of those tribes. But his apprehensions were not shared by the directors, and no additional troops appear to have been provided.

We now approach one of the most memorable episodes in the French annals of Louisiana, viz, the war with and destruction of the Natchez nation. The history of this strange and interesting people has been imparted to us by their destroyers; and we may therefore presume that all the more amiable and polished traits ascribed to them are true. They and their kindred, the Taensas (who disappeared as a distinct tribe before 1712), inhabited that range of sunny hills on the east side of the Mississippi, which constitutes one of the finest districts in the present State of Mississippi. Their traditions pointed to the fact that their ancestors had come from countries to the southwest. Their language, Sabianism, human sacrifices, and mound building, seem to connect them with the Toltecs of Mexico, or the Mayas of Yucatan. Their singular custom of distorting the head by compression corresponds with the description of the ancient Mexicans, by Bernal Diaz. They are described as mild, friendly and brave, though preferring peace to war, and as being very dissolute.

Compared with the Indians around them, the Natchez might be called a semi-civilized people. It is true that some barbarous customs prevailed among them, but these only indicate that a cruel and sanguinary superstition may taint the character and manners of a people, otherwise peaceable and humane. They had fixed laws or usages, gradations of rank, and an established worship, with temples dedicated to the sun. They were governed by a chief called the Great Sun, said to have been descended, in the female line, from a man and woman who came down from the sun, and built their first temple for perpetual fire, which was ever afterward maintained. This temple stood on a mound about eight feet high, with a pitched roof, and in it three logs were kept slowly burning. The power of the Sun-chief was absolute, as was that of the lesser suns, or male members of his family. Such was the idolatrous veneration in which the great chief was held by his subjects, that he was never approached by them without special marks of reverence. Next to the Suns were the subordinate chiefs or nobles. The common people, called *puants*, by the French, were apparently a mixed race of Choctaws and others. In war the Natchez used bows and arrows, clubs, and other Indian weapons, but they had no metals of any consequence. They dressed in buffalo, bear and other skins for winter, and in summer wore light robes made of flax, or the inner bark of the mulberry. They had various feasts, which were duly celebrated; and on the death of a chief killed many of his retainers to attend him in the future life. Their dead, after the practice of the Indians in general, were kept on raised platforms till the flesh was consumed, when the bones were buried.

"The Natchez," writes Mr. Gayarré, "were of a light mahogany complexion, with jet black hair and eyes. Their features were extremely regular, and their expression was intelligent, open, and noble. They were tall in stature, very few of them being under six feet, and the symmetry of their well-proportioned limbs was remarkable." This description, however, could hardly apply to any but the chiefs and nobles of that race. Originally a very numerous people, they occupied and ruled the country far up and down the Mississippi; but they began to decline before the appearance of the French among them, which has been termed "the era of their doom." The causes assigned for the dwindling of this race were, their frequent hecatombs of human beings, the state of warfare in which they lived with the neighboring tribes, the prevalence of lung diseases among them, and the ravages of the small-pox.

The existence of the Natchez was known to Europeans from the year 1560, when Don Tristan de Luna led a Spanish expedition into their country from the southern coast of Florida. La Salle, as we have seen, reached them in March, 1682, and d'Iberville was there in the spring of 1700. Soon after that, they were visited by English traders from Carolina. At this period they occupied a group of five villages, situated to the east and south-east of the present city of Natchez, and about three miles from the Mississippi River. The French both courted and dreaded this formidable people, and in their intercourse with them had need for the exercise of all their tact and skill in Indian diplomacy. In 1716, the Natchez having killed some Frenchmen and made prisoners of others, Bienville, as lieutenant of the province, coerced them to put to death certain of the murderers, and built Fort Rosalie there for the protection of the French settlers. In 1722 acts of hostility were renewed by the inconstant Natchez, when Bienville, as commandant-general, sent the Sieur Paillou, with a number of troops, to chastise them ; and in October, 1723, the governor himself conducted an expedition from New Orleans against that people. Upon arriving with his army at the Natchez, he destroyed two of their villages (White Apple and Gray Village), and compelled Stung-Serpent, the great chief of the nation, to bring him the heads of Oldhair, chief of the White Apple Village, and of a free negro, who had settled among the Natchez and made himself the leader of an insurrectionary party. Having thus brought the war to an end, the governor returned to the capital.* But the peace now made was insincere, and new

---

* Dumont's Memoir, in Hist. Coll's of La., vol. v.

troubles arose from time to time between the whites and the Indians.

The proximate cause of the war, which ended in the extinction of the Natchez as a nation, was due to the rapacity and tyranny of the Sieur de Chopart, or Chepart, who was appointed commandant of Fort Rosalie in 1726. He first made himself obnoxious to the French settlers at Natchez by various acts of oppression and injustice, and was ordered to New Orleans to undergo an investigation of his conduct. But, at the solicitation of influential friends, and with mistaken leniency on the part of Governor Périer, he was reinstated in his command. On his return to his post, in 1729, Chopart took with him some negro slaves, intending to establish a plantation in that locality. Not daring to dispossess any of the French settlers, he resolved to take possession of the Great Village of the Natchez, which was seated in a beautiful plain, intersected by the little river St. Catharine. With this intention, he sent for the Sun-chief, and by his interpreter, Papin, ordered him to remove his people from the Great Village, since it was needed for the erection of some large buildings. To so astounding a proposition the great chief replied, "that their nation had long been in possession of that village, and lived there; that the ashes of their fathers reposed there, deposited in the temples which they had built; that the French had never yet taken lands by force; that if they had settled on their lands, the nation itself gave them sites in the hope of obtaining protection and defense against their enemies; and that many Frenchmen had given goods to the Indians in payment for the lands they occupied." *

These representations made no impression on the mind of the rapacious commandant, who repeated his order, with the threat that, if it was not complied with, he would send the chief bound hand and foot to New Orleans. The great chief seeing that he could not move the commandant, pretended to yield to his demand, and only asked two moons (months) in which to choose and prepare a new vil-

---

* Dumont's Memoir, in Hist. Coll's of La., vol. v., p. 65.

lage for his nation. The time asked for was granted by Chopart, but on the condition that the inhabitants of the village should pay him a certain quantity of poultry, baskets of corn, pots of bear's oil and bundles of skins.

When the great chief returned to his village, he summoned a council of his principal chiefs and warriors to consider what means should be adopted to prevent their village and lands from being taken from them by the French. Many secret meetings and conferences were held, and it was finally resolved to massacre not only the commandant and garrison of Fort Rosalie, but all the French in their territory, and thus rid themselves of their hated presence. So soon as this barbarous resolution was taken, they sent deputies to the principal Indian nations in the province, requesting their aid in this supreme effort to preserve their independence. The Choctaws, the Chickasaws, and even the Illinois were invited to take part with them in their meditated scheme of vengeance. The Choctaws were the first and readiest to embrace the quarrel of the Natchez. They agreed to destroy all the French on the lower part of the Mississippi, and for the execution of this purpose fixed the day which ended the two moons granted by the commandant. But as these Indians could not count, they exchanged with each other as many little sticks or twigs as there were days, till that fixed for the butchery. After this negotiation, the Natchez deputies returned to their village, bearing the fatal bundle of sticks. These the great chief carried to the temple, and every morning he threw one of the twigs on the fire, which was kept burning there. The Indians, meantime, remained quietly at their Great Village, taking no steps to remove to another site.

Although kept very secret, the plot was nevertheless disclosed. The interpreter of the post, the sub-lieutenant of the garrison, and several others were warned of what was coming by certain Indian women, their mistresses. Even the day (St. Andrew's-eve) of the bloody execution was foretold. But when this was reported to Chopart, the commandant, he refused to believe it, and went so far as to order those who brought him the disquieting news to be placed under arrest. " Warned as he was, he might very easily have prevented the misfortune which happened, had he chosen to do so; it would have been enough to put the troops under arms, and fire a cannon even without ball. But either because wine and the table had troubled his judgment, or that he was unfortunately prejudiced in favor of the Indians, or that he believed them incapable of daring to execute such a design, he would not take any measures to thwart it; and as his injustice provoked, so his obstinacy crowned the evil and made it remediless."*

The fatal day for the outburst of the smothered vengeance of the savages, according to the count kept by the Natchez, was the 29th of November, 1729. On the morning of that day the Sun-chief set out from his village, attended by a numerous body of his warriors, with their weapons concealed under their clothing, and with the calumet raised aloft, they marched to the house of the commandant, bearing the promised tribute of poultry, corn, bear's oil, etc. The soldiers of the garrison were abroad in fancied security, and the savages immediately seized the gates of the fort, so as to exclude them from access to their arms. At the same time the houses of the French, and a boat at the landing, were surrounded. The work of blood now began, and before noon nearly all the Frenchmen cantoned among the Natchez were slain. Two men only were spared—one a carter and the other a tailor—and a few others escaped. Such was the abhorrence and contempt of the Natchez for Chopart, that none of their chiefs would kill him, and a Puant warrior was deputed to perform that service.

It is related that the Sun-chief took his seat under the projecting roof of the store-house belonging to the India Company, and complacently smoked his calumet, while the heads of the Frenchmen were brought one after another and laid at his feet. Among the more prominent victims

---

*Dumont's Historical Memoir, before cited. He was a lieutenant in the French service, and a participant in some of the events he narrates.

of this treacherous massacre were, Father du Poisson, a Jesuit missionary among the Arkansas; Father Soulet, a Capuchin missionary to the Natchez; the Sieur de la Loire des Ursins, who had been judge and commissary at Natchéz; M. de Koly and son, who had arrived only the day before to visit their concession on St. Catherine's Creek; and the Sieur Codere, commandant of the post on the Yazoo, who happened to be at Fort Rosalie at the time. The French garrison of twenty men, at Fort St. Claude, on the Yazoo, also shared the fate of assassination; but this was not until some weeks later, for the Natchez did not, at first, admit the Yazoo Indians into the secret of their plot. The total number of men killed was reckoned at not less than two hundred and fifty. Several of the French women, who attempted to defend their husbands or brothers, were cut down by the pitiless savages; but the greater part of the women and children were held up as captives, and the negro slaves were kept for menial purposes.

When the tidings of this horrible massacre were carried to New Orleans and Mobile, it created a general consternation. But Governor Périer promptly took measures of defense and retaliation. A vessel was dispatched to France for additional troops and military stores, and messengers were sent with the news, by way of Red River and the Arkansas, to Fort Chartres, in the Illinois. The town of New Orleans was hastily fortified by a ditch and embankment, and each house was furnished with arms. The governor assembled a force of regulars and militia to move up the river against the Natchez, and confided the command of it to the Chevalier de Lubois, king's lieutenant.

Governor Périer also sent the Sieur de Lery,* a capable officer, familiar with the Indian languages, to sound the Choctaws, and gain over that inconstant tribe to the French interest. The Choctaws were piqued at the Natchez for having made their attack upon the French two days in advance of the time fixed by their fagot of sticks, and, moreover, were dissatisfied with the reception accorded by the

---

* Or Le Sueur, according to some authorities.

Natchez to their deputies, who had been sent thither a few days after the massacre. Under these circumstances, the Sieur de Lery, by distributing presents among the Choctaw chiefs, easily induced them to serve the French in the campaign, and he was followed across the country by over twelve hundred of their dusky warriors. Entering the Natchez territory, and advancing to the vicinity of the Great Village, Captain de Lery and his Choctaw army encamped about the 28th of January, 1730, to await the arrival of the French army from New Orleans. Still exulting in their triumph, and not expecting to be attacked so soon, the Natchez were spending their time in idle festivities and carousals. Early the next morning (the 29th), the Choctaws rushed upon their village, liberated some of the captive French women (whom they stripped of every thing the Natchez had left them), and brought away a number of prisoners and scalps.

In the following February the colonial troops arrived from the capital, under the command of the Chevalier de Loubois, who laid siege to the fort of the Natchez on St. Catherine's Creek. In the meantime the Natchez made preparations for a determined resistance; but upon the appearance of so superior a force, and hearing the discharge of French cannon, they humbly sued for peace, offering to restore the prisoners remaining in their hands, and forsake the country. Anxious to save the captive women and children, Loubois consented to postpone the attack for one day. During the night of the truce, however, the Natchez withdrew from their fort and village so quietly as not to disturb the slumbers of their enemies. Their escape was due to a want of vigilance on the part of the French officers, who may have connived at it, and the war was consequently prolonged. Leaving a detachment of one hundred and twenty men to rebuild Fort Rosalie, which had been destroyed by the Natchez, the French commander embarked with the remainder of his army for New Orleans.

Some of the fugitive Natchez sought shelter and homes with the Chickasaws; but the main body of the nation, under the lead of the Sun-chief, crossed the Mississippi and established a new village and fort on Black River, from whence they continued their acts of hostility. Thither they were pursued by Governor Périer in January, 1731, with a force of one thousand French and Indians; and on the 25th of that month, partly by assault, and partly by strategy, he reduced their stronghold, capturing the Sun, his brother and nephew, forty warriors, and three hundred and eighty-seven women and children. These were sent to New Orleans, whence they were shipped to St. Domingo, and sold as slaves for the benefit of the "company." A remnant of the tribe, fleeing farther westward, came in conflict with the Natchitoches, by whom they were repulsed with loss, aided by the French under the veteran St. Denis; after which they joined the Chickasaws, and kept up a desultory warfare on the French settlers.*

"Thus perished the nation of the Natchez. Their peculiar language, which has been still preserved by the descendants of the fugitives, and is, perhaps, now on the point of expiring—their worship (of the sun), their divisions into nobles and plebeians, their bloody funeral rites— invite conjecture, and yet so nearly resemble in character the distinctions of other tribes that they' do but excite, without gratifying, curiosity." †

---

*The Natchez never again appeared as a distinct nation. After a considerable time they moved to the Muskogees, and in 1835 were reduced to 300 souls, retaining their own language and line of Suns, but without restoring their temple or sun-worship. For their language, the only materials are the words preserved by Le Page du Pratz and other early French writers, and a vocabulary taken by Gallatin, in 1826, from the chief Isahalateh. Dr. Brinton traced the analogy between it and the Maya.—Amer. Encyclo., vol. xii., p. 158.

† Bancroft's History, vol. iii., p. 364.

Note.—In the vicinity of the modern city of Natchez there are, or were formerly, two or three groups of ancient mounds of considerable size, from which have been taken numerous relics, such as stone weapons, pipes, earthen vessels covered with figures, fragments of pottery, etc. It has been a question among local antiquaries whether these tumuli were in any way the work of the Natchez Indians. But the probabilities are, that while they may have been used as places of sepulture by these or other Indians, yet that, if not mere natural elevations, they were originally the work of the more ancient mound builders.

The heavy expenditures incurred in prosecuting the war against the Natchez, the consequent loss of trade with other tribes, the inadequate returns from its commerce and mines, and the financial embarrassments following Law's failure, induced the Company of the Indies to solicit leave of the king for a surrender of its charter in Louisiana. The petition was granted; and on the 10th of April, 1732, by proclamation of Louis XV., the jurisdiction and control of the government and commerce of the colony reverted directly to the French crown. The Company of the West and its successor, the Royal India Company, had held actual possession of the Louisiana wilderness for fourteen years, which, upon the whole, were years of prosperity. During this period the white population of the province had increased from something over one thousand to five thousand, and the number of negro slaves from twenty to two thousand. New Orleans had been made the seat of the provincial government and the chief mart of trade. The extravagant hopes at first entertained in regard to the precious metals had not been realized, but the search for them had attracted hither many immigrants, some of whom had now made such progress in agriculture as to be self-sustaining. Illinois contained at this time several flourishing settlements, the inhabitants of which were more exclusively devoted to the cultivation of the soil than in any other part of the province.

It has been observed by an Illinois historian, that all industrial enterprises were, to a great extent, paralyzed by the arbitrary exactions of the "company;" that the agriculturists, the miners, and the fur-traders of Illinois were held in a sort of vassalage, which enabled those in power to dictate the price at which they should sell their products, and the amount they should pay them for imported merchandise; and that the interest of the company was always at variance with that of the producer.

All of this might have been, and perhaps was, substantially true. But "whoever takes a correct view of the transactions of the Mississippi Company," says Major Stoddard, "must be convinced that it was of infinite utility to

Louisiana, perhaps the preservation of it."* Judge Breese also takes a very favorable view of the rule of the great corporation in the Illinois. He writes:

"Their sway here was more in name than in fact; for, setting aside their power to grant lands, all real control of the people (in Illinois) was with the Jesuits. Their business pursuits were but little interfered with, and no arbitrary or forced exactions of their little abundance were made. They did not find, as is too often the case in others, in this overshadowing monopoly, whose sole principle of aggregation was wealth, a cruel and heartless tyrant, ready and willing, in the various modes such corporations can devise, to plunder them of their small revenues, or oppress them in any form. In their relations to it, it was as the benefactor to the benefited; and though the fortunes of its proprietors were wrecked, the colony itself received a new and immense impulse from its varied operations."†

---

* "Historical Sketches of Louisiana." (Phila., Pa., 1812), p. 61.
† "Early History of Illinois," p. 180.

CHAPTER XV.

1732-1752.

LOUISIANA UNDER THE DIRECT GOVERNMENT OF THE CROWN.

When the Royal India Company, successor to the Company of the West, gave up its charter and vast privileges to the crown, another government was at once organized for the Province of Louisiana, which severed it from New France, and continued Illinois as a dependency of Louisiana. By letters patent of the 7th of May, 1732, the Superior Council of the province was re-organized, with Périer as governor, Salmon as intendant commissary, and Loubois and d'Artaguette (Diron) as king's lieutenants. The ecclesiastical affairs of the colony were under the more immediate supervision of a vicar-general, residing in New Orleans.

In 1733 the Canadian, Bienville, much to his own satisfaction and that of his friends, was re-appointed governor of Louisiana in place of Périer, who was promoted to the rank of lieutenant-general as a reward for his important services in the colony. The new commandant-general reached New Orleans early in 1734, and the Sieur Périer, resigning the government into his hands, immediately embarked for France.

During that year Captain Pierre d'Artaguette was appointed by Governor Bienville major-commandant for the district of the Illinois, with head-quarters at Fort Chartres. He was a younger brother of Diron d'Artaguette, the *commissaire ordonnateur* of Louisiana, and one of the most conspicuous men in the province. Pierre d'Artaguette had served with gallantry in the Natchez war, and was afterward sent by Périer to command at the new fort, which was built on the site of the old one at Natchez.* After his transfer to the Illinois he had no pleasant path to tread, as was the case with his predecessors.

The Chickasaw Indians—the Iroquois of the South—had all along preferred an alliance with the English colonists of Carolina, and had been stimulated by artful emissaries of the latter (if they required any stimulus) to repeated deeds of rapine and blood against the French, who were waiting a favorable opportunity to make them feel the weight of their resentment. The Chickasaws were known to Europeans, or at least to the Spaniards, from the time of De Soto. They inhabited the country intermediate between Upper and Lower Louisiana, extending eastward from the Mississippi River into Alabama, and northward through Western Tennessee. They were a less numerous people than the Cherokees, or even the Choctaws, but they made up in craft and pugnacity what they lacked in numbers. The presence of the Chickasaws in roaming bands on the eastern banks of the Mississippi not only rendered navigation perilous, but seriously interfered with trade between Kaskaskia and New Orleans, and many of the French boatmen and *voyageurs* successively fell victims to their muskets and tomahawks. Such, indeed, was the animosity of this people that they sent emissaries to the tribes of the Illinois to detach them from their long-established friendship with the French settlers, and to persuade them to make war upon and exterminate the latter. But the Illinois rejected the proposition with scorn, and sent a

---

* The new Fort Rosalie, as seen and described by Captain Pittman, in 1766, stood on the east side of the Mississippi, about six hundred and seventy yards from the river, and at an elevation of one hundred and eighty feet above the usual water line. The fort was an irregular pentagon, without bastions, and was built of sawn or hewed plank five inches thick. The buildings within the walls were a store-house, a house for the officers, a barrack for the soldiers, and a guard-house. These houses were constructed of framed timbers, the spaces between being filled with mud and Spanish moss. The fort was surrounded on three sides by a dry ditch, and the fourth or north side was fenced with pickets. Some traces of the ruins of this fort are said to be still visible at Natchez.

deputation, headed by their principal chief, Chccagou, to New Orleans to offer their services to the governor. In an interview with Bienville the chief presented the pipe of friendship, saying: "This is the pipe of peace or war; you have but to speak, and our braves will strike the nations that are your foes."*

By authority of the King of France an invasion of the Chickasaw country was now projected, with the three-fold purpose of re-establishing safe communication between the northern and southern districts of the province, of reducing those truculent savages to submission, and of driving the English traders from among them. The French were not wanting in a plausible pretext for commencing hostilities. Many of the Natchez Indians who escaped the war of extirpation against them had taken refuge among the Chickasaws, and become incorporated with that nation, where they continued to cherish their hatred of the French. Before the beginning of the year 1736, Governor Bienville made a demand on the Chickasaws for the surrender of those fugitives, and foreseeing that his demand was not likely to be complied with, he assembled an army to march against them. Great preparations were made, considering the military strength of the colony, to render the expedition successful. In addition to the regulars and militia raised in Southern Louisiana, the Governor sent Captain Leblanc up the river to Fort Chartres with orders to the Sieur d'Artaguette, commandant of the district, to get in readiness the troops under his command, together with such of the Illinois and other Indians as could be induced to join the expedition. D'Artaguette was further ordered to be in the Chickasaw country, with his forces, by the 10th of the ensuing May, and to there await the arrival of the commander-in-chief and his army from the south.

On the 4th of March, 1736, Bienville embarked at New Orleans, with a force of five hundred and fifty-four Frenchmen and forty-five negroes, for Fort Mobile, the rendezvous of the troops. Resting here until Easter-day, the first of April, the army began to ascend the river in bateaux

---

* Bancroft's History, Vol. III, p. 365.

and pirogues, which moved in line by force of oars. On the 20th the army reached a place called Tombecbé (Tombigbee), to which the governor had sent a company of soldiers nine months before to build a fort, intending it as a place of defense and a depot of supplies. This fort was on the Tombigbee River, and within the territory of the Choctaws. The artillery which the French had brought with them was now placed in position, and its discharge broke, for the first time, the stillness of the surrounding forest. Here the Choctaw chiefs, in consideration of a certain quantity of merchandise, joined Bienville's expedition with over six hundred of their warriors. Re-embarking on the 4th of May, and continuing to ascend the river, the troops reached the place of debarkation on the 24th of that month. They were now within seven or eight leagues of the nearest and principal Chickasaw village, which was situated only a few miles from the present county town of Pontotoc, in Northern Mississippi,—a town which still preserves the name of the Indian stronghold.

On the 25th of May (two weeks behind the prearranged time), the commander formed his army in two columns, and marched to within two leagues of the Chickasaw village, when he halted for the night. Early the next morning the impetuous Choctaws rushed forward upon the village, expecting to take it by a *coup de main*. But they found the Chickasaws awake and ready to receive them; and not only so, but protected by a strong fortification of earth and timbers, which had been constructed under the supervision of some resident English traders. During that day Bienville made two vigorous attempts to carry the enemy's works by storm, but was repulsed both times, and sustained a loss of thirty-two killed and sixty wounded, including several commissioned officers. He was, therefore, compelled to draw off his army, leaving his dead on the field of battle.

During the night of the 26th, a party of Indians arrived from another village, as they claimed, to present the calumet and a letter to Bienville; but, provoked by the reverses of the day, he refused to receive them, and ordered his Indians to attack them, which they did.* By this rash conduct, the commanding general probably lost his only opportunity of opening communication with D'Artaguette and his associate officers, who were then prisoners in the hands of the Chickasaws.

On the next day there was some skirmishing between the Choctaw and Chickasaw warriors, but without any decisive result. Discouraged at his unexpected failure, convinced of his inability to reduce the enemy's formidable works without cannon and the means of siege, and hearing nothing from the army that was to co-operate with him from the Illinois, Bienville now reluctantly abandoned the expedition. Dismissing his Indian auxiliaries, he made a retrograde march to his boats, and descended the river to Fort Tombecbé. On arriving there, it is told that he threw the iron cannon belonging to the fort into the river, to prevent their falling into the hands of the enemy, and returned to New Orleans covered with humiliation at his disastrous defeat.

Prior to these occurrences, however, Major d'Artaguette had set out from Fort Chartres in the last week of February, with thirty regular soldiers, one hundred volunteers (including the Jesuit father Sénat) and two hundred Illinois and Missouri Indians, and descended the Mississippi to the site of Fort Prudhomme, at the Third Chickasaw Bluff. Here he was soon after joined by the Sieur de Vincennes, from the Wabash, with twenty Frenchmen and about one hundred Miamis braves. The Sieur de Moncherval was also daily expected, with a contingent of Cahokias and Michigamies from the Illinois. Leaving a detachment at the river landing, to guard the canoes and heavier baggage, Major d'Artaguette set forward on his march into the Chickasaw country, and advanced by slow stages in order to give Moncherval a chance to overtake him. But that officer did not arrive in time to participate in the approaching battle. Having reached the appointed rendezvous, which was on the head-waters of the Yalobusha, on the 9th of May, D'Artaguette waited ten days

---

* Dumont's Historical Memoir of Louisiana.

for the appearance of the commander-in-chief, ready to unite with him attacking the enemy.

Meanwhile, according to Mr. Gayarré, a courier reached his camp with a letter, said to have been written by Bienville, stating that in consequence of unexpected obstacles and delays, he would not be able to reach the Chickasaws at the time designated, and authorizing him to act on his own military judgment. D'Artaguette thereupon convened a council of war, composed of his principal officers and the Indian chiefs, and at this council it was resolved to make an immediate attack upon the enemy's stronghold. Accordingly, about the 20th of May, having formed his impatient forces in order of battle—forces who had the courage to strike, without the discretion to wait the proper time—the commander led them against the Chickasaws. The charge was daring and impetuous, and the enemy was successively driven from two of his intrenched positions, but in the assault upon the third D'Artaguette was severely wounded and disabled, at the moment when the victory seemed within his grasp. Panic-struck at the fall of their leader, his Indian confederates, the Illinois and Missouris, precipitately retreated, and were hotly pursued for twenty-five leagues by the Chickasaws, in the flush of triumph. The Miamis, from the Wabash, appear to have been guilty of deliberate treachery, they having been previously tampered with by English agents.*

Father Sénat and the chivalrous DeVincennes might have both escaped, but the former, true to his profession, stayed to console the wounded and dying, while the latter was so devoted to his unfortunate chief, that he would not leave him in peril, "preferring rather to share his captivity, and, if necessary, to die by his side." As a consequence, they, with some fifteen other Frenchmen, including a brother of Captain Louis St. Ange, fell into the hands of the Chickasaws. The prisoners were, at first, civilly treated by their captors, who expected to receive a large reward from

---

* See " History of Louisiana," by Chas. Gayarré (New Orleans, 1885), 3d ed., vol. II., pp. 485–6.

the French for their safe return. But, after the discomfiture and retreat of Bienville's army, the Chickasaw chiefs abandoned hope of securing an adequate ransom for their prisoners, and prepared to make them the victims of a savage triumph. To this end they were taken to a neighboring field and bound by fours to stakes; and neither valor nor piety could save them from being tortured to death by slow and intermitting fires. Two of the number were reserved to be exchanged for a Chickasaw warrior, who had been made prisoner by the French.

After this cruel manner perished the gallant D'Artaguette, the faithful Sénat, and the heroic De Vincennes. We would not withhold the meed of sympathy due them in their direful fate. At the same time it must not be forgotten that, in hazarding an assault upon the enemy in his fortified position, before the arrival of the main army under Bienville, they invited the very fate that befell them, and destroyed the chances of French victory in that campaign.

The Chickasaws were now more defiant than ever, and being elated with vanity over their success in repelling the attacks of two French and Indian armies, they sent a deputation of chiefs to announce their triumph to the English authorities in Carolina, with whom they renewed their alliance, and by whom they were supplied with arms and ammunition, as well as merchandise.

Ambitious to retrieve his own military reputation, and also to recover the lost prestige of the French arms in Louisiana, Governor Bienville resolved upon a second campaign against the Chickasaws; but it was not until after receiving reinforcements from France that he was able to renew this arduous enterprise. In the spring of 1739, having previously obtained the sanction of the French Minister of Colonies, he again began active preparations for the subjugation of that fierce tribe, which had so successfully defied his power and authority. Orders were sent out to commandants of the various military posts in the province to furnish as many troops as possible, which resulted in the assembling of the largest and best appointed army hitherto seen in Louisiana. The general rendezvous was at first fixed on the St. Francis River, just above its junction with the Mississippi, where a fort and cabins were erected to serve as a basis of operations. The commandant-general arrived at this post toward the end of June, and in August he embarked his army and moved up to the mouth of Wolf River, a small stream which falls into the Mississippi near the present city of Memphis. Here, on the bluff, another and larger fort was built, with a house for the commandant, barracks for the soldiers, store-houses, etc. It received the name of Fort Assumption, because the troops landed here on that day.

At this fort the army received reinforcements from the north. The first to arrive was the Illinois force, composed of about two hundred Frenchmen and three hundred Indians, commanded by Alphonse de Buissoniere, who had succeeded the unfortunate D'Artaguette as commandant at Fort Chartres. After that came Captain de Céleron and Lieutenant de St. Laurent, with thirty cadets from Canada, and a large following of Indians. These united troops made a formidable army, numbering twelve hundred Frenchmen, and double as many Indians and negroes. Owing in part to the difficulty in procuring supplies, which had to be brought a long distance, this large body of troops was allowed to remain here in inactivity for six months.* In the meantime, provisions became so scarce that they had to kill and eat their horses, and sickness breaking out in the camp carried off a great number. Such were the ravages of disease and famine, that by the first of March, 1740, not more than two hundred French soldiers were fit for active service.

In these straits, Governor Bienville sent the Sieur de Céleron, with a body of French and Indian troops, to the Chickasaws, with orders, in case they sued for peace, to grant it in his name. When Céleron arrived with his force in sight of the enemy's fort, the Chickasaws, believing him to be

---

* Mr. Gayarré attributes Bienville's inaction to his jealousy of Noailles, who had been sent to command the army.

followed by the whole French army, sent to him to ask for
peace, promising to renounce their English alliance and resume friendly relations with the French. To confirm this
agreement, a party of their chiefs returned with Céleron to
Fort Assumption, and there entered into a treaty of pacification with the governor, which was ratified with the customary Indian ceremonies. Bienville now dismissed his
Indian auxiliaries, having first paid them off in goods, after
which he demolished his two forts, as being of no further
use, and re-embarked for New Orleans.*

So ended, in April, 1740, the second campaign against
the Chickasaws. It was less inglorious and disastrous
than the first, but its results were far from satisfactory, and
by no means commensurate with the costly preparations
that had been made. Having failed to redeem his tarnished
military record, and the prestige of the French arms in the
colony, the commandant-general thereby incurred the displeasure of his sovereign, and for this and other reasons he
was, in no long time, removed from office. Toward the
close of the year 1742, he was superseded by Pierre Francois de Rigaud, Marquis de Vaudreuil-Cavagnal, a native
of Quebec, and a man of distinguished family and social
connections.

Thus closed the official career of Jean Baptiste le
Moyne, Sieur de Bienville, in Louisiana,—a career which,
with some interruptions, extended through a period of
forty-three years, and which is without a parallel in French-
American history. Born at Montreal, in February, 1680,
he was nineteen years the junior of his celebrated brother,
D'Iberville, who introduced him when a mere lad into the
naval service, took him with him to Hudson's Bay, and
afterward on his first colonizing expedition to the Mississippi. Age and care had now cooled the ardor and energy
of Bienville's prime, and the luster of the honors achieved
in former years was obscured under a cloud of court censure, some of which, at least, was undeserved. In May,

---

* For more detailed accounts of this Chickasaw war, see Dumont's,
Martin's, and Gayarré's Histories of Louisiana. The account by Dumont is the earliest and most authentic.

1743, he sailed from New Orleans for France, thus leaving Louisiana forever. Although under the displeasure of the court the colonists were loud in expressing their regrets at his departure; and whatever errors or mistakes, inseparable from human nature, he may have committed, his popularity in the province, where he had mostly lived from early manhood to old age, had never been seriously shaken. He has been justly styled the Father of the Louisiana colony, of which his brother D'Iberville was the founder. He left behind him a code, sometimes called *Le Code Noir*, which was first promulgated in 1724, regulating the condition of the slaves, banishing the Jews, and prohibiting the exercise of every religion except the Roman Catholic. This code, with some modifications, remained in force in Louisiana until the cession of that country to the government of the United States, when it was abolished, excepting so much of it as related to the African slaves. After returning to France, Bienville lived for over twenty years in dignified retirement at Paris.

But to return to Louisiana. After the peace of 1740 with the Chickasaws, all the other aboriginal tribes in the immediate Valley of the Mississippi recognized the dominion of France, and became allies or friends of her colonists. Trade with the natives was now renewed and enlarged, and agriculture, freed from former restrictions, took on a new life. The culture of fruit became general. The orange, the lemon, and the fig tree began to blossom about the houses on the Lower Mississippi, and near the shores of the gulf; while farther to the north the apple, the peach, the apricot, and the plum were successfully grown. The sweet potato and the melon, extending over a wide range of latitude, also contributed largely to the sustenance of the people. Sugar-cane was brought by the Jesuits from St. Domingo as early as 1744, and was first cultivated by them in their gardens at New Orleans.* It was before this

---

* In 1758, M. de Breuil opened a sugar plantation on a large scale, and erected the first sugar mill in Louisiana. His plantation occupied the lower part of New Orleans, known as the suburb of St. Marigny.— *Reynolds' Pioneer History*, second edition, p. 64.

time that indigo began to be raised for export. The cotton plant was not introduced until some years later, when it was successfully cultivated as far north as the Ohio. Every vessel arriving from France added to the population of the southern settlements; and many Canadians, fleeing from the rigor of their northern winters, sought homes and happiness in the more genial climate of the Illinois. Under the stimulus of private and associate enterprise, commerce between the northern and southern districts of the province, and between New Orleans and foreign ports, was largely augmented. Cargoes of flour, bacon, tallow, pelts and lead were annually transported in *bateaux* to New Orleans, and thence reshipped to the West Indies or to France, in exchange for rice, sugar, indigo, and goods of European manufacture. The different districts of the province were mutually dependent, and, by means of the Mississippi and its numerous large tributaries, supplied with facility each other's wants. Upon the whole, the decade from 1742 to 1752 was one of unwonted prosperity in the French history of Louisiana.*

After some ten years of comparative peace and quiet, the Chickasaws, notwithstanding their existing treaty obligations, renewed their depredations upon the French colonists, and again interrupted their trade on the Mississippi River. To curb the marauding disposition of these savages, and coerce them into submission, Governor de Vaudreuil undertook another armed expedition to their forest fastnesses. Embarking at New Orleans, in 1752, with seven hundred regular soldiers, he was joined on the way by a horde of Choctaw braves, ready for the fray. His route was up the Mobile and Tombigbee Rivers, the same as that taken by Bienville in 1736. He had cannon, munitions, and supplies in abundance; yet, like his predecessor, he failed to vanquish the stubborn Chickasaws, who avoided an open battle, and shut themselves up in their fortresses. The French commander, however, destroyed some of their deserted

---

* Davidson and Stuve's History, p. 127.

villages, and left a strong garrison at Fort Tombecbé to hold them in restraint.

Reference having been made to the Sieur de Vincennes, and to the sad fate that befell him in the first campaign of the Chickasaw war, the inquiring reader may desire to know something more of his history, and also of the origin of the French village (now city) which is indissolubly linked with his memory. Jean Baptiste Bissot, Sieur de Vincennes was the tenth child of M. Francois Bissot, a leading merchant of Quebec, and was there born in January, 1688. He appears to have been a relative of Joliet, the explorer, who was probably an uncle by marriage. Early bred to the profession of arms, young De Vincennes was sent out to the West, where he soon became noted for his activity and enterprise. In 1704, with a party of Canadian troops, he attacked an Ottawa band, and rescued from them some Iroquois prisoners that had been taken in violation of treaties, thus averting a cause of war with the latter nation. In the autumn of 1705, he was sent by Governor de Vaudreuil* on a mission to the Miamis, who then principally occupied the territory immediately to the north-west of the Upper Wabash. In 1712 he took part in the defense of Detroit from an invasion of the Fox Indians, and during that year was again sent as an agent to the Miamis.

As early as 1719, De Vincennes probably established, or aided in establishing, the trading post on the Wabash which still bears his name; for it was about this time that Fort Ouatanon, higher up the river, was also founded by the French. A more ancient date than this has been claimed for the first settlement at Vincennes, but it doubtless originated in the confounding of the Wabash and Lower Ohio together as one stream.

"Before the close of the year 1702 (says Dillon's History of Indiana, p. 21), the Sieur Juchereau, a Canadian officer, assisted by the Jesuit missionary Mermet, made an

---

*This was Philippe de Rigaud, Marquis de Vaudreuil, who had been appointed governor of Canada in 1703, to succeed M. de Callieres. He was the father of that Marquis de Vaudreuil, who became successively governor of Louisiana and of Canada.

attempt to establish a post on the Ohio, near the mouth of that river; or, according to some authorities, on the Wabash at the site now occupied by Vincennes." But La Harpe,* and after him Charlevoix, fix the position of that post at the mouth of the Ouabache (Ohio), which discharges itself into the Mississippi. It was probably on the site of the more modern Fort Massac, and the date of its establishment is fixed by some French writers in the year 1700.

The neighboring Mascoutins, who later became associated with the Kickapoos, soon gathered about this post on the Ohio for the purpose of barter, and Father Mermet undertook, without success, to convert them to Christianity. In 1705, or thereabouts, the post was broken up in consequence of the increasing hostility of the Indians, and the French traders fled, leaving their effects behind them.†

---

* " In 1702 M. Juchereau, a French officer of Montreal, accompanied by thirty-four Canadians, attempted to form a settlement at the mouth of the Ouabache, to collect buffalo skins."—Extract from La Harpe's Journal, dated Feb. 8, 1703, cited in Dillon's Hist. of Ind., p. 400.

†"Acording to the authority of La Harpe, and the later historian Charlevoix, the French, in the year 1700, established a trading post near the mouth of the Ohio, on the site of the more modern Fort Massac, in Massac county, Ill., for the purpose of securing buffalo hides. The neighboring Mascoutins, as was customary with the Indians, soon gathered about it for the purpose of barter. Their numbers, as well as the expressed wish of the French traders, induced Father Mermet to visit the place and engage in mission work. At the end of four or five years, in 1705, the establishment was broken up on account of a quarrel of the Indians among themselves, which so threatened the lives of the Frenchmen that the latter fled, leaving behind them their effects and thirteen thousand buffalo skins which they had collected. Some years later, Father Marest, writing from Kaskaskia, relates the failure of Father Mermet to convert the Indians at this post on the Wabash; and on the authority of this letter alone, and although Father Marest only followed the prevailing style of calling the Lower Ohio the Wabash, some writers (the late Judge Law being the first) have contended that this post was on the Wabash and at Vincennes. Charlevoix says 'it was at the mouth of the Wabash which discharges itself into the Mississippi.' La Harpe, and also Le Sueur, whose personal knowledge of the post was contemporaneous with its existence, definitely fix its position near the mouth of the Ohio. The latter gives the date of its beginning, and the former narrates an account of its trade and final abandonment. In this way an antiquity has been claimed for Vincennes to which it is not

When the French first explored the Wabash, they found the land on either side of the lower course of that stream in possession of the Piankashaw Indians; and Vincennes was first known to the former as a Piankashaw village, by the name of *Chip-pe-coke*, or Brushwood. It was a secluded spot on the eastern bank of the river, about one hundred miles above its mouth. It was far removed from the French settlements on the northern lakes and on the Mississippi, and during many years it was a mere halting place for the missionaries and fur-traders, who chose to travel southward by the way of the Maumee and the Wabash. Of this sequestered post very little was known to the outside world until some time after the Sieur de Vincennes became its commandant. The priests and traders of Kaskaskia and Cahokia kept up some intercourse with the place, but there was no regular communication with it. The route thither by river was circuitous and dangerous, while the Indian "trace" or trail across the intervening wilderness of Illinois was beset by roving bands of bloodthirsty Kickapoos.

Under the auspices of De Vincennes, who built an earthen fort there about the year 1725, this Wabash post gradually assumed importance. He appears to have granted lands, in small parcels, to the French settlers for cultivation, and from the neighboring Indian chiefs they received a gift of more than two thousand acres, which they appropriated chiefly as "commons." * It is conjectured by Breese that the land on which the village was built, and the "common field" as well, were originally granted to De Vincennes by the India Company, or by the governor of Louisiana after the dissolution of the company in 1732, and that he, as

---

historically entitled."—"History of Vermilion County, Illinois," by H. W. Beckwith (Chicago, 1879), p. 102, *note*.

* "In 1742, some years after the foundation of the post of Vincennes, the natives of the country made the French and their heirs an absolute gift of the lands lying between the point above and the river Blanche (White) below the village, with as much land on both sides as might be comprised within the said limits."—Dillon's Hist. of Ind., p. 402. See also Memorial signed by sixteen of the inhabitants of Vincennes, dated November 20, 1793, and addressed to the president of the United States.

commandant, parceled it out in small allotments to the villagers. But however this might be, it was all included within the dependency of the Illinois, and differed but little from the other villages in this provincial district.

The Sieur de Vincennes* was still commanding at this post in 1735, and until the spring of 1736, when he was summoned by Major d'Artaguette to join him, with a force of French and Miamis, in his expedition against the Chickasaws, from which neither of these French officers ever returned. But the post village which the former had founded was thereafter variously known as Post de Vincennes, Au Poste, Post Vincent, Post St. Vincents, and finally Vincennes. Louis St. Ange de Bellerive succeeded De Vincennes in command of the post, though in what year is undecided. During his lengthy incumbency, and as early as the year 1749, he made some grants or deeds conveying small lots of land to different settlers in the village. These were executed on coarse paper, and were signed by "St. Ange, commandant *au poste* Vincenne."

In 1749, a mission was established, under charge of the missionary Meurin, at the Piankashaw village, which stood near the site of Post Vincennes. In the course of the next year, 1750, a small stockade fort was built at that place, and another light fortification was erected about the same time at the confluence of the Wabash and the Ohio. Between the years 1754 and 1756 the white population of Post Vincennes was considerably augmented by the arrival of immigrants from Detroit, Kaskaskia, and New Orleans. During this period the French settlers at Post Vincent, Ouatanon,† and the

---

* There is some little reason for supposing that there were two men of this name who figured in the Valley of the Wabash at or near the same time. In a letter addressed to the Council of Marine, written at Quebec, and dated October 28, 1719, M. de Vaudreuil says: "I learn from the last letters that have arrived from the Miamis, that the Sieur de Vincennes having died in their village, these Indians have resolved not to remove to the river St. Joseph." After citing the above extract in his history, page 402, Mr. Dillon observes: "This report of the death of Vincenne was untrue; or there was soon afterward, in the West, another French officer who bore the name of M. de Vincenne."

† Ouiatenon, Ouatanon, or Watanon, stood on the north side of the

Twightee village near the site of Fort Wayne, enjoyed a state of almost unlimited ease and freedom. Living in the midst of the forest wilderness, without taxes or church rates, and in friendship with the neighboring Indians, they spent their days in hunting and fishing, and in trading for pelts and furs, raising a few vegetables and a little maize for the sustenance of their families. Many of them intermarried with the daughters of the red men, whose amity was thereby secured and strengthened.*

Wabash, not far below the present city of Lafayette. When Colonel George Croghan visited this post in July, 1765, he found there fourteen French families residing within the stockade. According to his printed journal, Vincennes then contained from eighty to ninety families, and was a "place of great consequence for trade." The fort was garrisoned by only a few soldiers.

* Dillon's Hist. Ind., pp. 55 and 109.

CHAPTER XVI.

1742-1756.

PROGRESS OF EVENTS IN THE DEPENDENCY OF ILLINOIS.

In 1742, when the Marquis de Vaudreuil was made governor of Louisiana, Captain Benoist de St. Clair was major-commandant of the Illinois, having been appointed two years before to succeed La Buissoniere. But, early in 1743, St. Clair was superseded by the Chevalier de Bértel, or Bérthel, who held the position until 1748-9.

Among the earlier acts of his provincial administration, Governor de Vaudreuil confirmed to the inhabitants of Kaskaskia their right of "commons"—a right for which they had petitioned the Royal India Company, through their commandant, De Liette,* in 1727, but which had been until now wholly disregarded. It will be remembered that in 1719 M. de Boisbriant, as commandant at the Illinois, had granted a right of commons to the citizens of Kaskaskia, but had neglected to put his grant in writing, and that upon the surrender of the India Company's charter, in 1732, the whole country became united to the royal domain, so that the poor villagers continued in a state of painful uncertainty for sixteen years. At length, in June, 1743, these loyal subjects of the French king addressed a respectful petition to the new provincial governor to confirm their title; and in August they received a favorable response thereto in writing, of which the following is the more important part:

"Pierre de Rigault de Vaudreuil, governor, and Edme. Gatien Salmon, commissary orderer of the Province of Louisiana:—

"[Having] seen the petition to us presented on the 16th

---
* Breese writes this name *De Lielte*, and Mason *De Siette*.

day of June of this present year, by the inhabitants of the parish of the Immaculate Conception of Kaskaskia, dependence of the Illinois, tending to be confirmed in the possession of a common which they have had a long time for the pasturage of their cattle, in the point called *La Pointe de Bois,* which runs to the entrance of the river Kaskaskia, We, by virtue of the power to us granted by his majesty, have confirmed and do confirm to the said inhabitants the possession of the said commons, on the following conditions.

[Then follow the conditions in detail, which are omitted here.]

" Given at New Orleans, the 14th day of August, 1743.
(Signed) " VAUDRIEUL.
" " SALMON."

Concerning the above act of confirmation, Breese writes: " This confirmation took from the inhabitants the islands in the Mississippi, and the land on the east side of the Kaskaskia River, which the benevolent Boisbriant had verbally granted to them; nevertheless, they were content, as it secured to them nearly seven thousand acres of rich pasture and woodland, for *house-bote, plough-bote, fire-bote,* and *estovers,* and yielding, also, in great profusion, grapes, plums, persimmons, the lucious papaw, the delicate pecan, and other rich and delicious nuts; whilst the 'common field,' by this arrangement, did not embrace less than eight thousand acres of the richest, deepest, blackest loam, capable of itself of sustaining a numerous people.*

Kaskaskia continued from the first to be the most considerable of the Illinois villages, and carried on a profitable trade by the river with Natchez and New Orleans. From Kaskaskia, as a parent hive, small swarms of colonists were sent out, at intervals, to people the neighboring localities.

As early as the year 1735, according to tradition, a few French Canadian families had fixed their abode on the western bank of the Mississippi,† attracted thither, no doubt,

---

* Breese's Early Illinois, p. 187.
† The first military settlement of the French, in what is now the

by the salt springs and lead mines, which had been opened in that vicinity. This hamlet was located on the low river bottom, and took the name of *Misère*, signifying poverty or misery, but only in a comparative sense, when contrasted with the older and more flourishing establishments on this side of the river. After the great flood in the Mississippi, in 1785, which completely inundated their village, the inhabitants removed to the present site, on a bluff, three miles north or north-west of the old one. The new village received the name of Ste. Genevieve, by which it has ever since been known.* It is still a place of considerable importance, with a noticeable admixture of the original Gallic element in its population. The town has long been the seat of justice of Ste. Genevieve county, Mo., and by the last United States census, contained fifteen hundred and eighty-six inhabitants.

The population of the French and Indian villages in the district of the Illinois, at the period of which we write, is largely a matter of conjecture and computation. Father Louis Vivier, a Jesuit missionary, in a letter dated June 8, 1750, and written from the vicinity of Fort Chartres, says:

"We have here whites, negroes, and Indians, to say nothing of the cross-breeds. There are five French villages, and three villages of the natives within a space of twenty-five leagues, situate between the Mississippi and another river called (Kaskaskia). In the French villages are, perhaps, eleven hundred whites, three hundred blacks, and sixty red slaves or savages. The three Illinois towns do not contain more than eight hundred souls, all told." †

This estimate does not include the scattered French settlers or traders north of Peoria, nor on the Wabash. It is stated that the Illinois nation, then dwelling for the most part along the river of that name, occupied eleven different villages, with four or five fires at each village, and each fire warming a dozen families, except at the principal village, where there were three hundred lodges. These data would

---

State of Missouri, appears to have been at Fort Orleans, on the site of Jefferson City, in 1719.

* Switzler's History of Missouri, p. 143.

† *Lettres Edifiantes et curieuses*, Paris, 1781.

give us something near eight thousand as the total number of the Illinois of all tribes.

It may be as well to observe here that the form of government, if not the character of the civilization, instituted by the French in Canada and Louisiana, was materially different from that contemporaneously established by the English on the Atlantic seaboard. The government of France was bureaucratic, and more on the feudal type; a government in which all power was concentrated in the officers who administered it, while the *paysans*, or common people, had nothing to do but to obey the edicts and orders of their rulers. It was a system more conducive to the general equality and contentment of the people, than to their individual freedom and progress.

In the Province of Louisiana the governor and commandant-general, the intendant commissary, and the royal council exercised supreme authority in both civil and military affairs, and were accountable only to the king from whom they received their appointment. The governor was invested with a great deal of power, which, however, was checked on the side of the crown by the intendant, who had the care of the king's rights and whatever pertained to the revenue, and on the side of the people it was restrained by the royal council, whose duty it was to see that the colonists were not oppressed by the one nor defrauded by the other. The council was styled *Le Conseil Superieur de la Louisiane*. It was composed of the intendant, who sat as first judge, the procureur-general or king's attorney, six of the principal inhabitants, and the registrar of the province; and they judged in all civil and criminal matters. Every citizen had the right to appear before this body and plead his own cause, either verbally or by written petition, and the evidences of each party were submitted to and examined by the council.

The commandants in the various districts of the province were appointed by the governor, for no fixed period, and exercised all such executive duties as the exigencies of their respective districts required, though not without personal accountability to the power appointing them. The

major-commandant, as he was styled, was usually connected
with the governor by interest or relationship. "He was
absolute in his authority," writes Captain Pittman, "except
in matters of life and death; capital offenses were tried by
the council at New Orleans. The whole Indian trade was
so much in the power of the commandant, that nobody was
permitted to be concerned in it but on condition of giving
him a part of the profits. Whenever he made presents to
the Indians in the name of the king, he received peltry and
furs in return; (and) as the presents he gave were to be
considered as marks of his favor and love for them, so the
returns they made were to be regarded as proofs of their
attachment to him. Speeches, accompanied by presents,
were called *paroles de valeur;* any Indians who came to the
French post were subsisted at the expense of the king
during their stay, and the swelling of this account was no
inconsiderable emolument.

"As every business the commandant had with the Indians was attended with certain profit, it is not surprising
that he spared no pains to gain their affections; he made it
equally the interest of the officers under him to please them,
by permitting them to trade, and making themselves agents
in the Indian countries. If any person (or persons) brought
goods within the limits of his jurisdiction, without his
particular license, he would oblige them to sell their merchandise at a very moderate profit to the commissary, on
the king's account, calling it an emergency of government,
and employ the same goods in his own private commerce.
It may be easily supposed, from what has before been said,
that a complaint to the governor at New Orleans would
meet with very little redress. It may be asked if the inhabitants were not offended at this monopoly of trade and
arbitrary proceedings. The commandant could bestow
many favors on them, such as giving contracts for furnishing provisions, or performing public works; by employing
them in his trade, or by making their children cadets, who
were allowed pay and provisions, and he could, when they
were grown up, recommend them for commissions. They
were happy if, by the most servile and submissive behavior,

they could gain his confidence and favor. Every person capable of bearing arms was enrolled in the militia, and a captain of the militia regulated the *corveés* and other personal service.

"From this military form of government, the authority of the commandant was almost universal. The commissary (district) was a mere cipher, and rather kept for form than any real use; he was always a person of low dependence, and never dared to counteract the will of the commandant."*

Subordinate to the major-commandant of the district, each village had its own local commandant, who was usually a captain of the militia. "He was as great a personage," says Breese, "as our city mayors, superintending the police of the village, and acting as a kind of justice of the peace, from whose decisions an appeal lay to the major-commandant. In the choice of this subordinate though important functionary, the adult inhabitants had a voice, and it is the only instance wherein they exercised an elective franchise."

About the year 1751, for the furtherance of justice, the so-called "Court or Audience of the Royal Jurisdiction of the Illinois" was instituted at Kaskaskia. The proceedings of this court were carried on before a single judge, without the assistance of a clerk, sheriff, or lawyers, the judge himself entering his decisions in a book called "The Register." Following is one of the decrees extracted from it, being the opinion of the court by Justice Bucket:

"Between Louis Chancellier, plaintiff, by petition on the 18th of this present month—stating that having abandoned the prosecution of the suit which he had formerly brought against the defendant hereinafter named (on the subject of his negro woman, to whom a fright caused by the son of the defendant has produced dangerous consequences, since the said negro is afflicted with a falling sickness in consequence of this fright)—on the one part, and Pierre Pillet, called De la Londe, defendant, who plead that

* Pittman's "State of the European Settlements on the Mississippi" (London, 1770), pp. 53, 54.

he would not answer for the deeds of his son, but would say in defense of his son that this negro woman fell sick of this sickness before the fright, and, therefore, the plaintiff could not claim any damages on account of the fright which his son gave her, since the cause of her sickness is anterior to that which he pretends to rely upon.

"The parties having been heard, we condemn the defendant to make proof within eight days of what he advances, in order that it may be made to appear to whom the right belongs.

"Done at Kaskaskia. Court held 20th May, 1752.—Bucket."

Here is another case of a later date, arising *ex contractu*, against an administrator:

"Between Raimond Brosse, called Saint Cernay, inhabitant of Kaskaskia, plaintiff, to the effect that the defendant, Charles Lorain, be made to acknowledge a note for sixty francs, executed by the deceased Louis Langlois, and of Louise Girardy, his widow, and now wife of Charles Lorain, the aforesaid defendant, on the other part.

"The said note being examined, the parties heard, and all things considered, we condemn the defendant to pay, without delay, to the plaintiff the sum of sixty francs (livres), the amount of the said note, and also the costs of suit, which we have taxed at twenty-eight francs and ten cents (sols).

"Done at New Chartre, in our hearing, we holding court, Saturday the fifth of June, 1756.—Chevallier." *

The practice, or mode of procedure, in this and other courts of the province was after the forms of the civil law, very simple and brief, and probably as well calculated to promote the true ends of justice as the more cumbrous forms of the English common law, filled with technical jargon. Trial by jury was unknown here; the law and the facts in every case being decided by the presiding judge.

---

* Breese's Early History, pp. 217-219. At the time Judge Breese wrote, the record of the proceedings of this high-sounding court was yet extant, and it may be still.

Judgments and decrees were executed by the captain of militia, or the provost marshal, and no "stay laws" or "valuation laws" impeded its operation, nor was there any "redemption after sale." Occasion, however, did not very often arise for the exercise of the judicial authority, as litigation was expensive, and the people in general were peaceable, honest, and punctual in their dealings with each other. In fact, the most common mode of settling small difficulties and disputes about money, etc., was by referring them to the arbitration of friends and neighbors, or else by the mild interposition of the village priest.*

Thus were exercised the executive and judicial powers in the provincial district of Illinois; of legislative powers there were none. The laws in force were the edicts and ordinances of the King, and the "usages of the mayoralty and shrievalty of Paris." These were introduced by France into all her American colonies, but they were changed or modified, more or less, by the ignorance or caprice of those whose business it was to construe and apply them. The peculiar local customs of the colony, also, had the force of law.*

The pernicious system of monopolies still prevailed in the province. In August, 1744, Gov. de Vaudreuil conceded to a Frenchman named Déruisseau the exclusive right of trading in all the country watered by the Mississippi River, and the streams falling into it. This privilege, which seems to have embraced the entire district of the Illinois, was for a term something in excess of five years, beginning January 1, 1745, and terminating on the 20th of May, 1750. Several conditions were annexed to the grant, such as the maintenance of the posts on the Missouri, and the regulation of the prices at which goods were to be supplied to the settlements. One of the reasons assigned by De Vaudreuil for granting this monopoly to Déruisseau was to deprive the colonists in the Illinois district of all means of carrying on any commerce with the Indians, and thus

---

* Breese's Early Illinois, pp. 221, 222.

force them into the cultivation of the soil, and the raising of produce for the southern market.*

In 1749, the Sieur de St. Clair was re-appointed major-commandant at the Illinois, but, in the autumn of 1751, he was supplanted by the Chevalier Macarty, or Makarty, an Irishman by birth, and a major of engineers. Macarty served about nine years, and then yielded the position to Capt. Neyon† de Villiers.

Early in 1753, after a popular and successful administration of over ten years, the Marquis de Vaudreuil-Cavagnal relinquished the governership of Louisiana to accept the higher honor of governor-general of Canada. His successor in the former office was M. de Kerlerec, a captain in the royal navy. He arrived in New Orleans the 3d of February, 1753, and on the 9th of that month, was installed as chief executive of the province.

Let us now take a cursory view of contemporaneous military events, occurring beyond the confines of Louisiana. In 1744, war was again declared between France and Great Britain, and their trans-Atlantic colonies speedily became embroiled in the armed conflict, which is known as the Third French War. The active military operations, so far as they affected the French-American possessions, were chiefly confined to the eastern seaboard. But to guard against surprise, or any sudden irruption of the Chickasaws and other unfriendly tribes, some fresh levies of troops were made in Louisiana, and the garrisons were strengthened at the principal posts in the province.

The most noteworthy episode of this foreign war was the capture of the fortress of Louisburg, situated upon Cape Breton Island, by an army of four thousand men from Boston, under the command of Colonel (afterward Sir) William Pepperell, in June, 1745. The reduction of this stronghold, which had hitherto been considered impregnable, was a heavy blow to the French power, and during the succeeding year a powerful fleet was fitted out

---

* Gayarré's Hist. of La., Vol. II, pp. 23, 24.
† Written *Noyon* in old French documents.

in France to recover it and chastise its captors. The fleet, however, was delayed, and its aim was frustrated by a storm. But by a provision of the treaty of Aix-la-Chapelle (1748), Louisburg was restored to the possession of France in exchange for certain territory that England desired in India,—an arrangement very displeasing to the New Englanders.

The peace of 1748, which conferred increased prosperity on the Province of Louisiana, was not destined to be of long duration. Of the various causes at work to bring about a renewal of hostilities between the two rival powers, it is unnecessary now to speak, as we shall hereafter take occasion to pass them in review. But the fear that the English might eventually gain a foot-hold in this great Valley of the Mississippi was ever present to the minds of the intelligent French inhabitants. And the suggestion was made by De Bértel, commandant at the Illinois, to the governor in New Orleans, and through him to the king, that additional means of defense were required for the protection of these valuable possessions, hinting at more troops and larger and stronger forts.

Nothing appears to have been done at the time, however, excepting to enroll those able to bear arms into companies of militia, and to provide for the maintenance of garrisons at the more exposed places.

It was not until the year 1753, when Macarty was major-commandant, that the rebuilding of Fort Chartres was begun, in accordance with plans and specifications furnished by M. Saucier, a French engineer.* This huge structure of masonry, an object of wonder and curiosity to all who ever beheld it, was reared at an estimated cost of over five millions of livres, or about one million dollars. It was so nearly completed by the beginning of 1756, that

---

* See *Letters of Travel* through Louisiana, by M. Bossu, captain in the French Marines, and afterward Chevalier of the Order of St. Louis. Imprinted at Paris, 1768; English ed., London, 1771, p. 127. Of the fort itself, Bossu says (p. 158): "It is built of freestone, flanked with four bastions, and capable of containing (or housing) a garrison of three hundred men."

it was occupied by the Illinois commandant, and the archives of the local government were deposited therein. Thenceforth, the fortress was popularly known as "New Chartres."

"As a means of defense," writes Breese, "except as a citadel to flee to on any sudden attack of the savages, the erection was wholly unnecessary. Official emolument must have prompted it, and some of the many millions of livres, it is said to have cost must have gone into the commandant's pocket, or into those of his favorites, and they enriched by this mode of peculation."

This extensive fortification was constructed during Kerlerec's administration of the government of Louisiana, and he probably shared in the profits of the erection. Makarty was then major-commandant of the Illinois, and the Abbé de Gagnon, of the order of St. Sulpice, was chaplain at the fort.

M. de Kerlerec held the office of provincial executive from February 9, 1753, until June 29, 1763, when he was superseded by Mons. d'Abbadie*—not as governor, but as director-general, etc.—and was ordered to return to France. He was accused of various violations of duty and assumptions of power, and, in particular, was reproached with having spent ten millions of livres in four years, while M. Rochemaure was intendant-commissary, under the pretext of preparing for war. Upon his arrival in Paris, he was incarcerated for some time in the Bastile, and is said to have died of vexation and grief shortly after his discharge from that gloomy state prison.†

In Captain Pittman's "Present State of the European Settlements on the Mississippi," already cited, is contained an excellent description of Fort Chartres, as seen by him in 1766, while it was yet in its prime. He writes:

"Fort Chartres, when it belonged to France, was the seat of government of the Illinois. The head-quarters of the English commanding officer is now here; who, in fact, is the arbitrary governor of the country. The fort is an irregular quadrangle; the sides of the exterior polygon are

---

* Otherwise written *Abadie*.

† Gayarré's Hist. of La., II., p. 95; and Martin's Louisiana, I., p. 343.

four hundred and ninety feet. It is built of stone plastered, and is only designed as a defense against Indians; the wall being two feet two inches thick, and pierced with loop-holes at regular distances, and with two port-holes for cannon in the faces and two in the flanks of each bastion. The ditch has never been finished. The (main) entrance to the fort is through a very handsome rustic gate; within the walls is a small banquette, raised three feet, for the men to stand on when they fire through the loop-holes.

"The buildings within the fort are the commandant's and commissary's houses, the magazine of stores, *corps de garde*, and two barracks; they occupy the square. Within the gorges of the bastions are a powder magazine, a bake-house, a prison, on the lower floor of which are four dungeons, and in the upper two rooms, and an outhouse belonging to the commandant.

"The commandant's house is thirty-two yards long and ten broad. It contains a kitchen, a dining-room, a bed-chamber, one small room, five closets for servants, and a cellar. The commissary's house, now occupied by officers, is built in the same line as this; its proportions and distribution of apartments are the same.

"Opposite these are the store-house and guard-house. They are each thirty yards long and eight broad. The former consists of two large store-rooms (under which is a large vaulted cellar), and a large room, a bed-chamber, and a closet for the store-keeper; the latter of a soldier's and officer's guard-rooms, a chapel, a bed-chamber and closet for the chaplain, and an artillery store-room.

"The lines of barracks have never been finished. They at present consist of two rooms each for officers, and three rooms for soldiers. They are good, spacious rooms of twenty-two feet square, and have betwixt them a small passage. There are five spacious lofts over each building, which reach from end to end. They are made use of to lodge regimental stores, working and intrenching tools, etc.

"It is generally allowed that this is the most commodious and best built fort in North America.

"The bank of the Mississippi next the fort is continually falling in, being worn away by the current, which has been turned from its course by a sand-bank, now increased to a considerable island, covered with willows. Many experiments have been tried to stop this growing evil, but to no purpose. When the fort was begun in 1756, it was a good half-mile from the water side. In the year 1766 it was but eighty paces. Eight years ago the river was fordable to the island; the channel is now forty feet deep."

The story of the subsequent dilapidation and ruin of this historic fortress, which was intended to secure the empire of the French in the West, may be told in a few sentences. In the spring of 1772, a great freshet in the Mississippi, which submerged all the adjacent bottom, made such inroads upon the crumbling river bank, that the western wall and one of the bastions of the fort were undermined and precipitated into the raging current. The British garrison then abandoned it, and took refuge at Fort Gage, on the high bluff of the Kaskaskia, opposite to and overlooking the old town of that name. Thither the seat of government was transferred, and Fort Chartres was never again occupied. It was left to become a ruin, and such of its walls and buildings as escaped destruction by succeeding inundations were torn down and removed by the neighboring villagers for building purposes.

After the flood of 1772, "the capricious Mississippi devoted itself to the reparation of the damage it had wrought. The channel between the fort and the island in front of it, once forty feet deep, began to fill up, and ultimately the main shore and the island were united, leaving the fort a mile or more inland. A thick growth of trees speedily concealed it from the view of those passing on the river, and the high road from Kaskaskia to Cahokia, which at first ran between the fort and the river, was soon after located at the bluffs, three miles to the eastward. These changes, which left the fort completely isolated and hidden, together with the accounts of the British evacuation, gave rise to the report of its total destruction by the river. . . . But this is entirely erroneous; the ruins (or part of them) still remain; and had man treated it as kindly as the elements, the old fort would be nearly perfect to-day."*

Now and then a curious tourist or an antiquary made his way thither. In 1804, the fort was visited by Major Amos Stoddard,† of the U. S. Engineers, who described it as in a good state of preservation. In 1820, Dr. Lewis C. Beck, and Nicholas Hansen, of Illinois, made a careful drawing of the plan of the fortress, for insertion in Beck's "Gazetteer of Illinois and Missouri." At that time many of the rooms and cellars in the buildings, and portions of the outside walls, showing the opening for the main gate, and loop-holes for the musketry, were still in a state of tolerable repair. According to their measurements, the whole exterior line of the walls and bastions was 1,447 feet. The area of the fort embraced about four acres; and the walls, built of solid stone, were in some places fifteen feet high. In 1851, ex-Governor Reynolds visited the remains of the old fortress, concerning which he thus writes:

"This fort (situated in the north-west corner of Randolph county) is an object of antiquarian curiosity. The trees, undergrowth, and brush are so mixed and interwoven with the old walls that the place has a much more ancient appearance than the dates will justify. The soil is so fertile that it has forced up large trees in the very houses which were occupied by the French and British soldiers." ‡

The same writer was there again in October, 1854, and found what was left of the fort "a pile of moldering ruins," the walls having been torn away in many places nearly even with the ground. Moralizing upon the scene of desolation thus presented to his gaze, he quaintly wrote: "There is nothing durable in this world, except God and Nature." Later tourists to this interesting spot have seen

---

* Paper read before the Chicago Historical Society, by Hon. E. G. Mason, June 16, 1880.

† It was Stoddard who took possession of Upper Louisiana for the Government of the United States, in March, 1804, under the treaty of purchase from France.

‡ Reynolds' *Pioneer History*, 2d ed., p. 46.

the outlines of the external walls and ditches, and scattered heaps of broken stone; also the vaulted powder magazine, a piece of solid masonry, existing almost entire.

It is much to be regretted that this large and commodious fortress—the only great architectural work of the French in the entire basin of the Mississippi—over which, in succession, had long and proudly floated the flags of two powerful nations, should not have been built upon a firmer and more elevated site, where it might have been preserved, as an impressive and historical monument of the past, even unto the present time.

CHAPTER XVII.

1753-1760.

THE MEMORABLE SEVEN YEARS' WAR.

We now approach that momentous contest popularly known as the "Old French and Indian War,"* or the "Seven Years' War," in which France and Great Britain stubbornly contended for the final possession of this continent. The French, having begun their wonderful career of conquest and colonization in the early part of the seventeenth century, had gradually extended a chain of military and trading posts from Quebec up the river St. Lawrence to Lake Ontario, and thence westward along the great connecting lakes to the head of Lake Michigan; thence diagonally through the country of the Illinois to the Mississippi, and down that interior water-way to the Gulf of Mexico. The English, in the meantime, had been planting along the Atlantic seaboard—a reach of over two thousand miles—the most prosperous and powerful colonies in the New World. And it was the extension of their growing power and settlements across the Appalachian range of mountains, which had hitherto constituted their western boundary, that first brought them into controversy and collision with the French Canadian authorities.

France claimed the entire Valley of the Mississippi, including that of the Ohio as well, which her enterprising fur-traders and missionaries had been the first to explore and formally occupy, but which she had as yet only very sparsely peopled. In furtherance of this claim of exclusive jurisdiction, the alert French went so far as to carve their national *fleur-de-lis* on the forest trees, and to bury metallic plates, stamped with the arms of France, at various places

---

* It was really the fourth French and Indian war.

in the Ohio Valley. On the other hand, England, in virtue
of the primal discovery of the country by the Cabots,
maintained the right to extend her possessions on the
Atlantic coast indefinitely westward, and in conformity
with this view the charters of some of her colonies were
so worded as to reach across the entire breadth of the continent. The English sought to further strengthen their
title by annexing to it the pretense of their Indian allies,
the Six Nations,* who claimed, by right of conquest, all
that part of the northwestern territory lying south of the
great lakes and between the Alleghany Mountains and the
Mississippi.

So long as France and Great Britain were at peace,
which was never many years at a time, this standing,
national controversy gave rise only to a series of border
disputes, petty encroachments, and intrigues with the fickle
aborigines, neither party being numerous enough to colonize the territory which both coveted. But when war existed between the two parent countries, their respective
American colonies likewise engaged in murderous conflict,
which, because of the savages enlisted in it, was fearfully
destructive of life and property.

By the opening of the year 1753 affairs had reached a
crisis, and France, in order to fix a barrier to the westward
march of English colonization, and thus protect her wide
possessions in the West and South, determined to run a line
of detached posts from Niagara and Lake Erie to the head
of the Ohio, and down that river. The Indians were the
first to take alarm at this movement; and in April, when
the news reached the Upper Ohio that a French force was
on the way to erect forts in that region, the Mingoes, Delawares, and Shawnees met in council at a village called
Logston, on the Ohio, and sent an envoy to Fort Niagara
to protest against the French occupation, but their protest
was unheeded. In pursuance of a pre-determined plan,

---

*The Five Nations were increased to six by the addition of the
Tuscaroras from North Carolina, in the first quarter of the eighteenth
century.

the French soldiery, under General Pierre Paul, Sieur de Marin, built Fort Presque Isle on the south-eastern shore of Lake Erie, near the present city of Erie, and Fort le Boeuf on the head waters of French Creek, fourteen miles southeast of the former fort, and then opened a wagon road between the two. They also converted into a military station the Indian village of Venango, situate at the junction of French Creek with the Alleghany River; but when they undertook to erect a fort at the forks or head of the Ohio, they came into collision with representatives of the Ohio Company. This company, which had been formed in Virginia as early as 1750, was authorized by the Virginia Council to select five hundred thousand acres of land on both sides of the Upper Ohio for the purpose of settlement, and had caused surveys to be made of the lands and built some houses thereon. The French troops, however, seized several of the English agents and traders and sent them prisoners to Canada, and warned others away,—an arbitrary and unfriendly proceeding. The company thereupon made complaint to Robert Dinwiddie, governor of Virginia, who commissioned young George Washington (then adjutant-general, with the rank of major, of the provincial militia in the northern division of the colony) to be the bearer of a letter to the commander of the French forces on the head waters of the Ohio, requiring him to peaceably withdraw from that territory, which was claimed as a part of Virginia, and as belonging to the crown of Great Britain.

Major Washington started on his difficult mission from Williamsburg (the old capital of Virginia) on the 31st of October, 1753, first stopping at Fredericksburg to engage a French interpreter, and proceeded via Alexandria to Winchester, where he procured horses and baggage, and thence journeyed to Wills Creek. Here he employed a guide and four men as servants, and, continuing his journey over the mountains in a north-westerly direction, reached the junction of Turtle Creek and the Monongahela on the 22d of November, and the forks of the Ohio on the 23d. The next day he went down the river to Logstown, several miles below the forks, and there held a conference with the Indians friendly to the English cause. From thence, attended by a small native escort, he traveled up the valley of the Alleghany, and its tributary of French Creek, to Fort le Boeuf,* whither he arrived on the 11th of December. Presenting his credentials and letter to Jacques le Gardeur de St. Pierre, who had succeeded the Sieur de Marin (then recently deceased) in command of the French troops in that quarter, Washington was politely received and entertained by the commander and his staff. Some days later, on taking his departure from the fort, he was handed a letter by St. Pierre in answer to that of the Virginia governor.

Major Washington and his party set out on their return home the 16th of December, and after a most disagreeable and dangerous winter journey, made partly on horseback and partly afoot, he reached Williamsburg on January 16, 1754. Calling without delay upon Governor Dinwiddie, he delivered to him the letter of reply from the French commander, with which he had been intrusted, and of which the following is a translation:

"SIR: As I have the honor of commanding here in chief, Mr. Washington delivered to me the letter which you wrote to the commander of the French troops. I should have been glad that you had given him orders, or that he had been inclined, to proceed to Canada to see our general; to whom it better belongs than to me to set forth the evidence and the reality of the rights of the king, my master, to the land situate along the river Ohio, and to contest the pretentions of the King of Great Britain thereto.

"I shall transmit your letter to the Marquis du Quesne. His answer will be a law to me. And if he shall order me to communicate it to you, sir, you may be assured I will not fail to dispatch it forthwith to you. As to the summons you send me to retire, I do not think myself obliged to obey it. Whatever may be your instructions, I am here by virtue of the orders of general; and I entreat you, sir,

---

* Or *Fort sur la Rivière au Boeuf.*

not to doubt one moment but that I am determined to conform myself to them with all the exactness and resolution which can be expected from the best officer. I do not know that in the progress of this campaign any thing has passed which can be reputed as an act of hostility, or that is contrary to the treaties which subsist between the two crowns, the continuation whereof interesteth and is as pleasing to us as to the English," etc.

(Signed)   " LE GARDEUR DE ST. PIERRE.
" Dated *December* 15, 1753." *

When this rather defiant letter had been read and considered by the governor and council of Virginia, an order was issued to raise a regiment of mounted militia, for the double purpose of driving the French intruders from their territory, and of completing and garrisoning the post at the confluence of the Alleghany and Monongahela Rivers, the erection of which had been already begun by the agents of the Ohio Company. The command of this regiment was assigned to Colonel Fry, with Washington as lieutenant-colonel, and they were speedily equipped and on their way across the mountains. But the object of this expedition was thwarted in the main by the prompter action of the French under Captain Antoine Pécody Contrecoeur, who, in the month of April, in anticipation of the arrival of the Virginia troops, moved down to the head of the Ohio with a force of about one thousand regulars and Indians, and eighteen pieces of cannon. After dispersing the employés of the company and a small body of militia, whom he found there, Contrecoeur proceeded to finish the fort which they had commenced, and named it Duquesne, in compliment to the commander of the French forces in Canada.

Lietenant-Colonel Washington had meantime pushed forward, with one-half of the Virginia regiment, in advance of the rest, to a place called the Great Meadows, fifty miles north-west of Wills Creek (afterward Fort Cumberland),

---

* *Vide* " Diaries of Washington," edited by Benson J. Lossing, N. Y., 1860, p. 247.

and there erected a rude stockade fort, which received the name of Fort Necessity. While he was thus engaged, N. Coulon de Jumonville, a young French officer, was sent from Fort Duquesne, with a detachment of thirty men, to reconnoiter his movements and notify him to surrender the fort. On being apprised by his scouts of the approach of the French party, Washington planned to fall upon them by surprise. Accordingly, on the evening of the 27th of May, with a part of his provincials and a few Indian allies, he suddenly surrounded De Jumonville's camp, at a secluded spot called the Little Meadows, and ordered his men to open fire. In the brief action of a quarter of an hour that ensued, the Virginians had one man killed and three wounded; while, on the side of the French, ten men were either killed or wounded, and the remainder made prisoners. Among the slain was M. de Jumonville,* who commanded the French party. The killing of this brave young officer, who bore on his person a summons to the Virginians to surrender, caused much excitement in Canada and France, where it was claimed to be a violation of the law of nations, and it contributed to kindle into a flame the embers of war.

So soon as intelligence of this bloody encounter was brought to the Illinois, Neyon de Villiers, a brother of the deceased Jumonville, and captain of a company then stationed at Fort Chartres, solicited leave of Makarty, the major-commandant, to go and avenge the death of his relative. Permission being given, De Villiers set out with a considerable force of French and Indians. Passing down the Mississippi and up the Ohio to Fort Duquesne, he was there joined by M. Coulon de Villiers, with other forces, bent upon the same stern errand. The French on the Ohio, being thus re-inforced, took the offensive.

Some little time before this Colonel Fry had deceased, and Washington succeeded to the full command of his regi-

---

* M. Jumonville de Villiers was born in Picardy, France, about 1725. He was one of seven brothers, all soldiers, six of whom, it is said, were killed during this war. His death was made the theme of a short epic poem by M. Thomas, a French poet.

ment. Finding himself confronted by a superior force of the enemy, he now fell back to Fort Necessity, at the Great Meadows, which he strengthened as well as he could in the brief time allowed him. Here, on the 3d of July, he was attacked by De Villiers, with an army of some six hundred Frenchmen and over one hundred Indians. The Virginia troops made a stubborn defense, and withstood the irregular fire of the French and their allies (who sheltered themselves behind the forest trees), from ten o'clock in the morning until sunset. At length, fearing the failure of his ammunition, and not desiring to sacrifice the lives of his men by storming the fort, De Villiers sent in a flag of truce offering moderate terms of capitulation. In view of his critical situation, Colonel Washington, after some parleying over details, accepted the terms offered. By these he was allowed to march off his troops with the honors of war, and to carry away his baggage, but was required to leave his cannon, and to surrender all of his prisoners previously taken. In this frontier battle the French are said to have lost only three men killed and a few wounded, while the Virginians, penned up in the stockade fort, lost over thirty men killed and wounded.

When the news of these stirring events reached England and France, both nations prepared to settle their territorial disputes by the arbitrament of the sword, though war was not formally declared by the King of Great Britain until May, 1756. Among other sources of irritation between the two governments at this time was the alleged encroachment by French colonists upon the domain of the English in Acadia, or Nova Scotia, which had been ceded to England by the treaty of Utrecht, in 1713, but the boundaries of which remained unadjusted.

To the mere superficial observer the impending contest seemed a very unequal one. The population of the Anglo-American colonies aggregated about one million and a quarter, with wealth and military resources in proportion; whereas, the French, all told, did not count more than one hundred thousand souls. But the latter were difficult to be reached, for the reason that their forts and settlements were situated at remote points in the wilderness, and surrounded by numerous Indian allies, who could be quickly summoned to their aid; and from these forest retreats they menaced the entire western English frontier. Moreover, the regular British army of that day was an unwieldy machine, incumbered with heavy baggage and munitions, commanded by brave yet conceited officers, who were inexperienced in the wild tactics of Indian warfare, and in constant danger of being surprised and defeated by a lighter equipped, more agile and vigilant foe.

In February, 1755, General Edward Braddock, who had been given the chief command in the English colonies, arrived at Alexandria, Virginia, with two regiments of regular troops. During the following April he met there the governors of five of the leading provinces, and concerted with them a general plan of campaign. Three separate expeditions were planned; one against Fort Duquesne, to be commanded by Braddock in person; the second, against Forts Niagara and Frontenac, to be led by Governor William Shirley, of Massachusetts; and the third, against Crown Point, by General (afterward Sir William) Johnson.

Early in May, General Braddock set out with his army from Alexandria upon his luckless expedition. Arrived at Fort Cumberland, on the Upper Potomac, he was there joined by several hundred Virginia militia, under the lead of Colonel Washington, whom he had invited to serve as one of his *aides de camp*. Being thus reinforced, and having now completed the equipment of his army, the general resumed his march on the 10th of June. But the difficulty and delay attending the opening of a military road across the mountains induced him, partly at the suggestion of Washington, to leave his wagon train and heavy cannon behind with a guard of eight hundred men, under Colonel Thomas Dunbar, and to press forward with the main body of his army, over twelve hundred strong, in order to reach the French fort before its garrison could be reinforced. After reaching and fording the Monongahela

River, Braddock marched rapidly to the north down the valley of that stream.

Meanwhile, Daniel Lienard de Beaujeu, who had practically, if not formally, supplanted Captain Contrecoeur in the command at Fort Duquesne, being advised by his scouts of Braddock's approach, marched out with a force of two hundred and fifty Frenchmen, and six hundred and fifty Indians, to intercept his advance. Proceeding up the Monongahela seven miles from the fort, the French and Indians concealed themselves in the thick woods on the brow of a ridge overlooking the banks of the river, along which Braddock was expected to pass, and there uneasily awaited his coming.

In the forenoon of the 9th of July, the British force recrossed the river near the mouth of Turtle Creek,* and without taking any adequate precautions to guard against an ambuscade, boldly climbed the first bank, and advanced along a defile of the second, above and near which the enemy lay in ambush. And now, at a preconcerted signal, the Indians raised their hideous yell, and a deadly volley was poured upon the front column, which checked its advance, and caused it to fall back on the center, and the center on the rear, which was hemmed in by the river. Thus this brave army, which might have advanced and driven the enemy from his covert, speedily became involved in inextricable confusion, and, after a murderous conflict of three hours, was utterly routed and put to flight. Of the fourteen hundred and sixty officers and men who went into the battle on that hot July day, only five hundred and eighty-three came out uninjured. The carnage was frightful among the officers, who were picked off by the French sharp-shooters. General Braddock himself fought with great intrepidity, but, after having three or four horses shot under him, received a mortal wound, of which he died a few days later.†

---

* Lieutenant-Colonel Gage, who led the advance column, first forded the river, and sent back word that no enemy was in sight, whereupon the rest of the army followed after him.

† This imprudent and unfortunate commander was born in Perth-

The French loss, not counting that of their Indian allies, was less than forty; but it included their skillful commander, Captain Beaujeu, who had planned the ambuscade, and who was killed early in the action.*

Colonel Washington's clothing was riddled with bullets, and he escaped, as it were by a miracle, from that field of slaughter. His Virginia riflemen, despite Braddock's injudicious orders to the contrary, took positions behind trees and rocks, and maintained the unequal fight until more than half of them were killed and wounded. With those that remained, the dauntless and self-possessed colonel covered the retreat of the routed army. Happily for the fugitives, the Indian auxiliaries of the French were too intent upon the spoils of the battle field to pursue them beyond the river; and never before, in a single engagement, had the savages reaped such a harvest of scalps and booty as was gathered here. The panic of the defeat was quickly communicated to the rear-guard, commanded by the pusillanimous Colonel Dunbar, who abandoned his heavy artillery and baggage, and fled over the mountains to Philadelphia, leaving the frontier settlements defenseless.

Owing partly to the discouragement produced by Braddock's defeat, the other expeditions that had been planned by him and the colonial governors, for that year, also ended in failure. The attempt of Governor Shirley against Forts Frontenac and Niagara wholly miscarried. The governor, with a force composed principally of raw

---

shire, Scotland, about the year 1695, and had risen to the rank of major-general after forty years of meritorious service in the British army. It is affirmed, on what seems to be good authority, that Braddock was fatally shot in the side or back at the battle of the Monongahela, by one of the provincials, whose brother had been stricken down by the irate general for refusing to obey orders; yet it is equally probable that the shot was accidental. General Braddock expired in the camp of Colonel Dunbar, on the 13th of July, and was buried in the military highway, seven miles east of Uniontown, Pa., where his grave is still shown.

* For some old French accounts of this celebrated battle, see "*Relations Diverses sur la Bataille d' Malanguele, Gagné le 9th a Jouillet*, 1755, *par le Francais sous M. le Beaujeu, Commandant du Fort du Quene, sur les Anglois sous M. Braddock, Général en chef des troupes Angloises*," pp. xv., 9–51, N. Y., 1860 (—Cramoisy Series of Relations relative to the French in America).

militia, marched to Oswego, on Lake Ontario; but, in consequence of the lateness of the season, and the difficulty of procuring provisions and transports, he abandoned the expedition and returned to Albany.

It is true that the Acadians of Nova Scotia were reduced to subjection, by a fleet fitted out for that purpose at Boston, with a land force of over two thousand men under the command of Colonel John Winslow, of Massachusetts. After the treaty of 1748, the French inhabitants of that peninsula, living on the disputed territory, had not only refused to take the oath of unqualified allegiance to the King of England, but had contributed material aid to their own countrymen in the existing war. They were now (in August, 1755) inhumanly punished for their contumacy. Their petty forts at the head of the Bay of Fundy were taken and demolished; their villages were burned, and their farms laid waste. As many as three thousand of the poor Acadians—men, women and children—were forcibly put on shipboard and transported to the other English colonies, where they were distributed around as paupers. Some of these unhappy exiles, as we shall see, eventually found an asylum in Lower Louisiana, where they established a thrifty and permanent settlement.*

The army, under General Johnson, which was intended to operate against Crown Point, on Lake Champlain, reached the south end of Lake George in the latter part of

---

* Longfellow has graphically portrayed the touching scenes in this deportation of the unfortunate Acadians, and thrown around it the halo of romance, in the polished stanzas of his "Evangeline," beginning with these lines:

"In the Acadian land, on the shores of the Basin of Minas,
Distant, secluded, still, the little village of Grand Pré
Lay in the fruitful valley."

The history of the Acadians is long, varied and interesting. They were, in truth, the sport of fortune from the time of DeMonts (1604) until the treaty of Paris, in 1763. Their descendants, however, are still numerous in northern Nova Scotia. The name of this peninsula was first changed from Acadia to Nova Scotia in 1621, when Sir Wm. Alexander obtained a grant of the country from James I., and undertook to colonize it with Scotchmen.

August, (1755), when information was received that two thousand of the enemy, commanded by Baron Dieskau, who had recently arrived with fresh troops from France, were marching against Fort Edward, on the Hudson. General Johnson thereupon detached Colonel Williams, with a strong force, to intercept this movement of the French. Colonel Williams unexpectedly fell in with the army of Baron Dieskau, on the 8th of September, when a bloody action took place, in which the English were defeated and put to flight, and Williams himself was slain. But when the French, flushed with their success, advanced to attack the main body of Johnson's army, they were warmly received, and, after an obstinate conflict, were driven from the field with heavy loss, Dieskau himself being mortally wounded and taken prisoner. Satisfied with this hard-won victory, General Johnson gave over the further prosecution of his movement against Crown Point. Soon after these events, the English constructed a regular fort at the head of Lake George, and called it Fort William Henry.

In July, 1756, Lord Loudon arrived in America, as commander-in-chief of the British forces. An army of about twelve thousand men was raised this year, which was better prepared to take the field than any other that had been assembled within the colonies. But the change of commanders delayed military operations, and nothing of any consequence was accomplished by the English army. The French, however, under the able conduct of the Marquis de Montcalm, struck at least one vigorous blow. This was directed against Fort Ontario, at Oswego, on Lake Ontario. In the early part August they attacked this fort, with a strong armament, and quickly compelled its surrender, with a garrison of over one thousand men, and a large quantity of artillery and valuable stores. By the loss of Oswego, and the defeat of Braddock in the preceding year, all the western country was laid open to the ravages of the enemy; and the Indians, sustained and encouraged by the French, now wasted the frontiers of Pennsylvania and Virginia, in particular, with a pitiless and desolating war.

The next year, 1757, was marked by the same inactivity and inefficiency on the part of the English, and by another successful expedition on the side of the French. The English colonists, as a rule, displayed great energy in raising men and money for the war; but their efforts were paralyzed by the want of concert with each other, by the necessity of awaiting orders from England, and by the dilatory and do-nothing policy of the incompetent generals sent over to command them. On the other hand, Montcalm, as general-in-chief of the French, not being obliged to take counsel with any one (unless it was the governor of Canada), speedily collected a force of about eight thousand men, including Canadians and Indians, with which he passed up lakes Champlain and George, and laid siege to Fort William Henry. The garrison here was nearly three thousand strong, commanded by Colonel Monroe, a brave officer, and General Webb was at Fort Edward, only fourteen miles away, with four thousand more. But the latter made no effort to succor the beleagured fort, and manifested so much indifference to its fate that he was suspected of treachery. After standing a close siege for six days, and seeing that he was to have no relief from General Webb, Colonel Monroe capitulated on terms honorable to himself and the garrison. But the savage auxiliaries of the French, paying no regard to the articles of capitulation, nor to the entreaty of Montcalm, fell upon the English after the surrender, robbed them of their baggage and other effects, massacred their sick and wounded, and killed and scalped the Indians in their service.

The unexpected capture of this valuable post, together with the Indian atrocities attending it, caused great alarm throughout New York and New England, and, when too late, large re-inforcements of militia were assembled and sent forward to Albany and Fort Edward. Meantime, however, General Montcalm, after ravaging the settlements on the Mohawk River, retired into Canada.

Thus far the war had been very disastrous and discouraging to the English. After three consecutive campaigns, the French not only retained every foot of the disputed territory, but had captured Oswego, driven their antagonists from Lake George, and, through their Indian confederates, had carried the brand and tomahawk into the heart of the English settlements. To remedy this series of defeats in America, as well as elsewhere, William Pitt, afterward Earl of Chatham, was called to the head of the English ministry. He took the helm in June, 1757, and by his vigor and consummate ability, soon gave a new and surprising turn to affairs.

In the spring of 1758, General Abercrombie, who had been appointed to the chief command in place of Lord Loudon, found himself at the head of about fifty thousand fighting men, one-half of whom were regulars. This was the largest force that had ever been seen in America, and from it was expected great results. On the other hand, all the French Canadians capable of bearing arms did not exceed twenty thousand, and they had been so constantly in the service that agriculture was neglected, and the horrors of partial famine were added to those of war.

On the 28th of May a powerful armament, which had been fitted out in England, sailed from Halifax for the reduction of Louisburg—the Dunkirk of New France—which was defended by the Chevalier de Drucourt, with 3,100 men. The English fleet, consisting of twenty ships of the line and eighteen frigates, besides numerous transports, was commanded by Admiral Boscawen, and carried a land force of fourteen thousand men, under General Amherst. Arrived before Louisburg the 2d of June, a close investment was begun of the town both by sea and land. After a stubborn defense, the French garrison surrendered on the 27th of July, and, together with the sailors and marines (amounting in all to 5,737 men), were transported prisoners of war to England. The loss of this colossal fortress, with all its cannon, mortars, military stores, and shipping in the harbor, was the most effectual blow that France had received since the beginning of the war. It made the English masters of the entire coast from

Halifax to the mouth of the St. Lawrence, and greatly facilitated their conquest of Canada.*

Early in July of that year, General Abercrombie moved with an army of fifteen thousand effective men against Fort Ticonderoga, on Lake Champlain. Montcalm had meantime thrown himself with a strong force into the fort, and had so obstructed the approach to it by an abatis of felled trees that it was impregnable, except by the processes of a regular siege. The English troops, with more courage than calculation, attacked the enemy's lines in front, and, after a desperate conflict of four hours, were routed with heavy loss, and retreated precipitately to their camp at the foot of Lake George. To offset this mortifying defeat, the result of bad generalship, Colonel John Bradstreet was shortly detached, with a force of three thousand provincials, on an expedition against Fort Frontenac. He crossed the outlet of Ontario Lake, landed within a mile of the fort, planted his batteries, and speedily compelled the surrender of its garrison and munitions. By the capture and demolition of Fort Frontenac, the English gained practical control of Lake Ontario, and cut off the main line of communication between Montreal and the French posts in the West.

While these momentous events were transpiring in the north, General Joseph Forbes, who had been appointed to command the expedition to the Ohio, was slowly advancing, with an army of seven thousand men (including wagoners, sutlers, and camp-followers), to the conquest of Fort Duquesne. The British general left Philadelphia in June, and was joined *en route* by Colonel Washington, with two regiments of Virginia militia. In consequence of the serious obstacles encountered in opening a new road across the Alleghanies, this army was greatly retarded in its march,

---

* The fortifications at Louisburg (which stood on the south-eastern side of Cape Breton Island) had been thirty years in building, and had cost the French government over $5,000,000. After this second capture by the British, the fortress was demolished and never again re-built. The town itself was ruined during the siege, and its present population comprises only a few fishermen.

and did not reach the head of the Ohio till the 25th of
November.

In the meantime Colonel Grant, commanding a detachment from the main army, had pushed ahead to reconnoiter the situation of the fort. But he was suddenly attacked and driven back with considerable loss, by M. Aubry,
who had recently arrived with a reinforcement of French
troops from the Illinois.

When General Forbes reached Fort Duquesne, he found
it deserted and burned. The French garrison, numbering
about five hundred men, had set fire to the wooden building
on the preceding night, and fled down the river in boats,
carrying with them their ordnance and stores. Taking
quiet possession of the burnt fort, Forbes caused it to be
forthwith repaired, and changed its name to Fort Pitt, in
compliment to the English prime minister. At the same
time he sent out a body of men to the battle-ground on the
Monongahela, to bury the dead soldiers of Braddock's
army, whose bones had been left to bleach there for three
years on the hillsides.

Leaving two regiments of provincials as a garrison at
Fort Pitt, General Forbes returned by short marches to
Philadelphia; but his constitution was so broken by the exposure and fatigues of the campaign, that he died shortly
after his arrival thither. And now the Indian nations,
throughout the region of the Upper Ohio, seeing that the
French were losing ground, and ever ready to join the
stronger side,* made overtures of peace to the English. A
treaty of pacification was accordingly entered into with
them, which gave security for a few years to the border
settlements in Pennsylvania and Virginia.

In passing down the Ohio from Fort Duquesne, M.
Aubry, the French commander, made a halt about thirty-six miles above its mouth, and there on the site of a former
fortlet, on the northern bank of the river, commenced
building a fort, at which he left one hundred men for gar-

---

* In this particular, they were not unlike many of the more civilized
descendants of Adam.

rison duty, and returned with the rest to Fort Chartres. The new post was called Fort Massac, in compliment to M. Massac, or Marsiac, the officer who first commanded there. This was the last fort erected by the French on the Ohio, and it was occupied by a garrison of French troops until the evacuation of the country under the stipulations of the Treaty of Paris, in 1763.*

---

* Monette's "Valley of the Mississippi," vol. i, p. 317.

Note.—The early French history of Fort Massac dates back to the beginning of the last century, but it is obscured by time and fiction. Dr. Lewis C. Beck, in his "Gazetteer of Illinois and Missouri" (Albany, N. Y., 1823, p. 114), describing the place, says: "A fort was first built here by the French when in possession of this country. The Indians, who were then at war with them, laid a curious stratagem to take it, which answered their purpose. A number of them appeared in the daytime on the opposite side of the river, each of whom was covered with a bear-skin, and walked on all-fours. Supposing them to be bears, a party of the French crossed the river in pursuit of them. The remainder of the troops left their quarters, and resorted to the bank of the river in front of the fort to observe the sport. In the meantime a large body of warriors, who were concealed in the woods near by, came silently up behind the fort and entered it without opposition, and very few of the Frenchmen escaped the carnage. They afterward built another fort on the same ground, and called it Massac (or Massacre), in memory of this disastrous event." This romantic story is repeated by Judge Hall, in his "Sketches of the West," and by other western writers. Ex-Governor Reynolds, in his "Own Times" (2d ed., p. 16), writes more specifically of the fort, as follows: "Fort Massac was first established by the French about the year 1711, and was also a missionary station. It was only a small fort until the war commenced in 1755, between the English and the French. In 1756 (1758), the fort was enlarged and made a respectable fortress, considering the wilderness it was in. It was at this place that the Christian missionaries (first) instructed the southern Indians in the gospel precepts, and it was here also that the French soldiers made a resolute stand against the enemy." Fort Massac was subsequently maintained by the United States government as a military post, and a few families resided in the immediate vicinity, until after the close of the war of 1812-14. During this later period of its history it was sometimes called the "old Cherokee Fort," from the river of that name, better known as the Tennessee. In 1855 Reynolds visited the place, which, in his "Own Times," he thus describes: "The outside walls were one hundred and thirty-five feet square, and at each angle strong bastions were erected. The walls were palisaded, with earth between the wood; a large well was sunk in the fortress; and the whole appeared to have been strong and substantial in its day. Three or four acres of graveled walks were made on the north of the fort, on

Stimulated by the brilliant successes that had attended their arms in the campaign of 1758, the British ministry resolved to make a supreme effort the next year for the complete conquest of Canada. The Anglo-American colonies, zealously seconding the exertions of the home government, brought into the field twenty thousand provincials, and raised a large sum of money for their equipment and sustenance. At a general military council, held early in the year 1759, it was decided to invade Canada with three different armies, which should enter the country by three separate routes, and commence offensive operations at about the same time. The command of the first and principal expedition, which was destined against Quebec, was intrusted to General James Wolfe, a young brigadier of great enterprise and promise, who had distinguished himself by his valor and conduct at the reduction of Louisburg. Of the two subsidiary expeditions, one, under General Sir Jeffrey Amherst, was to proceed by way of Lake Champlain to Montreal, and the other was to march against Fort Niagara.

General Amherst's operations were impeded and restricted by a lack of vessels and transports. Yet Ticonderoga and Crown Point successively fell into his hands without a struggle—the danger to Quebec having caused the withdrawal of the greater part of their French garrisons—and a detachment of his army attacked and burned the Indian village of St. Francis, whence many of those scalping parties were believed to have issued, which had ravaged the frontiers of New England. General Prideaux was unhappily killed by the bursting of a gun at the siege of Niagara; but his successor in command, Sir William Johnson, on the 24th of July; defeated a force of twelve hundred French and Indians, who had advanced to relieve the fort, and he pressed the siege so vigorously that the garrison soon capitulated. Johnson should then have

---

which the soldiers paraded. These walks were made in exact angles, and are beautifully graveled with pebbles from the river. The site is one of the most beautiful on *La Belle Riviere,* and commands a view that is charming."

passed down Lake Ontario and the St. Lawrence, to co-operate with Wolfe in the attack upon Quebec, but the want of facilities for transporting his troops prevented the execution of this purpose.

In the latter part of June, General Wolfe appeared in the St. Lawrence, below Quebec, with a powerful fleet, and an army of eight thousand regular soldiers. His force, though hardly equal in number to that of the French, was better equipped and provisioned; but the latter had the advantage of one of the strongest natural fortresses in the world, which had been greatly strengthened by art, and they were commanded by a general of consummate ability, who had merited the first honors in war. So long as Wolfe sought to bombard Quebec from his batteries at Point Levi, on the opposite height of the St. Lawrence, or assaulted the French intrenchments below the city, along the St. Charles, his efforts were easily frustrated by the tact and vigilance of Montcalm. But, after trying various expedients, the British general at last hit upon the bold design of moving his forces from the Isle of Orleans (his base of operations) up the river, and then dropping down at night, in flat-bottomed boats, and silently scaling the high plateau known as the Heights of Abraham, at a point about one mile above the citadel of Quebec. This critical movement was as skillfully executed as it had been daringly planned, though the aclivity was so steep and rugged that the soldiers could, with difficulty, climb it by clinging to the projecting rocks and roots of trees. Learning with surprise and chagrin that the English had thus gained a position in his rear, where his defenses were rather weak, and seeing that a battle was unavoidable, Montcalm drew out his army of five thousand men on the sloping plain behind the town, and put the fate of Canada on the hazard of a single engagement. Nor was the issue long in doubt. After some skirmishing in front by a body of light armed Canadian and Indian marksmen, the French advanced briskly to the charge. The English received them with firmness, but reserved their fire until the enemy was near, and then

delivered it with decisive effect. The French fought with
valor and determination until the fall of their general and
his second in command, when they retreated, and were pursued almost to the gates of the city.

This famous battle was fought September 13, 1759.
The English lost in killed and wounded six hundred men,
and the French nearly one thousand. Generals Wolfe and
Montcalm were both mortally wounded, the former dying
on the field of conflict, and the latter on the next day within
the city walls.* On the 18th of that month the citadel of
Quebec was formally surrendered, and received a British
garrison of five thousand men. The royal ensign of France,
which, with a single interval of three years, had waved
over this fortress for a century and a half, was now lowered from its staff, and in its place was unfurled the victorious cross of St. George.

But the submission of Canada did not immediately
follow after the fall of Quebec. The war was further protracted. The Chevalier de Lévis succeeded to the command made vacant by the death of Montcalm, and strove
to retake the city by a *coup de main*. Another pitched
battle was fought a few miles above Quebec, on the 28th
of April, 1760, in which the French army gained the advantage, and they made the most strenuous yet unavailing
efforts to recover their lost citadel and seat of power. It
was not until the 8th of September, 1760, when the united
British forces were concentrated before Montreal, that articles of capitulation were signed by the governor-general,
the Marquis de Vaudreuil. By these terms Canada and
its dependencies were surrendered to the English crown,
with a reservation to the French inhabitants of their civil
and religious privileges.

Equally unsuccessful, both in Europe and America, and
exhausted by her great and protracted exertions, France
now made overtures of peace. These were favorably con-

---

* After receiving his mortal wound, Montcalm was carried into the
city; and when informed that he could survive only a few hours, he
replied: "So much the better; I shall not then live to see the surrender of Quebec."

sidered by England, and every thing seemed in a fair way of adjustment, when the negotiations were suddenly broken off by the attempt of the court of Versailles to bring in the affairs of Spain and Germany. A secret compact of the Bourbon princes to support each other, in peace and in war, had rendered Spain averse to a treaty which weakened her ally, and this induced France to once more try the fortunes of war. As the interests of these two nations were thus identical, it only remained for the King of England to proclaim hostilities with Spain. The New England colonies, being interested in the reduction of the West Indies, on account of their commerce with them, furnished a liberal quota of men and means for continuing the war; and a great fleet was dispatched from old England, bearing a land force of some sixteen thousand men. These combined forces acted with such vigor and celerity that, before the end of the next year, Great Britain had gained possession of Havana (the key to the Gulf of Mexico), Grenada, Martinique, St. Lucia, St. Vincent, and the Caribbee Islands.

The rapid progress of her conquests, which threatened the remaining possessions of France and Spain, was arrested, however, by the exchange of preliminary articles of peace at Fontainebleau, toward the close of the year 1762. On the 10th of the ensuing February, 1763, a definitive treaty of peace was signed at Paris, and it was soon after ratified by the respective powers. By this memorable treaty, France ceded to Great Britain all the conquests made by the latter in North America during the war. The western boundary of the British possessions was fixed to run along the middle of the Mississippi River, from its source down to the Iberville, and thence along the center of that river or bayou, and through Lakes Maurepas and Pontchartrain to the Mexican Gulf. All of Louisiana lying west of the Mississippi, together with the district of New Orleans on the east, had been ceded from France to Spain by a private treaty, executed at Fontainebleau on November 3, 1762, which was permitted to stand.* By the treaty of Paris,

---

* See Article seventh of the Paris treaty in Chap. XIX of this work.

England also acquired large territorial possessions in India and elsewhere.

Such was the final outcome of this prolonged and sanguinary war, whereby the great power of the French monarchy in America was permanently annihilated. The struggle was computed to have cost the Anglo-American colonies thirty thousand lives, and over sixteen millions of dollars, of which only five millions were ever reimbursed to them by the government of Great Britain. Among the more direct advantages accruing to the colonies from the war, was a marked increase in their trade and population; while the indirect benefits, such as unity and concert of action in emergency, and knowledge and experience in military science, prepared the way for the War of Independence.

NOTICE OF MONTCALM.

Louis Joseph, Marquis de Moncalm-Gozon de St. Vérain, the most celebrated soldier in French-American history, was born at the chateau of Candiac, near Nismes, in the south of France, on the 29th of February, 1712, and died in Quebec, Canada, September 14, 1759. His education was directed by one Dumas, a natural son of his grandfather, and at the age of fourteen he entered the French army as an ensign, in the regiment of Hainault. He served with gallantry and distinction in Italy and Germany, and was promoted from one position to another until he attained the rank of general. In the spring of 1756 he was appointed to succeed the Baron Dieskau in command of the French forces in North America, and arrived at Quebec about the middle of May. His subsequent eventful career is written in the history of that war. It is believed that if he had received timely reinforcements from his home government, he could have maintained the authority of France in Canada. General Montcalm is described as a man of small stature, with a fine head, a vivacious countenance, and a rapid, impetuous speech. He had a nice sense of honor and ardent patriotism, combined with the tastes of a scholar, and a love of rural pursuits. He possessed true military genius, and as a commander stands very high, though not in the highest rank. His last years were embittered, and his popularity impaired, by contentions with the governor of Canada, the Marquis de Vaudreuil, who, during the life of his rival, and after his death, lost no opportunity of traducing him. (Appleton's Cyclop. of Amer. Biog., vol. iv., p. 364.) Upon the final overthrow of the French power in Canada, the friends of the dead general preferred serious charges to the king against Governor Vaudreuil, who was thereupon summoned to appear and answer them in France. But, after a full investigation of the acts of his administration by a competent tribunal, he was exonerated. Having lost his property, he died in Paris, October 20, 1765.

On the 20th of November, 1827, during Lord Dalhousie's administration in Canada, when the animosities and race prejudices, engendered and perpetuated by centuries of cruel warfare, had been in a measure obliterated, the corner-stone of a monument to the joint memory of Montcalm and Wolfe was laid, with military and Masonic ceremonies, in the Palace Garden, formerly attached to the old Castle of St. Louis, in the Upper Town of Quebec. This appropriate monument—built of gray granite in the form of an obelisk—is sixty-five feet high, and bears upon its pedestal the following Latin inscription:

> Wolfe—Montcalm.
> Mortem Virtus Communem,
> Famam Historia,
> Monumentum Posteritas.
> Dedit A. D. 1827.

Which, being freely rendered into English, reads thus: "Military virtue gave them a common death; History a common fame; Posterity a common monument."*

---

*In 1832 Lord Aylmar, governor-general of Canada, caused to be erected on the Plains of Abraham, at the spot where Wolfe fell, a granite monument ten feet high. But it became so broken and defaced in a few years by relic hunters, that it was replaced in 1849 by a Doric column, inclosed by an iron fence. This beautiful pillar was erected at the expense of the British Army in Canada; and on the west side of its pedestal, as on the former monument, are inscribed the words: "Here died Wolfe Victorious, Sept. 13, 1759."

CHAPTER XVIII.

1760-1765.

INDIAN CONSPIRACY AND WAR OF PONTIAC.

During the prolonged and bitter struggle between France and Great Britain for supremacy on this continent, as hereinbefore succinctly narrated, the French settlements in Upper and Lower Louisiana, being remote from the principal theater of warfare, were but slightly affected by its various fluctuations, though most of the garrisons in this western province were withdrawn, from time to time, to participate in the ensanguined contest. The dread of British conquest no doubt operated to dull the energies and cloud the future of these detached colonists; yet they lived on in comparative tranquillity and happiness, no scenes of rapine and bloodshed occurring in their midst to disturb the even tenor of their lives. It was only when the war between the two rival kingdoms had ceased, and after the peace of Paris, that its wide reaching results were brought directly home to them.

M. Neyon de Villiers* was then major-commandant of the Illinois, and the Sieur d' Annville was king's advocate and judge, doing duty as commissary. Among the few records extant of their official acts, we find the grant of a certain tract of land, for use as a stock farm, to one Joseph Labusciere, who had made written application therefor "at New Chartre, the 22d September, 1761."†

---

* DeVilliers had been taken prisoner by the English at Fort Niagara, in July, 1759, but was afterward exchanged or released.

† Appended to Labusciere's application appears the following official indorsement:

"In consideration of the above declarations and others from other quarters, we have granted and do grant to Joseph Labusiere the land (called *la belle fontaine*) situated between the hills and Outard's marsh,

We now proceed to recount the military transactions that took place in the West after the capitulation of Montreal. On the 12th of September, 1760, Major Robert Rogers, a gallant colonial officer of New Hampshire, received orders from General Amherst to ascend the lakes with a strong detachment of rangers, and take possession, in the name of his Britannic majesty, of Detroit, Mackinac and other western posts still held by the French. While Rogers' flotilla was on its way up Lake Erie, being delayed by stormy weather, he dispatched a courier in advance to inform Captain Belestre, the French commandant at Detroit, that Canada had surrendered, and that an English force was on its way to relieve him of his command. Taking umbrage at the informality of the notice, and doubtless wanting a pretext for delay, Belestre incited the Indians around the post to measures of resistance. Accordingly, when Major Rogers reached the head of Lake Erie, he found a force of about four hundred warriors ready to dispute his farther progress. But through the active intervention of Pontiac, or Pondiac, the great Ottawa chief (with whom Rogers had recently held an interview on the lake shore), he and his men were allowed to advance unmolested to Detroit. They arrived thither in the last week of November, and on the 29th of that month, this military and trading post, the most considerable in the central lake region, passed into the hands of the English. The French garrison, composed of three officers and thirty privates, quietly laid down their arms, to the astonishment of the Indians present, and were sent prisoners of war to Montreal. The Canadian residents of the district were left in the undisturbed possession of their houses and lands, but

---

prayed for by him, according as it is explained and described in the present petition, on condition that the said land shall be subject to the public charges, and that it shall be put to profit or built upon in the course of the year beginning from this day, under the penalty of being again reunited to the king's domain.

"Given at Fort Charte, this fourth day of January, 1762.
    (Signed),   " NOYON DEVILLIERS.
                                 " D'ANNVILLE."

were required to take the oath of allegiance to the British crown.

As heretofore remarked, the first permanent military settlement of Detroit was made by Antoine la Mothe Cadillac, in July, 1701. He had previously been in command of the post at Mackinac, and in his voyages up and down the lakes had observed the strategic value of the place, commanding the passage between Lakes Erie and St. Clair. Returning to France in 1699, he laid the matter before Count Pontchartrain, minister for the Colonies, who authorized him to erect a fort on the strait. It was built on the plain adjoining the western brink of the river, and at or near the site of the older fortlet of St. Joseph, erected by Du L'hut in 1686. It was named by Cadillac, Fort Pontchartrain, but it early assumed the name of Detroit, which, in French, means a strait. From that time until the close of the Anglo-American war of 1812-14, the history of this post is one of marked vicissitudes—of sieges, captures, battles, and bloodshed. As the fort slowly grew into a village, with a fixed population, it was inclosed with a quadrangular, wooden stockade, having two gates as the only entrances.

At the beginning of the English possession, the French-Canadian population of Detroit, including their settlements along the river, was estimated as high as twenty-five hundred persons, but the number soon diminished. The fort, then embracing the entire town, is described as a stout palisade, twenty-five feet in height, furnished with bastions at the four angles, and block-houses over the two gateways. A short distance below the fort, on the same side of the strait, stood a village of the Pottawatomies. To the southeast, on the opposite bank, was that of the Wyandots, and five miles above the latter, on the same bank, lay the village of the Ottawas. The river, half a mile in width, ran through a landscape of singular beauty, and in its pellucid waters were mirrored the outlines of the stately forest trees that stood on either bank. Back from the full-flowing stream rose the whitewashed cottages of the settlers, while in the distance were clustered the Indian wigwams, from which curling columns of smoke rose high into the pure northern atmosphere. At the *Isle a la Pêche*, near the outlet of Lake St. Clair, dwelt Pontiac, "the master spirit of this sylvan paradise, who, like Satan of old, revolved in his powerful mind schemes for marring its beauty and innocence." Here, according to Rogers' journal, he lived with his squaws and children, and here, no doubt, he might have been often seen reclining on a rush mat, like any ordinary warrior.

Directly after the British occupation of Detroit, Major Rogers sent officers to take possession of Forts Miami on the Maumee, and Ouatanon on the Wabash. The major himself started to relieve the French posts on the upper lakes, but was prevented from carrying out his purpose by the early approach of winter. During the ensuing spring of 1761, however, the forts on the Straits of Mackinac and St. Mary, at the head of Green Bay, and on the river St. Joseph, were all garrisoned by small detachments of British troops. But the flag of France still waved over the posts in Illinois and Louisiana, which had not been included in the stipulations of the surrender at Montreal.

The English were now in military possession of the whole of Canada; yet the task of maintaining their authority in this vast region was found to be one of no small difficulty, because of the general dissatisfaction with the change of rulers pervading its inhabitants. The French settlers, who formed the ruling element, having their national hatred intensified by years of warfare, were irreconcilable, and many of the more discontented left their Canadian homes and removed to Illinois and Louisiana, which still belonged to France. Here they continued to cherish their animosity and foment resistance, still hoping that Canada might be again restored to France. Illinois thus became a place of refuge and a center of French intrigues against the British rule. Canadian traders and refugees went every-where among the north-western tribes, whose good will they had long before secured by a conciliatory policy, and incited them to take up arms against the English, who, it was declared, were seeking to compass their destruction by hedging them round with forts and settlements, and by stirring

up the Cherokees and Chickasaws to attack them. To give
the greater efficacy to their arguments, the French traders
liberally distributed among the Indian chiefs guns and ammunition, which the English refused to do, and otherwise
treated them as inferiors. It should be observed that fire-
arms, blankets, and other articles of European fabric had
been so long supplied by the French to the western Indians,
that they were now become a necessity to the existence of
the latter.

Under these altered circumstances, Pontiac, who still
hated the British, although he had interfered on their side
so far as to permit Major Rogers to take peaceable possession of Detroit, soon began to show his old partiality for the
French. He was now some fifty years of age, and in the
full prime of his powers. Pontiac was born on the Ottawa
River about the year 1712, and was, it is said, the son of an
Ojibwa or Chippewa woman. It has been claimed that he
was of Sac lineage, but he belonged, by adoption at least,
to the Ottawa tribe.* As the Ottawas were in alliance with
the Ojibwas and Pottawatomies, he became in time the principal chief of the three tribes. In 1746 he defended the
chief post of Detroit from an attack of some discontented
tribes of the north, and in 1755 he appears to have commanded a band of Ottawa warriors at General Braddock's
defeat. During the war between France and England he
fought valiantly on the side of the former, and for his
courage and devotion was presented with a full French
uniform by the Marquis de Montcalm, only a short time before the fall of Quebec.

After the final defeat of the French and the surrender
of Canada, Pontiac at first manifested a disposition to cultivate the friendship of the conquerors, but was disappointed

---

* Reynolds says, in his "Pioneer History," that Pontiac had French
blood in his veins; and his alleged light complexion and strong bias
toward the French lend credence to the assertion. The traditional descriptions of this Indian chief vary in regard to his features and the
color of his skin, but all concur in depicting him as a savage of sym-
metrical and noble form, of proud and haughty demeanor, and of commanding address.

Planning of the Conspiracy. 347

in the advantages he expected to derive from their favor. In the now changed state of affairs, his sagacious mind discerned the danger which threatened his race. The equilibrium that had hitherto subsisted between the French and English gave the Indians the balance of power, and both parties were compelled to respect their rights to some extent. But, under British domination, their importance as allies was gone, and their doom sealed, unless they could restore the power of the French and use it to check the encroachments of the English. Inspired with this idea, as well as by ambition and patriotism, he sent trusty messengers to the nations of the upper lakes, to those on the Illinois, the Mississippi, and Ohio, and southward to the Gulf of Mexico. In the autumn of 1762 his emissaries, bearing the red-stained hatchet and war-belt as symbols of their mission, passed quickly from tribe to tribe, and everywhere the dusky denizens of the forest assembled, eager to hear the fiery message, which had been prepared by the leader for the occasion. The attending chiefs and warriors, moved by these stirring appeals, pledged themselves to unite in the league and war against the common enemy of their race.*

Thus, by his own superior energy, activity, and address, Pontiac became the acknowledged head and front of the most extensive confederation of Algonquin nations ever before known in Indian history. He not only conceived the great scheme of uniting all these nations in a league or conspiracy against the English colonists, but of simultaneously attacking all the accessible forts of the latter, and, after butchering their garrisons, to turn upon the defenseless settlements and continue the death-dealing work until the entire English population should be exterminated, or driven into the sea. The conspiracy was planned or matured at a council of the Ottawas, Pottawatomies, Chippewas, and Hurons, held near Detroit about April 27, 1763, when Pontiac made a speech recounting the wrongs and indignities that had been suffered by the Indians, and

---

*See Davidson & Stuve's Hist. of Ill., pp. 140, 141.

prophesied their extermination. The plot was well laid, and it was more successfully executed than might have been expected, considering the limited resources of the natives, and the rankling jealousies and enmities that prevailed among the different tribes.

Prior to this, on February 10, 1763, was signed the treaty of Paris, by which all the territorial possessions of France east of the Missisipi were ceded to Great Britain. During the following spring, in pursuance of this act of cession, all the French posts in Southern Louisiana, on the east side of the Mississippi, but not including the district of New Orleans, were occupied by English garrisons. The immediate occupation of Illinois, however, was not deemed practicable, owing to the strong barrier of hostile Indians surrounding the forts there, and the French officers then in command were therefore authorized by Sir Jeffrey Amherst, the British commander-in-chief, to retain their posts until formally relieved. In the exercise of this trust they seem to have been guilty of a breach of faith, both in furnishing the Indians with arms and supplies, and in concealing from them the transfer of the country to the English.* But for this misplaced confidence, or want of soldierly foresight on the part of General Amherst, the war that ensued might have been abbreviated, and thus divested of some of its barbarities.

According to the plan concerted by Pontiac and his council of war, the last of May (1763) was designated as the time for the general uprising, when each tribe was to

* "It now appears from the best authorities (says a Report of Sir William Johnson, Superintendent of Indian Affairs, to the Board of Trade, December 26, 1764), and can be proved by the oaths of several respectable persons, prisoners among the Indians of Illinois, and from the accounts of the Indians themselves, that not only many French traders, but also French officers, went among the Indians, as they said, fully authorized to assure them that the French king was determined to support them to the utmost, and not only invited them to visit the Illinois, where they were plentifully supplied with ammunition and other necessaries, but also sent several canoe loads at different times up the Illinois River to the Miamis, as well as up the Ohio to the Shawanese and Delawares."

attack the garrison of the nearest English fort, and the secret was so closely kept that two-thirds of the posts attacked were captured, either by surprise or stratagem. The taking of Detroit was to be the preliminary task of Pontiac himself, and the date of its execution was set for the 7th of May. He accordingly attempted, with a band of trained warriors, to seize that post, but was foiled in his design by the vigilance of Major Henry Gladwin, the English commandant, who had received information of the plot the day before, from a young Chippewa woman, who had formed an attachment for him and wished to save his life.*

The assault upon Detroit was renewed by Pontiac, with an augmented force, on the 12th of May, but, failing in this, he turned it into an irregular siege. The garrison, meantime, obtained food from the neighboring Canadian settlers, who likewise supplied the Indians in turn. In consequence of the largely increased number of his followers, Pontiac found it necessary to make regular levies on the French farmers for provisions, and in lieu of other compensation, he gave them his promisory notes, scrawled on pieces of birch bark and signed with the figure of an otter, the totem of his family. This imitation of the practices of civilized men might have been suggested to him by some of the farmers themselves, yet it is related to his credit that all of these notes were afterward paid.

Supplies and reinforcements were sent to the beleaguered fort in small schooners, by way of Lake Erie; but these were mostly captured by the Indians, who compelled their prisoners to row them to Detroit in hope of surprising the garrison. At length, however, the garrison was reinforced, and thereupon took the offensive. On the 31st of July the English attacked Pontiac at his camp near the mouth of a little stream known as Bloody Run; but in this engagement the assailants were defeated, and retreated to

---

* It may be hoped that no iconoclast will arise, as in the case of Pocahontas, to demolish this traditional story of the devoted Chippewa maiden.

the fort with a loss of fifty-nine men in killed and wounded. The siege of Detroit was maintained in a desultory manner until about the 10th of October, when the ammunition of the natives fell short, and they became discouraged.

Although failing in all their efforts to capture this coveted post, the Indians were more successful elsewhere. It is true that Forts Pitt and Niagara, which they also attacked, proved too strong for their destruction; but between the first and twentieth of June, they took Fort Venango, LeBœuf, Presque Isle, Sandusky, Miami (on the Maumee), St. Joseph,* Mackinac and LeBaye,† and either murdered or made prisoners of their respective garrisons, only a few effecting their escape. The destruction of life and property at these widely separated posts was but the prelude to a general Indian war, which carried terror and desolation into many of the fairest and most fertile valleys of Virginia, Pennsylvania and New York.

General Amherst had now become aware that the occupation of the Illinois forts by French garrisons was contributing to prolong and intensify the contest, and he would gladly have displaced them at once, but still found it impracticable to break through the cordon of hostile tribes by which they were environed. His only expedient, therefore, was to write to Neyon de Villiers at Fort Chartres, instructing him to make known to the Indian chiefs and warriors their altered relations under the treaty of cession. That French officer, being thus compelled to divulge what he had long concealed, reluctantly wrote to Pontiac, saying, "that he must not expect any assistance from the French; that they and the English were now at peace and regarded each other as brothers, and that the Indians should abandon their hostilities, which could lead to no good result."‡

---

* On Lake Michigan, formerly called Ft. Miami.
† At the head of Green Bay.
‡ At or before that time DeVilliers wrote to D'Abbadie, at New Orleans, that it was the fault of the English if the Indians manifested such enmity to them. "The English," said he, "as soon as they became aware of the advantages secured to them by the treaty of cession, kept no measures with the Indians, whom they treated with harshness

This letter was a grievous disappointment to Pontiac, who relied for ultimate success upon the continued support of the French, and it proved the entering wedge toward the breaking up of his prodigious power and influence. Shortly after its reception, he departed from Detroit, with a number of his followers, and went southward to the country of the Maumee, intending to return and renew the contest the next spring.

The winter of 1763-4 passed without any very noteworthy occurrence. In the early summer of 1764, the English authorities fitted out two considerable expeditions; one to operate against the savages in the central lake region, and the other for the punishment of those in the Valley of the Ohio. The command of the latter column was entrusted to Colonel (afterward General) Henry Bouquet, who marched from Fort Pitt, and, encountering the warlike Delawares and Shawnees on the banks of the Muskingham, soon defeated and reduced them to submission. This efficient officer required these Indians to surrender all of their white prisoners. In compliance with his demand, they reluctantly brought into camp a large number, principally women and children, some of whom had been captured during the early part of the French war, and had been in captivity so long as to have almost forgotten their native tongue and the homes of their childhood or youth.

Colonel Bradstreet, who commanded the other expedition, proceeding up the southern shore of Lake Erie, wrested Sandusky from the hands of the hostile Indians and reinforced Detroit. He then sent Captain Thomas Morris, with some Canadians and friendly Indians, to induce the Illinois and their allies to make peace with the English. The captain and his party ascended the Maumee River to the vicinity of Pontiac's camp, and thence went as far as Fort Miami, which had been captured by the Indians in the preceding year. But, after experiencing great hardships, and being subjected to gross indignities by the Miamis

---

and the haughtiness of masters, and whose faults they punished by crucifixion, hanging, and every sort of torment."—Gayarré's Hist. of La., Vol. II., p. 98.

and Kickapoos, Morris was glad to escape from their grasp with his life, and returned to Detroit without having effected the object of his perilous journey.*

Previously to this, in the early part of February, 1764, Major Arthur Loftus, then doing duty with the 22d regiment at Pensacola, Florida,† was ordered to proceed to the Illinois and take military possession of the posts there. He accordingly sailed from Pensacola with four hundred men for that purpose, but on his arrival in New Orleans some of them deserted him. On the 27th of February he re-embarked his troops, with thirty-seven women and children, in ten heavy boats and two pirogues, and started up the Mississippi. Advancing slowly, he reached Davion's Bluff, near Tunica Bend, on the 19th of March, when he was fired upon by a party of Tunica Indians, who had ambushed both sides of the river. They killed six and wounded seven of the English soldiers, and thus stayed the farther progress of the expedition. The suspicion was strong among the English that the French, at Pointe Coupée, had aided the Tunicas with their slaves in this murderous attack. Returning to New Orleans in a rage, Major Loftus accused Governor D'Abbadie of complicity with the Indians; but it does not appear that the governor was in any way responsible for the unfortunate occurrence. On the contrary, he had furnished the British officer with an interpreter, and had sent orders to the commandants of the French posts on the river to afford him needed aid and protection, and, in fine, had done all in his power to insure the success of his expedition. The truth is, that Loftus himself was partly to blame for his failure, since he took little pains to conciliate either the French or Indians.‡

Soon after this abortive effort to reach Fort Chartres,

---

* In a letter written during this adventurous trip, dated La Prairie des Mascoutins, September 2, 1764, and addressed to Colonel Bradstreet, at Detroit, Captain Morris suggestively says: "I am certain, sir, that a few presents to the chiefs would have a good effect. Kind treatment will infallibly open a way to the Illinois country."

† In the treaty of Paris, Florida had been given by Spain to England, in exchange for Havana.

‡ See Gayerré's History of Louisiana, Vol. II., pp. 102, 103.

Captain Pittman started from Mobile to make a second attempt, but on his arrival in New Orleans he was deterred from proceeding farther, owing to the excited state of feeling among the Indians along the Mississippi. During the ensuing summer, Major Robert Farmer was dispatched from Mobile, with a part of the 34th regiment of foot, upon the same mission, yet he did not advance far before he was stopped by the hostile savages. It was not, indeed, until the first week in December, 1765, and after the final surrender of Fort Chartres, that he arrived with his force in the Illinois.

Such was the continued great influence of Pontiac, and such the strength of the combination he had formed among the aboriginal tribes of the Mississippi Valley, that General Gage (who had succeeded Sir Jeffrey Amherst as commander-in-chief of his Britannic Majesty's forces in North America) now became convinced that it would be impossible to eradicate from the minds of the Indians the idea of French assistance, so long as the forts in Illinois remained in the hands of French officers. He therefore undertook to put a period to this tedious and humiliating war, by removing the principal cause of its continuance. After the failure of the attempts of Majors Loftus and Farmer, it was determined to send troops to the Illinois by way of the Ohio River. To facilitate this design, Colonel George Croghan, a deputy of the Superintendent of Indian Affairs, and an experienced trader among the western Indians, together with Lieutenant Alexander Fraser, of the English army, were sent out in advance, to prepare the savages by negotiation for the advent of the projected military expedition. They started from Philadelphia in February, 1765, attended by a small mounted escort, and carried with them an ample assortment of goods for use as presents in conciliating the natives. After a difficult and fatiguing journey over the mountains, obstructed with snow and ice, they reached Fort Pitt (now Pittsburg) in March, but had the ill-luck to loose the larger part of their goods at the hands of the "freebooting borderers" of Pennsylvania. Colonel

Croghan tarried at Fort Pitt a number of weeks, in order to complete his preparations, and to confer with the sachems of the Delawares and Shawnees, along whose southern borders the armed expedition would have to pass.

Meanwhile, to expedite the main business of the mission, Lieutenant Fraser, with more boldness than discretion, embarked in a canoe, with a trader named Sinnott, and descended the Ohio and ascended the Mississippi to Kaskaskia. Arrived thither in the forepart of May, he experienced very rough treatment from the Illinois Indians. He was buffeted and his life threatened, and finding his position neither agreeable nor safe, he fled in disguise down the Mississippi River to New Orleans.

Pontiac was then encamped in the vicinity of Fort Chartres, whither he had come some time before, with a train of four hundred warriors, to demand arms and ammunition of the French for the further prosecution of his war against the English. About the 18th of April, on being received into the fortress and presented to St. Ange, the commandant, he addressed him in the following elevated strain:

"Father, we have long desired to see you and enjoy the pleasure of taking you by the hand. While we refresh ourselves with the soothing incense of the friendly calumet, we will recall the battles fought by our warriors against the enemy, which still seeks our overthrow. But while we speak of their valor and victories, let us not forget our fallen heroes, and with renewed resolves and more constant endeavors, strive to avenge their deaths by the downfall of our enemies.

"Father, I love the French, and have led hither my braves to maintain your authority and vindicate the insulted honor of France. But you must not longer remain inactive, and suffer your red brothers to contend alone against the foe who seek our common destruction. We demand of you arms and warriors to assist us, and when the English dogs are driven into the sea, we will again in peace and happiness enjoy with you these fruitful forests and prairies, the noble heritage presented by the Great Spirit to our ancestors."

St. Ange was constrained by circumstances to decline giving the expected aid; but he accompanied his refusal with soothing compliments, and added a few gifts to appease Pontiac's bitter disappointment.

But to return to Colonel Croghan. On the 15th of May, 1765, having completed his conferences with the tribes about Fort Pitt, he started down the Ohio with two bateaux, or long boats, and a small party of white men. Early the next day he was joined at Chartier's Island by several deputies of the Senecas, Shawnees, and Delawares, whom he had persuaded to accompany him. Proceeding on his way, with occasional short stoppages for refreshment, Croghan arrived the first of June at the head of the Falls of the Ohio, where he landed and encamped for the night. On the following morning his party passed the Falls or rapids; but as the river was quite low at the time, they had to lighten their boats in order to get safely through the channel on the Indiana side. Continuing their expeditious voyage, they reached the mouth of the Wabash on the 6th, and found there a rude breastwork, supposed to have been erected by the Indians. Six miles below the Wabash, they put to shore and encamped at a place known as the "Old Shawnee Village," some little distance above the present Shawneetown.* From this landing place Croghan dispatched two of his Indians across the country to Fort Chartres, with letters to Lieutenant Frazer, who was supposed to be still at that post, and to Captain St. Ange de Bellerive.

At day-break, on the 8th of June, while yet in camp, on the site of the old Indian village, Croghan's party was suddenly surrounded and fired upon by a band of eighty Kickapoo and Mascoutin warriors, who had been watching his movements for several days. They killed five of his company, two white men and three Delaware Indians, and

---

*The time occupied in this downward trip from Fort Pitt was twenty-one days, and the distance traveled, eight hundred miles, by the sinuosities of the river. It will thus be seen that they moved with unusual celerity, averaging about forty miles per day.

wounded several others, including the leader himself; then made him and the rest of the whites prisoners, and proceeded to despoil them of every thing they had. The excuse afterward given by the assailants for this unprovoked and murderous attack was, that they had been told that Croghan was coming into their country with an armed escort of Cherokees, their mortal enemies. But a better reason was to be found in their instinctive love of blood and plunder. Having quickly divided the spoils of Colonel Croghan's camp, the Kickapoos and Mascoutins,* fearing the arrival of another marauding party, whom they suspected to be on their trail, left such heavy articles as they could not carry away, and set off in haste, with their prisoners, for their villages on the Upper Wabash. Their course lay on and through the heavily wooded river bottom, which was so intersected by morasses and beaver ponds, as to render traveling slow and laborious.

On the 15th they reached Post Vincennes, where a halt was made of two days for rest and refreshment. Here Croghan had some new apparel made for himself and men, and purchased a few horses of the Piankashaw Indians, promising them payment when he should reach Detroit. In his printed journal he gives but a poor character to the French at Vincennes, whom he describes as a "lazy people, a parcel of renegades from Canada, and much worse than the Indians." He further says: "They took a secret pleasure at our misfortune, and the moment we arrived they came to the Indians, exchanging trifles for our valuable plunder." But Croghan was hardly in a frame of mind to do those French settlers justice, for they refused him permission to write to any one but the commandant at Fort Chartres.†

Arriving at Fort Ouatanon on the 23d of June, he was set at liberty, and took up his temporary quarters there, where he found a number of French families living.

---

* Called "Musquatimes" by Croghan.

† Journal of George Croghan, "who was sent in 1765 to conciliate the Indian nations that had hitherto acted with the French." Burlington (N. J.) reprint, 1831; small 4to, pp. 38.

This palisaded fort, as he informs us, was located on the north side of the Wabash, about two hundred and ten miles above Post Vincent, by the windings of the river. It derived its name from a tribe of Weas, or Ouiatanons, whose principal village stood on the south bank of the Wabash, a few miles below the site of what is now Lafayette, Indiana. The fort was maintained as a trading post with the Indians until June, 1791, when it was destroyed by an American force, under the command of General Charles Scott, of Kentucky.

During Croghan's stay here, a messenger arrived with a letter from Captain St. Ange, inviting him to visit Fort Chartres and arrange matters for the withdrawal of the French garrison from that place. As this request coincided with his own previous intentions, he set out with an Indian escort, on a journey thither across the prairies, but had not traveled far before he was met by Pontiac and a numerous retinue of his dusky warriors, on their return from the Illinois. This astute chief, perceiving at last that the great confederation he had formed among the Indian nations in the west was falling to pieces, and that he had nothing more to hope for from the French, was coming to make terms with the accredited agent of the English; and for the purpose of further conference on the subject they now returned together to Fort Ouatanon. Having hastily convened the neighboring chiefs and braves in council, Pontiac produced the calumet of peace, and made a plausible speech to them. He declared, among other things, that the French had misled him with the story that the English purposed to stir up the Cherokees against his brethren of the Illinois, to conquer and enslave them. He allowed that the English might take possession of Fort Chartres and the other posts in the Illinois, but suggested that as the French settlers had never bought their lands of the Indians, and lived on them by sufferance only, their successors would have no legal right of possession. The amicable disposition shown by such of the Illinois warriors as were present at this council, with other sufficient reasons, induced

Croghan to forego his intended trip to Fort Chartres, and to turn his attention to the tribes on the north-east.

Having adjusted matters satisfactorily with the natives at and about Fort Ouatanon, he departed thence on the 25th of July, being accompanied by Pontiac and a number of his followers. Proceeding on horseback up the Valley of the Wabash to the portage between that river and the Maumee, Croghan stopped to visit a small village of the Twightees near Fort Miami. He thence continued his journey to the main Twightee village, situated on the St. Joseph's River,* which unites with the St. Mary to form the Maumee, or Miami, as it was called by him. Arrived thither, he met a friendly reception from the Twightee chiefs, and, after completing his conference with them, set out on the 6th of August for Detroit, descending the Maumee in a canoe to Lake Erie. On the 17th he landed at the battle-scarred post of Detroit, which he incidentally describes in his journal, as a "large stockade, inclosing about eighty houses." During his stay here, he held frequent consultations with the chiefs of the Chippewas, Wyandots, Pottawatomies, and other congregated tribes, from whom the fear of condign punishment, and the privations they had endured in consequence of the long suspension of the fur-trade, had driven all thoughts of further hostility. They had had enough of war to curb their restless spirit for the time at least, and were anxious to make terms with the English authorities. At a general meeting of the sachems and warriors, convened in the Council Hall on the 27th of August, Croghan was present, and in imitation, or rather exaggeration, of that figurative forest eloquence with which he had become so familiar, thus addressed the convocation:

CHILDREN,—We are very glad to see so many of you present at your ancient council fire, which has been neglected for some time past. Since then high winds have blown, and raised heavy clouds over your country. I now, by this belt (of wampum), rekindle your ancient fire and

---

* The above mentioned river St. Joseph should not be confused with another and larger stream of the same name, which flows westward into Lake Michigan.

throw dry wood upon it, that the blaze may ascend to heaven, so that all nations may see it and know that you live in peace with your fathers, the English. By this belt I disperse all the black clouds over your heads, that the sun may shine clear upon your women and children, and those unborn may enjoy the blessings of this general peace, now so happily settled between your fathers, the English, and you, and all your younger brethren toward the sunsetting.

"Children, we have made a road from the sunrising to the sunsetting. I desire that you will preserve that road, good and pleasant to travel upon, that we may all share the blessings of this happy reunion."

The council reassembled the next day, when Pontiac, in behalf of his people, replied to Croghan's address as follows:

"Father, we have all smoked out of this pipe of peace. It is your children's pipe; and as the war is all over now, and the Great Spirit,* who has made the earth and every thing therein, has brought us all together this day for our mutual good, I declare to all the nations that I have settled my peace with you before I came here, and now deliver my pipe to be sent to Sir William Johnson, that he may know I have made peace and taken the King of England for my father, in presence of all nations now assembled; and whenever any of these nations go to visit him, they may smoke out of it with him in peace.

"Fathers, we are obliged to you for lighting up our old council fire for us, and desiring us to return to it, but we (the Ottawas) are now settled on the Maumee River not far from hence; whenever you want us, you will find us there. Our people love liquor, and if we dwelt near you in our old village, our warriors would be always drunk, and quarrels would arise between us and you." †

---

* Pontiac probably derived his correct notions of the Great Spirit mainly from association with white men; and there is no doubt but that his speeches were revised and improved somewhat by the English scribes.

† *Vide* "History of the Conspiracy of Pontiac," by Francis Parkman, Boston, 1868; 4th edition, pp. 555, 556.

The conciliatory mission of Colonel Croghan being at last brought to a happy fruition, he started on his return to the East toward the close of September, going first to Fort Niagara, and thence to report to the commander-in-chief. Before quitting Detroit, however, he had exacted from Pontiac a promise to repair to Oswego, New York, and enter into a treaty of peace and amity with Sir William Johnson, the Indian Superintendent, on behalf of those western tribes with whom he had been leagued in the late war. In fulfillment of his promise, the veteran chief proceeded, with a few attendants, to Oswego in the early summer of the next year (1766), and there, in presence of a large gathering of whites and Indians, he thus addressed the representative of the British crown: "Father, we thank the Great Spirit, who has given us this day of bright skies and genial warmth to consider the great affairs now before us. In his presence, and in behalf of all the nations toward the sunsetting, of which I am the master, I now take you by the hand. I call upon him to witness that I have spoken from my heart, and, in the name of the tribes which I represent, I promise to keep this covenant as long as I live."

After the execution of the treaty at Oswego, Pontiac returned to his home, on the banks of the Maumee River, and for the ensuing three years buried his ambition and disappointment in the seclusion of its somber forests, providing, as a common hunter, for the wants of his family and dependents.

In the meantime Captain Thomas Stirling, following upon the mission of Croghan, embarked in boats at Fort Pitt, with one hundred veteran Highlanders, of the 42d English regiment, and descended the Ohio to its mouth. Pushing thence up the Mississippi, he arrived at Fort Chartres in the early part of October, 1765, and on or about the 10th of that month took military possession of the fortress. "The flag of France descended from the rampart, and, with the stern courtesies of war, St. Ange yielded up his post, the citadel of Illinois. In that act was consummated the double triumph of British power in in America. England had crushed her hereditary foe; France, in her fall, had left to irretrievable ruin the savage tribes to whom her policy and self-interest had lent a transient support."*

On assuming command of the fort and country, Captain Stirling caused to be posted and published the following proclamation, which had been carefully prepared some months in advance, and was intended as a kind of constitution of government for the Illinois:

"By his Excellency. Thomas Gage, Major-General of the King's armies, Colonel of the 22d Regiment, General, commanding in chief of the forces of His Majesty in North America, etc.

"Whereas, by the peace concluded at Paris, on the 10th of February, 1763, the country of the Illinois has been ceded to His Britannic Majesty, and the taking possession of the said country of the Illinois by troops of His Majesty, though delayed, has been determined upon, we have found it good to make known to the inhabitants,

"That His Majesty grants to the inhabitants of the Illinois the liberty of the Catholic religion, as it has already been granted to his subjects in Canada; he has, consequently, given the most precise and effective orders, to the end that his new Roman Catholic subjects of the Illinois may exercise the worship of their religion, according to the rites of the Roman Church, in the same manner as in Canada;

"That His Majesty, moreover, agrees that the French inhabitants or others, who have been subjects of the Most Christian King, may retire in full safety and freedom, wherever they please, even to New Orleans, or

---

* Parkman's "Conspiracy of Pontiac," p. 559.

[FRENCH COMMANDANTS AT ILLINOIS.]

Note.—By way of recapitulation, we here present a list of the successive French commandants at the dependency of the Illinois, with the years, as near as may be, of their respective service, beginning with Boisbriant:

Pierre Duqué de Boisbriant	1718-1725
Captain de Tisné (temporarily)	1725-1726
The Sieur de Liette	1726-1730
Louis St. Ange de Bellerive	1730-1734
Pierre d'Artaguette	1734-1736
Alphonse de la Buissoniere	1736-1740
Benoist de St. Clair	1740-1743
The Chevalier de Bértel	1743-1749
St. Clair, again	1749-1751
The Chevalier de Macarty	1751-1760
M. Neyon de Villiers	1760-1764
St. Ange, again	1764-1765

any other part of Louisiana, although it should happen that the Spaniards take possession of it in the name of His Catholic Majesty; and may sell their estates, provided it be to subjects of His Majesty, and transport their effects, as well as persons, without restraint upon their emigration, under any pretense whatever, except in consequence of debts or criminal process;

"That those who choose to retain their lands, and become subjects of His Majesty, shall enjoy the same security for their persons and effects, and liberty of trade, as the old subjects of the king;

"That they are commanded, by these presents, to take the oath of fidelity and obedience to His Majesty, in presence of Sieur Stirling, Captain of the Highland Regiment, the bearer hereof, and furnished with our full powers for this purpose;

"That we recommend, forcibly, to the inhabitants, to conduct themselves like good and faithful subjects, avoiding by a wise and prudent demeanor all cause of complaint against them;

"That they act in concert with His Majesty's officers, so that his troops may take peaceable possession of all the posts, and order be kept in the country; by this means alone they will spare His Majesty the necessity of recurring to force of arms, and will find themselves saved from the scourge of a bloody war, and of all the evils which the march of an army into their country would draw after it.

"We direct that these presents be read, published, and posted up in the usual places.

"Done and given at head-quarters, New York. Signed with our hand, sealed with our seal-at-arms, and countersigned by our Secretary, this 30th of December, A. D. 1764.*

"By His Excellency, THOMAS GAGE, [SEAL.]
"G. MARTURIN, Secretary."

---

*The attentive reader of American history will remember that it was General Gage who, some ten years later, precipitated the War of the Revolution, by sending out from Boston, Massachusetts, the expeditionary force that led to the battle of Lexington.

CHAPTER XIX.

1764-1769.

OCCURRENCES IN LOWER LOUISIANA.

On the 15th day of June, 1764, M. Neyon de Villiers, having become impatient at the delay of the British conquerors in arriving to take possession of Fort Chartres, and disgusted with his position, relinquished the office of major-commandant at the Illinois, which he had filled nearly four years, and departed down the Mississippi, accompanied by six officers, sixty-three soldiers, and eighty French inhabitants of Illinois, including women and children.* He reached New Orleans on the 2d of July, and there temporarily fixed his quarters. Not long after this, he was requited for his fidelity and services to the French crown with the insignia of the Cross of St. Louis, a distinction corresponding to the more modern Legion of Honor.

Mons. d'Abbadie was then acting governor or director-general of Louisiana, having superseded Governor Kerlerec in June, 1763. As heretofore observed, Western Louisiana, and the island district of New Orleans, had been abandoned to Spain by a private treaty † (Nov. 3, 1762), which was

---

* Many of these "inhabitants," who were induced to move to Louisiana by assurances from De Villiers that they would receive lands there in lieu of those they had abandoned, soon afterward found reason to repent of their haste in quitting the Illinois.

† Without any apparent reference to this separate and private treaty, the boundaries between the French and British possessions in North America were defined by the definitive treaty of peace between the Kings of France, Spain and England, signed at Paris on the 10th of February 1763; which article reads as follows:

"*Article VII.* In order to re-establish peace on solid and durable foundations, and to remove forever all motives for dispute respecting the limits of the French and British territories on the American continent, it has been agreed that the limits between the states of his most Christian majesty and those of his Britannic majesty, in that part of the

kept a state secret *for eighteen months*. On the 21st of April, 1764, the French prime minister addressed the following note to the Spanish ambassador on the subject of the cession of Louisiana:

"VERSAILLES, *April* 21, 1764.

"*To the Conde (Count) de Fuentes:*—Sir, the king has caused the necessary orders to be issued for the surrender of the country of Louisiana, with New Orleans and the island on which the said city stands, into the hands of the commissioner whom his Catholic majesty may appoint to receive them. I have sent the papers to the Marquis d' Ossun, who will have the honor to present them to his Catholic majesty. Your excellency will see that the king's orders are entirely conformable with the acts signed in 1762, and that his majesty has caused some articles to be inserted equally conducive to the tranquillity of the country after it is in possession of his Catholic majesty, and to the happiness of its inhabitants.

"I have the honor to be, with great esteem, your excellency's most humble and obedient servant.

"THE DUC DE CHOISEUL."

At the same time a letter was written by or in the

---

world, shall hereafter be irrevocably fixed by a line drawn along the middle of the river Mississippi, from its source to the river Iberville; and thence by another line through the middle of that river, and of the lakes Maurepas and Pontchartrain, to the sea; and for this purpose, the most Christian king cedes to his Britannic majesty, and guaranties to him, the entire possession of the river and port of Mobile, and of all that he possesses or should have possessed on the left bank of the river Mississippi, with the exception of New Orleans, and of the island whereon that city stands, which are to remain subject to France; it being understood that the navigation of the Mississippi River is to be equally free to the subjects of Great Britain and of France, in its whole breadth and extent, from its source to the sea, and particularly that part between the said island of New Orleans and the right bank of the river, as well as the entrance and departure by its mouth. It is moreover stipulated, that the vessels belonging to the subjects of either nation are not to be detained, searched, nor obliged to pay any duty whatsoever. The stipulations contained in the fourth article, in favor of the inhabitants of Canada, are to be of equal effect with regard to the inhabitants of the countries ceded by this article."

name of Louis XV., King of France, to M. d'Abbadie, Director-general of Louisiana, instructing him to acquaint the inhabitants of that province with the act of cession, and to turn over the government to the officers of Spain, when they should arrive to receive it. We give place here to an English copy of this historical state paper:

"*Monsieur d'Abbadie :*—Having, by a special act, passed at Fontainebleau, November 3d, 1762, ceded, voluntarily, to my dear and well-beloved cousin, the King of Spain, his heirs and successors in full right, completely and without restriction, the whole country known under the name of Louisiana, as well as New Orleans and the island on which that town is situated; and the King of Spain having, by another act, passed at the Escurial, on the 13th of November, in the same year, accepted the cession of the said country of Louisiana town and island of New Orleans, according to the annexed copies of these acts; I write this letter to inform you that my intention is, that on the receipt of this letter and the copies annexed, whether it reaches you through the officers of his Spanish Majesty, or directly by the French vessels charged with its delivery, you will resign into the hands of the governor (or officer) therefor appointed by the King of Spain, the said country and colony of Louisiana and its dependencies, with the town and island of New Orleans, in such state as they may be at the date of such cession, wishing that in future they belong to his Catholic majesty, to be governed and administered by his governors and officers as belonging to him, in full right and without exception.

"I accordingly order, that as soon as the governor and troops of his Catholic majesty arrive in the said country and colony, you put them in possession, and withdraw all the officers, soldiers and employes in my service in garrison there, to send them to France, and my other American colonies, or such of them as are not disposed to remain under the Spanish authorities. I moreover desire, that, after the entire evacuation of said port and town of New Orleans, you collect all papers relative to the finances and administration of the colony of Louisiana, and come to France and account for them.

"It is, nevertheless, my intention that you hand over to the governor, or officer thereto appointed, all the papers and documents which especially concern the government of the colony, either relative to the colony and its limits, or relative to the Indians and the various posts, after having drawn proper receipts for your discharge, and given said governor all the information in your power to enable him to govern said colony to the reciprocal satisfaction of both nations.

"It is my will that there be made an inventory, signed in duplicate by you and his Catholic Majesty's commissary, of all artillery, effects, magazines, hospitals, vessels, etc., belonging to me in said colony, in order that, after putting said commissary in possession of the civil edifices and buildings, an appraisement be made of the value of all the effects remaining in the colony, the price whereof shall be paid by his Catholic Majesty according to such appraisement.

"I hope, at the same time, for the advantage and tranquillity of the inhabitants of the colony of Louisiana, and I flatter myself, in consequence of the friendship and affection of his Catholic Majesty, that he will be pleased to instruct his governor, or any other officers employed by him in said colony and said town of New Orleans, that all the ecclesiastics and religious communities shall continue to perform the rights, privileges, and exemptions granted to them; that all the judges of ordinary jurisdiction, together with the Superior Council, shall continue to administer justice according to the laws, forms, and usages of the colony; that the titles of the inhabitants to their property shall be confirmed in accordance with the concessions made by the governors and ordinary commissaries of said colony; and that said concessions shall be looked upon and held as confirmed by his Catholic Majesty, although they may not as yet have been confirmed by me; hoping, moreover, that his Catholic Majesty will be pleased to give his subjects of Louisiana the marks of protection and good will which they have received under my government, which would have been made more effectual, if not counteracted by the calamities of war—

"I order you to have this, my present letter, registered by the Superior Council at New Orleans, in order that the people of the colony, of all ranks and conditions, be informed of its contents, and that they may avail themselves of it, should need be; such being my sole object in writing this letter. I pray God, M. d'Abbadie, to have you in his holy keeping.

"Given at Versailles, April 21, 1764.

[Signed] "LOUIS.
[Countersigned] "THE DUC DE CHOISEUL."

It was not until October of that year that Governor d'Abbadie reluctantly published the foregoing letter. His health was already declining, and the mental distress attending the performance of this official duty hastened his death, which occurred in New Orleans on the 4th of the following February, 1765. He was a patriotic and popular magistrate, just to all, and firm in his enforcement of the laws. At a meeting of the leading citizens of New Orleans, held shortly after his decease, a feeling tribute was paid to his memory.

M. d'Abbadie was succeeded in office by Captain Charles Aubry, the senior military officer of the province, on whom was now devolved the humiliating duty of handing over the government of Louisiana to the Spaniards. By his valor in the war with England, Aubry had won high praise and the Cross of St. Louis, and was also respected for his social virtues; but though a good grenadier, he had few qualities to fit him for properly governing a colony situated as Louisiana then was.*

---

* Memoir of Louisiana, by the Chevalier de Champigny. He was a contemporary and acquaintance of Aubry's, and has drawn his portrait in no flattering terms. Here it is: "M. Aubry was a little, dry, lean, ugly man, without nobility, dignity, or carriage. His face would seem to announce a hypocrite, but in him this vice sprang from excessive goodness, which granted all rather than displease; always trembling for the consequences of the most indifferent actions, a natural effect of

Between the first of January and the 15th of May, 1765, about six hundred and fifty Acadian exiles arrived in New Orleans from the English colonies, to swell the population of that part of Louisiana still nominally remaining to the French. At this juncture of affairs, their coming was regarded as a misfortune, since it imposed a fresh burden upon the unhappy colonists. Nevertheless, the claims of kindred humanity could not be ignored, and the poor exiles were sent by the acting governor to form settlements in the districts of Attakapas and Opelousas. In the following February (1766), two hundred and sixteen more Acadians arrived to join their brethren in Louisiana. They were authorized to make settlements on both sides of the Mississippi, from below Baton Rouge up to Point Coupée. Hence originated the epithet of "Acadian Coast," which is still applied to the banks of the river between those two points. As these refugees were destitute of supplies, the same rations were issued to them by the provincial commissary, during the first year of their residence, as were allowed to the troops in the province. They were an industrious and frugal people, strongly attached to the French interest and the Catholic religion, and they prospered almost from the start in Louisiana.

When the treaty-cession of Louisiana to Spain was at last made public, it created surprise and indignation at New Orleans and elsewhere in the province, and a general feeling of despair would have ensued, if the people had not been buoyed up with the hope that the transfer would never actually take place. Early in the year 1765, a meeting of the principal citizens and planters from the different parishes was convened in the city of New Orleans for the purpose of considering the subject of their distracted condition,

---

a mind without resource or light, always allowing itself to be guided, and thus often swerving from rectitude; religious through weakness rather than from principle; incapable of wishing evil, but doing it through a charitable human weakness; destitute of magnanimity or reflection; a good soldier, but a bad leader; ambitious of honors and dignity, but possessing neither firmness nor capacity to bear the weight."— *Vide* Hist. Coll's of La. (Fifth of the series), p. 153.

and of sending to the throne of France a united appeal for royal interposition in their behalf. At this meeting La Frenière, attorney-general of Louisiana, made an eloquent speech on the situation of the colony, and presented a resolution earnestly supplicating the king not to sever the colony from the parent .country. The resolution was promptly adopted, and Jean Milhet, of New Orleans, was selected to carry the petition to the foot of the throne.

Upon his arrival in Paris, Milhet went to the residence of the aged Bienville, who, by his request, accompanied him to Versailles. Waiting upon the Duke de Choiseul, the prime minister of Louis XV., they were courteously received and their statements attentively listened to ; but the resolution of the minister was unshaken, and he replied to them, in substance, as follows:

" Gentlemen, I must put an end to this painful scene. I am deeply grieved at not being able to give you any hope. I have no hesitation in telling you that I can not address the king on this subject, because I myself advised the cession of Louisiana. Is it not to your knowledge that the colony can not continue its present precarious existence, except at an enormous expense, of which France is now utterly incapable? Is it not better, then, that Louisiana should be given away to a friend and faithful ally, than be wrenched from us by an hereditary foe? Farewell. You have my best wishes ; I can do no more."

This interview is depicted by Mr. Gayarré as an affecting one, and the pathetic appeal of Bienville on behalf of Louisiana as not unlike that of a father pleading for the life of his child ; yet, under the then circumstances, it was of no avail. The excitement attending his effort, and grief at the loss of his beloved colony, seem to have loosened the feeble chords that bound him to life, and he died not very long afterward in his eighty-seventh year.* He had sur-

---

* Bienville deceased March 7, 1767, and was buried with military honors in the cemetery of Montmartre. His engraved portrait, from an oil painting belonging to the Le Moyne family mansion at Longueil, Canada, presents him with a martial figure and a noble head, in keeping with his record.

24

vived all of his eminent brothers. He had seen Canada, the land of his nativity, pass from the possession of the crown of France to that of Great Britain, and must now witness the transfer of Louisiana, with its future proud metropolis, which he had founded and fostered, to the dominion of Spain. All that the patriarch had most loved and cherished on earth was gone before. Hence, it was not desirable for him to longer live, and he departed to join the shade of his favorite brother, Iberville, in the spirit world.*

The primary motive of France, in voluntarily ceding Western Louisiana to Spain, appears to have been to indemnify the latter for her expenses in the war then just closed. Another incentive was to prevent Louisiana from falling into the hands of Great Britain. Moreover, the province had become a burden to the French government, of which it was anxious to be disincumbered. It has been computed that France, in her prolonged attempt to colonize Louisiana, expended directly, or indirectly, nearly twenty millions of dollars, without receiving any proportionate return; and if she had continued to hold the country, it would have been necessary for her to have incurred a large additional outlay. "Hence," says Gayerré, "the anxiety of the French government to part with a territory, which, at a later period, in abler hands, was destined to astonish the world by its rapid and gigantic prosperity."

The Duke de Choiseul having refused to address the king on the question of revoking the transfer of Louisiana to Spain, and having denied Milhet access to his majesty, the commissioner returned to New Orleans, and reported the failure of his mission. Still hoping that the treaty of cession would never be carried into execution, Jean Milhet was again sent to France, but returned with a like result. His next voyage, as we shall hereafter see, was as a state prisoner to Moro Castle, in Cuba.

The French colonists, however, did not altogether lose hope, in which they were sustained by the delay of

---

* Gayarré's Hist of La., Vol. II, pp. 128-9.

the Spanish government in taking possession of the country. It was not until the middle of the year 1765, that the Court of Madrid appointed Captain Don Antonio de Ulloa— a man of high reputation, and descended from a family distinguished in the maritime annals of his country—to assume the government of Louisiana. Some months in advance of his arrival in the province, Ulloa wrote from Havana to the Superior Council at New Orleans the following brief letter, announcing his mission:

"*Gentlemen*—Having recently been instructed by his Catholic Majesty to repair to your town and take possession of it in his name, and in conformity with the orders of his Most Christian Majesty, I avail myself of this occasion to make you acquainted with my mission, and to give you information that I shall soon have the honor to be among you, in order to proceed to the execution of my commission. I flatter myself beforehand, that it will afford me favorable opportunities to render you all the services that you and the inhabitants of your town may desire; of which I beg you to give them the assurance from me, and let them know that in acting thus, I only discharge my duty and gratify my inclinations.

"I have the honor to be, etc.,
"ANTONIO DE ULLOA."
"Havana, July 10, 1765."

The Spanish governor arrived at the Balize,* with some Capuchin friars and eighty soldiers, on the 28th of February, 1766, and, proceeding up the Mississippi, landed in New Orleans on the 5th of March. He was received by the French inhabitants with every superficial mark of courtesy and good will; but such was their aversion to Spanish rule, and such the lack of tact and administrative talent of Ulloa himself, that he could not openly exercise his authority.† The French troops continued to serve

---
* A small port or settlement at the outlet of the Mississippi, on the west side, in French times. It took its name from the Spanish word *baliza*, a beacon.

† The mistake of the Spanish government, at this time, was in not sending an adequate military force to sustain Ulloa's authority.

under their national flag; the council acted in the name of
the King of France; and all orders emanated from Aubry,
the *de facto* French governor, who practically governed the
colony for the King of Spain. The Spanish flag was unfurled at the Balize, on the banks of the river Iberville, at
the post opposite Natchez, and at the Missouri; but at all
the other posts in the province, the French colors were
kept up as before.

Governor Ulloa was apparently so desirous of conciliating those over whose affairs he had come to preside, that
on his arrival he promised to keep at a fixed rate the depreciated paper currency of the province, which then
amounted to about seven millions of livres. He also ascertained the resources and wants of the country, and
agreed to discharge the most pressing demands against it.
On the 6th of September, 1766, the governor published an
ordinance of the Spanish government regulating and limiting the commerce of Louisiana, but permitting a direct
trade with the French West Indies. This, together with
subsequent commercial restrictions, produced great discontent and excitement at New Orleans, and Ulloa, fearing
an attempt on his life, retired for safety to the Balize.
Here (January 20, 1767) he effected an arrangement with
Aubry, by which the latter resigned to him the colony of
Louisiana, but agreed to govern it for the time being. This
act was signed by the two governors in duplicate, and was
to be exchanged by the two courts of Paris and Madrid.*

In the meantime a conspiracy was set on foot by
Lafrenière, Foucault, Marquis, Noyon, Villeré, Milhet,
Petit, Caresse, Poupet, Boisblanc, and others, to drive Ulloa and his Spaniards from the province. To this end, at a
delegate convention of planters, merchants and tradesmen,
held in New Orleans on the 28th of October, 1768, a petition was signed by five hundred and thirty-six persons, praying the Superior Council for a restoration of their former
rights and privileges, and for the expulsion of the Spaniards from the country. This petition was presented to the

---

* Champigny's Memoir of Louisiana.

Council on the next day (the 29th), and, despite the formal protest of Aubry, the French commandant, a decree was passed that Ulloa and the Spanish troops should leave the colony within three days. Governor Ulloa did not stand on the order of his going, but embarked on the evening of the 31st of October, with his few troops, and sailed for Spain, where he arrived on the 4th of December following.

The news of this ill-starred revolution soon reached Spain, and the king (Charles III.) called a meeting of his ministers to determine upon the fate of Louisiana. At this cabinet council it was decided that possession of that province should be taken by force, if necessary. Apprehending considerable resistance from the French inhabitants, the king issued orders for the fitting out of a formidable expedition, and gave the command of it to General O'Reilly, whom he also appointed governor and captain-general of the province.*

---

*Don Alexandro O'Reilly was born in Ireland about the year 1735, and when quite a young man went to Spain, and entered the Spanish military service. Joining a body of his native countrymen called the "Hibernia Regiment," he served a campaign in Italy, where he received a wound which lamed him for the rest of his life. In 1755 he obtained permission from the king to enter the Austrian army, and made two campaigns against the Prussians. In 1759 he volunteered in the army of France, in which he distinguished himself by his soldierly qualities, and was recommended by the Duke de Broglie to the King of Spain, who commissioned him to the rank of lieutenant-colonel; and, as such, he served with distinction in the war with Portugal. He was afterward promoted to the rank of brigadier-general, and on the conclusion of the peace of 1762 was raised to the rank of major-general, in which capacity he was sent to Havana to rebuild the fortifications of that city, which had been demolished by the British. O'Reilly stood high in the confidence of the king, notwithstanding the prejudice existing against him among the Spaniards on account of his foreign birth. He was a man of flexible disposition and conciliatory manners, yet stern and unyielding of purpose. We are not informed of the precise nature of his instructions on being sent to Louisiana; but the substance of them is embodied in a royal order addressed to Don Pedro Gracia, under date of January 28, 1771, in which the king says: "But those inhabitants having rebelled, . . . I commissioned Don Alexandro O'Reilly, lieutenant-general of the army, and inspector-general of all my infantry, to proceed thither, take formal possession, chastise the ringleaders (informing me of all), establish the said government, uniting the province to the

Governor O'Reilly arrived at the mouth of the Mississippi on the 24th of July, 1769, with a fleet of twenty-four ships and transports, bearing an army of twenty-six hundred choice troops,—a force so large as to render all attempts at resistance hopeless. On the same day he dispatched his aid to Aubry, the acting French governor, to announce his arrival, and to notify him that he was duly authorized to receive possession of the Province of Louisiana.

The coming of the Spanish armament excited a great commotion in New Orleans; and on the 27th the citizens sent delegates to O'Reilly to implore his clemency. They returned to the city the next day with assurances from the governor that he was disposed to be lenient. On the 17th of August he reached New Orleans, and on the next day took military possession of the government.

Governor O'Reilly entered upon the duties of his responsible office with every outward manifestation of respect for all classes of the citizens; but, while promising pardon to those who quietly submitted, he had resolved in his own mind to punish the principal actors in the late revolution. This determination, however, was concealed until he had procured from Aubry, the retiring French governor, a full report of that event. On the 21st and 22d of August, after receiving Aubry's communication, he caused to be quietly arrested and imprisoned twelve chiefs of the revolution that had expelled his predecessor, Ulloa. They were, Nicholas Chauvin de la Frenière, ex-procureur-general of the province, and senior member of the Superior Council; Jean Baptiste Noyon, his son-in-law, a young man of great worth and promise; Pierre Carèsse, captain of militia; Pierre Marquis, a knight of St. Louis; Jean and Joseph Milhet, father and son; Joseph Villieré,* captain in the

---

rest of my dominions; all of which he did, adapting its laws, and after proposing to me that which he judged proper for the commerce of the country, and for the extinction of the council by which it is governed, and establishing a *cabildo* in the place of said council, and taking other measures, all of which were approved by me," etc.—Hist. Coll's of La., Fifth Series (N. Y., 1853), p. 247.

* Villeré resisted arrest, and died in prison three days after, from

militia; Joseph Petit, merchant; Balthauser de Masan, captain in the French service; Jerome Doucet, lawyer; Hardi de Boisblanc, assessor to the Council; and Pierre Poupet, merchant.*

These sudden arrests produced extreme uneasiness and trepidation among the French inhabitants. To quiet their fears, the Spanish governor, on the 23d of August, issued a proclamation of amnesty,† and a call inviting the people to appear before him on the 26th, and take the oath of allegiance to his Catholic majesty.

Something over a month after their arrest, the prisoners were arraigned before a semi-military tribunal, constituted for the purpose, on the charge of treason and rebellion, the deceased Villeré being represented by an attorney in fact. They were tried and convicted under Spanish law, and their property was confiscated to the state, after

---

the effect of wounds received in his struggle with the Spanish *gendarmes* for liberty.

* M. Foucault, president of the Superior Council, and commissary of the province, was also placed under guard; but at his request, and in deference to his official position, he was sent to France for trial. He is described as a wily man, who acted with singular duplicity toward the revolutionists in Louisiana.

† [*O'Reilly's Proclamation of Amnesty.*]

" In the name of the King, we, Alexander O'Reilly, commander of Benfayan, in the order of Alcantara, major and inspector-general of the armies of his Catholic majesty, captain-general and governor of the Province of Louisiana, in virtue of the orders of his Catholic majesty, and of the powers with which we are invested, declare to all the inhabitants of the Province of Louisiana, that whatever just cause past events may have given his majesty to make them feel his indignation, yet his majesty's intention is to listen only to the inspirations of his royal clemency, because he is persuaded that the inhabitants of Louisiana would not have committed the offense of which they are guilty, if they had not been seduced by the intrigues of some ambitious fanatic, and evil-minded men, who had the temerity to make a criminal use of the ignorance and excessive credulity of their fellow-citizens. These men alone will answer for their crimes, and will be judged in accordance with the laws. So generous an act on the part of his majesty might be a pledge to him that his new subjects will endeavor every day of their lives to deserve by their fidelity, zeal, and obedience, the pardon and protection which he grants them from this moment."

the payment of their debts. The sentence of the court was pronounced by the governor himself, October 24, 1769. Five of the number, viz., Lafrenière, Noyon, Carèsse, Marquis, and (Joseph) Milhet, were condemned to death on the gallows; but as no white hangman could be found in the colony, they were shot (October 24th) in the yard of the barracks. The memory of Villeré was declared infamous. It has been observed, and perhaps truly, that these men died victims to their love of liberty rather than of devotion to France.

The six remaining culprits were sentenced to varying terms of imprisonment. Petit was sentenced to imprisonment for life; Masan and Doucet to ten years; Boisblanc, Milhet (Jean), and Poupet to six years each, with the understanding that none of them should ever be permitted to live in any of the dominions of his Catholic majesty. They were shortly after transported to Havana, and incarcerated in Moro Castle; but they were subsequently pardoned by the King of Spain, on the intercession of the French ambassador at that court. After their release, it is said that they went to reside at Cape Francois, in St. Domingo.*

The extreme punishment thus meted out to a few leaders, while a free pardon was extended to the mass of the people, though conformable to Spanish ideas of justice and clemency, aroused a deep feeling of indignation among the French inhabitants of Louisiana, and evoked much unfavorable criticism in Old France.

O'Reilly now proceeded to abolish the laws of France in the province, and to substitute those of Spain. On the 21st of November, he issued his proclamation for the abolition of the Superior Council, which had been deeply implicated in the insurrection against Spanish authority. In place of the Superior Council, he established the *Cabildo*, which was both a high court and a legislative council, and at which the governor presided. In its judicial capacity, it only exercised appellate jurisdiction in appeals from the

---

* For a circumstantial account of this remarkable state trial, see Gayarré's Hist. of La., Vol. II, pp. 303-343.

Alcalde courts, which were established in New Orleans and the various villages.

He appointed lieutenant-governors for the several districts of the province; and a commandant, with the rank of captain, was appointed for each parish or settlement, with authority to exercise a mixed civil and military jurisdiction.

He also caused to be published, in French, an abridgment of Spanish law, which he promulgated for the government of the province until the Spanish language should be better understood by the colonists. This publication, known as the "Ordinances and Instructions of Don Alexander O'Reilly," was afterward approved by the "Council of the Indies." The Spanish language was henceforth that in which the judicial proceedings were conducted and records kept throughout the province. The black code, or *code noir*, which had been previously in force in the colony, was modified and re-enacted for the government of the slaves. Foreigners were prohibited from passing through the country without passports from the governor, and the inhabitants were prevented from trading with the English colonies. The colonists were at first permitted to emigrate, and many availed themselves of this privilege; but, finding that the province was losing some of its valuable citizens, O'Reilly refused to issue any more passports.

In accordance with an enumeration made during Gov. O'Reilly's administration, the whole foreign population of Louisiana amounted to thirteen thousand, two hundred and thirty-eight souls, about one-half of whom were African slaves. They were distributed in the settlements as follows:

New Orleans * [district of], . . 3,190
From the Balize to town [N. O.] . . 570

---

* According to the lowest estimate, at this time, the number of houses in New Orleans proper was 468. Most of these were single story structures of brick or wood, having gardens attached, and cellars above ground. They were situated within the quadrilateral still known as "Old French Town."

Bayou St. John and Gentilly,	307
Tchoupitoulas [above New Orleans],	4,192
St. Charles,	339
St. John the Baptiste,	544
La Fourche,	267
Iberville,	376
Point Coupée,	783
Attakapas,	409
Avoyvelles,	314
Natchitoches,	811
Rapides,	47
Ouachita,	110
Arkansas [Post of],	88
St. Louis [adjacent to the Illinois],	891
	13,238 *

This aggregate seems small, considering the fact that the French had been in Louisiana seventy years; yet it must be remembered that the province was now shorn of all its territory lying north of New Orleans and east of the Mississippi River, including the Mobile, Natchez, and the Illinois. At this transition epoch, a majority of the French inhabitants chose to regard themselves as miserable exiles, and were only consoled by the hope of acquiring sufficient means to enable them to return to Old France to die. About the only contented white people in the province were the Acadians, and a colony of Germans, whom Law's company had sent here in 1722.

The Spanish government ratified and confirmed all of O'Reilly's official acts in Louisiana, but it took care not to continue him in command there after his work was done. He was accordingly recalled within a year from the date of

---

* Hist. of La. (Gayarré), Vol. II, p. 355.

The exports of the province during the last year of its subjection to France were as follows: Indigo, $100,000; deer skins, $80,000; lumber, $50,000; naval stores, $12,000; rice, peas, and beans, $4,000; tallow, $4,000. Total exports, $250,000.

Fate of Aubry, the Last Acting French Governor. 379

his appointment. During that brief period, however, he left an impress of his own and the Spanish character upon the laws and institutions of Louisiana, such as neither time, nor subsequent political changes, has wholly obliterated.

We must now return to M. Charles Aubry, whose fate was sad and tragical. Having at length transferred the government of Louisiana to Captain-General O'Reilly, Aubry prepared to return to France. Early in January, 1770, he embarked in the ship or brigantine called *Père de Famille*, bound for Bordeaux. On the 18th of February, when this vessel had entered the mouth of the river Garonne, she met a violent storm, and foundered near the Tower of Corduan. All on board perished, save the captain, a sergeant, and two sailors, who succeeded in reaching the land.

" The king, in order to show how much he appreciated the services of Aubry, granted a pension to the brother and sister of that officer. Aubry, before his departure from Louisiana, had been offered a high grade in the Spanish army, as a token of satisfaction at the liberal course which he had pursued toward that nation in the colony, but he refused it on the ground that he intended to devote the remnant of his days to the service of his native country. Some there were, who thought that if those whom they loved so dearly had been unjustly treated, it was mostly in consequence of the imprudent denunciations of that officer, and of his servility to O'Reilly and the Spaniards. By them his melancholy end was looked upon as an act of the retributive justice of Heaven." *

One of the most noteworthy events associated with the close of the French rule in Louisiana was the banishment of the Jesuits, which was effected by a decree of the Superior Council in 1763, followed by an edict of the King of

---

* Hist. of La. (Gayarré), Vol. II., p. 344.

Note.—The official correspondence of Aubry was deposited in the archives at Paris, but his private journal, with valuable papers belonging to the province, were lost with him in the shipwreck. This was to be regretted, since they contained much matter tending to illustrate the history of Louisiana during that troubled period.

France in 1764.* All the valuable property of that religious order in the province, including plate and vestments, was sequestered, confiscated, and sold, for the aggregate amount of $180,000—a large sum, says Mr. Gayarré, at that day—which, after deducting the expenses, was covered into the public treasury. The Capuchins, who had been established in Lower Louisiana since 1722, and had long contended at disadvantage with the Jesuits, were now freed from the presence of their formidable rivals, and had this field of labor to themselves.

In this connection, some historical notice of the famous *Societas Jesu* (Society of Jesus) may not be uninteresting or uninstructive to the general reader. It was founded in Paris by Ignatius Loyola, an ex-Spanish soldier and religious enthusiast, in the year 1534. The society was primarily established to promote the following objects, viz: "The education of youth, preaching of the Gospel, defending the Roman Catholic faith against heretics and unbelievers, and propagating Christianity among the pagans and other infidels." Its constitution and laws were perfected, it is said, by Laynez and Acquaviva, two generals of the order who early succeeded Loyola, and who much surpassed him in learning and the science of government. They framed and introduced that system of profound and artful policy—a singular union of laxity and rigor—which has ever distinguished the Jesuit order. After receiving the formal sanction of Pope Paul III., in 1540, the society spread rapidly throughout Europe, and flourished with ever-increasing vigor and activity for above two centuries. It overshadowed all other orders in the Church of Rome, and at length became so rich, haughty, and powerful as to excite the jealousy and alarm of the crowned heads of Europe.

But whatever may have been the errors, the follies, or the crimes of the Jesuits (individually or collectively), while playing their part in the devious politics and diplomacy of the Old World, it is generally conceded that their labors in

---

* See *note* in the next succeeding chapter.

the New were prompted by a spirit of genuine philanthropy. Robertson, the eminent historian, in alluding to their operations in America, and particularly among the aborigines of Paraguay, remarks:

"It is in the New World that the Jesuits have exhibited the most wonderful display of their abilities, and have contributed most effectually to the benefits of the human species. The (European) conquerors of that quarter of the globe acted at first as if they had nothing in view but to plunder, to enslave, and to exterminate its inhabitants. The Jesuits alone made humanity the object of their settling there. They set themselves to instruct and to civilize the savages. . . . But even in this meritorious effort for the good of mankind, the genius and spirit of the order have mingled and are discernible." *

With reference to the zeal of the Jesuits as champions of the Church of Rome, and to their qualifications as teachers and missionaries, Breese finely writes:

"They became most useful auxiliaries to the pastoral clergy in those times of the Church's greatest need. They labored with untiring zeal and industry in defending the faith, then so violently assailed by Luther and his associates, and in propagating it in the countries of the heathen.

"As spiritual teachers they had no equals; for they possessed all the learning of the age, and being in high favor with the pope, they easily became the conscience keepers of kings and nobles. Their arrogance and presumption, therefore, became excessive, and the dark and complicated intrigues of European politics found in them able, wily, persevering actors. In every royal court they possessed some power. Schools and colleges were founded and controlled by them, and schemes of future aggrandizement planned. . . .

"In the plenitude of their power, no men on earth possessed higher qualifications for heathen conversion than they; for to their learning was added zeal, fortitude and enthusiasm, acute observation and great address, and a re-

---

* Robertson's Charles V., Book VI.

markable faculty for ingratiating themselves with the simple natives of every clime and winning their confidence. They were meek and humble when necessary, and their religious fervor inspired them with a contempt of danger, and nerved them to meet and to overcome the most appalling obstacles. Alike to them were the chilling wintry blasts, the summer's heat, the pestilence or the scalping knife, the angry billows of the ocean and the raging storm; they dreaded none."*

But having fallen under the ban of the government of Portugal, the Jesuits were forcibly expelled from that kingdom in the year 1759. In like manner they were banished from the realm of France in 1764, and from Spain, Naples and Parma, in 1767. In December, 1768, the Bourbon courts of France, Spain, Naples and Parma united in a formal demand upon the Pope for the entire abolishment of the order; and on July 21, 1773, Pope Clement XIV. issued the famous brief, *Dominus ac Redemptor noster*, by which the Company or Society of Jesus was declared suppressed in all the countries of Christendom. The activity of individual members of the order, however, was not thereby abated, nor was its vitality permanently impaired. They continued their teachings in private, and strove against the liberal tendency of the times.

Attempts to revive the order under other names were made in 1794, when the ex-Jesuits DeBroglie and De Tournly founded the "Society of the Sacred Heart," and in 1798, when Paccarani established the "Society of the Faith of Jesus." This last, despite the defection of its founder, maintained its organization, and its members formed the nucleus of the restored society in France. The prospects of general restoration at length dawned with the the Pontificate of Pius VII. in 1800. Having been solicited thereto by Ferdinand IV., he authorized the introduction of the order into the kingdom of the Two Sicilies in 1804, and on the 7th of August, 1814, he issued the bull of restoration, *Solicitudo Omnium Ecclesiarum*.†

---

* "Early History of Ill.," pp. 69, 70.
† American Encyclopedia (1874), Vol. IX., p. 632.

Since their revival the Jesuits, while every-where meeting with prejudice and opposition, and experiencing all the vicissitudes of good and ill fortune, have managed to regain their former footing in most of the countries of Christendom ; and, to-day, though much less dreaded than formerly, they are more numerous, if not more powerful and influential, than ever before.

On account of the long, dark cloaks or robes worn by the Jesuit missionaries, they were universally known among the North American Indians as the "Black Gowns," and their officiating priests as the "White Capes." The Recollet or Franciscan Fathers, in allusion to the gray color of their outward apparel, were called the "Gray Gowns."

"The Jesuits (writes Mr. Butterfield, in his work already cited), intent upon pushing their fields of labor far into the heart of the continent, let slip no opportunity, after their arrival upon the Saint Lawrence, to inform themselves concerning ulterior regions, and the information thus obtained was noted down by them. They minutely described, during a period of forty years, beginning with the year 1632, the various tribes that they came in contact with; and their hopes and fears as to Christianizing them were freely expressed. Accounts of their journeys were elaborated upon, and their missionary work put upon record. Prominent persons, as well as important events, shared their attention. Details concerning the geography of the country were also written out. The intelligence thus collected was sent every summer by the superiors to the Provincials at Paris, where it was yearly published in the French language. Taken together, these publications constitute what are known as the 'Jesuit Relations.'"

They were collected, edited and republished in French, under the auspices of the Canadian government, by M. Augustin Coté, at Quebec, 1858, in three large volumes. Vol. I contains twelve relations of the dates 1611, 1626 and 1632-1641 ; Vol. II, fourteen relations, dated 1642-1655; Vol. III, seventeen relations, dated 1656-1672. The relations of each year are paged separately, and form forty-three distinct memoirs. Besides the above, there are some separate publications of a later date than 1672.

CHAPTER XX.

1764–1778.

ILLINOIS UNDER THE BRITISH DOMINATION.

We now return once more to the Illinois. In the month of June, 1764, on the resignation and withdrawal of M. Neyon de Villiers from Fort Chartres, the command of this stronghold was devolved upon Louis St. Ange de Bellerive, who had arrived from Post Vincennes to receive it. He was a veteran Canadian officer, possessed of rare tact and ripe experience, and in his early manhood had formed one of Charlevoix' escort in his travels through the West. As *ad interim* commandant of the fortress, St. Ange's position was both insecure and difficult to fill. It required no ordinary skill and address to save the isolated French settlements from being embroiled in renewed warfare with the English forces on the one hand, and from massacre by the hordes of restless savages that surrounded them on the other. He had been advised by his own government of the treaty of cession to England, and ordered to surrender his post on the arrival of her representatives to claim it. In the meantime he was repeatedly importuned by deputations from the martial tribes to the north and eastward, under the domination of Pontiac, for material aid in keeping up their futile struggle against the English, and, moreover, was constantly annoyed by the demands of the Illinois Indians for arms and ammunition. But the commandant managed to put off the importunities of the natives from time to time, with fair speeches and occasional presents, while he anxiously waited the coming of an adequate British force to relieve him from his critical situation. Before yielding up his office and authority, however, he instituted some prudent and salutary regulations respecting the titles of the French settlers to their lands, and otherwise aided him to the extent of his power.

Evacuating Fort Chartres in October, 1765, St. Ange, under orders from the provincial executive at New Orleans, conducted his little garrison, of about thirty officers and men, up and across the Mississippi River to the embryo village of St. Louis. This post, so named in honor to Louis XV. of France, was founded in February, 1764, by Pierre Lacléde* Liguest, and young Auguste Chouteau, of the firm of "Maxent, Lacléde & Company, merchants of New Orleans, who had obtained the year before a special license from Governor Kerlerec to trade with the Indians on the Missouri River.

Although France had relinquished to Spain her territory on the west of the Mississippi, no Spanish authority was as yet established there, and in January, 1766, at the request of the principal inhabitants of St. Louis, Captain St. Ange assumed the functions of military commandant. His acts were approved by Aubry, the French commandant-general, and he continued to exercise the duties of his office until May 20, 1770, when he was relieved by Lieutenant-Governor Don Pedro Piernas, the first Spanish commandant of the district. After that St. Ange was admitted into the Spanish regiment of Louisiana, with the same rank of cap-

---

* Pierre Lacléde was born in the South of France about the year 1724. In 1755 he sailed to Louisiana, and engaged extensively in merchandising. On August 3, 1763, he left New Orleans with his boat, heavily laden with goods, and started up the Mississippi. After a short stoppage at Ste. Genevieve, he proceeded to Fort Chartres, whither he arrived on the 3d of November. During the next month he traveled by land as far as the mouth of the Missouri, selected and marked out the site for his trading post, and then returned to Fort Chartres to spend the rest of the winter. On the opening of navigation in February, 1764, Lacléde sent Auguste Chouteau (then a youth under age) in charge of his boat, with a company of thirty men and boys, and with instructions where to land and make a clearing. Chouteau landed at the place designated on the 14th of February, and the next day put his men to work.—See "History of St. Louis City and County," by J. Thomas Scharf (Philadelphia, 1883), Vol. I., pp. 66, 67, note, and fragment of Chouteau's Journal.

tain as he had before held under the French, but on half pay.* It has been affirmed that he returned to Fort Chartres, after the asserted death of Captain Stirling, and that, on the solicitation of the English, he again exercised command there for a short time; but this story is wanting in proof and probability.

It was in April, 1769, while still commanding at St. Louis, that St. Ange received an unexpected visit from Pontiac, who had been living for three years in sullen retirement on the river Maumee, but was now come on some unexplained yet suspicious mission to the Illinois. The Indian chieftain appeared at the head-quarters of the French commandant arrayed in the uniform which had been given to him by General Montcalm in 1759, and which, it is said, he never wore except on occasions of ceremony. After being hospitably entertained at St. Louis for several days, Pontiac, contrary to the advice of St. Ange and others of the French inhabitants, who warned him of the danger he was incurring, re-crossed the Mississippi, with a few of his personal adherents, to attend a social gathering, or pow-wow, of the Indians at Cahokia. Upon arriving thither, he found them engaged in a drinking-bout, and, with his fondness for liquor, soon became drunk himself. The noisy meeting broke up late at night, when he started with some friends down the long village street, and on the way was heard singing medicine songs, in the mystic virtues of which he seems to have reposed implicit confidence.

The visit of this redoubtable chief to the Illinois was regarded with great distrust by the few English residents of the country, who justly dreaded his power for evil over the minds of his fellow red men. At this time, it appears, there was in Cahokia an English trader named Williamson, who determined to avail himself of the opportunity pre-

---

* St. Ange de Bellerive died at the house of Madame Chouteau, in St. Louis, on the evening of December 26, 1774 (having executed his last will on the same day), and was buried there in the parish cemetery. He had attained the ripe old age of about seventy-four years. See Billon's "Annals of St. Louis," p. 128.

sented to effect his destruction. For this sinister purpose, he bribed a vagrant Indian of the Kaskaskia tribe, for a barrel of liquor and the promise of further reward, to take Pontiac's life. The hired assassin accordingly followed the inebriated chief into the forest, and, gliding silently up behind him, stabbed him to the heart. Thus ingloriously ended the notable career of the veteran Pontiac, whose extraordinary ability as a leader and organizer of the red men, his strategy and audacity in war, rendered him the terror of the English, and the typical hero of his race. When informed of this tragical occurrence, which created wild excitement in Cahokia, Captain St. Ange, mindful of his former friendship for the fallen chief, caused his body to be shrouded and brought to St. Louis, where it was interred with the honors of war, near the intersection of Walnut and Fourth streets. No mound nor tablet marks his forgotten grave, but his deeds are written, and his name is enduringly preserved in that of a thriving town in Illinois. Pontiac left several children, among whom were two sons of note in their tribe.*

The unfortunate killing of Pontiac—unfortunate if he was not seeking to stir up another race war with the English—aroused intense animosity against the Illinois Indians on the part of his numerous friends and followers among the more northern tribes. It was the occasion of a renewal of hostilities between the Sacs and Foxes and the Illinois, in which the latter sustained heavy losses and were finally driven south of the Illinois river. During this exterminating war, and about the year 1770, tradition says that a defeated band of Illinois warriors took refuge on the Rock of St. Louis, where, after a protracted siege, they were starved into submission and captured, thus giving rise to the legend of the "Starved Rock."

Just before and during the first years of the English

---

*An Ottawa tradition states that Pontiac took a Kaskaskia wife, with whom he had a quarrel, and that she persuaded her two brothers to kill him. But see Parkman's "History of the Conspiracy of Pontiac" (4th ed., 1868, pp. 571, 572, *notes*), where the various accounts of the great Indian's death are mentioned and discussed.

domination, there was a large exodus of the French inhabitants from Illinois. Such, in fact, was their dislike of British rule that fully one-third of the population, embracing the wealthier and more influential families, removed, with their slaves and other personal effects, beyond the Mississippi, or down that river to Natchez and New Orleans. Some of them settled at Ste. Genevieve, while others, after the example set by St. Ange, took up their abode in the village of St. Louis, which had now become a depot for the fur company of Louisiana. From the impetus thus received, as well as from its pleasant and advantageous situation for general trade, St. Louis soon outstripped the older French settlements on the eastern side of the Mississippi. Under successive mild administrations (French and Spanish), the village quietly grew and flourished, meeting with but few drawbacks, saving the attack by northern Indians, in May, 1780, the destructive inundation in 1785,* and the epidemic of 1801. It was not until after the Indian incursion that St. Louis was stockaded, and a regular fortification constructed at the upper end of the village. In 1770 there were one hundred wooden and fifteen stone buildings in the place. But no church edifice existed there prior to the year 1776, except a small log chapel which stood upon what was known as the Church Block. In 1794 the garrison and government house, situate on the second rise or bank of the village, was completed and occupied. In March, 1804, when the government of the country west of the Mississippi was transferred to the United States, the number of houses in St. Louis had increased to one hundred and thirty of wood, and fifty-one of stone, making a total of one hundred and eighty-one, of which one hundred and sixty were dwelling houses. These were one and two story structures, built upon the first bank of the river, with little or no pretensions to architectural embellishment. The population of the place was then rated

---

*The unusual inundation of 1785 was caused by the annual floods in the Mississippi and Missouri rivers occurring together. This was known as *L'année des grands eaux,* or "*the year of the great waters.*"

at nine hundred and twenty-five souls.* French influence was long dominant in St. Louis, and tended to retard her early development; but, in modern years, her growth and expansion into a great commercial and industrial city have been something phenomenal.

At the close of the year 1765, the whole number of inhabitants of foreign birth or lineage, in Illinois, excluding the negro slaves, and including those living at Post Vincent on the Wabash, did not much exceed two thousand persons; and, during the entire period of British possession, the influx of alien population hardly more than kept pace with the outflow. Scarcely any Englishmen, other than the officers and troops composing the small garrisons, a few enterprising traders and some favored land speculators, were then to be seen in the Illinois, and no Americans came hither, for the purpose of settlement, until after the conquest of the country by Colonel Clark. All the settlements still remained essentially French, with whom there was no taste for innovation or change. But the blunt and sturdy Anglo-American had at last gained a firm foot-hold on the banks of the great Father of Rivers, and a new type of civilization, instinct with energy, enterprise and progress, was about to be introduced into the broad and fertile Valley of the Mississippi.†

In Captain Pittman's valuable work, from which we have repeatedly quoted, is found a comprehensive account of the Illinois country and its inhabitants, with sketches in detail of the several French posts and villages situated therein, as personally viewed by him in 1766–7. Pittman was an officer of the British Royal Engineers, and was first sent out with a regiment to Pensacola, Florida, in 1763. From Pensacola he went to Mobile, and thence to New Orleans; after which he passed up the Mississippi, stopping at Natchez, and appears to have reached the Illinois early in the year 1766. Returning to Florida, he thence sailed for England in 1768. His book, we are told, was originally

---

* Billon's Annals of Early St. Louis.
† Davidson's and Stuve's History, 1st ed., p. 163.

written at the request and for the use of the Secretary of
State for the Colonies. It contains, in a compact form,
much useful and reliable information (nowhere else to be
found) concerning the Mississippi Valley and its people at
that transition period.*

Pittman describes the country of the Illinois as then
"bounded by the Mississippi on the west, by the river Illinois on the north, by the rivers Ouabache and Miamis on
the east, and by the Ohio on the south." Treating of the
villages *seriatim*, and beginning with Kaskaskia, he writes:

"The village of Notre Dame de Cascasquias is by far the
most considerable settlement in the country of the Illinois,
as well from its number of inhabitants as from its advantageous situation. It stands on the side of a small river,
which is about eighty yards wide, and empties itself with
a gentle current into the Mississippi, near two leagues below
the village. This river is a secure port for the large bateaux
which lie so close to its banks as to load and unload without the least trouble, and at all seasons of the year there is
water enough for them to come up. . . . Another
great advantage that Cascasquias receives from its river is
the facility with which mills for corn and plank may be
erected on it. Mons. Paget was the first who introduced
water-mills in this country, and he constructed a very fine
one on the river Cascasquias, which was both for grinding
corn and sawing boards; it lies about one mile from the
village. The mill proved fatal to him, being killed as he
was working in it with two negroes, by a party of Cherokees, in 1764.

"The principal buildings here are the Church,† and
Jesuit's House, which (latter) has a small chapel adjoining
it; these, as well as some other houses in the village, are
built of stone, and, considering this part of the world,

---

* *Vide* "The Present State of the European Settlements on the Mis-
sissippi; with a Geographical Description of that River, illustrated by
Plans and Draughts." By Captain Philip Pittman. London, 1770.
Quarto, pp. 107.

† The bell belonging to this quaint old church was cast at La Rochelle, France, in 1741.

make a very good appearance. The Jesuit's plantation consisted of two hundred and forty arpents (an arpent being 85-100 of an acre) of cultivated land, a very good stock of cattle, and a brewery; which was sold by the French commandant, after the country was ceded to the English, for the Crown, in consequence of the suppression of the order.* Mons. (Jean Baptiste) Beauvais was the purchaser, who is the richest of the English subjects in this country. He keeps eighty slaves; he furnished eighty-six thousand weight of flour to the king's magazine, which was only part of the harvest he reaped in one year. Sixty-five families reside in this village, besides merchants, other casual people, and slaves.

"The fort, which was burnt down in October, 1766, stood on the summit of a high rock opposite the village, and on the opposite side of the river. It was an oblong quadrangle, of which the extreme polygon measured two hundred and ninety by two hundred and fifty-one feet. It was built of very thick square timbers, and dovetailed at the angles. An officer and twenty soldiers are quartered in the village. The officer governs the inhabitants under the direction of the commandant at Fort Chartres. Here are also two companies of (French) militia.

"La Prairie des Roches† is about seventeen (fifteen) miles from Cascasquias. It is a small village, consisting of twelve dwelling houses, all of which are inhabited by as many families. Here is a little chapel, formerly a chapel of ease to the church at Fort Chartres. The inhabitants are very industrious, and raise a great deal of corn and every kind of stock. The village is two miles from Fort Char-

---

* The only Jesuit priest allowed to remain in the Illinois was Sebastian Louis Meurin, and he was required to sign a paper obligating himself not to acknowledge any other superior than that of the Capuchins at New Orleans. (Shea's "Catholic Church in Old Colonial Days.") Father Meurin died at Prairie du Rocher in 1778. He was a learned man and faithful missionary, who left in manuscript a large dictionary of the Indian and French languages.

† Prairie du Rocher is the only one of these old French villages that has continued to flourish until the present day. In 1890, according to the United States census, it contained a population of 408 souls.

tres. It takes its name from its situation, being built under a rock that runs parallel with the river Mississippi, at a league distance, for forty miles up. Here is a company of militia, the captain of which regulates the police of the village."

After giving a particular description of Fort Chartres,† Pittman's account continues: "In the year 1764, there were about forty families in the village near the fort, and a parish church served by a Franciscan friar, dedicated to St. Anne. In the following year, when the English took possession of the country, they abandoned their houses and settled at the village on the west side of the Mississippi, choosing to continue under the French government.

"Saint Phillippe is a small village about five miles from Fort Chartres, on the road to Kaoquias. There are about sixteen houses and a small church standing; all the inhabitants, except the captain of the militia, deserted it in 1765, and went to the French side (Missouri). The captain of the militia has about twenty slaves, a good stock of cattle, and a water-mill for corn and planks. This village stands on a very fine meadow, about one mile from the Mississippi.

"The village of Saint Famille de Kaoquias (Cahokia) is generally reckoned fifteen leagues from Fort Chartres, and six leagues below the mouth of the Missouri. It stands near the side of the Mississippi, and is marked from the river by an island (Duncan's) two leagues long. The village is opposite the center of this island; it is long and straggling, being three-fourths of a mile from one end to the other. It contains forty-five dwelling houses, and a church near the center. The situation is not well chosen, as in the floods it is generally overflowed two or three feet deep. This was the first settlement on the Mississippi. The land was purchased of the savages by a few Canadians, some of whom married women of the Kaoquias nation, and others brought wives from Canada, and then resided there, leaving their children to succeed them. The inhabitants of this

---

*See *ante*, Chapter XVI., p. 314.

place depend more on hunting and their Indian trade than on agriculture, as they scarcely raise corn enough for their own consumption; they have great plenty of poultry, and good stocks of horned cattle.

"The mission of St. Sulpice had a very fine plantation here, and an excellent house built on it. They sold this estate, and a very good mill for corn and planks, to a Frenchman (M. Gerardine), who chose to remain under the English government. They also disposed of thirty negroes and a good stock of cattle to different people in the country, and returned to France in 1764. What is called the fort, is a small house standing in the center of the village. It differs nothing from the other houses, except in being one of the poorest. It was formerly inclosed with high palisades, but these were torn down and burnt. Indeed, a fort at this place could be of little use." *

Concerning the soil, products, commerce, and aborigines of the country, Pittman says:

"The soil of this country, in general, is very rich and luxuriant; it produces all kinds of European grains, hops, hemp, flax, cotton, and tobacco, and European fruits come to great perfection. The inhabitants make wine of the wild grapes, which is very inebriating, and is, in color and taste, very like the red wine of Provence.

"In the late wars, New Orleans and the lower parts of Louisiana were supplied with flour, beef, wines, hams, and other provisions from this country. At present, its commerce is mostly confined to the peltry and furs, which are got in traffic from the Indians; for which are received in return such European commodities as are necessary to carry on that commerce and the support of the inhabitants.

---

* "The old fort has long since disappeared; no vestige of it can now be seen. The church still stands, and is probably the oldest house of worship west of the Alleghany Mountains. The village, instead of being 'near the side of the Mississippi,' is nearly a mile to the east of it. This change was mainly wrought by the general flood of 1844."—History of St. Clair Co., Ill., 1881, p. 327. "The old court-house was built (by the Americans) in 1795, or thereabouts, at which time Cahokia became the county seat. In 1814 the county seat was removed to Belleville."—Ibid., p. 329.

"The principal Indian nations in this country are the Cascasquias, Kahoquias, Mitchigamias, and Peoyas; these four tribes are generally called the Illinois Indians. Except in hunting seasons, they reside near the English settlements in this country. They are a poor, debauched and dastardly people. They count about three hundred and fifty warriors. The Panquichas (Piankashaws), Mascoutins, Miamies, Kickapous, and Pyatonons, though not very numerous, are brave and warlike people."

With regard to the hamlet of Prairie du Pont, of which Pittman makes no mention, Reynolds gives us this information:

"The village of Prairie du Pont was settled by emigrants from the other French villages, in the year 1760, and was a prosperous settlement. It is stated that this village, in the year 1765, contained fourteen families. They had their common field and commons, which were confirmed to them by the government of the United States. This village is situated about one mile south of Cahokia, and extended south from the creek of the same name for some distance. It is a kind of suburb to Cahokia."*

In order to further illustrate the history of the French settlements in Illinois, it is now requisite to give a succinct narration of the English rule over them. Captain Thomas Stirling began the military government of the country on October 10, 1765, with fair and liberal concessions, calculated to secure the good-will and loyalty of the French-Canadians, and to stay their further exodus; but his administration was not of long duration.† On the 4th of the ensuing December, he was succeeded by Major Robert Farmer, who had arrived from Mobile with a detachment of the 34th British infantry. In the following year, after

---

* Reynold's Pioneer History, second edition, p. 67.

† It appears that Captain Stirling did not die while in command at Fort Chartres, as related by the earlier historians of Illinois. On the contrary, he afterward fought his way up to a brigadier-generalship in the War of the Revolution, and finally died in England, in 1808, a baronet and a general of high rank.—Moses' History of Illinois (Chicago, 1889), Vol. I., p. 137; New York Colonial Docs., VII., 786, *note.*

exercising an arbitrary authority over these isolated and feeble settlements, Major Farmer was displaced by Colonel Edward Cole, who had commanded a regiment under Wolfe, at Quebec. Colonel Cole remained in command at Fort Chartres about eighteen months; but the position was not congenial to him. The climate was unfavorable to his health, and the privations of life at a frontier post increased his discontent. He was accordingly relieved at his own request, early in the year 1768.* His successor was Colonel John Reed, who proved a bad exchange for the poor colonists. He soon became so notorious for his military oppressions of the people that he was removed, and gave place to Lieutenant-Colonel John Wilkins, of the 18th, or royal regiment of Ireland, who had formerly commanded at Fort Niagara.

Colonel Wilkins arrived from Philadelphia and assumed the command September 5, 1768. He brought out with him seven companies of his regiment for garrison duty; but many of these soldiers succumbed to the malarious diseases of the country. Having been authorized by General Gage to institute a court of justice in Illinois for the civil administration of the laws, Wilkins issued his proclamation to that effect on the 21st of November. He next appointed seven magistrates or judges, who were to form a court, and to hold monthly sessions for the trial and adjudication of all controversies arising among the people in relation to debts or property. The first term of this honorable court was convened at Fort Chartres, December 6, 1768. It was the first court of common law jurisdiction established in the Mississippi Valley; and, although called by courtesy a common law court, it was, in fact, a very nondescript tribunal.

"It was a court of first and last resort; no appeal lay from it. It was the highest as well as the lowest, the only court in the country. It proved any thing but popular, and it is just possible that the worthy judges themselves, taken from among the people, may not have been the most en-

---

* Moses' History of Ill., Vol. I., p. 138.

lightened exponents of the law. The people were under
the laws of England, but the trial by jury—that great bulwark of the subject's right, coeval with the common law
and reiterated in the British constitution—the French mind
was unable to appreciate, particularly in civil trials. They
thought it very inconsistent that the English should refer
nice questions relating to the rights of property to a tribunal composed of tailors, shoemakers, or other artisans and
trades-people, for determination, rather than to judges
learned in the law. While thus, under the English administration, civil jurisprudence was sought to be brought
nearer to the people, it failed, because, owing to the teachings, and perhaps genius of the French mind, it could not
be made of the people.

"For nearly ninety years had these settlements been
ruled by the dicta and decisions of theocratic and military
tribunals, absolute in both civil and criminal cases; but as
may well be imagined, in a post so remote, where there was
neither wealth, culture, nor fashion, all incentives to oppress
the colony remained dormant, and the extraordinary powers
of the priests and commandants were (generally) exercised
in a patriarchal spirit, which gained the love and implicit
confidence of the people. Believing that their rulers were
ever right, they gave themselves no trouble or pains to review their acts. Indeed, many years later, when Illinois
had passed under the jurisdiction of the United States, the
perplexed inhabitants, unable to comprehend the to them
complicated machinery of republicanism, begged to be delivered from the intolerable burden of self-government,
and again subjected to the will of a military commandant."*

Subsequent to the treaty of Paris, on October 7, 1763,
George III., King of Great Britain, issued his proclamation for the government of the country wrested from France
in America, and dividing it into four provinces. In this
proclamation he prohibited his subjects from "making any
purchases or settlements whatever, or taking possession of

---

* Davidson & Stuve's Hist. Ill., 1st ed., p. 165.

any of the wild lands beyond the sources of any of the rivers which fall into the Atlantic Ocean from the west or north-west." The object of this inhibition was to reserve the vast and uncultivated region of the West as a hunting-ground for the use of the Indians, and, by the navigation of the great lakes, to place their enormous fur and peltry trade within English control. The policy of the home government then was to confine the English colonies to the Atlantic slope, within easy reach of the English shipping, which would be more conducive to trade and commerce; whereas the granting of large bodies of land in the remote interior would tend to separate the colonists, and render them more independent and difficult to govern.

But it was soon apparent that this narrow and restrictive policy of the government could not be strictly enforced. Indeed, one of the most noticeable features of Colonel Wilkins' administration was the liberality with which he parceled out large tracts of the domain over which he ruled to his favorites in Illinois, Philadelphia, and elsewhere, without other consideration than requiring them to re-convey to him a certain interest in the same. By the aforesaid proclamation of the king, the taking or purchasing of lands from the Indians in any of the American colonies was strictly forbidden, without special permission being first had and obtained. Under this prohibition, Colonel Wilkins, and some of his predecessors in office, treated the lands of the French absentees in Illinois as forfeited, and granted them away; but these transactions never received the sanction of the King, and by no royal or judicial act did their property become escheated to the British crown.*

Lieutenant Colonel Wilkins' government of the Illinois country eventually became unpopular, and specific charges were preferred against him, including a misappropriation of the public funds. He asked for an official investigation, claiming that he was able to justify his public conduct.

---

* Davidson & Stuve's Hist. Ill., 1st ed., p. 166.

But he was deposed from office in September, 1771, and sailed for Europe in July of the following year.*

Captain Hugh Lord, of the 18th regiment, became Wilkins' successor at Fort Chartres, and continued in command until the year 1775. It was during his incumbency, in the spring of 1772, that the great freshet occurred in the Mississippi, which undermined and partly destroyed the fortress, so that it was abandoned. The seat of the local government was then removed to Kaskaskia, and the garrison took up their quarters at the old fort on the rocky hill or bluff, over against the town. This fort, as herein before stated, had been destroyed by fire in 1766, but it was now repaired or reconstructed, and was named Fort Gage, in token of respect to the British commander-in-chief in America. At this time the British garrison here was quite small, comprising, it is said, only twenty men and one commissioned officer, though there were two companies of militia in Kaskaskia village.

On the 2d of June, 1774, Parliament passed an act enlarging and extending the province of Quebec to the Mississippi River, so as to include the territory of the Northwest; restoring to the people of Canada their ancient laws in civil cases; guaranteeing the free exercise of their religion, and rehabilitating the Roman Catholic clergy with the privileges stipulated in the articles of capitulation at Montreal in 1760. This act was popularly known as the "Quebec Bill." It was intended not only to conciliate the French inhabitants of Canada, and to firmly attach them to the English crown, but to counteract the growing opposition to the home government in the American colonies on the Atlantic seaboard. The measure was a master stroke of policy on the part of the British ministry, since it allayed disaffection, and tended to prevent the revolt of the Canadian provinces in the War of the Revolution.

Who was the immediate successor of Captain Lord in command of the Illinois, is not positively determined. It appears from a letter written by Governor Haldimand

---

*Moses' Hist. of Ill., Vol. I., p. 141.

Kennedy's River Voyage. 399

(July 8, 1781), that Captain Matthew Johnson received a salary of twelve hundred pounds sterling for services as lieutenant-commandant of the Illinois from May, 1775, to May, 1781; but we are not informed as to where that officer was stationed, or what duties he performed other than to draw his pay.*

It is clear, however, from the "Governor Haldimand Papers" (preserved in the Canadian Archives at Ottawa), that Philippe Francois de Rastel de Rocheblave was in command of the British at the fort near Kaskaskia as early as October, 1776, and that his conduct as such commandant was approved by his superior, Sir Guy Carleton.* Rocheblave was a native of Dauphiny, and had been an officer in the French service, but with the transfer of the country to Great Britain he changed his allegiance, and for this was promoted. He resided for many years in Kaskaskia, and was married there in April, 1763, as is shown by the parish records.

In Imlay's "Description of the Western Territory of North America," published at London in 1797, is contained the journal of a river voyage made by one Patrick Kennedy, with several *coureurs des bois*, in the summer of 1773, from Kaskaskia village to the head-waters of the Illinois, in search of copper mines. From this curious and interesting journal, we condense the subjoined statement descriptive of his journey, and of the then still wild country of the Illinois.

Kennedy and his party left Kaskaskia on the 23d of July, 1773, in a large canoe or bateau, and on the 31st of that month reached the mouth of the Illinois River, eighty-four miles from Kaskaskia, and eighteen above the junction of the Missouri. In ascending the Mississippi, they passed, on their right, the heavily timbered American Bottom as far as to the site of the present Alton, and thence skirted the chain of rugged rocks and high hills, which begins below the Piasa Bluffs and extends to and beyond the confluence of the Illinois. On quitting the Mississippi and enter-

---
* Mose's History of Ill., Vol. I., p. 142.

ing the Illinois, they found the latter river so low and its
borders so full of weeds and bushes that their progress was
much impeded, and they were obliged to row their boat in
the deeper water of the channel. The banks are depicted
by Kennedy as low on both sides; the course of the stream
as N., N. E.; and the bottom land as being well timbered
with pecan, maple, ash, button-wood, etc.* "There are
fine meadows," he tells us, "at a little distance from the
river, the banks of which do not crumble away as do those
of the Mississippi."

On the first day of August, after passing the mouth
of the Macoupin, or White Potatoe Creek, the voyagers
stopped to refresh themselves at an old wintering ground
of the Peorias. In this lower part of the river, they encountered several small islands, and saw many buffalo and
deer feeding. On the following day they passed an island
called *Pierre à Fléche*, which had its name from a large hill
on the west side of the stream, where the Indians procured
the stone from which they chipped their arrow-heads and
gun flints. On the 4th our voyagers passed the mouth of
the Sangamo, or Sangamon River,† putting in from the
east, and on the 7th they reached the southern extremity
of Peoria Lake; concerning which, and the remains of the
fort then standing there, Kennedy's Journal says:

"The morning being foggy, and the river overgrown
with weeds along its sides, we could make but little (head)
way. About twelve o'clock we got to the old Peoria fort
and village, on the western shore of the river, and at the

---

* "The kinds of timber most abundant (in Illinois) are oaks of various species, black and white walnut, ash of several kinds, elm, sugar-maple, honey-locust, hackberry, linden, hickory, cotton-wood, pecan, mulberry, buckeye, sycamore, wild-cherry, box-elder, sassafras, and persimmon. In the southern and eastern parts of the state are yellow poplar and beech; near the Ohio are cypress, and in several counties are clumps of yellow pine and cedar. The undergrowth is redbud, papaw, sumach, plum, crab-apple, grape-vines, dogwood, spice-bush, greenbrier, hazel, etc. The alluvial soil of the rivers produces cotton-wood and sycamore timber of amazing size."—Peck's *Gazetteer of Illinois*.

† To what extent, if any, the Sangamon was ever explored by the French does not appear of record.

foot of a lake called the Illinois Lake, which is nineteen miles and a half in length and three miles in breadth. It has no rocks, shoals, or perceptible current. We found the stockade of this Peoria fort destroyed by fire, but the houses standing.* The summit on which the fort stood commands a fine prospect of the country to the eastward, and up the lake to the point where the river comes in at the north end; to the westward are large meadows. In the lake is great plenty of fish, and in particular sturgeon and picamau."

Pushing on up the lake and river, Kennedy and party arrived at the entrance of the Vermilion, two hundred and sixty-seven miles from the mouth of the Illinois, on the 9th of August. The Vermilion River is described as thirty yards wide, but with such a rocky and uneven bed as not to be navigable. A mile above that the voyagers reached the rapids in the Illinois, and finding the water too shallow for their boat, they abandoned it and proceeded by land about forty-five miles farther. Having crossed a northern

---

* In the above citation, no reference is made to the time when this "old Peoria fort" was built by the French, though it must have been subsequent to Father Charlevoix' visit (1721), for he makes no mention of any fort there. As to the remains of Fort Crève-coeur, on the opposite side of the river, they had disappeared long before. From the time of La Salle and Hennepin, the southern extremity of Peoria Lake was a familiar locality to the French *voyageurs* and traders, as well as to the English who followed in their wake. There is, however, no authentic account of any continuous European settlement in this vicinity until 1778, when the village of *La Ville de Maillet* was begun on the north-western shore of the lake. It took its name from its founder, Hypolite Maillet, who is portrayed as a man "remarkable for his bravery, brutality, and enterprise." This small French settlement was subsequently changed to the old Indian village at the foot of the lake, on account of its greater salubrity and other advantages. The transfer was fully effected by the year 1797, and the new village received the name of Peoria. (See Ballance's History of Peoria.) In the fall of 1812, it was destroyed by a detachment of Territorial militia under Captain Craig, and its French inhabitants were forcibly transported to and below what is now Alton. In 1813 a wooden fort was erected on the site of the village, which was called Fort Clark. This fort was burned in 1818; and it was not until the next year (1819) that the place was permanently occupied by American pioneers.

tributary of the Illinois called the Fox River, they struck and followed a trail up the Illinois to an island, where some French traders were found encamped. The latter, however, could give Kennedy no information in regard to the copper mine he was seeking. He now hired one of the traders to take himself and party in a canoe back to the place where they had left their boat. From thence, on the way down the Illinois, they met with a Frenchman named Jeanette, who assisted them in a further search for the mine; but Kennedy finally returned to Kaskaskia without having discovered any copper. The meeting with French-Canadians on this expedition showed that they still hunted and trafficked with the Indians in this part of the country.*

In 1778, when Colonel George Rogers Clark, and his Virginia militia, numbering less than two hundred men, achieved the bloodless conquest of Illinois, not a single British soldier was found doing duty in the country, they having all been withdrawn to other and more important points. M. de Rocheblave was still in command for the English at Fort Gage; but, owing to his contumacious behavior, he was sent a prisoner of war to Virginia, where he was paroled and afterward broke his parole. In Kaskaskia and Cahokia the French militia were well organized, and they were utilized by Clark † in maintaining his conquest.

France had exercised sovereignty over the country of the Illinois for ninety-two years, commencing with the discovery by Joliet and Marquette, in 1673, and ending with the surrender of Fort Chartres, in 1765. The actual English possession lasted but thirteen years, or fifteen from the treaty of Paris in 1763 till 1778. In October of the latter year, the Virginia Legislature erected the conquered territory into the County of Illinois, and Colonel John Todd,‡ of Kentucky, was appointed lieutenant-commandant

---

* See "Description of Western North America," by Captain Gilbert Imlay: 3d ed., London, 1797, pp. 507–512.

† George Rogers Clark, the greatest character in the early American history of Illinois, was born in Albemarle county, Virginia, November 19, 1752, and died, unmarried, near Louisville, Ky., in February, 1818.

‡ Todd was subsequently killed at the battle of Blue Licks, Ky., in 1782.

thereof. Illinois thus became an integrant part of Virginia, and so remained until March, 1784, when it, with the rest of the territory north-west of the river Ohio, was ceded by the Old Dominion to the Government of the United States.

In July, 1778, when Colonel Clark took military possession of Kaskaskia, it is stated, on apparently good authority, that it comprised two hundred and fifty houses, with a proportionate population. This estimate, if not too high, shows a somewhat rapid and progressive growth from the time of Pittman's visit thither in 1766. Kaskaskia, however, continued to prosper, and maintained her rank and prestige as the leading town in the Illinois country down to the year 1820, since which date she has gradually dwindled to a mere skeleton of her former self. In April, 1881, the Mississippi and Kaskaskia Rivers became united above the village by a deep channel, which the former had cut across the peninsula that forms the southern extremity of the American Bottom, thus leaving what remained of the historic old place on an island.

"The very river," says a native of Kaskaskia, "upon whose placid waters they (the French settlers) paddled their light canoes, has become the bed of the wild currents of the Mississippi and Missouri Rivers, and that beautiful and rolling peninsula, whereon the old town was located, has become a desert island. The history of the world affords no parallel to the rapid and absolute desolation of old Kaskaskia. Towns and cities have gone down to ruin, but yet have left some traces of their former greatness; not so with old Kaskaskia. The very earth upon which she stood has become a desert and desolation. Night and ignorance have wrapped themselves around her, and she rests alone in the memories of the past. It is scarcely beyond the life of those now living, when she was the most important place in our western territories—the center of trade in Illinois, the capital of our territory, the capital of our state, and, with a population of some three thousand people, embraced a large proportion of the wisdom, learning, wealth and eloquence of Illinois. . . .

"There is a witchery attending the hallowed memories of old Kaskaskia; with it the dreams of romance become realized, and the prose of life is transformed into poetry."—Extract from an address, by Hon. Henry S. Baker, before the Illinois State Bar Association, Jan. 10, 1888.

CHAPTER XXI.

GENERAL DESCRIPTION OF THE FRENCH COLONISTS.

In this concluding chapter it is proposed to depict, with as much fidelity as possible, considering the distance of time and place, and the scantiness of authentic data, the village abodes, household and farming implements, occupations, dress, manners, customs, amusements, the social and religious life, peculiar to the early French communities in Illinois and Louisiana.

Unlike the English and American pioneers, who preferred sparse settlements and a free range on account of their desire to become land owners, the French settlers invariably established themselves in irregular yet compact villages, with such narrow streets between the houses that they could easily carry on their light and animated conversations across them. These villages were commonly located on the banks of some river, adjacent to a fort or other secure place, and convenient to both timber and prairie; the one furnishing them with firewood and building material, and the other with ground for tillage.

Their primitive habitations were doubtless little better than the Indian wigwams—a mere protection from the weather—but in process of time they erected more substantial houses. In general, their dwellings were one story high, built in a simple and inexpensive way, after the style brought from Canada, or France. The framework consisted of roughly hewn posts, firmly set in the earth, a few inches (sometimes a few feet) apart, and bound together by horizontal cross-timbers,—the spaces between being filled in with mortar, made of common clay and Spanish moss * or cut straw. The walls were whitewashed, both within

---

* This moss was found growing in great abundance on the forest trees of the country.

and without, which gave an air of neatness and comfort to the buildings. The floors were laid with puncheons, or cemented with clay mortar. The eaves were low and projecting, and the roofs steep and thatched with straw or wild grass, though some were covered with clapboards fastened with wooden pins; and on the comb of the roof a wooden cross was often placed. The doors were of plain batten work, and were mostly made out of walnut. The windows generally had some glass in them, and were hung on hinges; but in the earlier built houses, they used scraped skins or oiled paper as a substitute for glass. The chimneys, when attached to the dwellings, stood on the outside, with large fire-places opening within. Most of these domiciles, especially in Lower Louisiana, were surrounded with plain verandas, which protected them from the sun and rain, while the rooms within were cool and commodious, having little furniture, but with white walls and well scoured floors.

The mansions of the better sort were in the same peculiar style, though larger, stronger, and more pretentious in their architecture; these being often built of roughly dressed limestone, and then whitewashed. Few articles of luxury were to be found in any of their homes, though it was not uncommon to see in the best of them small services of china or plate, or a single piece of silverware (perhaps an heirloom), displayed on the top of the closet, or on a side table. The walls of the rooms were frequently decorated with cheap prints, illustrative of our Savior's passion, or of scenes in the life of the Virgin Mary, or some favorite saint. These pictures not only contributed to furnish their humble apartments, but served to inspire devotional sentiments in the hearts of a people inclined to piety and superstition.

Of the "commons" and "common fields," pertaining to the French villages, we have elsewhere treated in this work. To each villager was allotted a certain portion of the common field, the extent of which was usually proportioned to the size of his family. The lands thus apportioned were subject to the village regulations, and when the person in possession became idle or negligent so as to injure the common interest, he forfeited his claim. As accessions were made to families from time to time, by marriage or otherwise, portions of land were taken from the commons and added to the common field for their benefit. The time of plowing, sowing, and harvesting was subject to the enactments of the village council and commandant. Even the form and construction of the inclosures to their dwellings and other buildings were made a matter of special regulation by the local commandant, and were arranged with a view to defense in case of any sudden uprising of the Indians.

In the gardens of the villagers, the common culinary plants, with some medicinal herbs and small fruits, were cultivated by the side of the modest violet, the fragrant rose, and the stately sunflower. Here, too, the apple, peach, and pear trees blossomed and matured their delicious fruits; and the prolific grape-vine, trained along the inclosures or against the eaves of the cottages, yielded its rich vintage in its season. In addition to the varied products of their gardens, their tables were otherwise well supplied from the spoils of the chase.

There was always a considerable diversity of pursuits among the French inhabitants of Louisiana proper, but in the dependency of the Illinois, the colonists applied themselves mainly to agriculture. The principal crops raised were wheat, oats, rye, hops (for the breweries), and tobacco. The last named article was highly esteemed by the males for smoking, and by the elderly females also, when it was cured and pulverized into snuff. Indian corn was not much grown, except for hominy, and to fatten swine. For use as bread, the French entertained for it a settled aversion. Their horses, of which they did not have a great number, had been introduced chiefly from the Spanish settlements in Mexico, and were small, yet strong and hardy, performing well for their size. Horned cattle were easily and extensively raised. They were first brought into Illinois from Canada, and, though not large, were neat and well formed.

The farming implements of the colonists were of the crudest and most primitive pattern. They used wooden plows* for breaking and tilling the ground, hand-flails for threshing their grain, and rude wooden carts, without a particle of iron, in place of wagons. These implements were mostly the handiwork of the farmer himself, aided by his slaves (if he had any), or by those of his more fortunate neighbor. Oxen were employed in plowing or breaking the earth, and horses for riding and drawing the carts. The oxen were yoked by the horns instead of the neck, and were guided by strips or ropes of untanned hide. The horses were driven *tandem*, that is, one before the other, and were directed and controlled by the whip and voice, without the convenience of reins. The harness used was made of raw hide, since they had no tanned leather for any purpose.

Although cows were plentiful and milk abundant, the common churn was a thing unknown to these simple colonists, their butter being made by shaking the cream in a bottle, or breaking it in a bowl with a spoon. Nor were the spinning-wheel and loom (so common with the American pioneers) to be seen in their houses. The traders supplied all goods or stuffs for the use of both sexes, not from stocks exposed on shelves in stores, as at present, but from chests and trunks, or tied up in bales.

The costume of the early French settlers was somewhat motley in its composition, but they had an inherited predilection for the blue in color. For clothing, the men wore shirts and waistcoats of cotton, with coarse blue cloth or deer-skin trousers, and moccasins, after the Indian fashion. Over these was worn, in winter, the indispensable *capote*, or long woolen coat, with a blue hood attachment, which, in wet or cold weather, was drawn over the head, and at other times fell back on the shoulders as a cape, like

---

* "The old plow used by the French would be a curiosity at this day. It had no coulter, but had a large wooden mold-board. The handles were short, and stood almost perpendicular. The beam was nearly straight, and rested on an axle supported by two small wheels, which made the plow unsteady."—*Reynolds' Pioneer History.*

that of the *habitants* of Lower Canada. Among the *voyageurs* and traders, the head was more often covered with a blue cotton handkerchief, folded in the shape of a turban. In like manner, but neatly trimmed with ribbons, was formed the fancy head-dress worn by the young women at balls and other festive occasions. The dress of the matron, though plain and with the antique short waist, was neat and varied in its minor details to suit the diversities of womanly taste. Both sexes wore moccasins of Indian manufacture, which, for public occasions, were variously decorated with small shells, beads and ribbons, giving them quite a showy appearance.

Notwithstanding their tawny complexions, and an appearance of languor among the people, the effects in part of climate, there was nothing of that sickly, cadaverous look, and listless air and bearing so observable in the creoles of the West Indies and Central America. The countenances of the young maidens in particular were lively and engaging, with their black eyes, raven tresses, graceful forms, and quick, elastic steps, like that of the mountain maiden of whom Scott has sung:

"A foot more light, a step more true,
Ne'er from the heath-flower dashed the dew."

They were all essentially French in character, with something of the Spanish gravity, but the *tout ensemble* indicated cheerfulness and an agreeable composure.* A quick-witted people, they had a penchant for nick-names, both as applied to persons and places. For example, they first named Ste. Genevieve, Mo., *Misère*, as expressive of the misery or poverty of the place. Carondelet received the derisive name of *Vide Poche*, or Empty Pocket,† and St. Louis was long known as *Pain Court*, or Short-bread.

---

* Breese's Early Ill's, p. 193.

† Carondelet, Mo., was founded by Clement Delor de Tregette, as early as 1767, and was afterward named in compliment to the Baron de Carondelet, who was Spanish governor of Louisiana from 1792 till 1797. This French village is situated about six miles south of the county court house, in St. Louis, and now forms a part of the latter city.

Kaskaskia was familiarly called *Au Kas*, which became corrupted into Okaw.

Among these colonists, the mechanical occupations were confined to a few carpenters, tailors, stone-masons, boat-builders, and blacksmiths; which last could repair a firelock or a rifle. The artisans journeyed from village to village in quest of employment, and were ready to turn their hands to any kind of work. Now and then might be found among them a millwright, who could make or repair the running-gear of a water-mill, or build a horse mill. The only wind-mill in the country, of which we find any mention, stood on the road between Kaskaskia and Prairie du Rocher. Coopers were scarce, though they should have been in demand, for large quantities of flour were manufactured and shipped to the southern markets; but no other bagging appears to have been used in the packing and shipment of flour than that afforded by dried elk and deer-skins.

Aside from the business of hunting and small trafficking with the Indians, which attracted the more indolent, the most captivating and adventurous employment for the young or middle-aged Frenchman was boating on the Mississippi River. Success in this arduous calling demanded the combined exercise of many qualities, such as bodily activity, courage, capability of undergoing great fatigue, a quick eye, a steady hand, and withal good judgment. The voyage from Fort Chartres or Kaskaskia to New Orleans was the principal and most important one. It usually consumed about three months' time, and was more difficult and hazardous than a trip across the Atlantic, even at that day. The river, then as now, was tortuous and rapid, its deep channel being obstructed by snags and sawyers, and continually shifting its course. Nor were these the only difficulties to be encountered in navigating the stream. From Kaskaskia to the vicinity of New Orleans, there were no white settlements of any consequence, except at the Arkansas, Natchez, and, later on, Baton Rouge; and the route was more or less beset by marauding bands of Chickasaws and other Indians, whom French power had not been able to subdue.

The voyage was made in large *bateaux*,* each manned by from sixteen to twenty hands, and going in convoys for mutual safety. The boats were laden with the surplus productions of the Illinois country, which were exchanged for such necessaries and luxuries as their own labor or soil did not produce, or else converted into the gold and silver coinage of France. Accounts were all kept in livres; and, besides coin, good pelts, at a fixed rate per pound, were a recognized measure of values, and passed freely in commercial transactions throughout the province.

The upward or return voyage was very tedious and laborious, generally taking from three to four months. Every means was resorted to by the boatmen—by keeping in the eddies near the shore, by sometimes crossing the river, and by the frequent use of the tow rope—to make headway against the dead weight of the current. Under such circumstances an Indian ambuscade might be fatal to the crew of one boat, but as several went together the danger was proportionately lessened. Attacks from the savages, however, were less to be dreaded than the malignant fevers, which swept away numbers of the men annually.

The flotilla was usually commanded by an officer of the king's troops, when a suitable one could be had, or, if not, one was selected from among the more experienced of the boatmen themselves. To reach this distinction, or even that of captain of a single boat, was deemed an object worthy of ambition; yet but few attained this coveted prize of their perilous calling. Strict military discipline was enforced, and a regular guard was mounted at each stopping place at night. On returning from their protracted river voyages, the boatmen, like sailors the world over, were very prodigal of their earnings. "They were as liberal as princes, and valued money as nothing more than a means by which pleasure could be purchased and appetites indulged. Saving was no part of their economy." † In con-

---

* The *bateau* was a long and rather light built boat, of about twenty tons burden.

† Breese's Early Illinois, p. 208.

vival intercourse, they were much addicted to relating long stories about their voyages, adventures, and hair-breadth escapes among the savages.

For ordinary locomotion on water, the canoe was indispensable to the early French settler. Those in common use were mostly hollowed out of the trunks of trees, that of the cypress being preferred on account of its lightness and elasticity. The birch bark canoes came from the region of the high northern lakes, and were principally used by the Canadian *voyageurs* and fur-traders. They were constructed of a slight frame-work of cedar, incased with the flexible bark of the "Canoe Birch," and were remarkable for their lightness and buoyancy. Of different sizes, they were finished alike at both ends, and were built to carry from four to twelve persons. Charlevoix informs us that the Ottawa Indians were the most expert builders of these canoes, but that the French were more skillful in handling them.

Owing to their extraordinary tact for ingratiating themselves with the aboriginal tribes, by whom they were surrounded, the Illinois French escaped almost entirely those broils and border strifes which weakened and sometimes destroyed other and less favored European colonies. Whether navigating the interminable rivers of the country, or threading the solitudes of the wild forests and prairies in quest of game; whether at home in their villages, or as participants in the religious exercises of the same Catholic church, the red men became their every-day associates and assistants, and were treated with the kindness and consideration of brothers. The social condition of the early colonists was thus formed, to some extent, by the influence of their Indian neighbors with whom they maintained such friendly relations. But while the barbarism of the savages was, in some degree, softened by this intercourse, the morals of the French were not improved. Many of the original settlers, and particularly the trappers and traders, contracted marriages or temporary alliances with the Indian women, from which sprang the mixed progeny known as "half-breeds."* They made expert hunters and trappers, and indefatigable boatmen, but in their general characteristics partook more of the savage than the civilized man. The natural home of the "half-breed" is on the outskirts, the boundaries of American civilization, where he still flourishes as in days of yore.

The example of the Canadian and Illinois French in amalgamating with the Indians, although adopted more perhaps as a matter of policy and convenience, was not one to be commended; for time and experience have abundantly shown that all such intermixture of races degrade the superior without materially improving the inferior race. In the case of the French, they did not sink to the level of barbarism, yet they were left in a condition below that of true civilization. There are, it is true, some English and American half and quarter-breeds; but, as a rule, the Anglo-Americans have ever disdained to mingle their blood with a distinctively inferior race, and to this circumstance they owe, in no slight degree, their pre-eminence among the enlightened races of mankind.

In the early years of the French settlements in Louisiana, there was very little money of any kind in circulation, business being transacted by barter and exchange. After the collapse of Law's "credit system" (1720), the money in use consisted of gold and silver coins of the French and Spanish mints. The value of every thing was reckoned in livres; the livre being equivalent to the modern franc, five of which equal ninety-five cents. Then there was the *louis d'or*, a French gold coin, valued at $4.84, and the Spanish doubloon, a gold coin worth about $15.93. During Gov. Kerlerec's administration, a paper money called *bons* was extensively issued at New Orleans, but it never had much circulation in the dependency of the Illinois. It was emitted in sums of from ten *sous* or cents to one hundred livres, was signed by the governor and intendant of the province, and was so called from the first word on the

---

* In the French villages of Missouri, the half-breeds received the nic-name of "Gumbos."

face of the paper—*Bon pour la somme payable en lettre de change sur le trésor.*

Separated from their mother-land by the Atlantic Ocean, and by a thousand miles of interior navigation from Montreal on the one hand, and from New Orleans on the other, the French colonists of Illinois were obliged to rely upon themselves not only for the necessaries of life, but also for their amusements. Socially inclined, light-hearted and gay, their principal diversion was dancing, in which all classes freely joined, to the enlivening music of the violin. When parties were assembled for this purpose, it was customary to choose some of the older and more discreet persons to direct the entertainment, preserve order, and see that all present had an opportunity to participate in the pleasurable pastime. Whenever those in authority on such occasions decided that the entertainment had been protracted long enough, it was brought to a close, and thus excesses were avoided.

Then, again, the monotony of their existence was broken by the many *fêtes* or festal days connected with the Catholic church. All the people shared alike in the harmless merriment of shrove-tide, and in the fun and frolic of the carnival, and at its close repaired to the sacred precincts of the sanctuary to receive the sprinkling of ashes, typical of their conclusion. All, too, observed the same self-denying ordinances during the Lenten season, which terminated with the festival of Easter. Society, of course, had its divisions even here; but those artificial distinctions between the rich and the poor, which obtain in older and more polished communities, were not recognized or maintained among these secluded colonists.

In their domestic relations, they were in general exemplary and kind, affectionate to their children and lenient toward their slaves. In fact, the family circle was usually a very cheerful and happy one. The male servants worked in the fields with their masters, faring as well as they did, and had small plots of ground assigned them, and the use of their master's team to cultivate the same; thus mutual esteem and confidence were inspired. The females assisted their mistresses in the kitchen and nursery, and then, in neat attire, accompanied them to matins and vespers. When sick or disabled, they were nursed with tenderness and care; and, in fine, were the recipients of so much humane treatment as to be wholly unmindful of the fetters with which custom and state policy had bound them.

The language spoken by the commonalty was not pure French, but a *patois*, or corrupted provincial dialect. No common schools existed in the country, nor any system of public instruction. The Jesuits imparted some little of that learning, with which they were so richly endowed, to such young creoles as they found "thirsting for the waters of the Pierian spring;" yet no plan of general education was ever adopted, or even seriously considered, by those in authority. Hence the charge of illiteracy is laid against this people; but, as the poet Gray has said—

"Where ignorance is bliss, 't is folly to be wise."

The Roman Catholic creed, however, was instilled into the minds of all from their earliest childhood, and the tapering spires of its little churches or chapels arose in every hamlet. In them was performed the marriage ceremony, the priest consecrating the nuptial tie and recording the act, which was attested by witnesses. There the sacrament of baptism was administered to infants and adults; there, too, were held the last sad obsequies for the dead, and masses were said for the souls of those "not dying in the odor of sanctity." *

" Separated thus from all the world, these people acquired many peculiarities. In language, dress, and manners, they lost much of their original polish; but they re-

---

* Breese's Early Ill., p. 209.

Note.—"The inhabitants," writes Reynolds, "were devout and strong believers in the Roman Catholic Church. They were willing to fight and die for the maintenance of the doctrines of their church. They considered the Church of Rome infallible, emanating directly from God, and therefore all the dogmas were received and acted on without a why or wherefore."—*Pioneer History of Illinois*, p. 55.

tained, and (their descendants) still retain, many of the leading characteristics of their nation. They took care to keep up their ancient holidays and festivals; and with few luxuries, and fewer wants, they were probably as cheerful and as happy a people as any in existence."*

The foregoing descriptive account applies not only to the early French colonists in Illinois and all Northern Louisiana, but also, with only slight alteration, to their village settlements in Southern Louisiana. At New Orleans, the political and commercial seat of government, there was always a certain number of people of family and education. There were the rude semblance of a court, a kind of theater, and amusements of a higher grade than could be found elsewhere within the limits of the large province. The denizens of New Orleans were wont to look upon their rural countrymen in much the same manner as they themselves were regarded by the refined circles of Paris. Among the mixed population of that colonial metropolis, however, drunkenness, brawls, and dueling were unhappily too prevalent, both before and after the Spanish occupation of the country.†

Some few of the Louisiana colonists were of noble origin; many were military officers, while others were born gentlemen, and the ecclesiastics were all educated people. With but few exceptions, the original immigrants to Illinois had come by way of Canada from the north of France, and mostly belonged to the *bourgeois* and *paysan* classes. But many of those who afterward settled in Lower Louisiana were from the south-western provinces of France, bordering on the Pyrenees and the Atlantic. A number of these were well educated business men from the *larger cities and towns*, and some of them made their way up the Mississippi to Kaskaskia and St. Louis, where they founded influential families, still existing.‡ It was, perhaps, a fortunate trait, and certainly an amiable one, in

---

* *Sketches of the West*, by Judge James Hall, vol. 1, p. 150.
† Gayarré's Louisiana, vol. 1.
‡ Billon's Annals of Early St. Louis.

the French character, that such men could so readily resign the comforts and pleasures of civilized life in their natal land, and make themselves contented among savages in the remote and uncultivated regions of the Mississippi, where they seldom heard from their homes over the sea more than once in twelve months.

[AUTHORITIES.]

For the facts embodied in the foregoing chapter, we are indebted to various sources, but chiefly to the labors of Judge Sidney Breese and ex-Gov. John Reynolds, both of whom had early an excellent opportunities for observing the French character and manners. Breese resided in Kaskaskia from 1818 to 1835, and then at Carlyle, Illinois, until his death in 1878; while Reynolds lived in Cahokia from 1814 to about 1830, and afterward in Belleville, Ill., until the close of his life in 1865. It may be added here that Breese's "Early History of Illinois" was first given to the public in the shape of an extended historical address, in December, 1842, but it was not published in book form until after his decease, and, then, without his previous revision or correction. Reynolds' "Pioneer History," an entertaining and instructive work, first appeared in 1852.

Among modern writers on French-American history, the two most distinguished are Francis Parkman and the late Dr. John Gilmary Shea.* Their various and valuable publications cover the entire period of the French rule on this continent, and are characterized by profoundness of erudition and elegance of style. To these may now be added Dr. Wm. Kingsford, of Ottawa, Canada, whose elaborate and able "History of Canada from the Earliest Times to 1841," has taken rank among the standard publications of the day. But those who would become thoroughly informed concerning this early and intricate branch of American history, should study the writings of Charlevoix, Hennepin Le Clercq, Bossu, La Hontan, and the Jesuit missionaries.

* This eminent Catholic scholar, after a long and laborious literary career, died at his home in Elizabeth, New Jersey, the 22d of February, 1892, aged sixty-nine.

INDEX.

A.

Abenakis Indians, a band of near Fort Miami on Lake Michigan, *page* 130; they form a part of La Salle's colony on the Illinois River, 148.

Abercrombie, General, and commander-in-chief of the British army (1758), 332; repulsed by Montcalm at Ticonderoga, 333.

Acadia, settled by the French under DeMonts, 10, 11 ; origin of the name, 10, *note;* when changed to Nova Scotia, 329, *note.*

Acadians, deportation of to English colonies, 329 and *note;* settlement formed by in Lower Louisiana, 368.

Accault or Ako, Michael, companion of Father Hennepin on the Mississippi, 105; his wife the daughter of a Kaskaskia chief, 204.

Aix-la-Chapelle, Treaty of, 313, 329.

Akansea, or Akansa. (See Arkansas.)

Algonquins, on the St. Lawrence, 13 and *note;* mention, 34, 48.

Alibamons, location of, 265, *note.*

Allouez, Claude, founds the Jesuit Mission on Green Bay, 51 ; intrigues with the Miamis against La Salle, 92; re-establishes Marquette's mission at the great town of the Illinois, 196; his description of the town, 197; death at Ft. Miami, on Lake Michigan, 198.

Amusements of the early Illinois colonists, 413.

Anticosti Island, discovered by Cartier, 5; granted to Joliet, 68.

Aquipaguetin, a Sioux chief, the adopted father of Hennepin, 107.

Arkansas River, discovered by De Soto, 29.

Arkansas Post, 181, *note;* established by Henri de Tonty, 182; mention, 190, 242.

Arkansas, villages of the, 58, 138, 183.

Aubry, Charles, Chevalier de, defeats an English force near Fort Duquesne, 334; becomes acting French governor of Louisiana, 367; Champigny's portrait of, 367-8, *note;* he delivers possession of the province to O'Reilly, 374; perishes by drowning in the river Garonne, 379 and *note.*

Authorities cited in this work, 416, *note.*

B.

Bahamos, or Ebahamos, an errant tribe of southern Texas, 162, 167.

Bancroft, George, references to his History of the United States, 29, *note,* 205, 219, *note,* 285, 290.

Balize, a hamlet at the mouth of the Mississippi, 371, *note.*

Beaujeu, Captain or Count de, pilots La Salle's Sea expedition into Gulf of Mexico, 156; his bickerings with La Salle, 156-7; takes leave of the latter on coast of Texas, 159.

Beaujeu, Daniel Lienard de, plans defeat of Braddock on the Monongahela, 327; is killed in the battle, 328.

Belle Fontaine, lieutenant under Tonty at Fort St. Louis, of the Ill., 184.

Bellerive, Louis St. Ange de, commandant at Post de Vincennes, 302; he surrenders Fort Chartres to Capt. Stirling, 360; twice appointed commandant at Fort Chartres, 361, *note*; goes to St. Louis, Mo., and takes command there, 385; is admitted into a Spanish regiment, 385; dies in St. Louis at a ripe age, 386, *note*.

Bienville, Jean Baptiste, Sieur de, accompanies his brother Iberville to Louisiana, 213; succeeds Sauvolle in command at Fort Biloxi, and on the Mobile, 223; is appointed lieutenant-commandant under Crozat, 239; erects Fort Rosalie at Natchez, 241; commissioned governor of the Province of Louisiana, under the Company of the West, 260; founds the city of New Orleans (in 1718), 263; takes Pensacola from the Spaniards, 266-7; his first campaign against the Chickasaws 290; second campaign, 295; retires from office under a cloud, 296; sails for France regretted by the colonists, 297; his interview with the Duke de Choiseul, to protest against the transfer of Louisiana to Spain, 369; death and character, 369 and *note*.

Billons (F. L.) Annals of early St. Louis, 389, 415.

Boating on the Lower Mississippi, 409.

Bœuf, Fort Le, or *Ft. sur la riviere au Bœuf*, situation of, 321; Washington's winter journey thither, 322; mention, 350.

Boisbriant, Pierre Duqué de, arrives in Louisiana as king's lieutenant, 260; is sent to command at the dependency of the Illinois, 270; builds old Fort Chartres, 271; land grants executed by, 272-3; becomes governor *ad interim* of Louisiana, 276.

Bossu, M., Captain in the French marines, and Chevalier of St. Louis, his account of the Spanish-Mexican expedition into the country of the Missouri Indians, 269; and notice of the rebuilding of Fort Chartres, 313, *note*.

Bouquet, Col. Henry, conquers the Delawares and Shawnees on the river Muskingham, 351; releases many white prisoners, 351.

Braddock, Edward, British general, lands at Alexandria, Va., and marches against Fort Duquesne, 326; his disastrous defeat at Battle of the Monongahela, 327; sketch of his military career, 328, *note*.

Brébeuf, Jean de, one of the first Jesuit missionaries in Canada, 16, 18.

Breese, Sidney, references to and citations from his Early History of Illinois, 89, *note*; 96, *note*; 112, *note*; 147, 204, 273-4, 287, 305, 310, 314, 381, 408, 410, 414, 416, *note*.

Breuil, M. de, erects first sugar mill at New Orleans, 297.

British military governors of Illinois, 394, 395.

Buffalo Rock (60 feet high), on the Illinois River, about three miles above Starved Rock, 90.

C.

Cabots, John and Sebastian, early voyages of discovery to North America, 2 and 3.

Cadillac, Antoine de la Mothe, governor of Louisiana under Crozat, 238; sketch of, 239, note; founds the post of Detroit, 344.
Cadodaquis, an Indian tribe on Red River, 180, 188.
Cahokia, first settlement of, 207; Charlevoix' account of the mission at, 209; Pittman's description of the village, 392, 393 and note.
Canada, discovery of, 5; derivation of the name, 7, note.
Canoes, birch bark, how constructed, 411.
Carondelet, village of, when and by whom founded, 408, note.
Cartier, Jacques, French navigator, discovers and explores the St. Lawrence, 5; with Roberval he attempts a settlement on that river, 7; is rewarded for his services to the king with a patent of nobility, 8.
Cavelier, the Abbé Jean, a Sulpitian priest and brother of La Salle, 72; he accompanies La Salle in his last expedition, 155; deception practiced by him on Tonty, 186.
Cenis Indians, on Trinity River, Texas, visited by La Salle, 164; also by Joutel et al., 176.
Champlain, Samuel de, parentage and early career, 9; is sent by the governor of Dieppe on an exploring expedition to the St. Lawrence, 10; assists DeMonts in colonizing Acadia, 11; with Pontgravé he founds Quebec, 12, 13; surrenders that post to the English, and is carried a prisoner to England, 17; his return to Canada, and death at Quebec, 18: analysis of his character, 19.
Champlain Lake, when discovered, 14.
Charlevoix, Pierre Francois Xavier de, a distinguished Jesuit scholar and historian; references to and quotations from his works, 12, note; 16, note; 62, 65, note; 208–240, 263; biographical notice of, 211, note.
Chateaugué, Antoine le Moyne de, brother of Iberville and Bienville, 225.
Checagou, chief of the Kaskaskias, 290.
Chickasaw Bluffs, mention, 28, 137, 292.
Chickasaw nation, 289; French wars with, 290, 295, 298.
Chicagou or Chicago, site of wintered on by Marquette, 63; visited by La Salle on his way to the gulf, 135–6.
Choiseul, Duke de, prime minister of Louis XV., letter to the Count de Fuentes, 364; he refuses petition of the inhabitants of La., 369.
Clark, Col. George Rogers, his expedition to, and conquest of the Illinois country, 402 and note, 403 note.
Colbert, Jean Baptiste, a great minister under Louis XIV., favors La Salle's enterprises, 80, 81; decease of, 153, note.
Columbus, Christopher, mention, 2.
Comet of 1680, 120, note.
Commons, right of granted to the inhabitants of Kaskaskia, 304, 305.
Common Fields, description of, 273.
Copper mines, search for, 40, 46, 399.
Cortereal, Gaspar de (Portuguese navigator), voyages to Labrador, 3.
Cotton, when culture of introduced in Louisiana, 298.
Court of "Royal Jurisdiction" in the Illinois, 309, 310.
Court, first common law, in Illinois, 395.

Coureurs des bois, or runners of the woods, attempts of the Canadian government to suppress, 118, 195.

Courcelles, Daniel de Rémy, Sieur de, second Canadian governor under the royal provincial government, 20; recall of, 45.

Créve-coeur (See Fort Créve-coeur).

Craig, Captain Thomas, destroys French and Indian village of Peoria, 401, *note*.

Croghan, Colonel George, conciliatory mission to the Western Indians, 353; his journey over the mountains to Fort Pitt, 353; he descends the Ohio, 355; is captured by a band of Kickapoos below mouth of the Wabash, 355; taken as a prisoner to Vincennes, 356; released at Fort Ouatanon, 356; he meets and confers with Pontiac, 357; peace speech by to the Indians at Detroit, 358; success of his mission, 360.

Crozat, Antoine, Marquis de Chatel, is granted a monopoly of the commerce and government of Louisiana, 234; his letters patent, 234–237; mercantile and mining operations of, 238, 239; surrenders his charter to the crown, 240.

D.

Dablon, Claude, eminent Jesuit missionary, 42; notice of his life and writings, 43, 44, *note*.

D'Abbadie, M., succeeds Kerlerec as acting governor of Louisiana, 314, 363; death of in New Orleans, 367.

D'Artaguette, Diron, *commissaire ordonnateur* in Louisiana, 233, 288.

D'Artaguette, Pierre, serves in the Natchez war, 288; is made commandant at the Illinois, 288; leads an expedition against the Chickasaws, 292; wounded and taken prisoner, 293; perishes at the stake, 294.

Davidson and Stuvé's History of Illinois, references to, etc., 132-3, 286, 298, 347, 389, 396, 397.

D'Autry, the Sieur, explores passes of the Mississippi with La Salle, 144.

Delaware Indians, mention, 320, 351.

De Leon, Don Alonzo, expedition of from Mexico to Fort St. Louis, of Texas, 190.

De Luna, Don Tristan, leads a Spanish army of Invasion into West Florida, 33, 279.

De Monts, Pierre du Guast, Sieur, an officer of Henry IV.'s household, 10; under letter patent he plants the first French colony in Acadia, 11; loses his influence at court on death of that monarch, 15.

Detroit, founded by La Mothe Cadillac (in 1701), 344; its situation and early military history, 344; Indian siege of under Pontiac, 349.

De Villiers, Capt. Neyon, overcomes Washington at Fort Necessity, 325; is made commandant of the Illinois at Fort Chartres, 312, 342 and *note;* he resigns and goes to New Orleans, 363; receives the decoration of the Cross of St. Louis, 363.

De Vincennes (or Vincenne) Jean Baptiste Bissot, sketch of, 299; establishes the post of Vincennes, 299, 301; joins D'Artaguette in his expedition against the Chickasaws, 292; and shares that officer's lamentable fate, 293.

Index. 421

Des Ursius, Marc Antoine de la Loire, commissary and judge for the India Company in Illinois, 272, 273; killed at Natchez, 382.

Dieskau, Ludwig August, Baron, a German-French general in the Seven Years' War, 330; mortally wounded in battle near Crown Point, 330.

Dinwiddie, Robert, colonial governor of Virginia, sends Washington on mission to the French, 321; orders the raising of a regiment to drive the French from Virginia territory, 323.

Domestic Alliances of the French colonists with the Indians, 8, 204, 303, 412.

Donnacona, an Indian potentate at Quebec, 5; is carried by Cartier to France, 7.

Douay, Father Anastasius, Recollet missionary, 155; his account of La Salle's murder, 168*; ascends the Mississippi and Illinois with Abbé Cavelier, et al., 183–4; returns to France, 187; he accompanies D'Iberville in his colonizing expedition to the Mississippi, 215 and *note*.

Du Gay, Picard, companion of Hennepin in his Sioux captivity, 105, 107.

Duhaut, M., principal assassin of La Salle, 170; is himself slain in an altercation with Iliens, 177.

Du L'Hut, Daniel Greysolon, penetrates the Sioux country from Lake Superior, and effects the release of Hennepin, et al., 108; sketch of his adventurous career, 108, *note*.

Dumont's Historical Memoir of Louisiana, 267, 279, 280, 282, *note*, 292.

Durret's, R. T., Kentucky Centennial Address, 38.

E.

Edict of Nantes, when enacted and revoked, 248 *note*.

English, early efforts to discover the Mississippi, 38; surrender of the Illinois country to, 360; duration of their rule, 402.

"English Turn," on Lower Mississippi, origin of the phrase, 220.

Epinay, M. de L', succeeds Cadillac as governor of Louisiana, 245.

F.

Farmer, Major Robert, relieves Captain Stirling, in command at Fort Chartres, 394.

Florida, when discovered, 24; Soto's remarkable adventures in, 24–32; Narvaez's expedition to, 25.

Forbes, General Joseph, leads the second English expedition against Fort Duquesne, 333; death of, 334.

Fort Biloxi, or Maurepas, built by Iberville, 219; unfavorable site of, and removal of the colony from, 224; New Biloxi, 267, *note*.

Fort Chartres, first building of, 271; when rebuilt, 313; Breese's remarks on, 314; Pittman's description of, 315; subsequent history, 316–318.

Fort Créve-coeur, building of, 93; why so named, 94; described by Hennepin, 101.

Fort Duquesne, begun by agents of the Ohio Company, 323; completed and named by Captain Contrecoeur, 323; taken by the English under General Forbes, and name changed to Fort Pitt, 334.

Fort Frontenac, when built, 79; granted in seigniory to La Salle, 80;

---

* In this account, the date of La Salle's murder should read the 19th instead of the 9th of March, 1687.

captured and demolished by the English provincials under Colonel Bradstreet, 333.
Fort Gage, near Kaskaskia, removal of British troops to from Fort Chartres, 316; Pittman's notice of, 391; is taken by Colonel Clark, 402.
Fort Massac, or Marsiac, on the Lower Ohio, 335; brief hist. of, 335, *note.*
Fort Miami, at mouth of the St. Joseph, built by La Salle, 89.
Fort Prudhomme, on the Mississippi, 137, 145.
Fort Rosalie, at Natchez, when built, 242; rebuilt, 284; Pittman's description of 289, *note.*
Fort St. Claude, on Yazoo River, French garrison at massacred by the Natchez Indians, 283.
Fort St. Louis of Illinois, when built, 147; decline of, 195.
Fort St. Louis of Texas, 161; destruction of, 191.
Fort Louis de la Mobile, when first built, 224; site of changed, 227.
Fort Ouatanon, on the Wabash, mention, 299, 303, *note.*
Fort Tombecbé, on the Tombigbee River, built by Bienville, 291.
Fox River, of Wisconsin, discovered by Nicolet, 36; mention, 51, 195.
Foxes, or *Rénards.* (See Sacs and Foxes.)
Fowls, domestic, among the southern Indians, 38, 216.
France, New. (See New France.)
Francis I. of France, mention, 4, 7.
Franciscan friars, 96, *note.*
Fraser, Lieutenant Alexander, associated with Croghan, 353; he descends the Ohio to Illinois, 354; is buffeted by the Indians at Kaskaskia, and flees down the Mississippi to New Orleans, 354.
French-Canadian population at the beginning of long war, 325.
French Commandants at the Illinois, table of, 361.
French Colonists in Illinois and Louisiana, general description of, 404.
Frontenac, Louis de Buade, Count de, celebrated governor of Canada, 45; he sends Joliet to explore the Mississippi, 46; dispatch of relating to his discovery, 69; erects Fort Frontenac at the outlet of Lake Ontario, 79; recommends La Salle to Colbert, 80; indorses Tonty's petition, 232; expires in Quebec, 46.

G.

Gage, General Thomas, British commander, proclamation by to the inhabitants of Illinois, 361, 362, *note.*
Gayarré, Charles, references to and citations from his History of Louisiana (3 vols.), 213, *note,* 219, 293, *note,* 295–6, *notes,* 312, *note,* 351–2, *notes,* 369, 379, 415.
Gravier Jacques, one of the missionary founders of Kaskaskia, 198, 199.
Green Bay, discovered by Nicolet, 36; mission station at, 51, 61.
Griffin, construction of at Niagara, 86 and *note;* lost on the upper lakes, 88.
Growth of the French settlements in Illinois, 208, 271.
Gulf of California, mention, 59, 78.
Gulf of Mexico, long a closed sea to the French, 38, 154.
Gulf of St. Lawrence, explored and named by Jacques Cartier, 5.
Gumbos, a nickname for the half-breeds in Missouri, 412, *note.*

H.

Halifax, town of, British fleet sails from for the reduction of Louisburg, 332.

Havana, Soto's expedition sails from to Florida, 24; taken by the English, 339; restored to Spain, 352, *note;* French state prisoners sent to from Louisiana, 376.

Helena, Arkansas, mention, 59, *note*.

Hennepin, Father Louis, his nativity, 96; early monastic life and travels, 97; comes as a Recollet missionary to Canada, 98; his active life at Quebec, 98; joins La Salle's expedition to the West, 99; visits Niagara Falls, 99, *note;* makes a journey to the principal village of the Senecas, 100; embarks on the Griffin, 100; his account of Fort Créve-coeur, 101; his daring canoe voyage up the Mississippi, 105; is captured by a party of the Sioux Indians, 106; adventures among the Sioux, 107; is released from captivity, 108; return journey to Canada and France, 109; his expulsion from France, 110; withdraws into Holland, and enters the service of William III., 110; decease, 110; review of his writings, 111, 112; his conflicting estimate of La Salle, 171.

Henry IV. of France, issues letters patent to De Monts, 10.

Hiens, one of the conspirators against Moranget and La Salle, 107; murders Duhaut, 177.

Huguenots, 9; driven by persecution from France, 248.

Huron, Lake, discovered by Champlain, 16.

Huron Indians, mention, 16, 35, 39, 48, 109, *note*.

I.

Iberville, Pierre Le Moyne, Sieur de, early naval career of, 212; his colonizing expedition to the Mississippi, 213, 214; plants a colony in Lower Louisiana, 218; revisits his colony, 220, 224; decease and character, 226.

Illinois Indians, loose confederations of, 53; meaning of the word *Illini* or Illinois, 53; they are invaded by the Iroquois, 121, 122; they aid the French in the Chickasaw war, 292; are defeated by the Sacs and Foxes, 387; Pittman's notice of, 394.

Illinois country, explored by Joliet and Marquette, 53, 60; military occupation of by La Salle, 94; a dependency of Canada, 194; a part of Louisiana, 233; under M. Crozat, 234, *et seq.;* under Boisbriant and the Company of the West, 270; under the Royal government, 288; under the English sway, 384; conquest of by Col. Clark, 402.

Illinois River, mention, 43, 60, 77, 90, 105; Kennedy's voyage on, 399;

Imlay, Capt. Gilbert, work on North America, 399.

India Company, Royal, successor to the Company of the West, 272; surrender of the company's charter, 286.

Indian allies, value of to the French in war, 326.

Indian colony of La Salle on the Illinois, 148.

Intendant, office of, 40, *note*.

Iroquois (or Five Nations), 13; army of invade the Illinois country, 122;

burning of the great town of the Illinois, 124; massacre of women and children, 127.

J.

Jesuits, their first appearance in Canada, 16; missions of in Illinois, 63, 196, 199; are banished from Louisiana, 379.
Jesuit Order, history of, 380, 381; suppressed by Pope Clement XIV., 382; revived by Pius VII., 382.
Jesuit Relations, 383.
Johnson, Gen. Sir William, mention, 326, 330; report of, 348, *note*.
Joliet, Louis, commissioned to explore the Mississippi River, 46; his birth and education at Quebec, 46; is first sent by Talon to look for copper mines at Lake Superior, 46; with Father Marquette, he reaches the Mississippi, 52; descends that river to the vicinity of the Arkansas, 59 and *note*; returning, he ascends the Illinois, 60; stops at the Indian villages en route, 61; he loses his manuscripts in the rapids at La Chine, 67; reports his discoveries to Gov. Frontenac, 67; his marriage, 68; makes a trip to Hudson's Bay, 68; is given the Island of Anticosti, 68; surveys the coast of Labrador, 68; is granted the seigniory of "Joliette," 68; death and character, 68, 69.
Joliet, city of in Ill., named for the explorer, 69.
Joutel, Henri, soldier, accompanies La Salle's expedition to Texas, 154; his account of La Salle's assassination, 169; his *Journal Historique* of the expedition, 187.
Juchereau, Sieur de, a Canadian officer, 299, 300, *note*.
Jumonville, Sieur Coulon de, killed in action at Little Meadows, 324, and *note*.

K.

Kankakee (Te-a-ki-ki) River, a constituent branch of the Illinois, mention, 90, 135, 197, *note*.
Kappa, or Quappa, a noted village of the Arkansas on Lower Mississippi, 58 *note*, 138, 183.
Kaskaskia, Indian village on the Illinois River, first visited by Joliet and Marquette, 60; Mission of the I. C. V. founded there by Father Marquette, 63; re-established by Father Allouez, 198; removal of the mission and tribe to the site of the present Kaskaskia, 199; early history of the mission and settlement on the Mississippi, 204; Charlvoix' visit to, 209; Pittman's description of, 390; subsequent decline of the village, 403, *note*.
Kaskaskias, a leading tribe of the Illinois, mention, 60, 63, 196, 202, 209, 290, 394.
Kennedy, Patrick, his journey up the Illinois River in search of copper mines, 399.
Kerlerec, M. de, governor of the Province of Louisiana (1753–1763), 312; ordered to return to France, and incarcerated in the Bastile, 314; paper money issued under his administration, 412.
Kingsford, William, references to his History of Canada, 20, 67, *note*, 416, *note*.

Kiskakons, a christianized branch of the Ottawa Indians, disinter and remove Marquette's remains, 65.

L.

Labrador, visited by the Cortereals to, 3; coast of surveyed by Joliet, 68.
La Barre, Le Febvre de, governor of Canada (1683–1685), 149; he dedeposes La Salle from the command of Forts Frontenac and St. Louis, 152.
La Buissoniere, Alphonse de, succeeds D'Artaguette as commandant at the Illinois, and takes part in the second Chickasaw war, 295.
Laclède, Pierre Liguest, principal founder of St. Louis, Missouri, 385; sketch of, 385, *note.*
La Forrest, a lieutenant of La Salle, 118, 120, 153, 154, 195.
La Harpe, Bernard de, adventures of in the southwest, 260, 261; is sent by Bienville to form an establishment on the Bay of St. Bernard, 262.
La Hontan,* Armand Louis de Delondarce, Baron de, a noted French officer and traveler, 56, *note;* his curious account of Michilimackinac, 109, *note;* his notice of the priest Cavelier and his traveling party, 180, *note.*
La Motte, de Lusiére, an associate of La Salle in his first great exploring enterprise, 83, 85, 86.
La Salle, Robert Cavelier Sieur de, his Norman birth and parentage, 71; receives his education from the Jesuits, 71, 72; emigrates to Canada, 72; founds Lachine, above Montreal, 72; discovers the Ohio, 76; secures the patronage of Gov. Frontenac, 78; is granted the seigniory of Fort Frontenac, 80; builds the Griffin on the Niagara, 86; voyages with her through the upper lakes, 87; he enters the country of the Illinois, 89; difficulties with the natives and his men, 92; builds Fort Créve-coeur at foot of Peoria Lake, 93, 94; sends Hennepin to explore the Upper Mississippi, 95; his return journey to Fort Frontenac, 115; second expedition to the West, 118; its failure, 120; he negotiates with the Western tribes, 131; descends the Mississippi to the Gulf, 136–141; takes possession of the country for the King of France, 142; erects Fort St. Louis on the Illinois, 147; forms an Indian colony around it, 148; corresponds with Gov. La Barre, 149, 150; is dismissed from his command by that functionary, 152; he goes to Old France, 153; is given audience by the King, 154; sails with a colony for the mouth of the Mississippi, 156; lands at' Matagorda Bay, 158; builds a fort there, 160; wanderings in the wilderness of Texas, 162, 163; sets out for the Illinois and Canada, but returns, 164; he again sets forth and is assassinated on the way, 165; analysis of his character, 171 *et seq.;* concealment of his death, 183, 185; destruction of his colony, 191.
La Salle Co., Illinois, named in memory of the great explorer, 196.
La Tour, early French engineer in Louisiana, 263.
Lake Michigan, or *Lac des Illinois,* discovered by Nicolet, 35–6.
Lake Superior, mention, 39, 40, 48.

---
*Incorrectly printed La Houtan, in note on page 99.

Law, John, Scotch financier and adventurer, birth and education of, 249; his theory of banking, 249; is patronized by the Duke of Orleans, 250; he establishes a bank in Paris, 250; his Mississippi scheme, 251; public infatuation thereat, 252; progress of his credit system, 253; its collapse, 257; he flees from France, 258; dies in poverty at Venice, 259.

Lead mines in Missouri, worked by the French, 239; in Illinois, 275 and *note*.

League, French, length of, 52, *note*.

Le Clercq, Father Crétien, 104, *note;* his History of the Establishment of the Faith in New France, 112, *note;* his account of La Salle's last expedition by sea, 161, *note*.

Le Clercq, Father Maximus, Recollet missionary in Texas, 155, 192.

Lesdigueres, Duchesse de, mention, 211.

Le Sueur, Pierre, a French voyageur, mention, 201, 300, *note*.

Lévis, Chevalier de, successor to Montcalm, 338.

Letters patent to La Salle, 81; to M. Crozat, 234.

Liotot, surgeon, and one of La Salle's assassins, 170; his violent death, 177, 178 and *note*.

Loftus, Major Arthur, his unsuccessful attempt to ascend the Mississippi to Fort Chartres, 352.

Lord, Captain Hugh, English commandant at the Illinois, successor to Wilkins, 398.

Louisiana, Lower, permanent settlement of by the French, 212; cession of the country to Spain, 364, 365.

Louis XIV. of France, falls heir to the throne at the age of five years, 246; erects Canada into a royal province, 19; issues patent of nobility to La Salle, 80; demise of, 246; review of his reign and character, 247, 248.

Louis XV., cedes Western Louisiana by private treaty to Spain, 339, 363; his letter concerning the cession to Gov. d'Abbadie, 365, 366.

Louisburg, fortress of, taken by the English, 312; second siege and capture of, 332, 333, *note*.

Loyola, Ignatius, originator of the Order of Jesuits, 380.

M.

Macarty, Chevalier de, major-commandant at the Illinois during the rebuilding of Fort Chartres, 313; mention, 324, 361.

Major-commandants, functions of the, 308.

Manitou, Indian name for the Deity, 51 and *note*.

Maps, Marquette's, 50, 62; Joliet's, 67 and *note;* Franquelin's and Hennepin's, 93; Delisle's, 99, *note*.

Marest, Gabriel, missionary priest at Kaskaskia, 199; he transfers the mission of the Immaculate Conception from the Illinois River to the site of the present Kaskaskia, 199–203; extracts from his correspondence, 205, 206.

Margry, Pierre, French author, references to his works, 68, 76, *note*, 104–5, *notes*, 151, *note*, 191, *note*, 197, *note*.

Index. 427

Marquette, Père Jacques, born at Laon, France, 47; he enters the Society of Jesus, and is ordained to the priesthood, 47; sails as a missionary to Canada, and studies the Indian languages under Father Dreuilletes, 47; with Father Dablon, he founds the mission of St. Mary of the Falls, 48; is thence sent to St. Esprit near western extremity of Lake Superior, 48; returning, he founds the mission of St. Ignace at Old Mackinac, 49; with M. Joliet, he discovers and explores the Mississippi River, 50–60; table of the distances traveled, 61, *note;* his journal of their great canoe voyage, 61, 62; he establishes the mission of the Immaculate Conception on the Illinois River, 63; sets out from thence on his return to St. Ignace, 64; dies and is buried on the eastern shore of Lake Michigan, 65; removal of his remains to St. Ignace, 65; his religious and general character, 66.

Mascoutins, allied tribe of the Miamis, 51, 92.

Massac, or Marsiac. (See Fort Massac.)

Mason, E. G., his account of the Kaskaskia Mission, 200–203; also of the ruins of Fort Chartres, 316.

Maillet, M. Hypolite, founds French village on Peoria Lake, 401, *note.*

Membre, Zenobius, Recollet friar and follower of La Salle, 85, 87; his description of the Illinois Indians, 103; exciting experience with the Iroquois, 124, 125; he perishes at Ft. Louis of Texas, 192; notice of his life, 192.

Menard, Father René, first French missionary in the region of Lake Superior, 39 and *note.*

Mermet, Jean, a missionary priest on the Lower Ohio, 300 and *note;* and an associate of Father Marest at Kaskaskia, 205.

Meurin, Sebastian Louis, last Jesuit missionary in the Illinois, 391, *note.*

Mexico, French attempts at trade relations with, 240, 242.

Miamis Indians, a kindred tribe of the Illinois, 51, 132, 133, 299.

Michilimackinac, or Mackinac, 49 and *note;* mission of St. Ignace at, 49; visited by La Salle in the Griffin, 87; described by La Hontan, 109, *note.*

Mills, water, at Kaskaskia and Cahokia, 271.

Missionaries in Illinois and Louisiana, Jesuits, 63, 194; Recollets, 103, 121; Sulpitians, 393.

Mississippi Company, Laws, 251, 252; its advantages to the Province of Louisiana, 250, 286.

Mississippi River, Spanish discovery of the, 24; different names of, 28, *note;* French discovery and exploration of, 45.

Missouri River, discovered by Joliet and Marquette, 56; said to have been first explored by La Hontan, 56, *note.*

Missouri Indians, allies of the French, destroy expedition of the Spaniards from New Mexico, 268.

Mobile River, visited by De Soto, 26; French fort on, 224.

Mohegan Indians, band settle at Ft. Miami, 130; party of, follow La Salle to the outlet of the Mississippi, 135.

Monso, a Mascoutin chief, intrigues with the Illinois against La Salle, 92.

Montcalm, Louis Joseph, Marquis de, captures Fort Ontario and Fort William Henry, 330, 331; defeats Abercrombie at Ticonderoga, 333;

is vanquished by Wolf at Quebec, 337, 338; sketch of his brilliant career, 340, *note*.

Montmagny, Charles Huault de, succeeds Champlain in the government of the Canadian colony, 18.

Montreal, when settled, 22; religious origin and early annals of, 22, 23.

Moranget, Sieur de, nephew of La Salle, 155; murder of, 167.

Moses, John, History of Illinois, references to, 62, 207, 394, *note*, 395, 398, 399.

Mound Builders, ancient, 33, 285, *note*.

Morris, Captain Thomas, adventures with the Indians, 351, 252 and *note*.

Muscoso, Luis de, lieutenant and successor to De Soto, 31; conducts the remains of Soto's expedition to Panuco, Mexico, 32.

N.

Nadouessiouxs. (See Sioux.)

Narvaez, Pamphilio de, a Spanish adventurer in Florida, 25.

Natchez Indians, visited by La Salle, 140; their strange history, 277-279; they massacre the French at Fort Rosalie, 282; war with, 284; extermination of the nation, 285.

Natchitoches, post of, when established, 245; mention, 260, 378.

Natchitoches Indians, mention, 188, 242, 260, 285; New Chartres, when built, 313, 314.

New Orleans, origin of, 246; founded by Bienville, 263; named for the Duke of Orleans, 263; visited by Charlevoix (1721), 263, 264; is made by Gov. Bienville the capital of Louisiana, 164.

New France, a name originally bestowed by the navigator, Verrazano, upon the north-eastern coast of North America, 13; History of. (See Charlevoix.)

Niagara Falls, Hennepin's visit to and description of, 99 and *note*.

Nicanope, a chief of the Peorias, 92.

Nicolet, Jean, early life of, among the Ottawas and Nipissings, 34; his voyage of discovery in the North-west, 35, 36; he marries an adopted daughter of Champlain, 37; is drowned in the St. Lawrence, 38.

Nipissing Lake, discovered by Champlain, 16.

Nonville (or Denonville), Jacques René de Brisay, Marquis de, governor of Canada (1685-1689), 229, 231 and *note*.

Northmen, in North America, 1 and 2.

Nouvelle France, a name applied to all the French-Canadian country, 13, 19.

Nova Scotia. (See Acadia.)

O.

Ohio River, discovery of by La Salle, 76, 77.

Onondagas, a tribe of Iroquois, 76, 79, 123.

Onanghisse, a Pottawatomie sachem, noted saying of, 129.

Ortiz, Juan, interpreter for De Soto, 25, 29.

O'Reilly, Don Alexandro, Spanish military governor of Louisiana, 373; sketch of, *note*; his proclamation of amnesty, 375; he punishes the revolutionary leaders and reorganizes the government of Louisiana, 376, 377.

Index. 429

Osage Indians, mention of, 92, 268, 269.
Ottawa Indians, so called from the river on which they dwelt, 13, *note*; expert builders of bark canoes, 411.
Ouabouskigou, the Ohio, or Ouabache, of the French, 56.
Ouisconsing (Wisconsin) River, first descended by Joliet and Marquette, 52; mention, 95, 195.
Ouichita, or Ouachita (Washita), a river of Arkansas, explored by Bienville, 223.
Oumas, or Houmas, one of the bravest tribes on the Lower Mississippi, 217, 220; visited by Iberville, 217.
Outagamies, a name given by French explorers to the Foxes, 131.

P.

Paris, Treaty of, 339; seventh article of the treaty, 363, *note*.
Parkman, Francis, historian, references to and quotations from his works, 75, *note*, 77, 120, *note*, 137, 151, 165, 166, 188, 193, 229, 248, *note*, 361.
Pascagoula River, mention, 219.
Passes of the Mississippi, explored by La Salle and Tonty, 141; surveyed by La Tour, 263.
Pensacola, Florida, fort erected at by the Spaniards, 214; it is taken, retaken, and demolished by the French, 267; transferred to the English by the treaty of Paris, 352, *note*.
Peoria Lake, La Salle's first arrival in, 91; description of the lake, 94, *note*, 208.
Peoria Village, Indian, situation and extent of, 91, 100; Charlevoix' notice of the village, 208; Kennedy's visit to, 400.
Peoria Village, French and American, 401, *note*.
Pepperell, Sir William, captures Louisburg (1745) from the French, 312.
Périer, M. de, governor of Louisiana during the Natchez war, 277; is promoted to the rank of lieutenant-general, 288.
Piankashaws, village of on the Wabash, 301; mention, 356.
Piasa, pictured rocks at, 55 and *note*.
Pinet, Father Jacques, principal founder of Cahokia, 207; success of his mission there, 207.
Pirogue, an Indian canoe, 6, *note*.
Pittman, Captain Philip, sent to Pensacola, Florida (1763), 389; extracts from his account of the French settlements on the Mississippi, 390-394.
Pontchartrain, Count de, French minister of colonies, 220; his answer to the application of Huguenot families from Carolina to settle in Louisiana, 220.
Pontiac, celebrated Ottawa chief, interposes in favor of Major Rogers' advance to Detroit, 343; sketch of, 346; his conspiracy and war against the English, 347, *et seq.*; unsuccessful attack and siege of Detroit, 349; capture of other Western posts, 350; disappointed at lack of French support, 351; he marches into the Illinois, 354; speech by at Fort Chartres, 354; he yields to the inevitable and confers with Colonel Croghan at Fort Ouatanon, 357; his peace

speeches at Detroit and Oswego, 359, 360; retires to the shades of the Maumee, 360; his last visit to the Illinois, 386; is murdered by a Kaskaskia Indian at Cahokia, Illinois, and buried by Captain St. Ange in St. Louis, Missouri, 387 and *note*.
Population (foreign) of Illinois at the time of the British occupation, 389.
Population of the province of Louisiana at the beginning of the Spanish rule, 377, 378.
Pottawatomie Indians, first visited by Nicolet, 37; mention, 88, 128.
Prairie du Chien, village of, on the Upper Mississippi, 52, *note*.
Prairie du Pont, a suburb of Cahokia, 394.
Prairie du Rôcher, a village in vicinity of Fort Chartres, 276; Pittman's account of. 391, *note*.
Prudhomme, Pierre, with La Salle on the Mississippi, 137; fort named for, 137.

Q.

Quebec, city of, site first visited by Cartier, 5; founded by Champlain, 13; surrendered to the English under Captain Kirk, 17; restored to the French, 18; failure of Sir William Phipps' attack upon, 20; stone fortifications at, 21; the city is taken by the English under Wolfe, 337, 338; unsuccessful efforts of the French to retake the citadel, 338.
"Quebec Bill," its effects upon the French colonists.
Quinté, bay of on Ontario Lake, seat of a Sulpitian mission, 73 and *note*.
Quinipissas Indians (the Bayagoulas of Iberville and Bienville), La Salle's experience with, 141, 144; Tonty leaves a letter with one of their chiefs, 182, 216.

R.

Randolph County, Illinois, ruins of Fort Chartres in, 317.
Rasles, Sebastian, a noted Jesuit missionary in Illinois and Maine, 198.
Red River, of Louisiana, discovered by the Spaniards, 31.
Renault, Philip, Francois de, director-general of the mining operations of the Mississippi Company, 274; he founds the village bearing his name, 275.
Reynolds, John, Pioneer History of Illinois, references to and quotations from, 317, 335, *note*, 346, *note*, 394, 407, *note*, 414, *note*.
Ribaut, Jean, attempts to plant a Huguenot colony in East Florida, 9.
Ribourde, Gabriel de la, a Recollet friar with La Salle in Illinois, 84, 101, 104; is slain by a scouting party of Kickapoos, 126.
Richelieu, Cardinal, organizes the company of "One Hundred Associates," 17; charter of, when abandoned, 19.
Rio del Norte, or Rio Grande, reached and crossed by St. Denis, 243.
Rocheblave, Philippe Francois de Rastel de, commands for the British at Fort Gage, 399; is sent a prisoner to Virginia by Col. Clark, 472.
Rogers, Major Robert, takes military possession of Detroit, 343; and of other western posts, 345.
Roman Catholic Church, devotion of the French colonists to, 414 and *note*.
Rosalie. (See Fort Rosalie.)
Ryswick, Treaty of, 212.

S.

Sacs, or Sauks, and Foxes, mention, 36, 131, 299.
Sangamon River, mention, 400 and *note*.
Santa Fé, New Mexico, when settled, 267, *note*.
Sault de Ste. Marie, mission established at by the Jesuits, 48.
Sauvolle—M. de Sauvolle de la Villantry—a brother or associate of D'Iberville, and first colonial governor in Louisiana, 213, 219; his early death at Fort Biloxi, 223.
Sénat, a Jesuit Father and volunteer in D'Artaguette's southern expedition, 292; he is martyred at the stake by the Chickasaws, 294.
Shawnees, restless character of, 56, *note*.
Shea, John Gilmary, references to and quotations from his works, 12, *note*, 39, *note*, 64, 65, 76, *note*, 104, *note*, 113, *note*, 163, *note*, 197, *note*, 228; decease of, 416, *note*.
Ship Island, first landing-place of Iberville's colony, 214.
Sioux Indians, 48, 106 and *note*.
Slaves, Negro, introduced into Louisiana by Crozat, 238; number of at the close of the French rule, 337.
Soto, Hernando de, Spanish discoverer of the Mississippi, 24; his remarkable expedition through Florida, 24-32.
Starved Rock, legend of, 387.
Stirling, Captain Thomas, takes British possession of Fort Chartres, 360; what became of him, 394, *note*.
Stoddard, Major Amos, 317 and *note*.
St. Anthony's Falls, discovered and named by Hennepin, 107; description of, 107, 108, *note*.
St. Cosme, Jean Francois Buisson de, a missionary priest at the Natchez, 200; sketch of, 201, *note*.
St. Croix, or St. Charles, a tributary of the St. Lawrence at Quebec, 5, 7, 12.
St. Francis Xavier, name of the Jesuit mission on Green Bay, 51, 61.
St. Denis, or Denys, Louis Juchereau de, his adventurous overland journey to Mexico, 242-244; appointed commandant at the post of Natchitoches, 244; sketch of, 245, *note*.
Ste. Genevieve, Missouri, when settled, 306.
St. Louis Missouri, when and by whom founded, 385 and *note*; early history of the village, 388.
St. Lusson, Simon Francois Daumont de, sent by Talon on a mission to the upper lake region, 40; he holds an important conference with the North-western tribes, 41, 42.
St. Peter's (Minnesota) River, French fort erected on by Le Sueur, 221, *note*.
St. Philippe, a small village in the neighborhood of Fort Chartres, 275.
St. Pierre, Le Gardeur de, commanding officer at *Fort sur la riviere au Boeuf*, 322; his letter of reply to Governor Dinwiddie, 322, 323.
Sugar-cane, when introduced into Louisiana, 297.

T.

Talon, Jean Baptiste, first intendant of Canada under the government of the crown, 20; slight sketch of, 40, *note;* he recommends the appointment of Joliet to explore the Mississippi, 46.

Taensas Indians, a kindred tribe of the Natchez, La Salle's arrival among, 139; their habitations, life, and worship, 139, 140.

Tamaroas, one of the five tribes of the Illinois, mention, 105, 127; Jesuit mission established among, 207.

Tampa Bay, Florida, landing-place of De Soto, 25.

Tejas Indians, name of Texas derived from, 164, *note*.

Texas, country of claimed by Spain, 190; unsuccessful attempts of the French to plant colonies in, 194, 262.

Timber, kinds of most abundant in Illinois, 400, *note*.

Tombigbee River, ascended by Bienville in his expedition against the Chickasaws, 291; also by Governor de Vaudreuil, 298.

Tonty, Henri de, lieutenant of La Salle, 83; his early military career, 84; accompanies La Salle to New France (1677), 85; superintends the construction of the Griffin, 86; sails with his chief to Mackinac, 87; goes thence to Sault de Ste. Marie, 88; arrives in the Illinois, 89; is left in command at Fort Créve-coeur, 115; his perilous encounter with the Iroquois, 123; escapes with his party to the Pottawatomies, 128, 129; he descends the Mississippi with La Salle, 135, *et seq.;* assists in constructing Fort St. Louis on the Illinois River, 147; is given charge of the fort by La Salle, but superseded in command by De Baugis, 152; afterward reinstated, 182; his river voyage to the Gulf in search of La Salle, 182; establishes a post on the Arkansas, 182; heroic attempt to succor the remains of La Salle's Texan colony, 188; is continued in command at the Illinois, 194, 195; finally joins D'Iberville on the Lower Mississippi, 221; is sent thence on a mission to the Chickasaws, 228; dies at Fort Louis, on the Mobile, 228; summary of his character, 229; printed memoirs of, 230; his petition to Count Pontchartrain, 231.

Tonty, Alphonse de, brother of Henri, 229.

Trois Rivieres, town on the St. Lawrence, founded by Champlain, 18, mention, 37, 47.

Tunica Bend, scene of Major Loftus' attack by Tunica Indians, 352.

Tuscarora Indians, a sixth tribe of the Iroquois nation, 320, *note*.

U.

Ulloa, Don Antonio de, first Spanish governor sent to Louisiana, 371; letter of to the Superior Council, 371; his expulsion from the province, 373.

Ucita, an Indian town on Tampa Bay, Florida, 25.

Utica, Illinois, mention, 146, 196.

Utrect, Treaty of, 21.

V.

Vaca, Cabeca, or Cabeza de, an early Spanish wanderer in Florida, 29 and *note*.

Vaudreuil, Pierre Francois de Rigaud, Marquis de, governor of Louisiana (1742-1753), 296; prosperity of the province under his administration, 297; he is promoted to the governorship of Canada, 312; jealousy and contentions with General Montcalm, 340, *note;* charges preferred against him by friends of the latter, on which he is tried and acquitted, 340, 341, *note;* death of in Paris, *Ibid.*

Vega, Garcilasso de la, a Spanish historian of De Soto's Expedition, 30, 33, *note.*

Venango, Indian village and military post on the Alleghany River, 321, 350.

Verrazano, Juan, a celebrated Florentine navigator; early voyage of discovery to North America, 4.

Vexilla, or *vexilla regis prodeunt*, first line of grand Latin hymn, 144, 198.

Vicanque, ancient Indian town on the upper waters of the Arkansas, 29.

Vincennes, Jean Baptiste Bissot de. (See De Vincennes.)

Vincennes, Indiana, beginning of, 299; early history, 301, 302; visited by Croghan, 303, *note.*

Virginia, Illinois made a county of, 402.

W.

Wabash River, when French posts first established on, 299.

Washington, George, mission to the headwaters of the Ohio, 321; surrenders Fort Necessity, 325; gallant conduct at Braddock's defeat, 328.

Wars of the French with the Spaniards, 265-268; with the Natchez, 277-285; with the Chickasaws, 290-298; with the English, 20, 312, 319-339; Pontiac's war, 346-360.

West, Company of the, when organized, 252; operations of in Louisiana and Illinois, 259, 571; charter of surrendered to the crown, 286; benefits of its sway, 287.

William III. of England, sends two vessels to explore the outlet of the Mississippi, 113, 220.

Winnebago Indians, a branch of the Sioux or Dakota nation; Nicolet's visit to and account of, 36; mention, 41.

Wilkins, Lieutenant-Colonel John, succeeds Colonel Reed as English commandant at the Illinois, 395; account of his administration, 395-398.

Will of La Salle, 134, *note.*

Wolfe, General James, distinguishes himself at the reduction of Louisburg, 336; his siege of Quebec, 337; dies on the field of battle, 338.

Wolfe and Montcalm Monument, 341, *note.*

Wolfe's column, *Ibid.*

Y.

Yazoo River, De Soto winters at village on, 27; French Fort on, 283.

Yalobusha River, in Northern Mississippi, rendezvous of D'Artaguette in his unfortunate expedition against the Chickasaws, 292.

FINIS.

www.ingramcontent.com/pod-product-compliance
Lightning Source LLC
Chambersburg PA
CBHW022148300426
44115CB00006B/406